# EXPLORATIONS IN WHITEHEAD'S PHILOSOPHY

# EXPLORATIONS IN WHITEHEAD'S PHILOSOPHY

*Edited by*
LEWIS S. FORD
&
GEORGE L. KLINE

New York
FORDHAM UNIVERSITY PRESS
1983

LC 77–75800
ISBN 0–8232–1102–9 (*clothbound*)
ISBN 0–8232–1103–7 (*paperback*)



Printed in the United States of America

# CONTENTS

# ABBREVIATIONS

References to the principal works of Alfred North Whitehead will use the following abbreviations, followed by page numbers, placed in parentheses in the text.

AE—*The Aims of Education and Other Essays.* New York: Macmillan, 1929.

AI—*Adventures of Ideas.* New York: Macmillan, 1933.

CN—*The Concept of Nature.* Cambridge: Cambridge University Press, 1920.

ESP—*Essays in Science and Philosophy.* New York: Philosophical Library, 1947.

FR—*The Function of Reason.* Princeton: Princeton University Press, 1929.

IS—*The Interpretation of Science: Selected Essays*, ed. A. H. Johnson. Indianapolis: Bobbs-Merrill, 1961.

MT—*Modes of Thought.* New York: Macmillan, 1938.

OT—*The Organisation of Thought, Educational and Scientific.* London: Williams and Norgate, 1917.

PM—*Principia Mathematica*, 2nd ed. Cambridge: Cambridge University Press, 1925–1927.

PNK—*An Enquiry Concerning the Principles of Natural Knowledge.* Cambridge: Cambridge University Press, 1919.

PR—*Process and Reality.* New York: Macmillan, 1929.

R—*The Principle of Relativity.* Cambridge: Cambridge University Press, 1922.

RM—*Religion in the Making.* New York: Macmillan, 1926.

S—*Symbolism, Its Meaning and Effect.* New York: Macmillan, 1927.

SMW—*Science and the Modern World*, 2nd ed. New York: Macmillan, 1926.

UA—*A Treatise on Universal Algebra, with Applications.* Cambridge: Cambridge University Press, 1898.

# FOREWORD

All the authors of the sixteen essays gathered in this volume are concerned, in their different ways, to clarify, criticize, and develop key ideas and insights of Alfred North Whitehead (1861–1947), one of the towering figures of twentieth-century speculative thought, whose "process philosophy" has, in recent decades, aroused intense intellectual interest both in this country and abroad. The present volume is intended to complement, but not to duplicate, an earlier selection of important Whitehead studies: *Alfred North Whitehead: Essays on His Philosophy*, ed. G. L. Kline (Englewood Cliffs: Prentice-Hall, 1963).

With respect to their origins, our sixteen essays fall into four distinct groups, which do not coincide with the four topically arranged parts of the book reflected in the Table of Contents:

*Group One*: Six essays were written for the special Whitehead issue of the *Southern Journal of Philosophy* (Vol. 7, No. 4 [1969–1970]), edited by Lewis S. Ford. This group includes the essays by John B. Cobb, Jr., William J. Garland, Granville C. Henry, Jr., George L. Kline, Robert C. Neville, and Gene Reeves.

*Group Two*: Five essays have been selected from among the most stimulating work on Whitehead published in journals other than the *Southern Journal of Philosophy* during the past two decades. These papers, ranging in date of original publication from 1959 to 1972, include the essays by Justus Buchler, Donald A. Crosby, Charles Hartshorne, A. H. Johnson, and Ivor Leclerc.

*Group Three*: Three essays are drawn from books published during the last four decades. The slim volume by the late Stephen Lee Ely, *The Religious Availability of Whitehead's God* (1942), is reprinted in its entirety, with minor corrections and the addition of section numbers. Robert C. Neville's essay is drawn from his book *Creativity and God: A Challenge to Process Theology* (1980). Since the major portion of this essay had appeared in an earlier version in the Whitehead issue of the *Southern Journal of Philosophy*, the essay is also listed with the papers in Group One. Richard M. Rorty's essay, written before Rorty had taken his "linguistic turn," was originally published in the collective volume *The Concept of Matter*, ed. E. McMullin (1963).

*Group Four*: Three essays were written especially for this volume and have not previously been published. This group includes the papers by William A. Christian, Sr., and Lewis S. Ford, as well as Ford's "Afterword: A Sampling of Other Interpretations," which focuses on additional Whitehead literature published during the decade or so prior to the founding of the journal *Process Studies* (1971—), in which current writings on Whitehead are assessed in detail.

All of the previously published essays have been carefully revised, and where necessary corrected, for inclusion here. Standardized sigla have been introduced in all of the essays for references to Whitehead's works (see Abbreviations, p. vii). Johnson's article has been considerably abridged; Cobb's essay has been slightly abridged. Garland's essay has been extensively revised and somewhat expanded; Kline's essay has been substantially rewritten and greatly expanded.

The place and date of original publication of the previously published papers, and the extent to which they have been revised, abridged, or expanded, are indicated in the footnotes which appear on the title page of each of the individual chapters.

Thanks are due to the book publishers mentioned in the list of Abbreviations and to both the book publishers and the journal editors listed in the title-page footnotes to individual chapters for permission to quote from, or to reprint, copyrighted materials.

# I

# WHITEHEAD AS PHILOSOPHER

1

# Some Conversations with Whitehead Concerning God and Creativity

A. H. JOHNSON
*University of Western Ontario,*
Emeritus

IN THE FALL OF 1936 I came to Harvard hoping to clarify my understanding of Whitehead's theory of actual entities in general, and his discussion of eternal objects, objectification, God, and creativity in particular. Professor Whitehead agreed to meet with me once a week in tutorial session in the study of his home.

At every meeting, in accordance with his suggestion, I presented to him a typed "basis for discussion." Each was composed of several questions which were "set" in a series of background statements about, or quotations from, some phase of Whitehead's philosophy. These questions were of such a nature that I hoped Whitehead would be able to answer "yes" or "no." In cases when, after careful examination of the "discussion" sheet, and much thought, he did so, I noted this fact on my carbon copy of the "basis for discussion." When he provided additional comment, I recorded it as accurately as possible after the end of the tutorial session.

What follows here is a partial report of my discussion with Professor Whitehead on God and creativity.[1]

## I · GOD

Whitehead admitted that he did not get all his insights adequately organized with respect to the concept of God. In any case, he was not *primarily* interested in God. Rather, he "just brought [God] in to show He belonged." But God *does* belong, and hence Whitehead opposes those humanists who would "save" religion by eliminating essential features.

Whitehead remarked that he sought to strike a mean between Christianity and Buddhism. The traditional expression of ideas about God has been characterized by absurd exaggerations. (1) The reality of God has been stressed at the expense of diminished reality for finite actual entities. (2) God's "personality" has been exaggerated. Here Buddhism is saner in being satisfied with vaguer notions, but it diminishes the personality of God too much. "Personality" is a very difficult sort of thing to get hold of. There is (a) the immediacy of the present occasion (myself now) combined with (b) the objective immortality of an antecedent society (i.e., myself in the past). Personality is a line of dominant inheritance. When do you become a person? From conception, or from the first time you think? When you say that God is an actual person, you are using a very vague concept.

Turning now to to a more technical consideration of Whitehead's concept of God, I asked:

JOHNSON: "By God's *primordial* nature you mean his conceptual prehensions, and by his *consequent* nature you mean his physical prehensions, don't you?"[2]

WHITEHEAD: "Yes."

He then commented that God's primordial nature is not included among the categoreal notions, yet it should have been. In order to account for the origin of novelty, the fifth Categoreal Obligation of conceptual reversion was introduced. Later, when God's primordial nature is considered, this category may be dispensed with. This category is not as coherent as the others. Category 6, for example, explains a phase of "creative synthesis"; Category 5 does not.

The theory of conceptual reversion, which was introduced to account for novelty, implies that either (a) eternal objects stray about the universe in no relevant relationship to actuality, emerging from nowhere, or (b) there is an actual entity (God) prehending all unrealized eternal objects. Whitehead admitted that he should have introduced God's primordial nature sooner.

Whitehead emphasized that God as primordial has an aspiration to enter into history. He is both constructive and destructive. He is concerned to eliminate repetition, and to encourage new orders to emerge. In God as primordial there is an appetition to realize eternal objects in the world. But as primordial he is not the only or basic cause in the universe. If he were, our everyday decisions would make no difference, and moral decisions would be meaningless. While all the eternal objects are present in God's primordial nature as possibilities, God cannot tell what particular events will in fact happen, because each actual entity is "self-creating." He can foresee the "logical" consequences, after the event happens.

JOHNSON: "When you say that God is the 'principle of concretion' (PR 374), do you mean, more specifically, that God provides a 'pattern' (eternal object) which a new actual entity accepts as its subjective aim and uses as a guide in its process of concretion? In this sense God *provides*, not *is*, the principle of concretion. My problem is this: Is it wise to call an actual entity a 'principle'? (It is true that an actual entity is the exemplification of a principle.) Isn't a principle, as such, an eternal object?"

WHITEHEAD: "You are right."

God is not a principle. A principle is an eternal object (i.e., a possibility), while God is an actuality. The expression 'principle of concretion' is adopted from *Religion in the Making*,[3] and Whitehead admitted that his language was vague in that book.

Whitehead contended that while all possibilities (eternal objects) as such are present in God's nature as intellectually apprehended (conceptually prehended), the exemplifications of these eternal objects are not present in his primordial nature but in his consequent nature. God as primordial is not a distinct actuality; only the union of the primordial and consequent natures forms a distinct actuality. Whitehead admitted that he "wobbled" on that point. In one passage in *Process and Reality* he almost suggests that God as primordial might be a separate kind of actual entity. The principle of concretion when exemplified in God results in a maximum of vividness and a minimum of distortion.

Whitehead emphasized that in God's consequent nature the various actual entities do not retain their individuality as such, but the distinctness of elements of these actual entities is immortal in God's consequent nature. Whitehead's notion of the consequent nature is, in this sense, pantheistic. In God's consequent nature, the distinctiveness of the actual entities in the temporal world is lost. But the elements which were present in our experience are more vivid in God's, for he evaluates them more accurately. His experience is richer. The individuality of elements in our experience is enhanced in God. This is what Whitehead means by immortality.

JOHNSON: "I judge that when you refer to God retaining immediacy (PR 524–25) the 'immediacy' God 'retains' is his own, not that of the actual entities objectified in him. Some elements of their being are eliminated as they pass into God. When you say 'Nothing is lost', don't you mean that in God (as consequent) actual entities are transformed? 'Nothing is lost which can be saved' (i.e., is worthy of being saved)."

Whitehead commented that God's immediacy doesn't "die." There is no elimination in God's nature as such. There is, of course, elimination of some of the data presented for inclusion in God's nature. God's consequent nature is conditioned by data from the developing actual world. He can foresee all future possibilities but not exactly what the future will be. Whitehead explained that God's consequent nature is introduced to deal with moral and aesthetic problems. Further, the consequent nature accounts for God's experience of objective succession in the external world. In our own experience we have a "specious present" with only quasi-objective immortality. We cannot measure (stand off and observe) our successive stages of self-creation. We are always enmeshed in subjective immediacy. The "external" world must be regarded as separate from "my" intrinsic process of self-creation.

JOHNSON: "You refer to the everlasting nature of God, which is, in a sense, non-temporal, and in another sense temporal (PR 524–33). In what sense is God 'temporal'?"

Whitehead replied that by 'temporal' he here means '[exhibiting] growth', not coming to be and passing away. He stated that God grows, and thus in a sense is historical. God is everywhere (in time). God is not historical in the sense of having a definite "whereness" or existing as a merely "present" being who fades.

Whitehead added that God's primordial nature is prior, but not temporally. The primordial nature finds history and every fact of history finds it. The primordial nature influences the consequent nature, i.e., together with the individual decisions of other actual entities, it conditions the formation of the latter. As mentioned before, in God's consequent experience there is both the historical perishing of other actual entities and real immortality. Some of the "historical" past is lost. There is real "passing away," e.g., the details of our own past experience are not all retained in God. But the "past" elements in God's nature are never lost. These comments provide the necessary background for the discussion of tragedy in God's experience. There is always elimination when things are objectified in God. That is the tragedy which even God does not escape. A God perfectly satisfied with the tragedy of the world would be "damnable." God experiences evil as tragedy. God is tragic and noble, not perfect. In God, evil does not lose its character. It is not ultimately a neutral element in an all-inclusive perfection (as in Absolute Idealism).

Whitehead remarked that in the last part of *Process and Reality*, he was not clear on what he wanted to say. In the last chapter of *Adventures of Ideas* God's effect upon the world is considered in terms of "Peace," and the individuality of God is lost sight of. He hopes to bring these two discussions together. In a genuine sense, what is worthy of objectification is objectified in God, yet he is forced to leave out much. Furthermore, in God things are transmuted and transformed.

Whitehead then considered the meaning of several key expressions in the sentence: "[God] is the poet of the world, with tender patience leading it by his vision of truth, beauty, and goodness" (PR 526). 'Poet' is used in the sense of its Greek root, 'maker'. His "tender patience" by which he leads or persuades the world shows that he has the "pluck" to go to that experience which is most profound to obtain his insights. He relies on the total wealth of human experience.

The claim that "God's role is not the combat of productive force with productive force" (PR 525–26) does not mean that God has no efficient power. His superjective nature provides as much efficient causation as any other actual entity. But it is causation from such a high point of view and of such general scope as to harmonize the whole. It does not have the character of short-range combat with its limitation of aim. It is not the combat of force with force as in the case when you are confronted by a madman. Then you forget about the choir of heaven and the internal gyrations of the atom and concentrate on the immediate activity (which is limited in its scope of interest) of subduing the madman.

Whitehead contended that the proper notion of "power" is like that found in the British constitution. Neither the King, the Prime Minister, nor the electorate has absolute power. At best each can only be vividly persuasive.

JOHNSON: "Is it correct to say that God exerts only as much causal influence on the world as any other actual entity, by providing data for other actual entities, but not forcing data on them?"

Whitehead replied that God does not force data of any sort on other actual entities. However, God has more causal influence than other actual entities in the sense that he continues to exist, while others pass away. Whitehead added in an aside that perhaps Part III should come before Part II in *Process and Reality*, though he was not quite sure.

In general he contended that his view of God has more richness of content than the Buddhist nirvana. His philosophy of religion might be called an effort to "true up" the concept of nirvana.

Whitehead pointed out that *Religion in the Making* "takes a kick" at the liberal theologians of the nineteenth century. The universe is complex. They make it *too* simple. Whitehead considered his *Religion in the Making* a complete failure. Yet it has proved one of his most successful works. He had wanted to write a much longer book, but Dean [Willard] Sperry [of the Harvard Divinity School] had restrained him.

The discussion then turned to a consideration of more technical aspects of his theory of God. I pointed out that *in a sense* every actual entity has a definite locus, and asked: "Is it possible to indicate God's locus?"

Whitehead replied that in respect to the world, God is everywhere. Yet he is a distinct entity. The world (i.e., the events in it) has a (specific) locus with reference to him, but he has no locus with reference to the world. This is the basis for the distinction between finite and infinite. God and the world have the same [general] locus. It is a matter of emphasis which you pick out as occupying the locus. Whitehead does not want to set God over against the other actual entities, as they are (for practical purposes) located at specific (separate) loci with reference to one another.

JOHNSON: "Can you think of God (as consequent) as a 'society'?" Whitehead replied that he had considered the possibility, since a society is what endures, and an actual entity passes away. But,

WHITEHEAD: "The answer is no."

In a society the past is lost. One ordinary actual entity fades away and only some of its data are passed on to another actual entity. But in God, his past is not lost. Yet, in a sense, God is a society in that actual entities passing into God as consequent do provide a group or society of distinguishable components, even though the actual entities as such do not survive. This, however, Whitehead has not thought out.

JOHNSON: "Does not your description of God make it difficult for you to say that God is an actual entity in the *usual* sense of the term? For example, 'an actual entity has "perished" when it is complete' (PR 126) may be contrasted with: God retains immediacy and creative advance (PR 524–25), i.e., God is *never* complete in the sense that he 'perishes'."

WHITEHEAD: "Yes."

JOHNSON: "If God never 'perishes', how can he provide data for other actual entities? Data are only available after the 'internal existence' of the actual entity 'has evaporated' (PR 336)."

WHITEHEAD: "This is a genuine problem. I have not attempted to solve it."

JOHNSON: "Am I correct in assuming that for the purposes of your metaphysics, you hold that the metaphysical situation has always been as it is now, namely: actual entities, interacting creatively; eternal objects; God, with both primordial, consequent, and superjective natures? The fact that you discuss God's consequent and superjective nature at the end of *Process and Reality* does *not* indicate that God had only his primordial nature for a long time, nor do you hold that the consequent nature came into being only after the world of ordinary actual entities appeared, with the help of God's primordial nature, which came first. Is this a correct interpretation of your position?"

WHITEHEAD: "Yes."

He then commented that there is no sense in talking about a "beginning" of the universe. There is no temporal sequence of the sort Bidney[4] refers to, with Process (creativity), God as primordial, then God as consequent, in that order of appearance.

## II · CREATIVITY

JOHNSON: "As I understand it, you use the term 'creativity' to refer to the fact that a new actual entity arises by appropriating data provided by other actual entities. Creativity is a process of interrelations between actual entities. There is no actual 'creativity' apart from actual entities in process of self-origination (AI 303; 230). It is therefore evident that, when you use the term 'creativity', you do *not*, strictly speaking, refer to some stuff, reality, substratum, entity, from which actual entities emerge by a process of individualization (SMW 223–24; PR 10). Is this a correct interpretation of your use of the term 'creativity'?"

Whitehead answered affirmatively, commenting that every element of the universe is present in any actual entity. Therefore, creativity is too. The character "creativity" is *nothing* apart from fact, which is the entire universe (cf. PR 31).

JOHNSON: "You refer to 'creativity' as the 'universal of universals', a 'principle' (PR 31). You also use, by implication, the term 'form'. I judge that you would not object to the term 'essence'?"

WHITEHEAD: "Correct."

JOHNSON: "Yet, you speak of 'each event [as] an individual matter of fact issuing from an individualisation of the substrate activity' (SMW 103; cf. PR 32). Do you mean, more specifically, that the 'principle' or 'essence'—'creativity'—is *exemplified* in particular actual entities during their process of self-creative development? In this sense 'creativity' is a 'general metaphysical character which underlies all occasions' (SMW 255)."

WHITEHEAD: "Yes."

He admitted that he applies the term 'creativity' to both (a) the eternal object "creativity" and (b) the *exemplifications* of this eternal object. *Most* eternal objects are contingent potentialities, in the sense that they do have to be actually exemplified by an actual entity. (They are, however, present to God's primordial nature.) Ultimate principles like "creativity" are not contingent possibilities. They are exemplified in *all* actual entities, at all times.

Whitehead recognized that he should have included in the Category of the Ultimate a reference to the potentiality of contingency as closely allied to "disjunctive diversity" (see PR 31).

Disregarding more complex processes, propositions, etc., Whitehead sees two basic forms of actual creativity. (1) With reference to eternal objects, there is the transformation from essence (an eternal object) to exemplification. (2) Actual entities contribute to other actual entities by a "conformation" of character. There is also the sense of the "whereness" (the "from-out-thereness") which accompanies the prehending, the taking in by one actual entity of the content of another.

JOHNSON: "When you speak of 'a creature of creativity' (PR 47); God as a 'non-temporal accident of creativity' (PR 11); God as 'the outcome of creativity' (PR 135), am I correct in assuming that you do not refer to the emergence of God and other actual entities from some reality other than an actual entity, but to the fact that each actual entity is the outcome of a creative process, its internal process of self-creation? Is it in this sense that it is 'a creature of creativity'?"

WHITEHEAD: "Yes."

God, an actual entity, is necessary to the world of other actual entities and they are necessary to him. God is one actual entity immersed in the process of his own self-creation and in the process of self-creation of other actual entities. As far as *actuality* is concerned, God is on the same level as anything else in the universe. Whitehead denied the claim of Augustine and Aquinas, that the more important is therefore the more actual. There are two sides to actuality: (a) limitation to an historic moment, (b) everlastingness. The latter is accounted for by God's consequent nature.

JOHNSON: "I presume that you would say that creativity as essence is exemplified in *various* actual entities. Hence the use of the term 'accident'."

WHITEHEAD: "Not exactly."

By 'accident' he means 'decision', for an actual entity is the ultimate source of its decision. 'God as accident' expresses the development of God's consequent nature, which never loses its character as specious present. It is wholly controlled by (a) a decision as to the possibilities to be realized (accomplished by God's primordial nature), and (b) a decision as to how God is going to receive data from the historical world.

JOHNSON: "Wouldn't it be wiser to say that God's subjective aim decides? There is a related question: God's primordial nature is accidental: it is one ordering of the eternal objects, the only one we have. But is that particular systematization of 'possibilities' the only one he could have?"

Whitehead replied that he could not settle the question. But what God has decided *is* the realm of possibilities for the universe. What he has decided is the result of a free decision. It is a standard of perfection for the universe.

JOHNSON: "When you say that creativity is 'conditioned by its

creatures' (PR 30), do you mean that creativity can only take place through the medium of the activity of actual entities (creatures)?"
WHITEHEAD: "Yes,"
and remarked that this deals with causality. He would stress: the process, objective immortality, real potentiality, objectification. The concrete characters of creatures are the conditions, the data to be used in creativity. Hence the notion of "real" potentiality.
JOHNSON: "When you say that creativity is 'actual in virtue of its accidents' (PR 10), do you mean that the essence 'creativity' is exemplified in particular actual entities as its accidents?"
WHITEHEAD: "Yes."
He suggested that the phrase be emended to: "creativity is actualized in virtue of its accidents."

A graduate course with Whitehead served, above all else, to illuminate and illustrate his profound conviction about philosophy.

> Philosophy is at once general and concrete, critical and appreciative of direct intuition. It is not—or, at least, should not be—a ferocious debate between irritable professors. It is a survey of possibilities and their comparison with actualities. In philosophy, the fact, the theory, the alternatives, and the ideal, are weighed together. Its gifts are insight and foresight, and a sense of the worth of life, in short, that sense of importance which nerves all civilized effort [AI 125].

NOTES

1. The following material is an abridged and modified version of the last two sections (pp. 365–76) of my report "Whitehead as Teacher and Philosopher," *Philosophy and Phenomenological Research*, 29 (1968–69), 351–76. It has had the benefit of the editorial skill of Professor Lewis S. Ford.
2. This and other questions enclosed in quotation marks are a verbatim reproduction of what was before Whitehead in typed form as he answered a question and dealt with related issues.
3. Whitehead also used it (earlier) in *Science and the Modern World*: see SMW 250, 257.—Eds.
4. David Bidney, "The Problem of Substance in Spinoza and Whitehead," *Philosophical Review*, 45 (1936), 574–92.

# 2

# Whitehead's Philosophical Response to the New Mathematics

GRANVILLE C. HENRY, JR.
*Claremont Men's College*

## I · HIS MATHEMATICAL DEVELOPMENT

WHITEHEAD BEGAN his serious philosophical writings after years spent as a professional mathematician, during which time he was intensely concerned almost exclusively with mathematics or its foundations. His professional philosophical contributions came late in life and only after he was convinced that problems in the foundations of mathematics could not be solved mathematically. It could be fairly said that Whitehead approached his philosophical interests historically through his own involvement in mathematics. For us, a look at his mathematical development can help point out some aspects of his intended meaning concerning eternal objects, which from many perspectives within the general philosophical tradition are quite problematical.

We may classify Whitehead's general concern in mathematics as a search for the true nature of mathematical existence. For the professional mathematician Whitehead, this meant no more than an appropriate understanding of number, magnitude, geometrical figure, algebraic structure, etc., that would allow both old and new

An earlier version of this chapter appeared in *The Southern Journal of Philosophy* (7 [1969–70], 341–49).

mathematics to fit into some unified whole with all aspects of pure mathematics interpretable in some common mathematical medium. New mathematical developments, for many of which Whitehead himself was responsible, caused him periodically to revise his understanding of this common medium and ultimately forced him to a *philosophical* position that he thought adequate for the new mathematics. We shall trace his development in this regard.

In his first major work, *A Treatise on Universal Algebra with Applications*, published in 1898, Whitehead was very sensitive to the fact that the new algebras, which constitute the primary subject matter of the book, represented a definite break with past mathematics and were, consequently, looked on with suspicion by many mathematicians. Accordingly, he issued a plea in the preface for their inclusion as legitimate mathematics (UA vi). In order to show that these algebras, which he believed capable of unification in a Universal Algebra, have claim to be an integral part of mathematics proper, Whitehead defined the nature of mathematics as "the development of all types of formal, necessary, deductive reasoning" (UA vi). This definition shows his feeling for and continuity with the English formalist school, which attempted to free mathematical formulation from necessary intuitive content. The further clarification of this definition by the explication of the words 'formal', 'necessary', and 'deductive' is an excellent description of the working philosophy of this formalist school, and I recommend it to the reader. By defining mathematics in terms of a "high" formalism, Whitehead could insist that the new algebras discussed in *Universal Algebra* are a definite part of the subject matter of mathematics in that they conform to the definition.

Whereas Whitehead recognized and accepted and indeed vigorously affirmed the formal nature of mathematics as the "dealing with . . . marks" according to "conventional laws" (UA 11), and also accepted the existence of a multiplicity of different mathematical systems that may have no necessary relationship to number or quantity, capable of being produced by such formalistic procedures, his primary goal in *Universal Algebra*, as far as he was concerned with the foundations of mathematics, was to find a ground of unity for the multiple systems in some common *interpretation.* If one mathematical content could be found such that aspects of it would serve as interpretations of the various formal systems, unity could be had on two fronts, the formal and the intuitive.

The search for an intuitive content for mathematics by Whitehead may seem surprising, since it is often claimed that mathematical formalists seek at all costs to avoid such content. This is not the case. The difference between the English formalists at the time Whitehead was writing *Universal Algebra* and the Berlin school of mathematicians with whom Husserl worked was primarily a matter of emphasis. Both groups operated with symbols in terms of some content. Whitehead's conviction that there is always some ontological content corresponding to mathematical reality allowed him the freedom to create apparently "fanciful" formalistic constructions with safety, whereas the members of the Berlin school, Kronecker, Dedekind, Weierstrass, and others, had grave doubts that one could find a mathematical content that would *always* correspond to formalistic manipulations. For them there was the ever present possibility that a mathematical system that was rigorous in all respects might still be no more than "formalistic nonsense." Accordingly, they sought for and thought they had found the universal content of all mathematics—namely, natural number.

For both groups, however, the tension between the apparent legitimacy of new formal mathematical systems and an old content that was being rendered increasingly inadequate *by* the new systems became critical. In response to this problem both Whitehead and Husserl launched a mathematical and then philosophical quest to find a true content or kind of mathematical existence that could provide a unified interpretation for the new algebras and logics. The end result for Whitehead was his doctrine of *eternal objects*; for Husserl his *intentional objects.* As a professionally trained mathematician, Husserl was influenced philosophically by the same major crises in the foundations of mathematics that influenced

Whitehead. In particular it was Husserl's awareness that natural numbers could not form the content of all mathematics that precipitated his search for the true objects of mathematics and resulted in his phenomenological method for apprehending them. As we shall see, it was the breakdown of the thesis of *Principia Mathematica*—namely, that logic could form the content of mathematics—that led Whitehead to investigate further the nature of mathematical objects. I mention Husserl here and at other places in this paper because reference to his development at critical junctures can help us to understand better Whitehead's development and mature position.

In *Universal Algebra* Whitehead sought to uphold an old Western idea that the unity of mathematical systems can be secured by a generalized idea of space. A generalized concept of space is an abstraction from many areas of mathematics, and hence has an applicability to those areas of mathematics which in themselves have no apparent relationship to the "spaciness" of space. Though capable of forming the interpretation of many different algebraic systems—this is what Whitehead sought to show in *Universal Algebra*—historically the mathematical idea of space arose as an abstraction from geometry.

It would be foolish and inaccurate on our part to see Whitehead's project in *Universal Algebra* as the reduction of different algebras to any physical properties of space. Whitehead specifically declares that his higher spaces are mathematical spaces and separate in concept and structure from physical space. Yet we must not forget the difficulty which even the most powerful of mathematicians and philosophers of the late nineteenth and early twentieth centuries had in isolating the new mathematical systems, abstracted from geometry, from intuitions associated with geometry. Whitehead was attempting in *Universal Algebra* to make intellectually palatable the new and strange algebras that had recently been created, and the natural and traditional way to accomplish this was to show how they could be interpreted through an extension of the familiar medium of geometry. The medium, however, was not adequate as a content-ground for mathematics, and Whitehead moved slowly toward a new foundation for mathematics, the *logic* of *Principia Mathematica.*

In Whitehead's next publication after *Universal Algebra*, "On Mathematical Concepts of the Material World,"[1] which was first read before the Royal Society in 1905, he sought to provide a multiplicity of different mathematical systems (or general spatial concepts), each of which is adequate to characterize the physical world. In this paper we see the mathematician–physicist Whitehead producing systems in pure mathematics designed to represent the most general characteristics of time, of space, and of entities in time and space. Many aspects of these mathematical systems found their way into his philosophical positions. It might be helpful to pursue the influence that these systems had on Whitehead's later philosophy, but our present interests are focused on Whitehead's search for the true nature of mathematical existence. This was not the thrust of the paper under consideration, but certain developments within the paper do give us clues concerning Whitehead's modification of his views on mathematics.

The expression 'general space' and the term 'manifold', which played such an important part in *Universal Algebra*, are absent from the paper "On Mathematical Concepts. . . ." They are to be found there, however, under a new name, 'polyadic relations', where they serve a different function, specifically the description of the physical world. The change in terminology from 'general spaces' to 'polyadic relations' is a shift from the terminology of higher geometry to that of logic. In "On Mathematical Concepts . . ." Whitehead introduced almost all of the full-blown logical symbolism of *Principia Mathematica.* The shift was from the generality of mathematical spaces to the generality of logic. This was a shift in orientation from the mathematical objects which are tinged with geometrical intuitions to those which partake of logical intuitions.

*Universal Algebra* was not devoid of interest for logic. On the contrary, Boole's symbolic logic was presented in detail and the other algebras were studied "for the sake of the light thereby thrown on the general theory of symbolic reasoning" (UA v).

But there is a decided difference of emphasis in the use of logic between the two works. In *Universal Algebra* logic as a formalized tool was not used extensively. It was reflected, as a Boolean algebra, into a general space in order to find unity with other systems. In "On Mathematical Concepts . . . ," however, instead of symbolic logic being reflected into a general space and thereby partaking of spatial intuition as in *Universal Algebra*, it was used as the *means by which* a multiplicity of essential relations (or, if we prefer, general spaces) is presented. General spaces (essential relations) in "On Mathematical Concepts . . ." were understood in terms of logic and the intuitions relevant to it and *vice versa*, that is, logic understood in terms of general spaces, as was done in *Universal Algebra.* There is nothing unusual in the use of logic by Whitehead in "On Mathematical Concepts . . ." to present what is essentially a mathematical content. This has been the traditional procedure since Greek mathematics. The use of logic, however, not merely as the tool of mathematics but as the fundamental content of mathematics was a new position taken by Whitehead in *Principia Mathematica.*

In 1900 Whitehead and Russell went to France and heard Giuseppe Peano report on his recent work in logic. Peano had enormously increased the extent of symbolic logic by introducing symbols to represent the notions "there exists," "is contained in," "the set of all $x$'s such that," etc., that had found no adequate representation in the logic of Boole. By this symbolism he was able to present in the *Formulaire mathématique* a development of arithmetic which requires only the general principles of logic (adequately symbolized), the undefined terms: 'number', 'zero', and 'the successor of'; five postulates about these undefined terms, and definitions of certain fundamental arithmetical operations. The place of logic in Peano's system, however, appears to be essentially a classical one. Logic is a tool for the presentation of mathematical content. The concepts "number," "zero," etc., are undefined and presumed to constitute the elements of arithmetic and not the content of logic.

The transition that we have observed in Whitehead's thought from trying to ground mathematics in a generalized mathematical space to the clothing of spaces (or essential relations) in logical terminology is run full course in *Principia Mathematica.* Logic was affirmed to be the source of mathematical subject matter. The task of *Principia Mathematica,* "the mathematical treatment of principles of mathematics," was accomplished by "a backward extension into provinces hitherto abandoned to philosophy" (PM I v), i.e., into logic, which had traditionally been a part of philosophy. What was sought by this "backward extension" was a set of primitive ideas of logic, a set of definitions phrased exclusively in terms of these primitive logical ideas, and a set of primitive propositions (axioms) of logic by which the logical system created from these axioms is sufficient to deduce the ordinary propositions of arithmetic, algebra, geometry, analysis, etc., from the original primitive ideas.

The primitive logical ideas: "elementary proposition," "propositional function," "negation," "disjunction," etc., are assumed to have a direct intuitive presentation. They point to logical or mathematical objects which "reveal" themselves to the trained observer. The primitive ideas cannot, of course, be defined but "are *explained* by means of descriptions intended to point out to the reader what is meant" (PM I 95). Whitehead and Russell, however, showed no trust in self-evidence alone. Too many serious errors had been introduced into mathematics by accepting apparently self-evident premisses for them to ascribe any infallible quality to such "feelings" of certainty. In spite of many careful statements in *Principia Mathematica* about the possible unreliability of "self-evidence," largely motivated by the necessity of introducing the awkward Axiom of Reducibility into its framework, the axioms of *Principia Mathematica* on the whole do, in fact, partake of a degree of self-evidence that allows them to be accepted by many philosophers, even today, as the true intuitive ground of both logic and mathematics. Most well-trained mathematical logicians, however, can no longer accept the logistic thesis as presented by *Principia Mathematica.*

The breakdown of the thesis of *Principia Mathematica* occurred primarily, I think, for three reasons: an instability within *Principia*

*Mathematica* that became critical; the more thorough and more adequate formalization by subsequent mathematicians of the mathematics of *Principia Mathematica*; and the surprising results of Gödel. The instability was the famous Theory of Types formulated by Russell to handle Burali Forti's contradiction and others implicit within *Principia Mathematica.* Whitehead's original enthusiasm for Russell's solution, reflected in his statement "All the contradictions can be avoided,"[2] turned to cautious skepticism and then to outright rejection when he realized that "our only way of understanding the rule is nonsense" (ESP 103).

The further formalization of the mathematical system of *Principia Mathematica* has effectively separated the mathematical system as such from the assumed logical content that was presumed to be its ground. The mathematical system of *Principia Mathematica,* for example, can be presented mathematically by the set theoretic models of P. R. Halmos, where "predicates" are functions, "propositions" are constant functions, quantifiers are mappings, etc.[3] The natural relationship between propositions and the primitive elements of *Principia Mathematica* becomes a very unnatural one in these algebras. Yet these newer algebras allow a more powerful grasp of the mathematics of the original system than did *Principia Mathematica.* The philosophical position that sees mathematics as a natural generalization from logical reality is no longer necessary and may indeed hinder the acquisition of the true mathematical structure of *Principia Mathematica* itself.

Gödel's Incompleteness Theorem showed the impossibility of deducing all the theorems of arithmetic from *Principia Mathematica* or, for that matter, from any finite axiomatic system. Thus, the program of *Principia Mathematica* to deduce mathematics (all of it) from a simple set of logical axioms is now believed to be impossible.

It is difficult to ascertain exactly when Whitehead became aware of the full crisis of developments pertinent to the thesis of *Principia Mathematica.* One does notice that even during the period in which he affirmed without any major reservations that mathematics is simply an extension of logic, he also espoused a more formalistic position.[4] As in the past, however, Whitehead could not exclusively maintain a pure formalism. For him the formalism of mathematics and the reality to which it referred had to be explained in terms of the most general categories applicable to all things, i.e., metaphysics. "Even in arithmetic you cannot get rid of a subconscious reference to the unbounded universe" (ESP 103). We see Whitehead's formalism slowly giving way to a generalized content of mathematics that appears at one point as "relations," at another point as "patterns," and finally crystallizes in terms of his precise understanding of "eternal objects."

## II · ETERNAL OBJECTS

If we understand Whitehead's doctrine of eternal objects as found in *Science and the Modern World* and *Process and Reality* to be primarily a description of the ontological nature of *mathematical relationships* and only secondarily a description of other abstract entities like colors or even emotional feelings, much ambiguity and actual error concerning them can be cleared up. I grant that this is not the way Whitehead normally approaches the subject. Many beginning students of Whitehead have their first approach to the meaning of eternal objects through colors. There is no surprise then that a general uneasiness may emerge concerning their supposed radical abstractness or their unique individuality.

I do not think that our common knowledge of the abstract nature of colors or of emotional feelings has undergone any great change since the time of Plato. There is a natural abstraction "red" that we can make from red things. Most of us, however, have considerable hesitancy about declaring "redness" to be in any significant way independent of red things. So also are our feelings concerning particular shades and variations of "redness." How can we declare a certain exact red color to exist if there are not things which have that red color? The general criticisms of the Platonic tradition concerning abstract relationships still hold. Yet we hear Whitehead frequently speaking of both the radically abstract nature of eternal objects and their individual particularity. And eternal objects are held by him to be somehow independent of and prior to *ordinary* empirical things.[5]

Although our knowledge of color abstractions has not changed appreciably since Plato, our understanding of the nature of mathematical abstractions *has changed* and changed in the direction of reintensifying both their abstract nature and their individuality. These changes came primarily in the nineteenth and early twentieth centuries through the more adequate formalization of mathematics itself. Although recognizing that an understanding of the transcendence of mathematical form with respect to empirical reality has been a part of the Western tradition since Plato, Whitehead clearly assumed that there is a degree of abstraction available to the contemporary mathematician and philosopher that was not available to *any* pre–nineteenth-century mathematician. For example, geometry need have no necessary relationship to space. As he learned from the breakdown of *Principia Mathematica*, mathematical logic need not be involved with propositions or any aspect of ordinary language. And number may have nothing to do with counting. "It is only recently that the *succession* of processes which is involved in any act of counting has been seen to be irrelevant to the idea of number."[6] Mathematical relationships, for Whitehead, as "complete and absolute abstraction" (SMW 31–32), need not be part of *any* empirical situation.

Mathematics acquires its transcendence by being purely symbolic and axiomatic. By being symbolic it allows us to consider relationships which transcend their own exemplification in the physical world. By being axiomatic it allows us to consider relationships that are not observable in the world—and may never be. This is possible because we can manipulate the axioms of a system and thereby determine new relationships and hence new mathematics without having presentations of these relationships in intuition or in the physical world at all. Colors and emotional feelings share neither of these characteristics.

What Whitehead had in mind as an eternal object is not just the symbolism, however, but a metaphysically real relationship to which the symbolism refers. The referent of the symbolism may be found at times in the physical world, but if this is where we primarily look for it we are not in the "realm of complete and absolute abstraction" and, hence, are not dealing with pure mathematics. The precise ontological status of a mathematical eternal object is that of a potential relationship for entities in the world. When such a potential relationship is actualized—or, to use Whitehead's terminology, becomes ingredient—in the world, we are able to see it in and among the things of the world. In order to "see" it, however, we do not have to behold it in the world. One can apprehend a mathematical eternal object directly, according to Whitehead, through the symbolism of mathematics or, for that matter, just as it is in itself.

As abstract, eternal objects have their own individual identity.

> [E]ach eternal object is an individual which, in its own peculiar fashion, is what it is. This particular individuality . . . cannot be described otherwise than as being itself [SMW 229].

Whitehead's emphasis on the individual objectivity of mathematical relationships is derived from his knowledge of the successive failures of more generalized mathematical theories to explain thoroughly, or to ground, mathematics. As we have mentioned, neither geometrical figure, natural numbers (arithmetic), logic as formulated in *Principia Mathematica*, nor even set theory can form the general foundation for the totality of canonical mathematics. During the long course of mathematical history, the general assumption that individual mathematical relationships are dependent on or grounded in larger, more comprehensive theories effectively blurred the focus of concern on the individuality of the relationships themselves. With the breakdown of the thesis of *Principia Mathematica*, Whitehead saw that the individual mathematical entities could somehow be ontologically prior to their general systematic relatedness, i.e., prior to the general field of logic itself, and began to investigate this position in his philosophical works.

What happened to Whitehead's philosophical position concerning the individuality of mathematical relationships can be understood by those who know Husserlian phenomenology and especially by those who are familiar with Husserl's early works. The similarity of development between the two thinkers is striking. Husserl's phenomenological battle cry "to the objects themselves" (*zu den Sachen selbst*) was originally raised with respect to mathematical and logical objects and for the same reasons that motivated Whitehead. The philosophical transition for Husserl was far more violent than for Whitehead because Husserl had been attempting to explain mathematics in terms of a psychologically dominated philosophy based on his understanding, derived from the Berlin school, that mathematics itself could be adequately grounded mathematically in natural number and thereby understood in terms of the *acts* of counting. The breakdown of this understanding in mathematics forced Husserl into an almost complete revision of his philosophy, where the emphasis was on the priority of the *intentional* mathematical objects and there was a de-emphasis of their psychological conditioning. We all know that Husserl's emphasis on intentional *objects* in no way kept him from incorporating human subjectivity into his philosophy, which has been hailed by Quentin Lauer as the "triumph of subjectivity."[7] For Whitehead too the locus or metaphysical ground of mathematics, namely actual entities, became most intensely subjective in his later philosophy.

If there is no systematic mathematical or logical ground that *mathematically* can be the source of all mathematics, where then ontologically do we find mathematics? How can we understand that unity and logical relatedness which mathematics seems actually to possess? Whitehead worked out a metaphysical view that finally saw mathematical relationships as grounded in actual entities, by reference to which he could explain the place and unity of mathematics. The concept of "actual entity," for Whitehead, developed out of his earlier concept of "fact," which he had employed to show the relationship of the obvious mathematical aspects of science to sense experience. The radical subjectification of facts that occurred in Whitehead's final concept of actual entity, where mathematical relationships seen in the world were understood to be projected there in the mode of presentational immediacy, became necessary in considerable measure due to Whitehead's pointed concern with the nature of mathematical relationships as constructed entities. We could by further analysis show how Whitehead's understanding of the structural development of actual entities corresponded to his understanding of the relationship of human subjectivity to created mathematics, but further considerations of this topic are unwise in view of the intended length of the present paper.

If the concept of eternal objects in Whitehead's philosophy was modeled, as we maintain, primarily on his understanding of mathematical existence, and if his concept of actual entities was developed in large part to find a true ground for mathematics, how then are we to understand non-mathematical eternal objects like colors and feelings, in their relationship to actual events? Are these kinds of eternal objects of the same nature as the mathematical ones? The answer is both "Yes" and "No" and is, therefore, hardly satisfactory. We need a detailed phenomenological analysis to establish the similarities and differences between mathematical and non-mathematical eternal objects.

An analysis of the sort proposed is a very difficult one, however. Its difficulty is not peculiar to the specific philosophy of Whitehead, but is manifest in the analysis of any Western philosopher who has used contemporary developments in mathematics to clarify and structure essentially non-mathematical reality. The list of philosophers who have employed a new mathematical technique or understanding to produce a new philosophical position, technique, or insight is long and honorable: Plato, Aristotle, Descartes, Leibniz, Spinoza, Pascal, Locke, Kant, Russell, Husserl, Wittgenstein, and many others. In Western thought new mathematical discoveries have often opened up new ways of seeing non-mathematical aspects of the world. In this regard, the most successful philosophy of this century is the phenomenology of Husserl, which was initially developed for analysis of mathematical and logical objects but became immediately applicable to vast areas of non-mathematical content involving the scientific, historical, psychological, social, and religious disciplines. It seems that the very success of a philosophy that has employed mathematical tools or insights to present or clarify non-mathematical content tends to obscure the relationship between the mathematical and the non-mathematical. This is especially true during the period of the most important influence of the given philosophy. Subsequent further formalization and development of the mathematics may sharpen the boundaries between the purely mathematical and that which is not. We are capable of adequately making such distinctions in the philosophy of Descartes, for example. But for the philosophy of Whitehead in its present stage, the analysis which I think *must* be made should proceed cautiously and in awareness of the major mathematical developments since Whitehead.

The proposed analysis should, I think, first try to show the similarity of non-mathematical eternal objects to mathematical ones, and then if possible try to make the way of understanding the non-mathematical ones consistent with the way of understanding the mathematical ones. The only way we can understand their differences is to press forward to an understanding of their similarities. For example, Whitehead speaks of colors—e.g., the elemental sensa involved in the experience of a green leaf—as simple eternal objects (SMW 240; cf. PR 174). But there are no simple mathematical eternal objects. Points, lines, whole numbers, etc., which had been considered to be simple by many nineteenth-century mathematicians, are, in fact, *very* complex structures.[8] Can colors be simple eternal objects? In a consistent Whiteheadian perspective, I do not think so. They are necessarily complex. A detailed analysis will confirm, I think, that all eternal objects are complex. Through this analysis, however, we may be struck by some aspect of color that is in principle different from the qualities of mathematical eternal objects, perhaps its simplicity. When we attempt to grasp the tension between the necessary characteristics of mathematical eternal objects and the experiential aspects of sensory eternal objects, a sensitive phenomenological analysis can be of immense help.

## NOTES

1. Reprinted in *Alfred North Whitehead: An Anthology*, edd. F. S. C. Northrop and Mason W. Gross (New York: Macmillan, 1953), pp. 7–82.

2. "Mathematics," *Encyclopaedia Britannica*, 11th ed., XVII 881. (Also ESP 278.—Eds.)

3. Paul R. Halmos, *Algebraic Logic* (New York: Chelsea, 1962).

4. "Axioms of Geometry," *Encyclopaedia Britannica*, 11th ed., XI 730.

5. By the ontological principle, eternal objects have to be somewhere, and ultimately they are found in the primordial nature of God.

6. "Mathematics," *Encyclopaedia Britannica*, 11th ed., XVII 881. (Also ESP 280.—Eds.)

7. Quentin Lauer, S.J., *The Triumph of Subjectivity: An Introduction to Transcendental Phenomenology*, 2nd ed. (New York: Fordham University Press, 1978).

8. The complexity of a point may be seen in *Process and Reality*, Pt. IV, Ch. 2.

# II

# THE METAPHYSICS OF PROCESS

# 3

# Some Aspects of Whitehead's Metaphysics

William A. Christian, Sr.
*Yale University*,
Emeritus

After half a century the logical structure of Whitehead's speculative philosophy is a good deal clearer than it used to be, but there are reasons why this has been slow in coming.

He began the construction of his speculative scheme in the nineteen twenties, which was not the best of times to embark on such an enterprise. A different tide was setting in, and from then on through our own time speculative philosophy would have to make its way against stronger currents. Rightly or wrongly philosophers would be occupied with other sorts of questions, logical or epistemological or existential. Also his categories were novel and strange; hence much of *Process and Reality* had to be devoted to explication and development of them. Kant's remark about his exposition in the first critique, that he had to sacrifice intuitive clarity for the sake of discursive clarity, has an application to *Process and Reality* as well. Another reason is that his conception of the function of speculative philosophy differed from some traditional models for metaphysics. Indeed it is not very widely understood to this day. So all in all it is not surprising that it has taken some time to puzzle him out.

As contributions to the continuing process of puzzling him out I offer three reflections. The first has to do with his use of the term 'feeling'; the second deals with his treatment of becoming and time; the third is about the relation of his speculative scheme to our non-speculative judgments.

When I speak of Whitehead's categoreal scheme I refer to his exposition of the categories in *Process and Reality*, Part I, Chapter II, Section II. Whitehead's conceptual scheme or his speculative scheme, as I use these terms, includes not only the categoreal scheme but also the derivative notions introduced in Chapter III and the further developments of the categories and derivative notions later in *Process and Reality* and elsewhere. When I speak of Whitehead's speculative philosophy or his metaphysics, I am taking together (i) his assemblage of "items of experience" from perceptual experience, from the sciences, from moral experience, and from other sources, and his arguments for these, (ii) his construction of the conceptual scheme, and (iii) his derivations from the conceptual scheme of speculative interpretations of items of experience.

## I

Whitehead aimed at replacing Cartesian dualism with "a one-substance cosmology," meaning not that there is just one substance but that substances are of just one sort. He thought the fundamental categories should be capable of interpreting both bodies and minds, and borderline cases as well.

One motive for taking this tack was to give an account of how conscious and reflective beings can occur in nature. He says:

> . . . any doctrine which refuses to place human experience outside nature, must find in descriptions of human experience factors which also enter into the descriptions of less specialized natural occurrences. If there be no such factors, then the doctrine of human experience as a fact within nature is mere bluff, founded upon vague phrases whose sole merit is a comforting familiarity. We should either admit dualism, at least as a provisional doctrine, or we should point out the identical elements connecting human experience with physical science [AI 237].

So when he developed his conceptual scheme the concept of an actual entity had to be so constructed that it could be used to interpret both living things and non-living things, and both conscious beings and non-conscious beings. How did he go about this?

In Whitehead's categoreal scheme, an actual entity is a concrescence, literally a growing together, of a number of prehensions. A prehension is an operation in which an actual entity relates itself to some other entity. A prehension need not be conscious, and it is consistent with Whitehead's scheme to say that none of those actual entities which (in a Whiteheadian interpretation) constitute stones and trees has any conscious prehensions at all. This would agree with what we would ordinarily say about the main bulk of the physical world.

Some other indications of the subordinate and, one might say, incidental role of consciousness in Whitehead's categoreal scheme are worth noting. Saying that an actual entity is a subject, i.e., that it prehends other entities, does not commit one to saying that an actual entity is conscious. Further, saying that the concrescence of an actual entity is subjectively immediate does not do so either. For this only says that some of its prehensions are reactions to others of its prehensions, so that it "plays diverse roles in self-formation" (PR 38; see Categories of Explanation 21–23). Also, the "privacy" of a concrescence is a consequence of its subjective immediacy, and does not depend on any of its prehensions being conscious.

Now some prehensions are called feelings. What does this mean? Strictly speaking, not very much. Whitehead introduced the term 'feeling' into the categoreal scheme while making a distinction between positive prehensions, in which an actual entity takes positive account of other entities, and negative prehensions, in which an actual entity blocks out other entities from contributing to its concrescence. 'Feeling' is introduced as equivalent to 'positive prehension' (PR 35; Category of Explanation 12). So the term 'feeling', wherever it occurs in this categoreal use, could be eliminated by substituting the expression 'positive prehension'.

Hence we should not read into this use of the term 'feeling' the connotations it has in ordinary speech. To say that an actual entity has feelings is only to say that it takes some positive account of other entities. So it would be misleading to say that the actual entities which (in a Whiteheadian interpretation) constitute the history of a stone have feelings, if the categoreal sense of the term were not clear from the context of the utterance. And it would be even more misleading to say bluntly that Whitehead attributes feelings to stones. For this would short-circuit the process of speculative interpretation, confusing terms of ordinary speech and terms of the speculative scheme. Of course Whitehead often speaks of human feelings in the ordinary way. These are among the items of experience which his conceptual scheme is designed to interpret.

Correspondingly the categoreal use of the term 'feeling' does not do much to develop the conceptual resources needed to interpret both the laws of classical mechanics and, on the other hand, the wealth of qualitative significance in a simple perceptual experience, or a conversation between two human beings. Further conceptual resources are introduced in other ways, one of which is as follows.

A prehension has not only a subject, which prehends, and an object, which is prehended; it has also a "subjective form," which is the specific quality of the subject's reaction to the object. This is the point at which qualities are introduced into the scheme. This is the category which can be used to interpret both physical and emotional intensities. Indeed, in one of his later writings Whitehead goes so far as to say: "the energetic activity considered in physics is the emotional intensity entertained in life" (MT 231–32). This is certainly a misleading exaggeration, since it suggests that we should speak of the emotional life of an atom or a stone. That would be intuitively implausible and, what is more to the point, it is not required by Whitehead's conceptual scheme. All that needs to be said is that an actual entity which is, in a Whiteheadian interpretation, a constituent of the history of an atom or a stone, reacts in its own specific way to the other entities in its environment. For a "one-substance cosmology" all that is needed is a genuine analogy, however faint, between physical intensity and emotional intensity. The analogy can be a genuine one because the differences can be explained within the framework of the category of subjective forms. Incidentally, consciousness itself is construed as an element of subjective form occurring, rarely, in the concrescences of some very complex actual entities.

This is by no means the whole story of Whitehead's aim at a scheme powerful enough to replace Descartes' dualistic ontology. But it illustrates the main point I wish to suggest—namely, that we should not attribute more force to Whitehead's analogies between physical processes and human experience than his conceptual scheme bestows upon them. For Whitehead himself sometimes spoke of the physical world in a more romantic manner than his own conceptual scheme required him to do.

## II

My second reflection is on Whitehead's discussion of becoming and time, in particular on what he called the epochal theory of time.

One reason why his doctrines about becoming seem paradoxical is this: we have an inclination to begin by thinking of time as an ordered array of empty times ready and waiting for events to occur in them, just as we have an inclination to think of space as an ordered array of empty places. We have been taught that there is an entity called time, and what could there be in time itself but empty times? Long after we have had more sophisticated thoughts about the matter, this picture is evoked by the word 'time', and to this day its ghostly presence haunts many scholarly discussions of the epochal theory of time. But long before Whitehead embarked on the enterprise of speculative philosophy he had been carrying on a critique of these notions of space and time, beginning with a paper read before the Royal Society in 1905 and continuing in *The Principles of Natural Knowledge*, *The Concept of Nature*, *The Principle of Relativity*, and a number of papers in the teens and early twenties.

The best way to understand Whitehead's treatment of time is

to begin by thinking of the word 'time' (written with a small 't') as a heading on a page of a notebook, under which one might list certain features of common experience. We could state some of these as follows:

> Some things come into being.
> Some things come to an end.
> Some things endure.
> Some things succeed others.
> Some things exist along with others.
> Some things are repeated.
> We can think of smaller and smaller, and larger and larger, durations.

We would thus assemble under the general heading "time" various things we would want to say which we would be willing to argue for if necessary. Then we would ask what categories we need to introduce in order to give a coherent interpretation of these and other features of the world. The latter sort of operation is what Whitehead is doing when he constructs his conceptual scheme.

This way of going about a cosmology commits him to conducting his argument in two stages. In the first stage he must argue for the items on the list of interpretanda, for example that some real things come into being, without essential reference to his own speculative scheme. In the second stage of the argument he must show that the scheme of categories and derivative notions is coherent, and that it can yield adequate interpretations of the interpretanda.

The principal concept for interpreting becoming is the concept of a concrescence, a process in which a number of prehensions grow together into the unity of a complete actual entity. Categoreally speaking, a concrescence does not have to begin or end. But if we believe that some real things do indeed begin and end, then we will want to say that some concrescences of actual entities begin and end, thus introducing into the conceptual scheme the derivative notion of actual occasions. And if we believe that there are real connections between the past and the present, we will say that the concrescence of an actual occasion includes prehensions of actual occasions which are in its past and is thus conditioned by them.

This last development introduces into the scheme the concept of a process of a different sort, a process of transition, the succession of one actual occasion by another actual occasion. In a finite concrescence an actual occasion comes into existence; in a process of transition one actual occasion is succeeded by another. More particularly, in the succession of one occasion by another, the occasion which is succeeded ceases to have significance for itself, though it functions as an object for its successors and thus its achievement conditions the concrescences which succeed it. This strong sense of succession might be called 'exclusive succession', though Whitehead does not use this expression. It gives a meaning to saying that one thing is in the past of another.

Now, within a process of concrescence there is no succession in that sense. None of the prehensions within a concrescence ceases to be active as the concrescence proceeds. No prehension is past and done with, relative to other prehensions in that concrescence, in the way an actual occasion is past and done with relative to its successors. Within a concrescence there is no exclusive succession.

Thus a concrescence is a real process, but it is a process which does not involve succession in that sense of 'succession' which holds of a process of transition. None of the operations which constitute a concrescence occurs after some other such operation within the concrescence has ceased. So no prehension is in the past of any other prehension in that concrescence. This distinction between processes of concrescence and processes of transition is very clear throughout *Process and Reality*.

As a concrescence proceeds, more and more complex prehensions supervene until a single complex prehension, the satisfaction of the subjective aim of the process, is produced. But the simpler prehensions are not superseded by the more complex prehensions in the way that one occasion is superseded by another. Instead they are carried along in the process. They are coordinated and combined but none of them is left behind as, in a process of transition, one actual occasion is left behind by another.

The growth of a concrescence can be analyzed into earlier and later phases (or stages). However, it seems clear that saying that one phase of a concrescence succeeds another does not imply that prehensions succeed, in the strong sense, other prehensions in the same concrescence. The reason is as follows.

The real constituents of a concrescence are prehensions, and the concept of a phase of a concrescence is a concept of a set of prehensions. Now, relative to a successor phase, the prehensions constituting a predecessor phase are not past. Instead they are real constituents of the successor phase, along with other prehensions which originate in reaction to them. They are present in the successor phase *formaliter* (a term which Whitehead takes from Descartes), that is to say, non-abstractively. Thus some successor phase in a concrescence is different from a predecessor phase, not because the prehensions belonging to the predecessor phase are past, but by virtue of the fact that it includes, along with the prehensions constituting the predecessor phase, prehensions of those prehensions. These latter prehensions are more complex, and they organize the simpler prehensions into compatible contrasts until a single complex prehension, the satisfaction, eventuates. This is the real force of 'earlier' and 'later', when successions of phases in a concrescence are spoken of. So speaking of successive phases does not imply that some prehensions in a concrescence are in the past of some other prehensions in that concrescence, that some prehensions succeed others in the strong sense of 'succeed'. (See Category of Explanation 26.)

Historically considered, Whitehead's paper, "Time," for the Sixth International Congress of Philosophy in 1926, belongs to a transitional phase in the development of his conceptual scheme. There he speaks of successions of phases in a concrescence as "internal supersession," in contrast to supersession of one actual occasion by another. But in *Process and Reality* the term 'supersession' is restricted to the latter kind of case, that is, to transitions. Phases in a concrescence are spoken of as 'supervening' (see PR 248, 287).

These concepts of concrescences and transitions are some but not all of the conceptual resources which Whitehead develops for the purpose of speculative interpretation of those features of the world which would be listed on the page of the notebook under the heading "time." If the scheme to which these concepts belong is coherent, then the issue is whether we can derive from it adequate interpretations of those interpretanda.

The main trouble about understanding the epochal theory of time begins when we suppose, as even some serious readers of *Process and Reality* have been tempted to do, that concrescences and transitions must be understood in the framework of absolute time. We are predisposed to think of time as a uniform succession of durationless moments, prior to and independent of actual occurrences. So we are tempted to suppose that both concrescences and transitions must be understood to be regimented, in their occurrences, by this uniform flow of time. With this supposition, which Whitehead was setting aside when he said that in a concrescence the "genetic passage from phase to phase is not in physical time" (PR 434), readers of *Process and Reality* would become mired in hopeless perplexities.

The train of thought which we are thus tempted to board runs as follows: Since, we suppose, concrescences are structured in their occurrences by a uniform succession of moments, and since each moment leaves other moments behind it, in its past, a concrescence must reflect this pattern. So, in a concrescence, prehensions must leave other prehensions behind them, in their pasts. In this way we are led toward thinking of a process of concrescence as a series of successions in each of which a successor leaves its predecessors in its past, in the way that an actual occasion leaves its predecessors in its past. Thus we come to think of the process of concrescence as a series of internal transitions. So, on this supposition, the distinction between concrescences and transitions would break down, and then it would be no great feat to show that the epochal theory of time—and with it Whitehead's theory of finite actual entities (i.e., actual occasions)—is incoherent.

It would also follow, if the process of nature is uniform in some such way as this, that we could not understand how any novel real thing could come into being. To some philosophers that might be a welcome conclusion. But whether we should say that novel actualities come into being, and then develop categories for interpreting this, is the very question at issue.

So we mistake the point of the epochal theory of time if we think that Whitehead's conceptual scheme presupposes a homogeneous structure of succession, and that the occurrences of concrescences and transitions are supposed to be regimented by this uniform flow. That would put the matter the wrong way around. For Whitehead wanted to raise the question how the concept of physical time could be derived from the concept of a multiplicity of concrescences and transitions.

In Part IV of *Process and Reality* and elsewhere he gave just such a derivation in his theory of extensive connection, whose ancestor was the theory of extensive abstraction which he had developed in his earlier philosophy of nature. The earlier theory was formulated in terms of the overlapping of events. The later theory was formulated in terms of extensive connections among, and within, the non-overlapping four-dimensional regions (standpoints) of actual occasions. In both cases Whitehead was construing the uniformity of space–time as an abstraction from more concrete constituents of the world we experience. He thought that extensive continuity was just what needed to be explained. Philosophy is the criticism of abstractions, he said. Beginning with absolute space and time seemed an example of misplaced concreteness. There was no doubt whatever in his mind that extensive continuity is a feature of our environment. He thought that philosophers ought to ask how this comes to be so.

## III

Now consider Whitehead's conception of the place of speculative philosophy in the total range of our thought, and especially in relation to the common-sense view of the world, including ourselves.

As human beings we have a certain perspective on the world. Most of us are between three feet and seven feet tall and weigh between fifty and three hundred pounds. We live on a certain scale.

We handle, desire, avoid, or enjoy some fairly large chunks of the world. We endure through time, for a time, and our lives have some fairly large-scale rhythms: sleeping and waking, resting and working, adapting to the seasons of the year, and so on. We undertake to carry out some fairly long-range purposes and plans. We remember events which happened years ago, sometimes, we say, "as if it were yesterday."

Yet we are told, and there seems good reason to believe, that the large-scale bodies we handle and enjoy, including our own bodies, are constituted without remainder by a vast multiplicity of microscopic and sub-microscopic entities: atoms, electrons, and other even more puzzling constituents. And we are told that the large-scale rhythms we experience are constituted by multiplicities of briefer events, some of them very brief indeed, with subtle and complex rhythms and patterns of their own, of which we are not clearly aware.

Now if, knowing or believing all this, it is still not inconsistent to maintain the human perspective and to live on the human scale, then it would not be inconsistent both to maintain the human perspective and to think of the world, including ourselves, as constituted by a multiplicity of actual occasions organized into nexūs of various sorts.

The real questions about this are: Why should we, and how should we think of the world in such a way? What sort of argument could be offered for Whitehead's speculative assertions, and what is the force of the conclusions the argument would lead to?

Here some of Whitehead's own phrases have been gravely misleading, particularly the phrase 'descriptive generalization' (see, for example, PR 15–16), even though corrections are to be found in its contexts. Some readers have taken this to mean (i) that actual entities are observable and (ii) that the concept of an actual entity is arrived at by generalization from a number of such observations. This certainly mistakes what Whitehead is doing. His argument does not require the isolation of actual entities as discriminable and identifiable data of experience. In this respect Whitehead's actual entities and Leibniz's monads are on the same footing. In both cases we are offered concepts whose instantiations cannot be picked out and inspected as a natural historian inspects specimens in the field or in a museum. Nor is the concept of an actual entity arrived at by comparison of a number of observed instances and generalization from these. Speculative philosophy as Whitehead practiced it is not aptly characterized as a process of descriptive generalization.

Descriptions or, we might better say, pre-speculative accounts of features of our experience of the world—and arguments about them—certainly do come in. Whitehead argues with Descartes about our self-consciousness, with classical mechanism about our spatio-temporal experience, and with Hume about the experiences which give rise to discourse about causes and effects. The way these accounts, and arguments for them, are relevant is this: they belong to the assemblage of interpretanda, in view of which the conceptual scheme is to be constructed. Other accounts come in here too, for instance, well-founded scientific theories, accounts of moral practices, and religious intuitions. These too have to be interpreted. But the conceptual scheme is not derived from these pre-speculative accounts by inductive generalization; it is constructed with a view to interpreting them.

So the form of the argument for Whitehead's speculative assertions must be different from the form of arguments supporting descriptive generalizations. Instead, it must satisfy the following two requirements: (i) it must show that the conceptual scheme itself is reasonably clear and coherent, and (ii) it must show that from this scheme adequate interpretations of the various items of experience can be produced.

What then is a speculative interpretation, and when is a speculative interpretation adequate? Suppose we take some item of experience, say a perception of the fall of a leaf, or a resolution to undertake a certain course of action. We ask what we can say truly of this item quite apart from speculative categories. This pre-speculative account would include statements about the motion of the leaf, our enjoyment of its changing shapes and colors as it falls, the functioning of our body in relation to it, the associations which condition our reactions, and so on.

Then we ask whether we could match this account with a complex statement formulated in Whitehead's systematic terms in accord with his rules for their use (his Categories of Explanation). If we cannot match it, then at this point Whitehead's scheme is inapplicable. If we can match it, then the scheme is applicable. If we can go on matching pre-speculative accounts with Whiteheadian interpretations up to any point we choose, then the scheme has shown itself adequate up to that point. Of course we can never finish the process, somewhat as we can never complete the applications of a physical theory.

Notice that at every point what is now up for judgment is no longer a description or an interpretandum of some other sort but an interpretation. The question is whether the scheme can yield interpretations which are adequate to the pre-speculative accounts with which we begin. That is the way speculative philosophy comes in. So instead of asking for examples attesting the descriptive power of Whitehead's categories, one should look for tests of their interpretative power, as, for example, David Crocker does in his dissertation, "A Whiteheadian Theory of Intentions and Actions" (Yale, 1970). Otherwise one would be barking up the wrong tree.

Why should anyone be interested in such interpretations? What is their value? On the first page of the preface to *Process and Reality* Whitehead says that Part II, which is titled "Discussions and Applications," "shows the power of the scheme to put the various elements of our experience into a consistent relation to each other." From time to time we do indeed reflect on the relations of perceptual experience to physical theories, on the relation of moral experience to our biological constitution, and even perhaps on mathematics and the good. The problem is that these topics seem to lie in different domains of truth.[1] Different sets of principles of judgment, including rules for consistency, apply to them. How then could we know whether our beliefs about them are consistent or not?

This is not an idle question. Is not our uneasiness about this a motive for reducing moral truths to psychological truths, for example, or psychological truths to truths of physics? Such reductions, if they were successful, would mitigate anxiety about whether our beliefs are consistent or not. Not knowing, and not being able to know, whether our beliefs are consistent or not would be worse than knowing that they are not consistent.

But suppose we could derive from Whitehead's scheme—or from some other speculative scheme, for that matter—adequate interpretations of statements in different domains. Then if the scheme is coherent the pre-speculative statements are consistent. This would not tell us whether the pre-speculative statements are true, of course, for we are supposing that distinctive principles of judgment are involved in each kind of case. The use of a speculative scheme is not to decide historical questions or mathematical questions or questions of physics or moral questions, though if adequate speculative interpretations were available this might be of some help in getting the questions straight. Instead the use of the scheme is to enable us "to put the various elements of our experience into a consistent relation to each other."

NOTE

1. See my "Domains of Truth," *American Philosophical Quarterly*, 12 (1975), 61–68.

4

# Freedom in Whitehead's Philosophy

JOHN B. COBB, JR.
*School of Theology at Claremont*

THE PROBLEM OF FREEDOM is an exceedingly subtle one. Some philosophers have understandably asserted the fundamental unintelligibility of the notion of freedom. They have argued that when we carefully approach what is supposedly free with refined tools of inquiry, the freedom vanishes. The conclusion is sometimes drawn that freedom is unreal; sometimes, that intellectual analysis has limited applicability to reality. We seem to be driven to choose between rigorous rationality and freedom.

A brief discussion of the extreme difficulty of conceptualizing freedom will put the problem in appropriate perspective. First, we may suppose that every action, event, or occurrence (and every aspect of it) is either caused or uncaused. If it is uncaused, then it is purely random, spontaneous, or matter of chance. Applied to human thought or behavior this would mean that some aspect of what I do simply happens without reason of any kind. If freedom is defined negatively as the absence of determination, this would be "free," but such "freedom" has nothing to do with ethical concerns. For something totally undetermined in this sense, I have, by definition, no responsibility whatever. Hence in quest of the kind of experienced freedom associated with responsibility, we must

An earlier version of this chapter appeared in *The Southern Journal of Philosophy* (7 [1969–70], 409–413).

turn to caused acts. Clearly, if these acts are caused by agents outside myself, I am again without responsibility, but if they are caused by *me*, then responsibility seems to be intelligible. The freedom with which we are humanly concerned is not indetermination, or determination by others, but self-determination.

Everything then hinges on whether the notion of self-determination can survive analysis. What can it mean that I am in some measure the cause of my own thought and action? Does it mean that my decision in one moment determines my behavior in the following moment? If so, then the locus of responsible freedom should be sought in the moment of decision. But what of the decision? Is it caused or causeless? If causeless, then mere randomness rather than responsibility follows. If caused, then the cause is either outside myself or within. Assuming it to be within, where does it lie? If it lies in some earlier experience or action, say, in that of the preceding moment, then the questioning turns to it. Obviously such questioning leads to an infinite regress. What occurs in each moment seems to be *either* causeless *or* caused by what has occurred in previous moments. Even if we cling to the notion of self-determination, and hence limit consideration to the chain of causes that constitutes the life history of the self, we must eventually reach a point prior to the emergence of the self at birth or even conception. We are driven again to the view that all things were determined in the beginning or that they were partly determined and that the rest has been a matter of chance. Neither view makes sense of human freedom.

Is there another possibility? If so, it lies in conceiving self-determination much more rigorously. In the former analysis self-determination was interpreted as determination by the previous state of the self. If the cause must *precede* the effect, then there is no other possible conceptualization. The alternative is to think of cause and effect as simultaneous. If my action in a moment is an instance of true self-determination, then the agent and the act must occur together at once. If this is thinkable, then the act need be neither random nor determined by the past. But is this thinkable?

To answer this question, we will consider first the usual view of time and of process as a continuum.

In terms of a continuum of becoming, a moment can be thought of in two ways. The most natural view is that the moment is an instant. This means that, like a point on a line, it lacks all thickness. The point is, of course, represented visually by a mark which, however small, has extension, but this mark is recognized as representing something that lacks extension. In the same way an instant as represented in thought or memory seems to have some very limited, but nevertheless real, content, whereas on reflection we see that, strictly conceived, it must lack all temporal extension. Otherwise it could still be divisible into earlier and later instants, and would not truly be a single instant. In an extensionless instant no action can occur. Hence a moment thus conceived cannot be the locus of self-determination.

The alternative view, given the understanding of process as continuous, is that the moment has duration. This means that some segment of the continuous process constitutes, for some purposes at least, a single moment. Since our interest is with an act, we can take as an example an act of deciding to speak. We will conceive this decision as constituting a limited segment of the continuum as a single moment. We might then claim that my act of deciding to speak is *causa sui*, cause of itself, and that in that act I am in the strictest sense self-determining.

The problem with this view is that it seeks illegitimately to remove the moment from the continuum of becoming. Given the doctrine of the continuum, the identification as a single moment of the half-second required for the decision to speak is ultimately arbitrary. It has a certain phenomenological justification and a certain practical utility, but if we are concerned to ground moral responsibility ontologically, it fails. This half-second, like any duration of time, is subject to infinite division into parts which are arranged in temporal succession. If my act of decision participates in this temporal flow, it too is infinitely divisible. Furthermore, this divisibility is not for thought alone. It would correspond to reality.

The decision must have occurred in and through an infinite succession of instants. The unity of the act is ultimately illusory. In actuality, either an act of self-determination occurs in the extensionless instant (the view rejected above) or the causal flow is from earlier to later, and genuine self-determination is lost.

Given the view of process as continuous, there is only one escape from the illusoriness of freedom. This consists in positing a reality that transcends time and process. For example, one may affirm that what has been said applies to the phenomenal world, but that it is not relevant to the understanding of the noumenal world. The deciding and acting self is then exempt from the category of time, which category is admitted to render freedom unintelligible. This solution either declares the temporal world illusory or accepts a radical dualism. Further, it can provide no intelligible account of the noumenal world. If process is continuous, then freedom is unintelligible.

The argument has been that freedom must mean self-determination, that self-determination must be in a moment, and that if process is continuous, there are no moments in which such self-determination can occur. The alternative to this negative conclusion is to posit that process is non-continuous. Perhaps actual occurrences are unified moments to whose becoming the notion of temporal flow is inapplicable, but such that when the notion of time (derived from the relations of these momentary events to one another) is applied to them, they must be described as having temporal thickness. If this is intelligible, then a real occurrence with ontological unity may be conceived as in some measure determining itself. The individual occurrence could then be (in some measure) responsible for itself.

It is precisely this position which Whitehead developed in an exceedingly novel and creative way. In doing so he did not have the problem of human freedom and moral responsibility primarily in view, but he was quite clear that the proposal provided a new basis for understanding these phenomena as well as the phenomena studied by quantum mechanics and relativity theory.

We must now consider the criticism which has been raised by

Edward Pols.[1] That criticism operates on the assumption that the process of becoming of a single actual occasion is one in which causal determination moves from earlier toward later phases in just the way it operates in the macrocosmic process for which Whitehead reserves the term 'temporal'. Given this assumption, the detailed analysis of Pols is unnecessary. *If* the settled outcome of an actual occasion is determined in a process in which each phase is determined by antecedent phases, then all the difficulties briefly treated above inevitably apply also to Whitehead's philosophy. They could be resolved only if the act of self-determination could be located in an individual phase of the microcosmic process, but then the properties of this phase would have to be those attributed by Whitehead to an actual occasion. Much confusion would be engendered, and nothing would be gained, by this move. Somewhere there must be an act of self-actualization, and Whitehead gives to such an act the name 'actual occasion'.

In Pols's defense it must be admitted that, after Whitehead has stated his doctrine of discontinuous becoming and temporal atomicity, his analysis of the process by which actual occasions actualize themselves seems at times to treat this process *almost* as a temporal one. He speaks of earlier and later, antecedent and subsequent, phases of this process, and he discusses what occurs at each phase *almost* as if he thought of that occurrence as temporally preceding subsequent phases. Friendlier interpreters than Pols have been misled by this language! I say 'almost', for I do not believe that Whitehead ever entirely lost sight of the basic doctrine of the temporal all-at-onceness of the becoming of individual occasions. He never writes as if there were any other subject of prehensions than the occasion as a whole, and he does not grant existence to prehensions prior to their subject. He never attributes causal efficacy to earlier phases in their relation to subsequent ones. He never allows actuality to earlier phases except as they are included in the actualization of the whole. He never speaks of sub-acts of the one act of becoming that is the actual occasion in its unity. He insists that every mode of analysis of the one, unified, complex act of self-actualization yields ingredients which have no actuality apart from the actuality of the whole. An actual entity is indivisible in fact, although it is analyzable into parts which in some instances can be associated with sub-regions into which the regional standpoint of the given actual occasion *is* divisible.

Pols is aware of the passages in which these points are stated, but he *assumes* that the genetic analysis of the process of becoming yields ingredients which come into being successively in a temporal sense. For this reason he excludes the possibility that the subject–superject is the agent of its own becoming. This position is readily understandable. Whitehead's alternative view is strange to all our habits of thought. But if Pols's assumption is granted, a crucial element in Whitehead's vision is removed, and vast changes are required. Pols works out the changes entailed in such a way as to reject the ontological principle and attribute the fundamental agency in the universe to eternal objects. I doubt that this is the most appropriate reworking of Whitehead, even when the freedom of actual occasions is denied, but it is some indication of how drastic the changes must be. It is well to have this pointed out before Whiteheadians, under the pressure of common-sense notions of time, give up by a thousand qualifications Whitehead's epochal theory.

When one insists (following Whitehead) that the process of becoming of an individual occasion is *not* temporal, one is bound to give some account of how the successiveness of phases is to be understood. The alternative usually proposed (and dismissed as inadequate) is that the relation is a purely logical one. I agree that this is inadequate. Whitehead would not have described a purely logical relation as genetic. But are logical and temporal sequences the only kinds? Clearly Whitehead did not think so. His new model of reality required the introduction of a new concept of successiveness, a successiveness into which an ontologically single but complex event could be analyzed *without* affirming different subjects or agents as active in the successive phases. If one thinks one knows on some other grounds that temporal–causal successiveness and logical successiveness are the only possible types, then one will not try very hard to understand the peculiar kind of successiveness here envisaged—and without serious effort one is unlikely to succeed! Whitehead's conceptuality is not as foreign to common sense as is that of much of modern physics, but, in its attempt to mediate that foreignness, it partakes of the radical break with previous common sense that physics requires.

My suggestions for understanding are only pointers. They are based on the doctrine repeatedly referred to above that the act that occurs all-at-once is nevertheless a complex act. A complex act is analyzable, and hence describable, in terms of its ingredients. Since the act in its relatedness to other acts has four-dimensional extension, the analysis yields some features (simple physical feelings) which can be associated with spatio-temporal sub-regions, but the act as a whole as well as its subjective immediacy, its subjective form, its subjective aim, and its entire mental pole are exempt from association with spatial sub-regions. The association with temporal sub-regions is still more abstract, although for certain very restricted purposes it may be allowable.

The complex act can be analyzed into simpler elements and indeed in its complexity it can be understood only when so analyzed. The relation between the actual complex unity and its simpler but non-actual ingredients is one of involvement and presupposition. The complex act involves the simple ingredients and cannot occur without their occurring. In this sense, it presupposes them not only logically but actually (though not temporally). The complex act is one of creativity synthesizing the simpler ingredients, and it is hard to think of an act of synthesizing without thinking of the ingredients of the synthesis as temporally prior to that act. They are certainly "prior" in some sense, but not in such a sense that they lie in the past of the act of synthesis. Rather the coming into being of the ingredients presupposes the self-actualization of the whole synthesis just as much as the self-actualization of the whole presupposes the coming into being of the ingredients. Thus the whole is active in the becoming of its parts. Whole and parts come into being together. The whole is equally the subject of the one act of becoming and its superject or outcome.

Pols's argument (or assumption) that if something is the outcome of an act it cannot be its subject presupposes the rejection of Whitehead's understanding of an actual occasion. When one operates on Pols's assumptions, one rules out in advance not only a major feature of Whitehead's thought but also the intelligibility of self-determination in general, in that sense which alone can account for responsible freedom.

A final word is in order. Whitehead in his doctrine of the extensive continuum restores to extension the continuous character which he denies to process in his atomic theory of actuality. Just as one must be warned in reading Whitehead not to *begin* with the language of successiveness employed in one of the modes of analysis of microcosmic process (but instead to read this analysis in the context established by the epochal theory), so also one must be warned not to *begin* with the doctrine of the extensive continuum in coming to an understanding of time and then ask how microcosmic process operates within this continuum.

One must repeatedly remind oneself that what is actual is composed of actual occasions, each of which comes into being all at once. Some *aspects* of their relations to other entities are extensive. When we analyze that extensiveness *in abstraction* from how it has in fact been actualized, we find it to be continuous. This continuous extensiveness can be so analyzed as to yield geometrical knowledge. Geometry tells us something about the relations of actual entities, but what it tells us is *very* abstract. It does *not* tell us how actual entities come into being. Thus the continuous aspect of extensiveness is *not* to be a presupposition brought to bear upon the investigation of the genetic analysis of the process of concrescence, as it would have to be on a Newtonian account. To break out of this Newtonian common sense is essential if Whitehead's philosophy is to be understood.

NOTE

1. *Whitehead's Metaphysics: A Critical Examination of* PROCESS AND REALITY (Carbondale: Southern Illinois University Press, 1967).

# 5

# Being and Becoming in Whitehead's Philosophy

IVOR LECLERC
*Emory University,*
Emeritus

EVEN IN HIS EARLIER WORK Whitehead had been concerned with metaphysical issues, as he later fully appreciated. His explicit turning to metaphysics came, however, when he was driven by the rational exigencies of his earlier theories to the primary metaphysical problem, that of "being." And he had to face this in the most fundamental sense. He had put forward a theory which conceived the world in terms of "events" and "objects." Besides the more detailed problems which arose in connection with them, there was the more general question of their ontological status, and this became for Whitehead an increasingly burning issue. What *is* an "event," and what *is* an "object"? This, stated in traditional terms, is the question as to what kind of being they have, or are. But this involves the most fundamental problem, the ultimate problem, that of "being" as such. When we inquire into the being of an event or an object, what is meant by 'being'? This is the issue Whitehead had to face.

I do not wish to suggest that Whitehead tackled this problem in explicitly traditional terms. But the problem with which he was

An earlier version of this chapter appeared in *Kant-Studien* (51 [1959–60], 427–37).

concerned, in his own way, was precisely the traditional problem of "being." He has given us very little direct discussion of his wrestling with this issue; but the development from his early work through *Science and the Modern World*, *Religion in the Making*, and *Process and Reality* clearly evinces his having come to grips with it. In *Process and Reality* we have the outcome, the conclusion. Taking this in conjunction with the preceding works, it is clear that this problem had impinged on him as forcibly and profoundly as it had on Parmenides, on Plato, and on Aristotle in the ancient world, and on Leibniz and Spinoza in the modern. I shall attempt, very briefly, to elucidate the problem.

Parmenides had declared: "[That which is] is, and it is impossible for it not to be," and "it is possible for it to be, but it is not possible for 'nothing' to be."[1] These dicta have an everlasting importance, and anyone grappling with the basic metaphysical problem is compelled to come to terms with them. Aristotle, as a direct outcome of the work of Plato, decided that the fundamental issue is that as to *what* is. That is, what is it that is? or, in other words, what is that which is? We cannot here enter into any detail of the Aristotelian discussion. Suffice it that he took great pains to demonstrate that the term 'being' is an equivocal; not, however, one with no essential connection between its different senses, a term that is used πρὸς ἕν, that is, in reference to a primary sense.[2] This sense is that of "something," a "that" which *is* or *exists* by virtue of its very nature (οὐσία)—bearing in mind Aristotle's definition that "nature in the primary and strict sense is the essence [οὐσία] of things which have in themselves, as such, a source of movement."[3] That is to say, the "that" exists or is because it itself is the source of its existing or being; it exists because existing, being, is inherent in it, by its very nature. To say that its being is "inherent" is to say that it is not derivative or dependent. The "that" in question is *causa sui*—as Spinoza put it. It is, in Descartes' formulation, "an existent thing which requires nothing but itself in order to exist."[4] Aristotle had used the word οὐσία to designate this primary existent, the that which is—a word not only stemming from the verb 'to be', but which significantly in common speech had the meaning of 'property', 'possessions', especially in the form of livestock, i.e., things which in their own nature are able to move about and do things on their own, by their inherent power.[5]

The point I am trying to make is that Aristotle had come to the conviction that there is no being as such, itself the ultimate existent; being, in the metaphysically primary sense, is the being, the existence, of an entity which exists by virtue of its very nature.[6] "Being" is "existing," and existence cannot come from what has no existence—cf. Parmenides. Being, in the primary sense, is the being of an entity whose nature it is to *be*. Aristotle's basic doctrine is epitomized in his statement that the question What is being? is the question What is *οὐσία*?[7] All other senses of 'being', 'existing', have reference to the fundamental sense of the being of *οὐσία*. That is to say, in a full, concrete sense, only *οὐσία is*. *All other* entities, of whatever kind, are or have being in a sense dependent upon that of the being of *οὐσία*. I am not claiming that Aristotle carried through this doctrine with complete consistency. But it was a profound metaphysical insight to which he had come, a most important landmark in the development of thought. Thomas Aquinas in medieval times, and Spinoza in the modern era, especially recognized its particular importance, and sought its coherent adoption.

Whitehead, in his own way, came to the same conclusion as Aristotle had. He expressed this in *Process and Reality* by saying that "the general Aristotelian principle is maintained that, apart from things that are actual, there is nothing—nothing either in fact or in efficacy" (PR 64). Being, existence, is the being or existence of actual entities—Whitehead's term for what Aristotle called *οὐσίαι*. The existence of actual entities is the basic sense of existence, and accordingly, "whatever things there are in any sense of 'existence', are derived by abstraction from actual [entities]" (PR 113). This is so "because in separation from actual entities there is nothing, merely nonentity—'The rest is silence' " (PR 68).

Now, if it be maintained that "being," in the non-derivative, the primary sense, is the being or existing of an entity whose nature it is to *be*, what is this "nature" by virtue of which there is existence?

Whitehead is in full agreement with Aristotle, with Thomas Aquinas, Spinoza, and Leibniz, who had emphatically held this to be act, action, agency. That is to say, being, existing, in the ultimate sense, is acting. To exist is to act; and to act is to exist. There is no being, in any sense, apart from, in separation from, acting, agency. In Whitehead's words, already quoted, "apart from things that are actual, there is nothing." The things or entities that are "actual" are the "acting" things. Whence Whitehead's term '*actual* entity' for the primary existent, the *οὐσία*. An "actual" entity is an *acting* entity. It is or exists by virtue of its acting. Its being, its existence, is *constituted by* its acting.

Thomas Aquinas, following Aristotle, held that there is only one entity whose existence is not derivative, one entity whose being is constituted by its act. As he put it in the *De Ente et Essentia*,

> And since every being which exists through another is reduced, as to its first cause, to one existing in virtue of itself, there must be some being which is the cause of the existing of all things because it itself is the act of existing alone.[8]

This doctrine, like that of Aristotle, admits a plurality of agents. But only one of these is a being whose very nature it is to act, in the classical formulation, whose essence is existence; only one who, in the words of Thomas Aquinas just quoted, "itself is the act of existing alone" (*ipsa est esse tantum*). The other agents are thus derivative. Since their existence is derivative, their *agency*, their *act*, is derivative. That is to say, they exist in virtue of their agency, but that agency is not ultimate with them; it is derivative from the one ultimate agent. Now, this raises the problem as to how the derivative beings receive their agency. Aristotle sought the solution to this problem by the identification of act and form. Thomas Aquinas saw clearly, however, that this is open to the most serious objections; it is of the utmost importance that the distinction between act and form be maintained. St. Thomas' solution is that the act of the other entities is a donation of God: ". . . et illud esse receptum est per modum actus"[9] (". . . and that existence is received in the mode of act"[10]).

But this raises a profound problem, of which Spinoza in particular was keenly aware. How is the agency of the many derived from the agency of the One? In this doctrine the one act does not become many; the one does not pluralize itself in the many. The one act remains that one act, eternal. Yet it somehow gives rise to many acts. But how can it give rise to a many without that constituting a pluralization of itself? The answer of Thomas Aquinas is: by creation. But is act a kind of "thing" that can be created? Further, the difficulty is not resolved by the distinction between "potency" and "act," for "potency," as Spinoza saw, cannot be separated from "act"; to do so is to truncate agency. Potency is an aspect within a complete transaction. Spinoza accordingly came to put forward a most important alternative to the antecedent doctrines.

He too maintained that there is one ultimate, primordial agent, which *is* by virtue of its agency. But he conceived this agent as what H. F. Hallett, the eminent Spinozistic scholar, calls an eternal "potency-in-act" actualizing itself in determinate modes.[11] The modes are the enaction of the eternal act, the actualization of the eternal potency. The modes are the modes of acting of the one being; they are the determinate actualizations of the one infinite, eternal potency-in-act which, as such, is absolutely indeterminate. In Hallett's words, "Spinoza's philosophical intention, therefore, is to derive all things from a primordial infinite power or indeterminate potency self-actualized in an infinite and exhaustively determinate eternal universe."[12] That is to say, for Spinoza, being, existence, in its metaphysically ultimate sense, is constituted by the acting of an eternal agent, achieving determinate actuality in determinate actings, the modes.

But by denying that the many are οὐσίαι, has not Spinoza thereby also precluded them from being independent, responsible agents? What is at issue here is the general metaphysical problem of whether there can be genuine agents which are not οὐσίαι. Aristotle, Thomas Aquinas, and Leibniz do not think so, for they have all stood for a plurality of οὐσίαι. But they have not been able to make fully intelligible how there can be a plurality of agents as οὐσίαι.

Whitehead has put forward an important new theory which seeks to give the metaphysical explanation of a plurality of agents as *οὐσίαι* by accepting the advantages of the Spinozistic position.

Spinoza, as we have seen, was in agreement with Thomas Aquinas that the ultimate metaphysical act must be an act of creation, but he saw that the many acts could not be separate created entities. The determinate individual acts, he held, must be the determinate enactings of the one infinite act; they must be the determinate modes of the one infinite creative acting. Whitehead accepts with Spinoza the notion of a primordial ultimate "potency-in-act" actualized in determinate creative acts. He agrees with Spinoza in holding that if act, acting, be metaphysically ultimate, then this primordial indeterminate "potency-in-act" must achieve actualization in specific determinate acts. But, he maintains, this ultimate creative potency-in-act is not itself an actual entity, an *οὐσία*, as Spinoza thought. This ultimate potency-in-act does not exist except in the individual actualizations. It is these concrete, determinate actualizations, Whitehead holds, which are the *οὐσίαι*. That is, each such determinate actualization is itself an actual entity, a concrete agent. These individual determinate acts are not, as for Spinoza, the acts of a single primordial agent; each is itself an individual subject acting.

Thus for Whitehead the Spinozistic modes become the actual entities, the *οὐσίαι*. That is to say, in Whitehead's conception the finite, determinate actual entities are the actualizations of a primordial ultimate potency-in-act, of an ultimate creative activity. Whitehead's term for this is 'Creativity'. In his doctrine there is an ultimate creativity, individualized in determinate self-creative acts. The parallel with Spinoza is close. The ultimate creativity, considered purely as such, is, like the ultimate Spinozistic potency-in-act or substance, wholly indeterminate. As Whitehead puts it,

> Creativity is without a character of its own in exactly the same sense in which the Aristotelian [prime] "matter" is without a character of its own. It is that ultimate notion of the highest generality at the base of actuality. It cannot be characterized, because all char-

acters are more special than itself. But creativity is always found under conditions, and described as conditioned [PR 47].

The "conditioning" is constituted by the individualization of the ultimate creative activity into determinate acts, in the same sense in which the ultimate Spinozistic potency actualizes itself in determinate acts.

Thus what Whitehead has done is to transform the Spinozistic ultimate potency-in-act into the analogy of the Aristotelian category of prime matter. Creativity is that which takes determinate forms, thereby constituting the actual entities, the οὐσίαι. Each actual entity is or exists by virtue of its own agency. It does not *receive* its agency, and thus its existence, from another, for each is, as such, by its very nature, an individualization of the ultimate creativity or potency-in-act.

It must be emphasized that, though there is an analogy, the Whiteheadian actual entities are not to be thought of too strictly as Leibnizian monads. In two respects Whitehead's conception comes nearer to the Spinozistic modes than to Leibnizian monads. A prime characteristic of the Leibnizian monad is its individual independence: it is "windowless." The contrary is the case with the Spinozistic modes. They are modes of the one substance; thus there is an inherent interrelatedness of the modes. Likewise with the Whiteheadian actual entities. Their acting is an inter-acting. They act in reference to one another, and not in isolation. The specific Whiteheadian doctrine is that the acting of an actual entity is an act of relating itself to all other actual entities—immediately or mediately. The act constituting an actual entity is in its fundamental nature "prehensive," i.e., grasping, laying hold of—in the sense from which is derived the word 'apprehend', meaning 'to grasp by the intellect or senses'. The act of an actual entity is an act of prehending other actual entities, relating them to itself. Thus each actual entity is, as it were, a node in a web of interrelatedness. To conceive it as existing in isolation is to falsify its nature. Each actual entity is the unitary synthesis achieved by its prehending activity. Each actual entity is a one prehending the many. There are many ones, each achieving its unity by the synthesis of the many. What I wish here primarily to stress is that this scheme conceives an essential interrelatedness and interdependence of actual entities. That interdependence constitutes them a universe, in which they function, and have a function, in relation to one another. As Whitehead has stated his position:

> . . . Spinoza's "modes" now become the sheer actualities; so that, though analysis of them increases our understanding, it does not lead us to the discovery of any higher grade of reality. The coherence, which the system seeks to preserve, is the discovery that the process, or concrescence, of any one actual entity involves the other actual entities among its components. In this way the obvious solidarity of the world receives its explanation [PR 10].

The second respect in which Whitehead diverges from the Leibnizian conception is that Whitehead's actual entity, like the Spinozistic mode, is an actual*ization* of the ultimate creativity or potency-in-act. That is to say, the entity is not only a determinate act*ing*, but also a determinate achieve*ment*. The term 'actual', 'actuality', includes in its connotation the aspect of attainment, of end reached, of final outcome—a connotation derived from Aristotle's *ἐνέργεια*, in his use as standing in contrast with *δύναμις*, 'potency'. From Greek times the factor of completion, of finality, has been recognized as essentially involved in the notion of "being,"and in the Parmenidean–Platonic tradition this has even been carried to the extreme of final "perfection." Without himself going to that extreme, Aristotle was nevertheless strongly influenced by it in the development of his notion of *ἐνέργεια*, 'actuality', as in contrast to, and exclusive of, *δύναμις*, 'potency'. Thus Aristotle, and following him a considerable part of the philosophical tradition, has contrasted 'being' (which is equated with *ἐνέργεια*) with 'becoming' (equated with *δύναμις*), making them mutually exclusive.

Whitehead has rejected this mutual exclusion as a major error. He agrees that being involves a factor of completion, of finality, of attain*ment*. He accepts this quite explicitly as connoted by the term 'actuality', in his use of it. But, he holds, the attain*ment*, the end reached, the outcome achieved, cannot be separated (except in conceptual abstraction) from the process of act*ing* whereby that end is attained. There is one integral transaction which is acting–reaching–achievement. The achieve*ment* is the actual*ity*; and this is not separate from the acting, the attain*ing*, the process of becom*ing* actual. That is to say, "being" is not separate from "becoming." Being is *actuality* when the whole transaction is viewed in its terminal aspect. But being is equally *becoming*, when the whole transaction is viewed in its aspect of act*ing*, of power, of δύναμις, that is, in the aspect of attain*ing* actuality. Whitehead, as opposed to Aristotle, places the emphasis in being on becoming rather than on the terminal attainment, "actuality": for there is being, existing, in the metaphysically basic sense, only *in* the acting, *in* the becoming. Actuality is the acting in its terminal aspect. This means that actuality is a function of act*ing*. This is a point of the utmost significance, which will be clear when we have elaborated some of the implications of this conception.

The attain*ment*, actuality, we have seen, is an abstraction apart from the acting, as is also the acting apart from the attainment. And likewise, the acting and attainment are abstractions apart from the agent, for acting is the acting of an agent. The agent is the subject of the acting, and since the acting is not separable from the attainment, the agent is also the outcome of the acting. There is one integral transaction, realized *in solido*, which is the agent actualizing itself in the acting. It must be conceived as one epochal whole. An agent becomes as a whole, a quantum. Thus *actualization* (which as we have seen connotes attainment, terminal achievement), is the achievement, by an agent, of its own actuality.

Now the achievement of actuality implies that the act*ing*, having attained its end, is over; it has completed itself in its attain*ment*. And since that acting is an individualization of the ultimate creativity, its termination involves the commencement of a new act. Thus in the Whiteheadian doctrine actual entities are agents actualizing themselves, and upon actualization their subjective career as agents is over; they have ceased being agents (for they are agents only in the acting), and are superseded by novel agents. These in their turn perish as agents, giving place to further new agents, and so on. Thus a Whiteheadian actual entity, unlike a Leibnizian monad, is not an *enduring entity*, a self-identical subject having perpetually new acts. For this conception separates the agent from the acts and from the attainment. If we do not make that separation, Whitehead holds, then we have to recognize that the agent must itself be the outcome of its acting. This necessitates the conception of one integral whole, a quantum of becoming, which is the actual entity. Further, as Whitehead says, "this quantum is constituted by its totality of relationships and cannot move"; that is, "the creature cannot have any external adventures, but only the internal adventure of becoming. Its birth is its end" (PR 124). That is to say, in his words again: "In the organic philosophy an actual entity has 'perished' when it is complete" (PR 126).

In saying that it has "perished" Whitehead is maintaining that the actual entity no longer exists in the primary sense of existence or being, for in that sense an actual entity exists only in the acting. But though its act*ing* is over, its attain*ment* does not thereby simply vanish into nothingness, non-existence. It continues to exist, but in a secondary or dependent sense of existence. For, upon completion, that attainment is the basis of subsequent attainings by subsequent agents. These subsequent agents, it will be borne in mind, are prehending subjects. What they prehend are the antecedent attainments. Thus these attainments are the objects of the prehensions of subsequent agents as subjects. Accordingly, an actual entity, upon actualization, is "objectified" for others. As "objectified" it is objectively included or immanent in those others. As thus objectively existent in other subjects, an actual entity has what Whitehead terms 'objective immortality'. That is to say, while an actual entity of necessity perishes subjectively, it is immortal objectively, i.e., as an object immanent in subsequent subjects. In other words, while an actual entity ceases existing in the primary sense of existence, it continues existing in a dependent or derivative sense: its objective existence is dependent upon the existence of the prehending subject.

We can explicate this alternatively by recurring to the point made earlier about actuality as a function of acting. Actuality always has reference to the agent in question; that is to say, actuality is always the actuality of the agent of whose acting it is the determinate attainment. But when that attainment is an object for another, *qua* object it is not actuality; *qua* object that antecedent attainment is a *potentiality* for the attainment (i.e., actuality) of the new prehending subject.

Thus we have another reason why Whitehead in his conception of being does not place the emphasis on actuality, as Aristotle does. For in the Whiteheadian scheme the actuality of one agent becomes the potentiality for another.

In this two points are to be noted. Such potentiality is not a mere abstract possibility. It is a specific determinate possibility as *potential for* the subject in question. 'Potentiality' includes 'possibility' in its connotation, but potentiality in this sense is a determinate selection from pure abstract possibility. Such specific determination was effected by the antecedent agent through its actualization. And this determinate selection among possibilities is a potentiality *for* a subsequent acting, because actualization can never be simply for its own sake; actualization has a necessary reference beyond itself, signified by its being the correlative of potentiality. The purpose and function of actualization is to contribute to subsequent achievement as the potentiality for that subsequent actualization.

The second point to be noted is that actualization, as potentiality for another (which means, as objectified for another), is ingredient *in* that other. That is, it is an element in the constitution of that other, contributing toward its new actualization. It does not contribute by its own potency, its own agency, for that is over, terminated; but instead it contributes as a definite, determinate item among the data undergoing synthesis. That is to say, while the actual entity no longer exists in the primary sense, since its acting has ceased, it exists in a dependent sense, as objectively ingredient or immanent in another agent as its potentiality. Its objective existence is dependent upon the existence, i.e., acting, of the new agent, because it is object only as prehended by the new subject. As objective, as potential, it is thus a function of the new acting.

Besides that of objectified actual entities, there are two other main types of dependent existence or being which should be briefly considered. One is that constituted by the pure abstract possibilities —what Whitehead has called 'forms of definiteness' or 'eternal objects'. Whitehead, with Aristotle, rejects the Platonic theory that these entities are independent existents, existing by virtue of their very nature. That is, they are not *οὐσίαι*, actual entities. They are the forms of definiteness *of* actual entities. Thus they *exist as* the *forms of οὐσίαι*. Which is to say that their existence or being is a dependent existence. This must not, however, be interpreted as implying that actual entities "create" or "generate" forms. Forms are as primordial as creativity, for there can no more be an act without definiteness than there can be definiteness without that of which it is the form or character. A fuller treatment than is here possible would display form as the counterpart or complement of acting. Form is *what* is enact*ed*, the definiteness of the acting. The closeness of the relation of form to actuality is evident. This conception of form enables Whitehead to explain the conversion of actuality into potentiality. For, as I remarked earlier, potentiality is a determinate selection of abstract possibility, actualized by an act. A fuller treatment would show the interrelation of actual entities as enabled by, and as particular instantiations of, the inherent structure of relatedness of pure abstract possibility. Such a treatment would exhibit the mutual requirement by each other of act and pure possibility, and would elucidate the role of a unique actual entity in mediating that relationship. Here, however, I can give no more than this adumbration.

The other type of dependent existence which I wish briefly to consider is that of enduring things. In Whitehead's analysis enduring things, enduring entities, are not *actual* entities. They are entities constituted by strands of actual entities in supersession, or entire groups of actual entities in supersession, in each case the whole being treated as a unit. These are both instances of what Whitehead calls 'societies' of actual entities. It will not be necessary here to enter into his theory of "society" or "social order." Sufficient for our purpose that a society of actual entities constitutes a whole, and thus a unit. It has a unitariness by virtue of the members participating in a common character through being related in genetic derivation from one another. The details need not concern us now. The relevant point is that there is a vast variety of groups or societies which constitute units and are treated as such. We do so constantly throughout everyday living: a building, for example, or any kind of fabrication out of a multiplicity of components, is treated as one thing; a group or association of diverse human beings is treated as one, a club, a business corporation, a church, a university, etc. Now all these units exist, or have being, as single entities. But this being, this existence, is not being in the metaphysically basic sense. That is to say, none of these units exists by virtue of its own acting, for none is an integral agent; each exists only through the existence, i.e., acting, of its ultimate components. Thus its being or existence is a dependent existence; it is dependent upon, and derivative from, the existence of the individual component *acting* entities, which alone are proper agents.

It is clearly of the utmost moment to distinguish the dependent types of existence from the "actual" existence of acting entities. In Whitehead's view a failure in this respect has been at the root of much difficulty in antecedent philosophy. As he puts it: "It is the mistake that has thwarted European metaphysics from the time of the Greeks, namely, to confuse societies with the completely real things which are the actual occasions" (AI 262). In particular it has thwarted the analysis of acting, agency, and has hindered the development of a satisfactory theory of becoming. One prominent instance of this confusion of societies with actual entities is that of the enduring human personality. Aristotle, and most philosophers subsequently, have taken an enduring human personality as the paradigm of an actual entity, an *οὐσία*.

I shall conclude this paper with a few brief remarks on Whitehead's treatment of the enduring human personality. The clearly evident features here which require philosophical explanation are our awareness and conviction of an essential self-identity throughout a life-history, and the unquestionable fundamental relevance for one another of acts throughout that life-history, indubitably evidenced by the factor of moral obligation. The readiest explanation is, of course, that of a numerically self-identical agent which endures. Besides the serious difficulties of the notion of 'duration' involved, which we shall not attempt to discuss here, there is the age-old problem of rendering coherent the conception of a self-identically enduring agent. Such an agent is the subject of continuous acts. It is that which "has" the acts, and is thus a full agent antecedent to its acts; it is not the outcome of its acts as a *terminus ad quem.* Its acts must therefore be strictly accidental to its being, to its actuality, to *what* it is. Yet somehow the agent must be affected by its acts, which implies that *what* it is must after all be altered—for otherwise morality becomes completely unintelligible. But if it is altered by its acts, an agent must be the outcome of its acts, a *terminus ad quem.* This, however, contradicts the conception of the agent as a *terminus a quo.*

These difficulties are resolved by considering an enduring human personality, on the Whiteheadian basis, not as an actual entity, but as a "society" of actual entities. In terms of Whitehead's metaphysical categories, the present self is an agent achieving its actuality by its acting. By the category of objective immortality, the present self is the cumulation of the past agents making up the enduring personality up to that point. And upon achievement of its actuality, the present agent becomes the potentiality for the subsequent agent in the enduring personality.

It will be noted that the present self is not severed from the past, or from the future. By Whitehead's categories, as I have shown, there is a real identity of the present agent with its antecedents, precisely that identity of which subjectively we are so keenly aware. The present agent is the cumulation of its antecedents, and the ground for the future. Its enacting *now* is for the future, in order that the future *will be* in accordance with its present determination; this is the metaphysical basis of morality. The present determination is, of course, open to modification by the decision involved in the acting of the future agent.

This application of Whitehead's categories to a human personality is an illustration of their adequacy. It also serves to correct the interpretation of many critics who have seen in Whitehead's theory a radical atomism. This is an error, for an actual entity is not to be considered in isolation. Whitehead's is a philosophy of "process," of "becoming." The being of an *οὐσία* is its becoming, its becoming actual. And it becomes actual in order to be the potentiality for further *οὐσίαι*. Whitehead sees the universe as in rhythmical pulsation, from potentiality to actuality, and from actuality to potentiality, from the many to the one, and from the one to the many. For him the universe is to be understood as in the process, and not statically.

NOTES

1. Diels–Kranz, *Fragmente der Vorsokratiker* (fr. 2, 6) (Berlin: Weidmann, 1937, 1959); as translated by F. M. Cornford, *Plato and Parmenides* (London: Kegan Paul, Trench, Trübner, 1939), pp. 30, 31. Italics removed.
2. Cf. *Metaphysics*, 1003a33–34.
3. Ibid., 1015a13–14 (trans. D. Ross).
4. *Principles of Philosophy*, Part I, Princ. 51, in *The Philosophical Works of Descartes*, trans. E. S. Haldane and G. R. T. Ross (Cambridge: Cambridge University Press, 1911), I 239.
5. Cf. Gottfried Martin, *An Introduction to General Metaphysics*, trans. E. Schaper and I. Leclerc (London: Allen and Unwin, 1961), p. 123 and passim.
6. Cf. *Metaphysics*, Book III, Ch. 10, and Book X, Ch. 2.
7. Ibid., 1028b3–4.
8. Trans. Armand Maurer, C.S.B., as *On Being and Essence* (Toronto: Pontifical Institute of Mediaeval Studies, 1949), p. 47: "Et quia omne quod est per aliud reducitur ad illud quod est per se sicut ad causam primam, oportet quod sit aliqua res quae sit causa essendi omnibus rebus ex eo quod ipsa est esse tantum; . . ." (*De Ente et Essentia*, ed. M. D. Roland-Gosselin, O.P. [Le Saulchoir: Revue des sciences philosophiques et théologiques, 1926], p. 35).
9. *De Ente et Essentia, loc. cit.*
10. *On Being and Essence, loc. cit.*
11. Cf. H. F. Hallett, *Benedict de Spinoza: The Elements of His Philosophy* (London: University of London, Athlone Press, 1957).
12. Ibid., p. 9.

# 6

# Matter and Event

RICHARD M. RORTY
*University of Virginia*

## I · INTRODUCTION

MOST FUNDAMENTAL CONTROVERSIES about the nature and status of matter are episodes in a struggle between Aristotelian realism and the tradition of subjectivist reductionism which stretches from Descartes through Berkeley and Hume to Russell and Goodman.[1] This struggle has shifted ground many times, but there is a recognizable persistence in the sort of arguments employed, and the sort of distinctions invoked, on both sides. Realists hold that matter-*vs.*-form is going to have to be a basic distinction in any adequate cosmology, whereas reductionists hold that this distinction does more harm than good. If they give a place to matter, it is not matter-as-opposed-to-form, but matter in some meaning of the term which has little more than the name in common with what Aristotelians are talking about.

Whitehead viewed the grand opposition between these two schools as a reflection of the opposition between "two cosmologies which at different periods have dominated European thought, Plato's *Timaeus*, and the cosmology of the seventeenth century, whose chief authors were Galileo, Descartes, Newton, Locke" (PR ix). He thought of Aristotle as having filled in and rounded out the *Timaeus* (CN 24), and of the post-Kantian epistemological controversies between idealists and positivistic empiricists as the inevi-

An earlier version of this chapter appeared in *The Concept of Matter*, ed. Ernan McMullin (Notre Dame: University of Notre Dame Press, 1963), pp. 497–524.

table outcome of a search for the presuppositions and consequences of the Newtonian cosmology (PR 76–79, 123–26). He thought of "the philosophy of organism" as replacing *both* cosmologies, and as being as different from either as either was from the other.

Nevertheless, from the point of view of realistic philosophers, insisting upon the irreducibility of the distinction between substances and qualities, and between substances and relations, Whitehead's philosophy usually looks like one more variant of subjectivist reductionism. His cosmology, with its ingression of "eternal objects" into sub-microscopic "actual entities," seems one more attempt to blend hard-headed atomistic materialism with the elegance of Platonic logicism—a combination whose possibilities have fired the imagination of philosophers ever since the rise of modern mathematical physics (and have become dazzling since the invention of symbolic logic). To reduce substantial forms to "conceptual prehensions," and to reduce the particularity and concreteness of actualities to patterns of relatedness with other entities, as Whitehead seems to do, is apparently to abandon all hope of a *rapprochement* with Aristotelian realism. Whitehead's notion of "subjective aim" and his analysis of "concrescence" are, to be sure, reminiscent of some key Aristotelian terms and themes, but the resemblances do not seem to come to much. Whitehead's polemics against the quest for a "substratum," his assertion that "Creativity" should replace Aristotle's category of "primary substance" (PR 32), as well as many of his historical allusions and judgments, suggest that Whitehead viewed his system as climaxing the revolt against the Aristotelian world-view which Descartes, Newton, and Locke had begun. Further, the affinities of Whitehead's atomism of actual entities with the logical atomism of Russell and the nominalistic *Aufbauten* of Carnap and Goodman seem obvious.[2]

If one accepts these affinities at face value, however, one may lose sight of two other sets of affinities. In the first place, Whitehead's cosmology is at least as close to Bergson and James as it is to Russell and Goodman. One cannot ignore his Bergsonian insistence that taking time seriously—the substitution of process for stasis as the inclusive category—permits one to demolish Aristotelian substances in the *right* way, whereas everybody else (Russell and Goodman, as well as Descartes, Newton, Hume, et al.) has been demolishing them in the *wrong* way. In the second place, one needs to notice that Whitehead's criticisms of these wrong-headed attempts draw on the same sort of arguments as those employed by Aristotle's defenders. Most of the usual points made by Aristotelian realists against nominalists, materialists, skeptics, and the like are strongly echoed by Whitehead. Whitehead stands between two reductionistic philosophical movements—Bradley's and Bergson's (ESP 116)—in the same way in which Aristotle stood between Plato and the materialist successors of Heraclitus. Both men find themselves insisting, against the simplistic analyses of such reductionisms, that a "critique of abstractions" is required. (Cf. PR 253.)

Contrariwise, Whitehead and Aristotle are attacked by reductionists for the same reasons. Both make heavy use of the distinction between potentiality and actuality to resolve cosmological dilemmas, and "potentiality," as all reductionists know, is merely an anthropomorphic vestige of pre-scientific picture-thinking. (As is teleological explanation, to which Aristotle and Whitehead are equally devoted.) Aristotle, in the distinction between matter and form, and Whitehead, in the distinction between actual entities and eternal objects, make heuristic use of the actuality–potentiality distinction to bifurcate the universe in (so the reductionists say) arbitrary, unempirical, and unnecessary ways. ("Aristotle without specific forms" and "Whitehead without eternal objects" are almost equally popular slogans.) Thus one might expect, on the principle that one's enemy's enemy is, at least temporarily, one's friend, that Aristotle and Whitehead would have interestingly similar aims and strategies.

In this paper, I shall try to spotlight some of the anti-reductionist features of Whitehead's cosmology, in order to show how Whitehead's critique of the Newtonian world-view, and the philosophical systems which presuppose this world-view, resembles the critique offered by Aristotelians. Then, on the basis of these similarities between Aristotle and Whitehead, I shall discuss some differences between them. On the basis of these differences, I hope to exhibit the significance of Whitehead's "taking time seriously" for a discussion of the concept of matter.

## II · REDUCTIONISM AND DISTINCTIONS OF LEVEL

I have said that both Aristotle and Whitehead are realistic philosophers who build their respective cosmologies around distinctions which, in the eyes of reductionist philosophers, seem arbitrary. I now wish to define (dogmatically and curtly) "reductionism" and "realism" in terms of the presence or absence of a certain sort of distinction. These definitions are no more than rough hints, to be developed and given sense in what follows, but formulating them here will give us some pegs on which to hang the Whiteheadian doctrines which we need to extricate and examine.

*Reductionism*, as I shall use the term, is the position which adopts what Whitehead calls "the [unreformed] subjectivist principle"—the principle that "the datum in the act of experience can be adequately analyzed purely in terms of universals" (PR 239). Holding to this principle, and defining a "universal" as "that which can enter into the description of many particulars" (PR 76), leads to the dissolution of particularity itself. For any candidate for the status of an ultimate particular is confronted with the alternative of either disclosing itself as a congeries of universals or condemning itself to unexperienceability. Making a virtue of necessity, reductionism then claims that particularity is either unknowable or unreal. The history of philosophy since Descartes, in Whitehead's eyes, is the history of the failure of reductionism—of the foredoomed attempt to develop an adequate cosmology with only one type of basic entity—viz., *repeatable* entities. The notion of an "unrepeatable entity" has, since Descartes, been taken to be an absurdity, and the admission that such entities exist has been taken as either a proof of skepticism or the mark of an "incomplete" analysis—which is why the Cartesian tradition can end only in Humean skepticism or Bradleyan idealism. (Cf. PR 85.)

*Realism*, as I shall use the term, is the position which holds that an adequate cosmological account can be achieved in terms of an irreducible distinction between two sorts of entities—entities of radically distinct categoreal levels. The cash-value of the phrase 'distinct categoreal levels' is that entities of these two sorts are such that any given arrangement of the first sort of entities is logically compatible with any given arrangement of entities of the other sort. That is, realism is the insistence that explanation must always be in terms of a correlation of *independent* arrangements,[3] and cannot consist in a reduction of entities on one level to entities on another.

These abstract and stark definitions may be given some initial relevance to the usual meanings of the terms defined by noting that the leading candidates for the position of irreducibly distinct levels of entities are "things" and "properties," and that the best efforts of three hundred years of reductionist thought have been devoted to breaking down this distinction. The view that the essence of realism lies in the refusal to reduce kinds of things to the sets of qualia which form the criteria for the application of thing–kind names has become fairly familiar. The independence of the knower from the known, which forms the common-sense kernel of realism, becomes, in the light of philosophical analysis, the independence of the contexts and methods by which we *specify* things from those by which we *describe* them. Manley Thompson has argued (successfully, I believe) that the methodological analogue of the cosmological doctrine that "things are not collections of properties (nor, *a fortiori*, of sense-data, ideas, or the like)" is that the question "what *kind* of thing is it?" (which we answer by *specifying*) is not reducible to a series of questions of the form "which thing?" (which can be answered by *describing*).[4] Thompson suggests (and Whitehead would agree) that an attempt to perform the latter reduction can end only in a pragmatism which is indistinguishable from idealism.[5]

Thompson has further shown that specification can only be kept distinct from description if one erects an irreducible distinction between words which function as K-terms (members of a classificatory scheme which classifies things into kinds) and words which function as D-terms (names of properties), *even though* the same symbols may be used for both sorts of terms.[6] This distinction between two sets of terms, where the meanings of the members of one set are independent of the meanings of those of the other set, is the logical analogue of the distinction between thing and property. Whether the distinction is made metaphysically, methodologically, or logically, its import consists in the refusal to adopt, as it were, a "monism of explanation," in which to "explain" something is to reduce it to an instance of a class—a class definable in terms of universals.

The master argument which realists use against reductionists is that the reductionist position cannot be made intelligible without smuggling in a covert realism. If one attempts to take seriously the notion that all data can be analyzed in terms of universals, one finds oneself faced with the question "What *is* it that can be analyzed in terms of universals?" More specifically, if one adopts the view that all explanation is a matter of discovering which class a thing is a member of, then one sooner or later finds oneself faced with the problem "What is the analysis of the notion *member of a class*?" The "datum" or the "member" can only be a bare particular, a bare substrate. Just insofar as it is something more than this, it requires further analysis in terms of further universals. Just insofar as this analysis is *not* offered, a covert distinction between levels—the level of the repeatable universals and the level of the bare particulars—is being assumed. As soon as the challenge to reduce this distinction is accepted by the reductionist, however, a potentially infinite regress is generated. Each analysis of the level of particulars into a new pattern of universals calls forth the need for a new level of particulars in which the new pattern of universals can be exemplified. Awareness of this regress may lead the reductionist himself to question the notion of bare particularity. But if he does so, he is no longer able to give a clear meaning to the notion of "universal." Universals, as "repeatable," require something to distinguish their various repetitions.[7] The notion of repeatability is equivalent to the notion of "capable of entering into external relations"; if there are no particulars, there is no possibility of entering into such relationships. If objects are mere congeries of universals, then, as idealists never tire of pointing out, all statements which attribute characters to objects are necessary truths, signifying internal relations. We thus wind up with a metaphysical monism as a consequence of our insistence upon a "monism of explanation." Given such a monism, the problem of "mere appearance" or "mere error" takes the place, for the reductionist, of the problem of "bare particular," or "mere substrate," and is equally baffling.[8] This is the *reductio ad absurdum* of the reductionist's attempt simultaneously to explain the datum and to reduce it away, and the confirmation of the realist's contention that "order," "explanation," "knowledge," and "analysis" are intelligible only as long as we hold the entities *to be* ordered, explained, known, or analyzed apart from the entities *in terms of which* the ordering, explanation, knowing, or analysis is to be performed.

In what follows, I shall try to show how Whitehead's awareness of the need to avoid this sequence of reductionist absurdities led him to adopt certain key doctrines, and to show the analogies between these doctrines and certain key Aristotelian doctrines, adopted from the same motives. In the course of expounding these doctrines, I hope to put some flesh on the bare bones of the notion of "distinction of categoreal level" which I have introduced. Having done so, I shall be in a position to compare Aristotle's "form–matter" distinction with Whitehead's "eternal object–actual entity" distinction. Both distinctions are attempts to locate ultimate and irreducible categoreal distinctions whose discovery and exposition will provide a stable foundation for realism. I shall be arguing that Aristotle's hylomorphism was an attempt to establish such a distinction, and that this attempt failed because of Arisotle's identification of "definiteness" with "actuality." I shall try to show that Whitehead's substitution of "decisiveness" for "definiteness" as the criterion of actuality permits him to succeed where Aristotle fails.

Comparisons between Aristotelian and Whiteheadian concepts do not lend themselves to lucid exposition, for Whitehead's critique of alternative cosmologies is so radical as to transform systematically the meaning of almost every traditional philosophical term. This essay is intended as an attempt to plot these transformations.

## III · FINAL CAUSALITY AND ATOMISM

Early in *Process and Reality*, Whitehead remarks that "[F]inal causation and atomism are interconnected philosophical principles" (PR 29). The faintly paradoxical air of this remark is due to our habit of associating atomism (in its logical and psychological, as well as its physical, forms) with a doctrine of external relations. We associate teleology, on the other hand, with a doctrine of internal relations—a thing which is striving to realize its end constitutes itself by that striving, and would not be the same thing were it not so striving. Saying that atomism and final causality are interconnected, then, would seem to be saying that something can sustain external relations only if it also sustains internal relations, or the converse, or both. Now Whitehead does, in fact, want to say the former. He holds that only because actual entities sustain internal relations to goals—their "subjective aims"—are they capable of sustaining external relations to other actual entities.[9] What prevents an actual entity from being "reduced" to the sum of its physical prehensions of other actual entities (and thus what separates the "philosophy of organism" from Absolute Idealism) is the individuality and unrepeatability of its subjective aim. Whitehead holds that an actual entity cannot be analyzed without remainder either into its physical prehensions of other actual entities (the domain of efficient causality; cf. PR 134) or into its conceptual prehensions of eternal objects (the domain of final causality; cf. PR 159). Nor can these two poles be disjoined in order to be interpreted as two independent actual entities in their own right.[10] An actual entity can retain its integrity only by being interpreted in terms of both levels of entities—the eternal objects and the other actual entities—*at once.* Particularity is safe, and the reductionist implications of the "subjectivist principle" are avoided, only if this distinction of level is maintained (cf. PR 128, 228).

This Whiteheadian doctrine should be compared with Aristotle's doctrine that a material substance cannot be reduced either to its form or to its matter, that it has matter only because it has form, and that "the actuality of a substance is its goal" (*Metaphysics*, IX 1050a9).[11] Because a substance has a goal, a goal which is (in the case of "things which exist by nature") identical with its form, it cannot be analyzed as "the sum of its qualities," in the sense of the sum of the properties which form the criteria for specifying it as a substance of such-and-such a species plus the sum of the properties which describe its accidents. To form the sum here involves a breakdown of categoreal level—a "category-confusion" in Ryle's sense of the term. The attempt to form such a sum is based upon the "unreformed subjectivist principle" and the ensuing myth of a "bare substratum"—a substratum which supports "essential" and "accidental" attributes in the same external way. The "formula of the definition" of which Aristotle speaks does not name a complex property; it names the substance, and names it directly.[12] "Each thing itself . . . and its essence are one and the same in no merely accidental way" (*Metaphysics*, VII 1031b19). The internal relation of the substance to the species of which it is a member (and thus to its goal) is what permits the substance to retain its independence (its atomic character)—an independence which permits it to be externally related *to* its accidental properties, rather than dissolving *into* them.[13]

Both Aristotle and Whitehead invoke teleology in order to explicate the distinctions of level which save the primary actualities (the "atoms") of their respective cosmologies from dissolution. However, this resemblance is obscured by, so to speak, a difference of scale. It is pointless to compare a Whiteheadian "actual entity" with an "episode of accidental change" occurring in an Aristotelian substance. Although there is a sense in which these two notions do explicate the same pre-analytic phenomenon, the radical differences between Aristotle's and Whitehead's categoreal schemes make such a comparison produce only paralogisms and misunderstandings. The proper comparison is between an actual entity and an Aristotelian primary substance—a substance which, however, is distinctive in being a species unto itself (resembling, in this respect, angels as characterized by St. Thomas). No two Whiteheadian occasions have the same subjective aim (cf. Christian, p. 310), and thus there is no distinction in Whitehead between specification and individuation. There is, however, an analogue of the distinction between specification and description—namely, the distinction between an actual entity's description as "subjectively immediate" and as "objectively immortal" (cf PR 34, 38, 44). As we shall see in Sections VI and VIII below, this analogue preserves the requisite Aristotelian distinction of level, while dismissing the Aristotelian problem of the relationship between the secondary substance "X-hood" and the substantial forms of individual *X*'s. Thus, actual entities are, as it were, miniature Aristotelian substances; they owe their unity and their irreducibility (their "atomic" character) to their internal relationship to a goal—a goal which is characterizable only in terms of entities of a different categoreal level from those which characterize their external relations to other actualities.

## IV · UNITY AS REQUIRING CATEGOREAL DIVERSITY

A second crucial Whiteheadian doctrine is, to an adherent of the unreformed subjectivist principle, as paradoxical as the interconnection of teleology and atomism. This is the doctrine that the ultimate unit of actuality must be internally complex; a unit, in short, must be the *unity of* something. "Each ultimate unit of fact is a cell-complex, not analysable into components *with equivalent completeness of actuality*" (PR 334, italics added). The implications of this doctrine are spelled out in an explication of the "category of objective diversity":

> The category of objective diversity expresses the inexorable condition—that a complex unity must provide for each of its components a real diversity of status, with a reality which bears the same sense as its own reality and is peculiar to itself. In other words, a real unity cannot provide sham diversities of status for its diverse components. . . . The prohibition of sham diversities of status sweeps away the

> "class theory" of particular substances, which was waveringly suggested by Locke . . . , was more emphatically endorsed by Hume . . . , and has been adopted by Hume's followers. For the essence of a class is that it assigns no diversity of function to the members of its extension. . . . The "class," thus appealed to, is a mere multiplicity [PR 348; cf. Christian, p. 248].

The fundamental importance of this point for process philosophy is shown by Whitehead's statement that:

> This doctrine that a multiple contrast cannot be conceived as a mere disjunction of dual contrasts is the basis of the doctrine of emergent evolution. It is the doctrine of real unities being more than a mere collective disjunction of component elements. This doctrine has the same ground as the objection to the class-theory of particular substances [PR 349].

In this doctrine of internal diversity we have perhaps the clearest expression of Whitehead's rejection of the reductionist notion of explanation as "placing a datum within a class." As Christian says: "This principle of individuality [the subjective aim as defining a mode of togetherness of actual entities and eternal objects], in Whitehead's metaphysics, supersedes in importance the principle of classification" (Christian, p. 252). The "ontological principle" that "actual entities are the only reasons" (PR 37), combined with the definition of "actuality" as "decision amid 'potentiality' " (PR 68), produces the most fundamental justification of Whitehead's insistence on the irreducibility of categoreal levels. The attempt to find an ultimate unit without internal complexity and without the teleology involved in the "decision" of an actual entity is simply one more form of the search for bare particulars—for "vacuous actuality." The impulse for such a search can only be the confusion of ease of classification with cosmological priority,[14] and its outcome can only be a tyranny of internal relations and the loss of real unity.

This protest against the confusion of the distinction between unity and plurality with the distinction between simplicity and complexity is also to be found in Aristotle, in his protests against both materialistic reductions of form to matter[15] and Platonic reductions of matter to form.[16] In both sets of protests, he is led to insist upon the irreducible complexity involved in the hylomorphic analysis of substance, and the loss of unity which occurs when it is proposed to replace this analysis with something simpler. However, in Whitehead's eyes, Aristotle betrayed his own better insight when, in *Metaphysics* XII, he made room for the Unmoved Mover —the perfect case of a "vacuous actuality." Aristotle's break with the realistic requirement of a distinction of level in the case of the Unmoved Mover gave fatal encouragement to the assumption that "satisfactory explanation" demands that "substances with undifferentiated endurance of essential attributes be produced"—an assumption which Whitehead calls "the basis of scientific materialism" (PR 120; cf. PR 241).[17]

However, if we put the Aristotelian notion of "immaterial substance" to one side for the moment, we can see that both Aristotle and Whitehead are, in their theories of the nature of real unity, conforming to the demands which we outlined in Section II: the demand that recourse to bare particulars be avoided by establishing two categoreal levels, and that the unitary character of the ultimate cosmological unit should consist in its unification of those two levels —a unification which is possible, and is given meaning, only in virtue of their irreducible difference.

## V · POTENTIALITY AND ACTUALITY

The paradox involved in the phrase 'unity which is internally complex' fairly cries out for resolution by means of a distinction between potentiality and actuality, and both Aristotle and Whitehead do invoke this distinction for that purpose. Aristotle holds matter and form together in subsantial unity by the formula: "the proximate matter and the form are one and the same thing, the one potentially, and the other actually" (*Metaphysics*, VIII 1045b-18–19). Whitehead's use of the distinction is summed up in the following passage:

> Just as 'potentiality for process' is the meaning of the more general term 'entity' or 'thing'; so 'decision' is the additional meaning imported by the word 'actual' into the phrase 'actual entity'. "Actuality" is the decision amid "potentiality" [PR 68].

Aristotle and Whitehead agree that the actuality–potentiality distinction is unavoidable, but their application of it is so drastically different as to have called forth the suggestion that their respective systems may be transformed into each other simply by following the rule: "What is potential for Aristotle is actual for Whitehead, and conversely."[18] In the previous two sections we have dwelt upon anti-reductionist doctrines on which Aristotle and Whitehead concur. Here, we begin to see how Whitehead separates himself off from both Aristotle and reductionism in the quest for a better reply to reductionism than Aristotle achieved, and thus for a more adequate formulation of realism.

Whitehead claims that

> [S]ome chief notions of European thought were framed under the influence of a misapprehension, only partially corrected by the scientific progress of the last century. This mistake consists in the confusion of mere potentiality with actuality. Continuity concerns what is potential; whereas actuality is incurably atomic [PR 95].

The immediate thrust of this remark is against Newtonian notions of space and time, but the extent of the confusion in question is much wider. The confused notion of the distinction of act and potency against which Whitehead is protesting here is the assumption that there are two equally atomic sorts of things: actual *X*'s and potential *X*'s. This notion, on reflection, drives one to the paradox that (1) "certain possible so-and-sos are not actual so-and-sos," yet (2) "the only possible entities are actual ones."[19] When the absurdity of an attempt to resolve this paradox by finding the "extra something" which transforms a potential *X* into an actual one becomes evident, we are tempted to give up the actuality–potentiality distinction altogether. When we do give it up, as reductionists do, we lose the ability to make intelligible the notion of "unity which is internally complex," and thus we have to fall back upon "bare particulars." Whitehead tells us that if we are going to keep and use this distinction, we must start all over again. We must get rid of the notion of potential X's, substitute the notion of "potentialities *for* X," and abandon the assumption that "the only possible entities are actual ones." A possible entity, for Whitehead, is not a half-baked version of an actual entity; to think of it this way is like thinking of the datum about which one decides as itself a half-baked decision. The actuality–potentiality distinction is in danger, in Whitehead's eyes, whenever one attempts to use the vocabulary appropriate to atomic individuals in describing potentiality. The temptations exerted by language, a language built around pragmatically convenient abstractions,[20] will almost inevitably engender the reduction of the potential to the actual, and thus the loss of the distinction of categoreal levels upon which realism depends. The last person really to struggle with language in order to keep the distinction viable was Aristotle, who, Whitehead thinks, largely failed.[21] The key to his failure, and the reason for his acceptance of "vacuous actuality" in the doctrine of the Unmoved Mover, was the illicit transition from the doctrine of form-as-the-actuality-of-the-matter to the notion of form-as-the-actuality-of-the-composite-substance. This transition evolved into the notion of form-in-isolation contributing something called "actuality" to the composite substance, whereas matter-in-isolation contributed the element of "potentiality." For Whitehead, the point of the contrast between actuality and potentiality is lost as soon as one begins to think of "actuality" as something other than "actualization *of the potential*."

This analysis permits us to formulate a first rough sketch (to be revised in Section VII below) of the central contrast between Aristotle's and Whitehead's approach to the distinction between form and matter. For Aristotle, this distinction is a special case of the distinction between actuality and potentiality. For Whitehead, the form–matter distinction, when applied to the process of coming-to-be of an actuality, is the distinction between two sorts of potentiality. The criterion of actuality is found, for Whitehead, neither in pure form (eternal objects in themselves) nor in pure matter (the extensive continuum of real potentiality), but in the unification—under the conditions of the "category of objective diversity" (cf. Section IV above)—of both levels.[22] This unification is itself a member of neither level. In other words, Whitehead agrees with Aristotle that an irreducible distinction of level is requisite to realism, but for Whitehead such a distinction, in order to be irreducible, must be strictly correlative. By 'correlative' here I mean that each level must be essentially incomplete, and completable only by interpretation in terms of the other level—an interpretation which cannot be achieved wholesale and *a priori* by philosophical inquiry (or by God, for that matter), but only at retail and *pro tempore* by the concrescent activity of actual entities. (This latter point is illustrated by the fact that both 'order' [PR 128] and 'actual world' [PR 102] are, for Whitehead, token-reflexive terms.) Philosophy is thus not the study of "order" or of "the structure of the actual world"—such a proposal would be analogous to a proposal to study "here" or "the structure of yesterday"—but rather, so to speak, of the grammar of token-reflexive terms and its relation to the grammar of non–token-reflexive terms.[23] "Philosophy is explanatory of abstraction, and not of concreteness" (PR 30).

In place of Aristotle's contrast between form-as-actuality and matter-as-potency, Whitehead contrasts "pure" potentiality (the realm of eternal objects) with "real" potentiality (the "extensive continuum": "one relational complex in which all potential objectifications find their niche" [PR 103]). Both levels are required for the explanation of actualities, but neither level can do its job if the entities which compose it are thought of as quasi-atoms; as would-be actualities.[24] These two levels will be discussed in the next two sections, but first it will be useful to draw one more comparison between Whitehead and Aristotle. I have cited a suggestion that Whitehead attributes all the characteristics to actuality which Aristotle attributes to potentiality, and conversely. This suggestion cannot be explored in detail here, but there is much truth in it. The most signal instance of this inversion is, of course, that definiteness is for Aristotle a characteristic of form, and form is actuality, whereas for Whitehead definiteness is characteristic of eternal objects, which are pure potentialities. This identification of pure definiteness with pure potentiality seems paradoxical to Aristotelians because for Aristotle (in the *Metaphysics*, and thus in the "orthodox" Aristotelian tradition, though not in the scientific treatises) definiteness is the criterion of actuality. For Whitehead it is not. His criterion of actuality is *decisiveness*, which is not the same thing. This shift of the criterion of actuality is perhaps the most important feature of the difference between a realism built around the notion of *stasis* and one built around the notion of *process*. *Definiteness* in Whitehead's eyes is primarily a *logical* notion—although, to be sure, one which needs to be grounded in cosmological notions. The seed of the reductionists' confusion of logical simplicity with "priority in the process constituting an experient occasion" (cf. n. 14) are already present in Aristotle's inability (despite desperate efforts[25]) to avoid the Platonic mastery of λόγος, ἰδέα, and μορφή over φύσις—of the terms which are necessary to discuss actualities over the actualities themselves. An actuality is a decision about *how to be* definite—a decision which, from the point of view of *other* actualities for which the first is a datum, looks like one more instance of definiteness. But if this exterior point of view is adopted as the point of view of philosophical analysis, then the interior decisiveness of the actuality will be analyzed away into patterns of definiteness. It will begin to seem, as it did to Aristotle, that superior actuality consists not (as it does for Whitehead: cf. PR 142) in making more and more important and far-reaching decisions, but in being so definite as no longer to have to make decisions at all. From here, it is but a step to the "unreformed subjectivist principle" that "the datum in the act of experience can be analyzed purely in terms of universals."[26] Aristotle shrank from this step, and his attempts to avoid taking it have been the foundation of anti-reductionist thinking ever since, but the "misunderstanding of the true analysis of 'presentational immediacy'" (PR 43) which he shared with Plato left Aristotelianism too weak to withstand the assaults of the reductionist revolt of the seventeenth century.[27]

## VI · REAL POTENTIALITY: MATTER AS OBJECTIFIED ACTUALITY

For Whitehead, there are two ways of describing any actual entity—as the culmination of process and as potential for process, as present and as past. The Eighth Category of Explanation tells us that:

> [T]wo descriptions are required for an actual entity: (a) one which is analytical of its potentiality for "objectification" in the becoming of other actual entities, and (b) another which is analytical of the process which constitutes its own becoming [PR 34].

This distinction is, *prima facie*, the closest Whiteheadian parallel to the Aristotelian distinction between the-matter-in-a-substance and the form of that substance. If one calls the aspect described by (a) the "objective" reality of the actual entity and that described by (b) its "formal" reality (as Whitehead sometimes does[28]), then one can think of its objective reality as the entity considered *qua* matter and its formal reality as the entity considered *qua* form. Differences appear, however, when one pursues the analogy. If one takes the general difficulty about "potentiality" to be summed up in the question "How can one ever talk about potentiality, since all we ever find are actualities?" then one is tempted to translate this into Whiteheadian terms as the question "How can one speak of the objective reality of an actual entity, when all that it *really* is is a process of becoming?" On reflection, however, one should realize that this question is wrong-headed. The *objective* reality of an actual entity is precisely what, ninety-nine times out of a hundred, we *do* speak of. The real problem for Whitehead is how to speak of the *formal* reality of an actual entity. The inversion of modality which, as we have noted, characterizes the contrast between Aristotle and Whitehead, is here marked by replacing the question "How can you talk about potentiality?" with the question "How can you talk about anything else?" In place of the reductionist's paradox that "the only things that can possibly be encountered are actualities, but not all possibilities are actual," Whitehead asks us to reflect on the fact that everything that can be encountered by an actuality is *objectively* real, and thus is merely a potentiality, yet actualities *do* influence other actualities.

This inversion is not a mere verbal twist, although it might seem so. Both Aristotle and Whitehead, after all, seem to identify actuality with immediacy, and it might seem obvious that the immediately encountered—the "given"—is actual, and that its function as a potentiality for further process is derivative, the product of reflection and analysis. But this is not obvious to Whitehead; on the contrary, viewing the situation in this way is, as we shall see, a symptom of the failure to "take time seriously." For Whitehead, "immediacy" is of two sorts—the private subjective immediacy of present enjoyment, and the public objective immediacy of the given past. Although the former is a criterion of actuality, the latter is not. The objective reality of an actual entity is "the actual entity as a definite, determinate, settled fact, stubborn and with unavoidable consequences" (PR 336), but stubborn facticity is not the same as actuality, any more than is definiteness. The *decisiveness* which marks the *formal* reality of the actual entity is the *reason* for the objective reality of that entity being as stubborn as it is (cf. PR 68–69), but stubbornness is not the same as decisiveness.[29] In a system in which "Creativity" is "The Category of the Ultimate," "stubbornness" is a mark of potentiality, not of actuality. The inversion of modalities here, far from being verbal, is part and parcel of Whitehead's campaign against the confusion of logical simplicity with ontological priority, and against the (pragmatically useful, but cosmologically disastrous) confusion of a thing's consequences with its nature.[30]

The importance of this inversion appears when we turn to the traditional dilemmas about the notion of matter. "Matter" has always been asked to play two distinct, and apparently incompatible, roles. On the one hand, matter is supposed to be cuddly, malleable, and receptive—it seeks form as the female seeks the male. On the other hand, it is resistant, obstreperous and stubborn—it needs, Aristotle tells us, to be "mastered."[31] In Aristotle, emphasis teeters back and forth between these two roles. The first appears when "matter" (as "material cause") is being used to make substantial change intelligible, and the second when "matter" is being invoked to explain accidents, individuation, and monstrosities. With the subsumption, in the cosmology of the seventeenth century, of substantial change under changes of quantity and quality, matter adopts the second role almost exclusively. Now, when one focuses on this second role, one sees that matter is not resistant because of its indefiniteness, but precisely because of its definiteness. It is not because a lump of marble is "formless" that it resists the sculptor, but because it has the *wrong* form. Again, reflection from the seventeenth-century point of view on the malleability and feminine complaisance which Aristotle attributes to proximate matter makes one realize that these features are due not to the "materiality" of the material cause but simply to its possession of the "right" form. So, following the lead provided by the "unreformed subjectivist principle," it begins to look as if one could analyze both the cuddliness and the stubbornness of "matter" away into congeries of forms, and thus eliminate altogether the need to give indefiniteness an ontological status.

Thus, *if one identifies actuality with definiteness*, one finds it absurd to think of "potentiality" as anything but a name for the confusion among our ideas (which was how the seventeenth-century philosophers did think of it). The actuality–potentiality distinction thus evaporates altogether. Without the heuristic aid provided by this distinction, all distinctions of categoreal level tend to evaporate. But if, with Whitehead, one distinguishes between definiteness and decisiveness, then one can unite the two roles played, in Aristotle, by "matter" by saying that matter ("objectified actual entities") is definite, stubborn, and resistant precisely because it *is* potential; and conversely. Only the definite and resistant is malleable—that is, only a perfectly definite feeling (cf. PR 338) can be a datum for further feeling, but once a feeling *is* definite, it is over, past, and thus, though objectively immortal, *no longer* actual (cf. PR 130). Instead of interpreting the distinction between matter and form as one between real indefiniteness and real definiteness, Whitehead interprets it as the distinction between the past and the present.

## VII · PURE POTENTIALITY: PRIMARY MATTER AS ABSTRACT MULTIPLICITY OF FORMS

At this point, however, one may wish to raise questions of the following sort: Is there then no place for the vague, the indefinite, and the muddled in Whitehead's system? Is there any point in using the notion of "potentiality" if all one means by it is "past actuality"? Doesn't a philosophy of creativity entail real indefiniteness as an ultimate categoreal level?

The answer to these questions, I shall argue, depends once again upon the contrast between "definiteness" and "decisiveness." There is no such thing in Whitehead's system as "real indefiniteness," but there distinctly *is* real indecisiveness, and this indecisiveness does form a distinct categoreal level. For it is here that the eternal objects come into the act. The Whiteheadian analogue of "primary matter" is the "barren inefficient disjunction of abstract potentialities" (PR 64). Primary matter, in Aristotle, is the ultimate background against which substantial change—generation and destruction—takes place. In Whitehead, " 'Change' is the description of the adventures of eternal objects in the evolving universe of actual things" (PR 92), and it is against this background of the bare unstructured multiplicity of eternal objects that actualities evolve. The concrescent processes which are the formal realities of actual entities order this multiplicity, and change it from a *mere* multiplicity into a pattern of *relevant* potentialities. The measure of an actual entity's actuality is the measure of the extent to which it succeeds in establishing such a pattern.[32] The analogue of the Great Chain of Being which (for Aristotelians, if not for Aristotle[33]) stretches from Primary Matter to the Unmoved Mover(s) is a hierarchy stretching from "the-eternal-objects-as-mere-multiplicity" (an ultimate abstraction, which is precisely as inconceivable as "Primary Matter"[34]) to God (who *positively* prehends *all* the eternal objects, whereas all other actualities prehend positively only a tiny fraction of them). "Each occasion exhibits its measure of creative emphasis in proportion to its measure of subjective intensity. The absolute standard of such intensity is that of the primordial nature of God, which is neither great nor small because it arises out of no actual world" (PR 75). Each temporal actual entity inherits suggestions, as it were, about relevant patterns of form from past actual entities, and it rearranges these patterns in accordance with its own τέλος—its own subjective aim. The more inclusive its subjective aim, the more it will be able to do toward restructuring inherited patterns, and the more individuality, decisiveness, and actuality (three synonymous terms, for Whitehead) it will have. When we think in terms of "change" (that is, of the creative process in the large) rather than of "enjoyment" (the concrescence of an individual actual entity), we see the eternal objects as playing the role of that-which-becomes-arranged and the individual actual entities as doing the arranging. From this point of view, the whole creative process can be seen as the attempt to find the pattern of relevance among eternal objects which will produce the greatest subjective intensity of enjoyment.

Taking this conclusion together with the discussion of real potentiality in Section VI, we can now revise the description of the contrast between Aristotelian and Whiteheadian treatments of the form–matter distinction which we offered in Section V. Our new set of analogies is as follows:

(1) the *specific form* of an individual material substance *S* has no Whiteheadian analogue, since (cf. Section III) there is no distinction in Whitehead between specification and individuation;

(2) the *form* of *S* is analogous to the formal reality of an actual entity *A*;

(3) the *proximate matter* of *S* is analogous to *A*'s past—the actual entities from which *A* inherits, considered as objective realities (the "extensive continuum");

(4) the *matter-in-S* or *S-qua-matter* is analogous to *A*'s objective reality—that is, *A*-as-prehended-by-later-actual-entities;

(5) primary matter is analogous to the bare multiplicity of eternal objects, by reference to which *A* and its ancestors may be described, and which *A* "orders" by reordering its inheritance from its ancestors.[35]

In Section V we treated the extensive continuum (3) as the analogue of *matter* and the multiplicity of eternal objects (5) as the analogue of *form*, while treating (2)—the formal reality of *A*—as the analogue of *composite substance*. That treatment expresses the way the situation looks from, as it were, "inside" *A*'s concrescence: the real potentiality (3) is "matter" for the process of being felt under subjective forms dictated by a new "form" (the initial datum of *A*'s subjective aim[36]) plucked out from (5). The table of analogies above, on the other hand, expresses how the situation appears when we step outside of *A* and look at the whole creative process: from this perspective, we can see both (3) and (5) as "matter" and (2) as "form," thus re-establishing the Aristotelian identification of form with actuality.

This table of analogies, however, should not mislead us into thinking that a concrescent actual entity's contact with primary matter is only by way of the traces of primary matter left in the proximate matter which it is prehending, as the Aristotelian analogues might suggest. *A* faces both ways—toward the level of real potentiality (3) and the level of pure potentiality (5)—and plays each off against the other in the interest of its own heightened enjoyment. It is in the space between these two levels, so to speak, that creation gets room to occur. Further (to repeat the conclusion of Section III) it is by virtue of the independence of these two levels that actual entities can be genuine individuals. The irreducible individuality and novelty of each actual entity is made possible by the inexhaustible array of alternative subjective aims which its pure conceptual prehensions—its prehensions, that is, of eternal objects not yet exemplified among its ancestors—make available to it. Without such pure conceptual prehensions, the new actual entity would merely be the product of efficient causes (cf. PR 75, 134). On the other hand, without the physical prehensions of the realm of real potentiality constituted by the objectified past actualities, it would be merely the product of idiosyncratic final causes, and the solidarity of the universe would be lost.[37] On neither alternative can time be taken seriously: on the first, there is no reason to transcend the past, since it can only be reiterated; on the second, there is no past to transcend.

There is, perhaps, a certain flavor of paradox in our claim that the multiplicity of eternal objects is the analogue of primary matter. For are not the eternal objects consciously modeled on the Platonic Forms? (Cf. PR 69–70.) "Forms of definiteness" seem, offhand, about as far as one can get from primary matter, when the latter is viewed, as it usually is, as a sort of *Urschleim.* Here again, however, the appearance of paradox arises from our Aristotelian habit of identifying both form and actuality with definiteness. But definiteness does not decide anything; it is what gets decided *about.* Forms of definiteness are not forms of decisiveness, even though once a decision is made it can be analyzed into forms of definiteness. We think of definiteness as a mark of actuality because we think that whenever there is something definite, there must have been an indefinite substratum, and a decision which formed that substratum into this definiteness. But this preconception, although it seems like hard-headed realism, in fact leads one down the reductionist path toward the notion of "bare particulars." It is no more arbitrary and irrational for Whitehead to postulate the non-temporal existence of an infinite and unstructured multiplicity of forms of definiteness than it is for Aristotle to presuppose the eternal structure of a finite number of specific forms. After all, *any* cosmology which declines the Hegelian challenge to "deduce," e.g., the colors of the visible spectrum, is going to have to start by letting forms of definiteness in on the ground floor of speculation—as an irreducible categoreal level. The only question is: How, once let in, can they be restrained from swallowing up any other sort of entity to which one wants to assign coeval ground-floor status? That is to say, how can one maintain a categoreal distinction between forms of definiteness and definite actualities?

The most dramatic version of this last question is the Platonic one: if the Forms are as definite as all *that*, what excuse can possibly be found for the sensible world? If actuality is identified with definiteness, then this problem is insoluble. Aristotle, tipped off by Plato to the existence of the problem, but unwilling, in the end, to give up this identification, tried to solve the problem by letting just a *few* forms of definiteness in on the ground floor—viz., the thing–kind names of common sense and of primitive science—while consigning all the others to a vague cosmological dustbin called "matter." In doing so, he paved the way for reductions, for when a more advanced science made it thoroughly unclear where substantial change left off and accidental change began, philosophers promptly endowed the forms of accidents with definiteness, and thus with actuality. They thereby (cf. Sections V–VI) made both the matter–form and the actuality–potentiality distinctions seem pointless.

Whitehead, abandoning the identification of actuality with definiteness, solves the problem by letting in *all* forms of definiteness at once, and by making the criterion of degree of actuality consist in the extent and complexity of the choice among those forms. Using this criterion, the only danger involved in postulating forms of definiteness is that the forms might, all by themselves, exercise an influence upon the choices which are made concerning them. Insofar as such an influence *is* exercised, the totality of eternal objects would have to be counted as itself an actuality, and a dissolution of the distinction between categoreal levels would ensue. Whitehead was incautious about this danger in *Science and the Modern World.* In that book, he seems to think of each eternal object as being what it is by virtue of its place in a scheme of internal relations with all the other eternal objects. Such a scheme suggests that all the decisions have already been made, and that the concrescence of actual occasions must follow rigid guidelines, tiresomely reiterating pre-established patterns. (Cf. SMW 229–31.) In *Process and Reality* he takes just the opposite tack and treats the eternal objects, by themselves, as utterly unrelated to one another:[38] all "relationships" between eternal objects are now interpreted as derivative from choices ("valuations") made by actualities.[39] Since *every* possibility of order is itself an eternal object (and therefore incompatible possibilities of order are equally possible) and since there can be no such eternal object as Order-in-general (corresponding to The Form of the Good),[40] the multiplicity of eternal objects remains as unstructured as ever Primary Matter was. To sum up, Whitehead's insight is that "pure potentiality" is to be found not in the *absence* of definiteness, but in piling definiteness on definiteness until no guidelines for decision between these alternative definitenesses remain.

## VIII · CONCLUSIONS

In this concluding section I shall try to tie what I have been saying together by answering the question: What does Whitehead's philosophy of process contribute to a discussion of the topic of matter? For this purpose, I shall return to my original distinction between realism and reductionism in Section II, where I said that reductionism tries, and fails, to analyze experience exclusively in terms of *repeatable* entities. The contrast between the repeatable and the unrepeatable—between the universal and the particular—is traditionally explicated by both Aristotelianism and common sense in terms of the distinction between form and matter. When one attends to the macroscopic objects of common sense, it seems obvious that *man*, for example, is a repeatable form, but that Socrates is unique and unrepeatable, and so we consider *man* as Socrates' form, and his unrepeatability as due to his matter.

The most obvious and dramatic difference between process philosophy and common sense is that the units of actuality, for process philosophy, are no longer such macroscopic objects. They are replaced by sub-microscopic unrepeatable entities. Taking time seriously means taking the break between past and present as the border between two different actualities.[41] If one does this, it becomes analytic that "only the non-actual is repeatable." Given this doctrine, it becomes clear that one must either (a) cease to use the matter–form distinction, or (b) deny that form is repeatable, or (c) deny that form is actual.

Aristotelians have fought against transferring the unit of actuality to this sub-microscopic level on the ground that, since such actualities do not change, one cannot preserve the distinction between matter and form. (This attitude has given Aristotelianism a bad name, since it has seemed to involve an unempirical insistence that science should always accommodate itself to philosophy, and never conversely.) Both the cosmology of the seventeenth century and Whitehead's process philosophy, on the other hand, accept this transference. But whereas the thinkers of the seventeenth century thought themselves well rid of the matter–form distinction, Whitehead is intent upon reinterpreting it so as to make it relevant to unchanging entities.

The way in which this reinterpretation proceeds will be clearer if we note the differences, within the cosmological tradition which we inherit from the seventeenth century, between rationalists and empiricists. Empiricists cling to the principle that only form is repeatable, but they deny that form is actual. They think of form as abstract, and of concreteness as inhering in an inexpressible and unintelligible "given." The "given" stands to form in the relation of "exemplification of," even as did Aristotelian matter, but unlike Aristotelian matter (which was describable, even if not "knowable" in the honorific sense of the *Posterior Analytics*), it is undescribable, and thus its postulation involves the absurdities inherent in the notion of "bare particulars." Rationalists, on the other hand, clinging to the identification of form with both repeatability and actuality, interpret the form–matter distinction by reference to the Platonic distinction between reality and appearance—so that "givenness," like "time" and "individuality," are treated as illusions. They thus can reply that the "given" is not truly concrete, and that only the Concrete Universal is truly actual. Although avoiding the absurdities of the notion of "bare particulars," rationalists encounter analogous absurdities in their attempt to explain how Reality manages to disguise itself as Appearance. Rationalists and empiricists thus either gratefully abandon talk of matter-*vs.*-form altogether, or else (following up certain Aristotelian leads, but neglecting others), they speak of matter-as-the-unfortunately-undescribable-actual (in empiricism) or of matter-as-unfortunate-and-non-actual-illusion (in rationalism).

Now Whitehead wants to say that:

(1) The seventeenth century was right, against Aristotle, in ceasing to regard middle-sized common-sense things as paradigmatic of actuality.

(2) Rationalists are right, against empiricists, in saying that the "given" is not actual.

(3) Empiricists are right, against rationalists, in saying that what is repeatable is not actual.

(4) Aristotelian realists are right in insisting, against everybody, that the form–matter distinction, or some analogue thereof which will preserve the ability of actualities to sustain both external and internal relations, is needed.

Whitehead's treatment of the relations between actual entities and eternal objects—that is, his reinterpretation of the form–matter distinction—is dictated by the need to reconcile these four positions. His point of departure is (3): the repeatable is not actual. Empiricists, having grasped this, are misled by their acceptance of the unreformed subjectivist principle into inferring that the actual is undescribable. What is required in order to get around this principle, Whitehead says, is the recognition that actualities are describable in terms of other actualities. (Cf. PR 76.) Empiricists, however, are afraid that such description will lead to idealism, and thence to monism. They fear that admitting that actualities are "present in" (cf. PR 79) other actualities will dissolve actualities into congeries of internal relations. Whitehead replies that a congeries of internal relations is not the same as a congeries of universals. Relations are as unrepeatable as anything can be (cf. AI 296; PR 349–50; Christian, p. 236), and an actuality which consists of internal relations to other entities is unrepeatable precisely by virtue of being a congeries of such relations. The idealist attempt to construe relations as universals is just another product of the unreformed subjectivist principle.

But this still leaves us without an account of external relations (without becoming involved in infinite regresses). Since entities which can sustain external relations must be repeatable, and since the repeatable is non-actual, we have to invoke repeatable potentialities to serve as "forms of definiteness" by which actualities, as terms of relations, may be characterized. But postulating such forms —the eternal objects—raises the traditional dilemma of the Platonic Forms: either (a) the forms postulated to characterize the actualities are so much like actualities as to make them indistinguishable from their actualizations, or (b) they are so different from actualities that they cannot do an adequate job of characterizing them. Now it is in the resolution of this dilemma that the significance of process philosophy emerges most clearly. The dilemma is resolved by distinguishing definiteness from decisiveness, a distinction which is unintelligble if one does not take time seriously. For if one does not, one will be unable to see a difference between the evaluative decision of a currently concrescent actual entity and the inheritance from that actual entity received by its successors—between, in other words, "formal" and "objective" reality. The latter *is* indistinguishable from a form of definiteness, and if all actual entities were past (or, what comes to the same thing, if they could be viewed *sub specie aeternitatis*) there would be no difference between the actual world and the extremely complex eternal object which described it. If time is taken seriously, however, and it is thus recognized that 'actual world' and 'actuality' are token-reflexive terms, then one can escape the first horn of the above dilemma by distinguishing between the definiteness of an entity's characterization (its "objective" reality) and the decisiveness of its concrescence (its "formal" reality). The latter is actual, and therefore non-repeatable. The former is "repeatable," and therefore potential, in the sense that it is related (externally to it, although internally to each entity which prehends it) to a potentially infinite number of subsequent actual entities by being "present in" them. The apparent dilemma is now seen to rest upon a confusion between past and present—between characterization and entity characterized.[42] Its second horn is escaped by replying that the difference between the characterization of the actual and the actual entity is no greater, though no less great, than the difference between past and present—which, if one takes time seriously, is precisely the difference which one would expect.

We saw in Section VI how the distinction between formal and objective reality resembles the traditional distinction between the form and the matter of a substance. In Section VII we saw how the multiplicity of eternal objects resembles primary matter. We can now see that the crucial *difference* between Aristotle's and Whitehead's doctrines of matter is that Whitehead retains the advantages of the matter–form distinction while avoiding the disadvantages of the species–individual and essence–accident distinctions. Specifically, he (a) retains Aristotle's categoreal distinction of level while avoiding both (b) the "unscientific" character of Aristotle's distinction and (c) the latent tendency toward the subjectivist principle (cf. Section V) inherent in Aristotle's use of teleology in regard to enduring and changing entities:

(a) The distinction between formal and objective reality permits one to save realism by (1) enabling the primary realities to bear both external and internal relations, (2) maintaining the independence of the level of pre-analytic (non-objectificatory) reference to an entity (the self-satisfaction of an actual entity in its subjective immediacy) and the level of its analysis (an actual entity as objectified, and thus as analyzable into a pattern of eternal objects); (3) uniting these two levels by the "two-way functioning of eternal objects" in conformal feeling (cf. PR 249), so that despite the utter privacy of an actual entity's subjective intensity, it is genuinely "present in" later actualities.

(b) The ordinary seventeenth-century objection to the Aristotelian form–matter distinction, interpreted as the distinction between the repeatable form of a species and the unrepeatable combination of accidents which individuate the species' members, was that since any given accident or congeries of accidents was as repeatable as a specific form, any distinction between the repeatable and the unrepeatable was arbitrary and unempirical. Whitehead's distinction between the decisiveness of formal reality and the definiteness of objective reality permits one to make sense of the notion of the ultimate unrepeatability of the actual, while his refusal of the gambit "But how do they differ *sub specie aeternitatis*?" protects him against reductionist efforts to make the repeatable either unintelligible or illusory. He is thus able, as Aristotelians are not, to welcome the seventeenth century's substitution of a law–event framework of scientific explanation for the Aristotelian species–individual framework.

(c) The Aristotelian identification of actuality with definiteness was a result of Aristotle's unwillingness to take time seriously. This unwillingness led him to postulate "immaterial substances," to identify form with actuality, and to lay the foundation for the tradition that satisfactory philosophical explanation must be in terms of "substances with undifferentiated endurance of essential attributes" (PR 120). Process philosophy, by breaking with this latter tradition, is able to avoid the reductionisms which flow from an acceptance of the unreformed subjectivist principle while preserving the links with modern scientific results which make these reductionisms so plausible. Whitehead's willingness to accept the Heraclitean view that 'actual world' is a token-reflexive term, and his consequent refusal to identify "actuality" with the results of an ideally long or ideally "objective" analysis in terms of universals, radically transforms the Aristotelian notions of form and matter. The history of futile debate between philosophies which presuppose the Aristotelian cosmology and philosophies which presuppose the cosmology of the seventeenth century shows, I think, that they badly needed such transformation.

## NOTES

1. I very much regret that I had not read Ivor Leclerc's "Form and Actuality" (in *The Relevance of Whitehead*, ed. I. Leclerc [New York: Macmillan, 1961]) at the time this paper was written. Any future comparison of Aristotle and Whitehead should take Leclerc's essay as a point of departure.

2. Cf. William A. Christian, *An Interpretation of Whitehead's Metaphysics* (New Haven: Yale University Press, 1959), who points out (p. 247) that in 1919 Whitehead was still toying with the "class-theory of particulars" (cf.

Section III below) characteristic of the Berkeley–Russell–Goodman tradition, but that by 1925 he had realized that he wanted to break with it. The Whitehead whom I shall be discussing in this paper is the Whitehead of *Process and Reality*, and I shall make no attempt to cover the shifts in Whitehead's views. (This, incidentally, is the reason why I refer throughout to "actual entities"—the term used in *Process and Reality*—rather than to "events," the term used in the earlier writings.) Christian's book, which I have used heavily, will be cited as 'Christian'.

3. On this notion of independence of categoreal level as a prerequisite for realism, cf. W. Donald Oliver, *Theory of Order* (Yellow Springs, Ohio: Antioch, 1951), chs. 1–3, where the notion is developed in great detail and with a precision which I cannot attempt here. I have attempted to apply the arguments which Oliver presents to problems concerning the nature of philosophical controversy in "The Limits of Reductionism" (in *Experience, Existence and the Good: Essays in Honor of Paul Weiss*, ed. Irwin C. Lieb [Carbondale: Southern Illinois University Press, 1961], pp. 101–16) and to problems of epistemology in "Pragmatism, Categories, and Language," *Philosophical Review*, 70 (1961), 197–223, esp. 217–20.

4. "On the Distinction Between Thing and Property" in *The Return to Reason: Essays in Realistic Philosophy*, ed. John Wild (Chicago: Regnery, 1953), pp. 125–51, esp. pp. 129–33.

5. Cf. Thompson, *op. cit.*, pp. 148–51. See also, for a critique of the notion of a "method of pure description," Oliver, *op. cit.*, ch. 4. For the resemblance between pragmatism (as usually conceived) and idealism (as usually conceived), cf. John Passmore, "The Meeting of Extremes in Contemporary Philosophy," *Philosophical Review*, 69 (1960), 363–75.

6. Cf. Thompson, *op. cit.*, pp. 130–33. This last point suggests the way in which the distinction between independent levels of entities which is central to realism must take account of the fact that language communicates just to the degree that it avoids the use of token-reflexive terms. The strong point of reductionism (and the reason why reductionism came into its own only with the "linguistic turn" and the adoption of the "formal mode of speech") is that any singular terms are always replaceable by descriptions. But, as Strawson points out, the employment of a language in which such replacement is consistently carried out will make *all* reference to particulars impossible (cf. "Singular Terms, Ontology, and Identity," *Mind*, N.S. 65 [1956], 449).

7. Cf. Charles Hartshorne, "The Compound Individual," in *Philosophical Essays for Alfred North Whitehead* (New York: Longmans, Green, 1936), p. 202: "[U]niversal and individual are ideas that are clear only in relation to each other, and where either conception is neglected the other will suffer also."

8. Cf. PR 78, on how the misinterpretation of the doctrine of universals paves the way for Kant's "degradation of the world into 'mere appearance'," and PR 85, on Santayanian skepticism or Bradleyan idealism as the only possible outcomes of reductionism. Cf. also PR 349–50.

9. As we shall see more clearly below, the external relations sustained by an actual entity *A* are not *A*'s prehensions of other actual entities which are

"objectified" by *A*; on the contrary, *these* relations are *internal* to *A*. The only external relations sustained by *A* are prehensions of *A* by "later" actual entities, for which *A* is objectified. The relation *X*-prehending-*Y* is always internal to *X* but external to *Y*.

10. For Whitehead's critique of the attempt to disjoin them in this way, cf. PR 108.

11. Compare also Aristotle's identification of ἔργον with both τέλος and ἐνέργεια, Whitehead's identification of "decision" with "actuality" (PR 68), and Leibniz's appeals to teleology against the mechanistic reductionisms of the Cartesians (in order to prevent the monads from dissolving into space–time points). For a comparison of these three philosophers on a related topic, cf. J. H. Randall, Jr., *Aristotle* (New York: Columbia University Press, 1960), p. 170.

12. Cf. Thompson, *loc. cit.*, p. 136, "K-terms . . . signify but a single kind of entity and thus have *simple and direct signification* which is neither denotation nor connotation." Wilfrid Sellars arrives at the same conclusion in connection with an analysis of the forms of Aristotelian substances; cf. "Substance and Form in Aristotle," *Journal of Philosophy*, 54 (1957), 695: ". . . thing-kind words are . . . common names of individuals, not proper names of universals. . . ."

13. The problem of how the difference between the relation of a substance to its form and its relation to its other attributes should be formulated is the major metaphysical problem which Aristotle willed to his heirs. (The trouble with taking seriously the *identification* of substance and essence is, of course, that such an identification seems to condemn the accidents, à la Plato, to the realm of "mere appearance.") We have the record of Aristotle's own unsuccessful struggles with this problem in *Metaphysics* VI–IX; see especially the discussion of the difference between τὶ σημαίνει and τὸ τί ἦν εἶναι in VII, Ch. 4, and compare Thompson, *op. cit.*, pp. 133–36.

14. Cf. PR 85, on "the assumption, unconscious and uncriticized, that logical simplicity can be identified with priority in the process constituting an experient occasion." At PR 202 Whitehead echoes Bergson in remarking that: "We may doubt whether 'simplicity' is ever more than a relative term, having regard to some definite procedure of analysis." For further polemics against reductionist notions of explanation, cf. PR 246, 253, 120.

15. Cf. *On Generation and Corruption*, I, Ch. 2, esp. 317a19–28.

16. Cf., e.g., *Metaphysics*, I.

17. For an account of what Aristotle *should* have said about God in order to avoid abandoning his commitment to categoreal diversity (an account with which Whitehead would be in hearty accord), see Randall, *op. cit.*, pp. 143–44.

18. Cf. Robert S. Brumbaugh, "A Preface to Cosmography," *Review of Metaphysics*, 7 (1953–54), 53–63. Cf. also Leo A. Foley, *A Critique of the Philosophy of Being of Alfred North Whitehead in the Light of Thomistic Philosophy* (Washington: The Catholic University of America Press, 1946), p. 120.

19. I borrow this formulation of the paradox from Nelson Goodman, *Fact,*

*Fiction, and Forecast* (Cambridge: Harvard University Press, 1955), p. 55. Chapter Two of this book—"The Passing of the Possible"—is a good statement of what becomes of the actuality–potentiality distinction when it is considered under the aegis of the unreformed subjectivist principle.

20. Cf. PR 253. For Whitehead's views on the relation between language and philosophical speculation, cf. PR 16–20, esp. 18: "A precise language must await a completed metaphysical knowledge."

21. Cf. n. 12 above. Whitehead's attitude toward Aristotle is full of mixed feelings. Although he regards the subject–predicate model as largely responsible for the popularity of "vacuous actualities," he seems to feel that it is medieval philosophers, rather than Aristotle himself, who are chiefly blamable. "The exclusive dominance of the substance–quality metaphysics was enormously promoted by the logical bias of the mediaeval period. It was retarded by the study of Plato and of Aristotle. These authors included the strains of thought which issued in this doctrine, but included them inconsistently mingled with other notions. The substance–quality metaphysics triumphed with exclusive dominance in Descartes' doctrines" (PR 209). Cf. also PR 45, 81, 85, 122; AI 356; A. H. Johnson, *Whitehead's Theory of Reality* (Boston: Beacon, 1952), pp. 123–24. Foley (*op. cit.*, p. 109) says that Whitehead is arguing only against the "Lockian or Cartesian" notion of substance as inert substrate, and not the Thomistic–Aristotelian notion of substance as activity. This is largely true. Whitehead knows that there is a difference between the two traditions, but he usually seems to think it not worthwhile to distinguish them, since he is convinced that the seeds of decay are already present in Aristotle's confusion of ἐνέργεια-as-ἔργον with ἐνέργεια-as-μορφή.

22. It is perhaps useful to point out the analogy with Kant, who takes "concepts" as "form" and "intuitions" as "matter," and then devotes himself to showing that *neither* can count as "experience," that both are merely analytic components of (potentialities for, as it were,) experience, and that skepticism (Hume) or idealism (Leibniz) are the result of speaking of either as if it could be, all by itself, a full-fledged experience. Whitehead, I think, conceives of himself as having done cosmologically and completely what Kant did epistemologically and incompletely: namely, developing the implication of the "reformed" subjectivist principle that "the whole universe consists of elements disclosed in the analysis of the experiences of subjects." (PR 252; on Kant, cf. PR 234–37.)

23. On the importance of token-reflexivity, cf. Hartshorne, "Process as Inclusive Category: A Reply," *Journal of Philosophy*, 52 (1955), 95–96.

24. The level of real potentiality is, of course, constituted by objectified actualities—past, but objectively immortal. But *as* past, and thus as potential, they lose their individuality. Having lost the power of decision, they become matter for decision. Because they *have been* actual, they are not would-be actualities, but simply suggestions to present actual entities about how to be actual.

25. Cf. Randall, *op. cit.*, p. 116.

26. Cf. Hartshorne, "The Compound Individual," p. 200: "Those who today defend Aristotelianism as the "commonsense philosophy" are simply inviting

us to begin the foredoomed process all over again. Every new Aristotle can only usher in a new Berkeley. . . ." Cf. also PR 79.

27. Whitehead's vision of the absurdities of modern reductionism as traceable to an initial misstep taken by Plato and Aristotle is very like Heidegger's. Cf. *An Introduction to Metaphysics*, trans. Ralph Manheim (New Haven: Yale University Press, 1959), pp. 180–94, esp. p. 182: "The crux of the matter is not that *physis* should have been characterized as *idea* but that the *idea* should have become the sole and decisive interpretation of being." Heidegger's analysis, both in *An Introduction to Metaphysics* and in *Sein und Zeit*, of Western ontology as dominated by the identification of "being" with "presence" (παρουσία, *Anwesenheit*) — cf. *Sein und Zeit*, sec. 6—should be compared with Whitehead's suspicion of the ultimacy of "presentational immediacy." Compare also Heidegger on *Zuhandensein*-vs.-*Vorhandensein* (*Sein und Zeit*, secs. 15–17) with Whitehead on causal efficacy-*vs.*-presentational immediacy.

28. Cf. PR 118. William P. Alston ("Internal Relatedness in Whitehead," *Review of Metaphysics*, 5 [1951–52], 535–58) equates "formal reality" with "existence" and "objective reality" with "actuality." The latter identification, I should want to argue, is very seriously misleading.

29. On the derivative status of stubbornness, compare Heidegger, *Sein und Zeit*: "Widerstandserfahrung, das heisst strebensmässiges Entdecken von Widerständigem, ist ontologisch nur möglich auf dem Grunde der Erschlossenheit von Welt. Widerständigkeit charakterisiert das Sein des innerweltlich Seienden. Widerstandserfahrungen bestimmen faktisch nur die Weite und Richtung des Entdeckens des innerweltlich begegnenden Seienden. Ihre Summierung leitet nicht erst die Erschliessung von Welt ein, sondern setzt sie voraus" (p. 210; italics removed). The attempt to construct *Erschlossenheit* out of *Widerständigkeit* is a product of the attempt to make *Vorhandensein* prior to *Zuhandensein* (cf. n. 27), as is the reductionism ensuing from an acceptance of the "unreformed subjectivist principle." (Compare also Peirce, on the impossibility of constructing "Thirds" out of "Seconds.")

30. Cf. PR 336: "The 'formal' aspect is functional so far as that actual entity is concerned: by this it is meant that the process involved is immanent in it. But the objective consideration is pragmatic. It is the consideration of the actual entity in respect to its consequences."

31. Cf. *On the Generation of Animals*, IV 769b11–770b27, 788a5–6.

32. Cf. Christian, p. 267: "[T]his ordering of eternal objects is an actual occasion's contribution to its future," and PR 132: ". . .'order' in the actual world introduces a derivative 'order' among eternal objects." (But this does not mean that the eternal objects are "changed" by being thus ordered; cf. n. 39 below.)

33. This parenthesis expresses my reservations about how seriously to take the (very rare) references to πρώτη ὕλη in the Aristotelian corpus—reservations, however, which need not be discussed here. Cf. Hugh R. King, "Aristotle Without *Prima Materia*," *Journal of the History of Ideas*, 17 (1956), 370–89.

Barrington Jones now argues that matter in Aristotle always designates the temporally prior particular actuality from which a substance comes into being, obviating any need for "primary matter": "Aristotle's Introduction of Matter," *Philosophical Review*, 83 (1974), 474–500. See also Lewis S. Ford, "Prime Matter, Barrington Jones, and William Brenner," *The New Scholasticism*, 50 (1976), 229–31; R. Rorty, "Genus as Matter" in *Exegesis and Argument*, edd. E. Lee, A. Mourelatos, and R. Rorty (Assen: Van Gorcum, 1973), and the articles by McMullin, Fisk, Nielsen, Bobik, and Sellars in Part II of *The Concept of Matter*, ed. E. McMullin (Notre Dame: University of Notre Dame Press, 1963).

34. Cf. Christian, pp. 265–66, the references there cited, and PR 42. As Christian points out, 'multiplicity' is used in a highly technical sense by Whitehead, and must be sharply distinguished from 'nexus' and 'proposition'. "[E]very statement about a multiplicity is a disjunctive statement about its individual members" (PR 45).

(I should like to note that this section could not have been written without the help of Christian's discussion of the doctrine of eternal objects in Part Two of his book. The reader is urged to consult this discussion for a full account of the process of "establishing patterns of relevance"—a subtle topic which can only be sketched in the present space.)

35. Whitehead himself was inclined to analogize "Aristotelian 'matter'" to "Creativity" (PR 46)—which, however, he also analogizes to "primary substance" (PR 32). The former analogy is probably due to his reading Aristotle as saying that a thing's matter is its internal principle of change—the sort of reading suggested by, e.g., Santayana's "The Secret of Aristotle" (in *Dialogues in Limbo* [New York: Scribners, 1926], pp. 173–93).

36. On the notion of the initial datum of a subjective aim (about which Whitehead is rather vague), cf. Christian, pp. 157–58, 215–16, 305–306.

37. Cf. PR 249: "The one eternal object in its two-way function, as a determinant of the datum [i.e., of the objectified past actual entity] and as a determinant of the subjective form [under which the present actual entity prehends the past actual entity], is thus relational. In this sense the solidarity of the universe is based on the relational functioning of eternal objects." (Cf. AI 236.) But if there is no datum other than the conceptually prehended eternal object itself, then there is nothing for this eternal object to relate.

38. As Christian (p. 262) has noted, Whitehead may be construed as speaking, in Chap. 10 of *Science and the Modern World*, of the eternal objects as they are related in the Primordial Nature of God. The latter—a "non-temporal actuality" which provides the primordial valuation of all eternal objects—raises many serious and complex problems for an analysis of Whitehead's cosmology. I shall make no attempt to go into these problems here, although a full defense of my argument in this paper would require that this Whiteheadian analogue of the Unmoved Mover (cf. PR 522–23) be discussed. I am here treating the Primordial Nature as simply one more actuality which transmits suggestions about relevant eternal objects to the future, just as temporal actual entities do.

39. I put 'relationships' in quotes as a reminder that one should not think of eternal objects as in any way "changed" by being thus re-evaluated. Despite

Whitehead's use of expressions like 'ingression of eternal objects' and 'adventures of eternal objects', it is clear that nothing ever "happens" to an eternal object. The order which Whitehead says is introduced among them is not some sort of quasi–spatio-temporal reshuffling, but is simply the "suggestions" about which eternal objects are more relevant than others made to a concrescent actual entity by its predecessor-actualities or by the Primordial Nature of God. To speak of "an order among pure potentialities" is always an elliptical way of referring to real potentiality. To say that an eternal object has been made more relevant to the creative process is not to say that anything has been added to it, nor that its "position" in the multiplicity of eternal objects (in some unintelligible sense of 'position') has changed, any more than to say that logarithms or ultrasonic vibrations have become relevant to human technology is to say that they have somehow suffered qualitative change or altered position.

40. This is because of the paradoxes of self-inclusion. Cf. PR 128, and Christian, pp. 271 72.

41. This is why time cannot be taken seriously until one ceases to think of the present as a knife-edge and begins to think of it as an extended duration.

42. Whitehead thus can be seen as replacing the distinction between "specification" and "description" (discussed in Section II above) with the distinction between reference-to-an-actual-entity-as-subjective-intensity and reference-to-an-object. The present–past distinction is thus substituted for the thing–property distinction.

# 7

# Form, Concrescence, and Concretum

George L. Kline
*Bryn Mawr College*

Whitehead is remarkably consistent in his use of such neologisms as 'concrescent', 'ingression', 'conceptual prehension', 'physical prehension', and 'subject-superject'. But he is much less consistent in his use of such traditional, and traditionally vague or equivocal, terms as 'actual', 'concrete', 'constitute', 'decision', and 'function/ing', all of which are of central importance for his thought. Thus, for example, he says that the "concrescence of any one actual entity involves the other actual entities among its components" (PR 10) and that "Each actual occasion defines its own actual world from which it originates" (PR 321). The term 'actual' in its *first* occurrence in both passages means 'active; in-process-of actualization'; in its *second* occurrence it means 'efficacious; already-actualized'. I shall distinguish these senses as 'actual$_1$' (='active and self-significant but-not-efficacious') and 'actual$_2$' (='efficacious and other-significant but-not-active'), respectively.[1] 'Actual$_1$' applies exclusively to concrescences, to subjects, to what is present; 'actual$_2$' applies exclusively to completed past actual entities—to what I call 'concreta' (pl.), 'concretum' (sing.).[2] Actuality$_1$ entails

An earlier version of this chapter appeared in *The Southern Journal of Philosophy* (7 [1969–70], 351–60). As published here it is substantially revised and enlarged. I have profited greatly from critical comments on various versions of this essay by Edward Casey, William A. Christian, William J. Garland, Victor Lowe, Donald W. Sherburne, and—especially—Lewis S. Ford.

actualization, a *process* of actualiz*ing*; $actuality_2$ entails actualiz*ed-ness*, the *state* or *condition* of having-been-actualiz*ed.*

What the two otherwise contrasted senses of 'actual/ity' have in common is the notion of "making a difference," of "making one's influence felt (by others)": what is $actual_1$ makes a difference by acting, by being an agent. As Whitehead says, "agency belongs exclusively to $actual_1$ occasions" (PR 46). What is $actual_2$ makes a difference by being (passively) efficacious, by providing what I call 'unrefusable data' for physical prehension by subsequent (present) concrescences (see pp. 127–28 below). Forms may also be called 'efficacious'—although Whitehead did not apply this term to them[3]—but they are not $actual_2$, since they are *non*-concrescent rather than *post*-concrescent entities; they make a difference, in a somewhat weaker sense, by providing "refusable data" for conceptual prehension by present concrescences.

Whitehead's regular use of '$actual_2$' (without making any explicit distinction between the two senses of the term) in the expression '[past] actual world' is particularly misleading, since Whitehead also calls this "world"—in my terms, the totality of concreta relative to a given concrescence—'*potential*', asserting that the past is characterized by "real potentiality."[4] Thus he speaks of the " 'real' potentiality, which is conditioned by the data provided by the $actual_2$ world" (PR 102; cf. also 34 [Cat. Expl. 6], 123, 147, 336, 340, 441, 470, 498, 508). Elucidating the expression 'real potentiality' as applied to the $actual_2$ world, Whitehead says that the term 'potentiality' refers to the "passive capacity" and the term 'real' to the "creative activity" (AI 230). If he had substituted 'stubborn efficacy' for 'creative activity' this definition would have been unexceptionable. But I shall return to this question in Section VII below.

Especially suggestive, but also misleading in the absence of a distinction between $actual_1$ and $actual_2$ is Whitehead's statement: "The systematic scheme, in its completeness embracing the $actual_2$ past and the $potential_p$ future, is prehended in the positive experience of each $actual_1$ entity" (PR 112). Entities which are $actual_2$ (efficacious) are indeed $potential_r$; but those which are $actual_1$

(active) cannot be potential in either sense; they are non-objectifiable and provide no data. In terms of the "actual/potential" polarity, only concrescences are $actual_p$ (and also, of course, $actual_1$); only concreta and forms are potential—the former, as $actual_2$, being $potential_r$; the latter, as neither $actual_1$ nor $actual_2$, being $potential_p$.

The "process/product" or "-ing/-ed" distinction will help to resolve the ambiguities of several of Whitehead's key terms (and concepts), including 'constitute', 'decision', 'determination', and 'transition'. The term 'constitution' has a double ambiguity: (1) a "semantic" ambiguity, which has been pointed out by Jorge Nobo:[5] 'constitute' sometimes means 'form' or 'create' (as 'constitutive'—the Kantian term, which Whitehead uses fairly often—means 'formative' or 'creative'), e.g., at PR 244, 335, 390, 448; AI 251, 328; but in other passages it means simply 'amount to', 'be', or 'comprise', e.g., at PR 63, 105, 244, 444; (2) a kind of "syntactical" ambiguity—the '-ing/-ed' ambiguity of many '-tion/-sion' words: 'Constitution' means: (a) 'the *process* of constitut*ing* or creat*ing*' and (b) 'the *state* or *condition* of having-been-constitut*ed* or creat*ed*'. These I distinguish as '$constitution_1$' and '$constitution_2$', respectively, where, as with '$actual_1$' and '$actual_2$', the subscript-1 form characterizes the concrescence, and the subscript-2 form, the concretum. Thus the Lockean phrase 'real internal . . . constitution', which Whitehead regularly uses to characterize actual entities, means '$constitution_1$'—'[process of] real internal [self-] creat*ing*' when applied to concrescences (cf. PR 43, 66, 71, 84, 335, etc.) but something like 'real internal state of having-been-[self-] creat*ed*', i.e., 'static structure or make-up', when applied to concreta (cf. PR 37 [Cat. Expl. 18], 43, 335). This second sense is close to what Locke intended, since 'real internal . . . $constitution_2$' is the Lockean definition of 'essence'. But the first, and for Whitehead more important, sense is surely quite remote from what Locke himself had in mind.[6]

Similarly, when Whitehead defines 'actuality' in terms of 'decision', it is necessary to distinguish between $actuality_1$, which is characterized by $decision_1$ (the *act* of decid*ing*) (cf. PR 75, 248, 423, 435) and $actuality_2$, which is characterized by $decision_2$ (the *state* of having-been-decid*ed*) (cf. PR 68, 69, 73, 227, 435). Whitehead himself implicitly recognizes this distinction, referring to what I call 'decision$_1$' as 'immanent' or 'immediate' decision and to what I call 'decision$_2$' as 'transcendent' decision (PR 248–49). (The term 'satisfaction' appears to be exempt from the '-ing/-ed' ambiguity: Whitehead uses it only in the '-ed' sense, meaning 'state or condition of having-been-satisfied or completed'.)

## I

Lewis S. Ford has convinced me that Whitehead uses the term 'concrete' in a second systematic sense in addition to the first systematic sense, which I characterized as 'concrete$_w$' in the earlier published version of this Chapter.[7] The first sense, which I shall now call 'concrete$_1$', applies to concrescences; the second sense ('concrete$_2$') applies to concreta. 'Concrete$_1$' means 'experient and actively self-relating'; 'concrete$_2$' seems to mean something like 'settled and determinate'. What is concrete$_1$ is also actual$_1$ (i.e., active and self-significant); what is concrete$_2$ is also actual$_2$ (i.e., passive and "other-significant").

I shall give examples of both senses, but wish first to state that in this paper I shall, because of the serious ambiguity of 'concrete' in Whitehead's usage, avoid the term altogether—along with its contrary, 'abstract',[8] and the cumbersome 'quasi-abstract' of my earlier paper—replacing these terms with 'concrescent', 'non-concrescent', and 'post-concrescent', respectively.

I pass over a number of texts (e.g., PR 32, 66, 94, 244, 321) in which the sense of 'concrete' is unclear or ambiguous, and cite several occurrences of 'concrete$_1$'. I admit that Whitehead does not say outright that concrescences are concrete$_1$, but I insist that in many passages he comes very close to making such a claim. Thus he speaks of "concrete$_1$ occasions of actual happening" (SMW 228), of the "full concreteness$_1$ of $\alpha$ [a concrescent occasion]" (SMW 246), of "a concrete$_1$ percipient entity [i.e., a concrescence]" (PR 261), and characterizes an event or unit-process as "the most $concrete_1$ $actual_1$ something," an end in itself, an entity "which is for its own sake" (SMW 136). Whitehead also declares that an $actual_1$ entity is "$concrete_1$ because it is . . . a particular concrescence [i.e., process of prehensive unification] of the universe" (PR 80).[9] He refers to a "concrescence which elicits a $concrete_1$ unity from [the] many [past] $actual_2$ occasions" (PR 322) and asserts that the "sole $concrete_1$ facts in terms of which $actualities_1$ can be analyzed are prehensions" (PR 444), that a prehension is a "$concrete_1$ element" in a given $actual_1$ entity (PR 35 [Cat. Expl. 11]), and that prehensions are the "most $concrete_1$ elements" in such an entity (PR 35 [Cat. Expl. 10]). The concrete in this sense is *quod concrescitur.*

To express this sense—'$concrete_1$'—Whitehead often uses the characteristic term 'concrescent', which is not, strictly speaking, a neologism, since it is defined in the larger dictionaries (e.g., *Webster's New International Dictionary*, 3rd ed.) as 'growing together', as in 'a flower with concrescent petals'—in company with the verb 'concresce' (='to coalesce') and the noun 'concrescence' (='a coalescence of particles').[10] In the lexicon of speculative philosophy, however, the term functions as a Whiteheadian neologism.

It seems clear that in other passages Whitehead uses the term 'concrete' in the sense of '$concrete_2$'—*quod concretum est*—applying it to the entities which I call 'concreta'. Thus he says that the "concrescence issues in one $concrete_2$ feeling, the satisfaction" (PR 66) and in a much-quoted passage characterizes "coordinate division" as "division [i.e., analysis] of the $concrete_2$ [i.e., the concretum or concreta]" in contrast to "genetic division," which is "division of the concrescence" (PR 433). Whitehead calls the "extensive continuum" a "specialized ordering of . . . $concrete_2$ occasions [i.e., concreta]" (PR 448) and says that the "notion of satisfaction" is a "notion of the 'entity [i.e., the concretum] as $concrete_2$' abstracted from the 'process of concrescence' " (PR 129). His most extreme and puzzling usage is in the rarely encountered expression '$concrete_2$ object' (PR 448). The concretum, though indeed an object, is precisely *not* $concrete_1$.

Such examples have convinced me that Whitehead does not associate a single systematic sense with the term 'concrete', but that he uses it, confusingly, in the two contrasted senses of '$concrete_1$' and '$concrete_2$'—as well as (occasionally) in the pre-systematic sense of 'particular', 'detailed', or 'down-to-earth'. Thus he refers to "more concrete concepts" (SMW 51); "more concrete intuitions" (SMW 126); "most concrete rendering of fact" (SMW 82); "a more concrete survey" (SMW 203); and "the most concrete mode of analysis" (PR 29; cf. SMW 107).

This is reason enough, I suspect, for the interpreter of Whitehead's speculative system to *avoid* use of the term 'concrete'; in any case, I shall avoid it for the remainder of this essay.

## II

The difference between a unit-concrescence or "concresc*ing* entity" and a concretum or "already concresc*ed* entity" is roughly that between a particular (present) *process*, and a particular (past) *product*, of actualization or partial self-creation. Concreta are not only non-$actual_1$ but also non-*actuel* in the French sense of the term, i.e., non-*present*, precisely because it is their "nature" to be *past*.

Whitehead uses the term 'concrescence' in three related, but distinct, senses: (1) As a synonym for 'particular $actual_1$ *entity*'—the sense in which I mainly use the term in this essay. (Cf. PR 66, 249, 374, 435, etc.) (2) As a synonym for 'particular concrescent *process*', in such expressions as 'concrescence of many [$actual_2$] entities into one $actuality_1$' (PR 33, 34; cf. 10, 130), 'process of concrescence' (PR 129, 130) or 'concrescent process' (PR 131), and 'insistent concrescence into unity' (PR 89), as well as in the claim that "each occasion [effects] a concrescence of the universe" (PR 481; cf. 80, 320). (3) As a synonym for the generic process of which concrescences in the first two senses are instantiations. Thus Whitehead speaks of "[particular] acts of [generic] concrescence" (PR 419; cf. 508) and, more explicitly, of an $actual_1$

entity as "an *instance* of concrescence" (PR 321; italics added).

When used in this third sense, the term might usefully be capitalized, to set it off from the other two senses. Thus one could say that "particular concrescences are instances of generic Concrescence" and even that "particular transitions are instances of generic Transition."

It seems to me that Whitehead, in developing his atomic or "epochal" theory of process, distinguished too sharply between concrescence and transition (and between Concrescence and Transition), and not sharply enough between concrescence and concretum. Concrescence and Transition are two "species of *one* process"; they are "inseparable, though distinguishable."[11] Transition is precisely the active relation of concrescence to concretum. Concreta provide the data which are "causally objectified" through physical prehension by individual concrescences.

The epochal theory of process or becoming can, I think, be defended as cogently in terms of the distinction between concrescence (in the first sense) and concretum as in terms of Whitehead's own less-than-lucid distinction between concrescence (in the second or third sense) characterized as 'microscopic' or belonging to the 'microcosm' and transition (in the second or third sense) characterized as 'macroscopic' or belonging to the 'macrocosm' (see PR 326, 327). It seems to me that transition (or Transition) is no less "microscopic" or "microcosmic" than concrescence (or Concrescence): both kinds of process or "fluency" (PR 320) occur at the *same* "ontological level."

What Whitehead calls 'eternal objects' are "pure potentials" for the definiteness or determinateness of "matters of fact"—of both concrescences and concreta. In this Chapter I shall be concerned only with what Whitehead refers to as 'eternal objects of the objective species' (PR 445–46) and for brevity I shall call them simply 'forms'.[12]

There are six kinds of relations among three kinds of relata, although Whitehead left nameless the relation between concreta and forms. I have suggested 'exhibition' and 'inherence'[13] as candidates to fill this terminological gap. See Table 1.

TABLE 1

| ORDER OF RELATA | MODE OF RELATION |
|---|---|
| 1.a Concrescence to form | 1.a Conceptual prehension |
| b Form to concrescence | b Ingression, ingredience |
| 2.a Concrescence to concretum | 2.a Physical prehension |
| b Concretum to concrescence | b Providing data for, functioning datively with respect to |
| 3.a Concretum to form | 3.a "Exhibition" |
| b Form to concretum | b "Inherence" |

Neither forms nor concreta are active; the relation between them is "static" or "passive." To say that a given concretum exhibits a given form or forms, or that a given form is inherent in a given concretum or given concreta, is to say no more than that the concretum in question is determinate in a particular respect or in particular respects. The relation of form to concrescence and of concretum to concrescence is an object-to-subject relation, the relation of a *timeless*, or a *past*, entity to a *present* entity. This relation is internal or "constitutive" (cf. SMW 230) with respect to the concrescence, but external ("non-constitutive") with respect to both the form and the concretum.[14] In Whitehead's words, any entity which enters into, or is patient of, external relations, functions as a datum "describable without reference to its entertainment" in the concrescence which prehends it (AI 226).

For Whitehead not every relation is a relat*ing*—an internal or "constitutive" relation—with respect to both, or all, of its relata. Some relations are simply states of being-related. That relatum (e.g., a form or concretum) with respect to which the prehensive relation is external, is simply "in relation" or passively relat*ed* rather than actively relat*ing*, as the concrescence is.

III

Table 2, which lists five characteristic features of forms, concrescences, and concreta, respectively, may be misleading to the extent that it appears to place all three types of entity on the same ontological level. In fact, the ontological distinction between concrescences and *concreta* (which are the *products* of concrescent *processes*) is less sharp than that between either concrescences or concreta and *forms* (which are *neither* processes *nor* products of concrescence).

I shall comment in turn on each of the five characteristics of forms.

(1) Forms are *non*-concrescent rather than *post*-concrescent, as concreta are. They are non-actual$_1$, i.e., both non-active and non–self-significant. As objects, non-subjects, forms are non-experient and have significance for, or "make a difference to," concrescent subjects alone. A given form does not have significance for, or make a difference to, itself, or to any other form. The form–concrescence relation is *external* ("non-constitutive") with respect to the form although *internal* ("constitutive") with respect to the concrescence.

Forms are passive; they are prehended or "enacted." They do not prehend or "enact" themselves. They are not agents; they do not, strictly speaking, *do* anything. Their "power"—like that of the concreta—is of the kind that Pols has called 'static'.[15] As data, they *are taken*; they do not "*give themselves*."

(2) It is misleading to say that forms "offer themselves" as data or "serve" as data—if 'offer' and 'serve' are regarded as active verbs. It would be better to say—as Whitehead himself sometimes does—that forms "function" (passively)[16] as "pure [in Kant's sense, i.e., non-empirical] potentials for the specific determination of facts" (PR 32 [Cat. Exist. 5]) or as "potentialities$_p$ of definiteness for any actual existence" (PR 63). They furnish or provide data, which are "taken," through conceptual prehension, by concrescent subjects. As objects, forms are *unconditionally* dative, in the sense that their availability for conceptual prehension does not presuppose any particular spatio-temporal occurrence (i.e., concrescence), as that of concreta does.

TABLE 2

| Forms | Concrescences | Concreta |
|---|---|---|
| 1. Are non-concrescent, non-experient, passive objects | 1. Are concrescent, experient, $actual_1$ (i.e., active but-not-efficacious) subjects | 1. Are post-concrescent, post-experient, $actual_2$ (i.e., efficacious but-not-active) objects |
| 2. Are unconditionally dative; they function passively as pure potentials | 2. Are non-dative; they do not function as potentials of any kind | 2. Are conditionally dative; they function passively as real potentials |
| 3. Are unconditionally repeatable; objectifiable (prehensible) and reobjectifiable | 3. Are non-repeatable, non-objectifiable, and non-prehensible | 3. Are conditionally repeatable and objectifiable (prehensible) |
| 4. Are "non-processive"; they neither become nor change | 4. Are "processive"; they become but do not change | 4. Are "post-processive"; they neither become nor change (although their *meaning* changes) |
| 5. Are timeless or atemporal; they do not become in the present and are not fixed in the past | 5. Are temporally active; they become in the present | 5. Are temporally static; they are fixed in the past |

(3) Forms are unconditionally objectifiable (prehensible) and reobjectifiable. They are "repeatable" in the sense that they can be "taken" (conceptually prehended) again and again. The same form is ingredient in many concrescences and inherent in many concreta, remaining self-identical in all of them. (The 'in' here does not, of course, designate a spatial relation.) The unconditional repeatability of forms is related to, but distinct from, what has traditionally been called 'universality'. As Whitehead notes, "every so-called 'universal' is particular in the sense of being just what it is, diverse [i.e., distinct] from everything else; and every so-called 'particular' [i.e., concretum but *not* concrescence] is universal in the sense of entering into the constitutions$_1$ of other [i.e., subsequent, present] actual$_1$ entities" (PR 76). In the traditional categories which Whitehead is here criticizing both concreta and concrescences would have to be classified as 'particulars', despite the important difference between them here expressed by calling concreta 'conditionally objectifiable' and concrescences 'non-objectifiable'. And forms could be called 'particular' in the sense that any given form is just what it is, distinct from everything else, although forms are, in a stronger sense, universals, since any given form enters into the self-creative activity (constitution$_1$) of *many* concrescences and into the determinate make-up (constitution$_2$) of *many* concreta.

(4) Forms are non-processive, although they are, of course, "in process" in the weak sense that they function as "non-processive ingredients of process." As a German philosopher might put it: *Sie sind im Werden, aber sie werden nicht.* Forms neither become nor change; they enter into differing relationships with differing relata, but remain constant and unmodified throughout all such (passive and external, i.e., non-constitutive) "adventures."

(5) Forms are timeless or atemporal; they do not become in the present, as concrescences do, nor are they fixed in the past, as concreta are. Their passive function is the provision of timeless data for present appropriation (conceptual prehension). For any form,

and for any concrescence, it "is" (tenselessly) the case that the form "is" (tenselessly) available to be conceptually prehended when the concrescent process begins. Although concrescences are partially self-creative, they do not in any sense create the objects of either their physical or their conceptual prehensions. In the case of conceptual prehension, a given concrescence takes or appropriates forms which, because timeless, "are" (tenselessly) available to it *whenever* it may occur.

IV

The principal characteristics of concrescences are listed in the second column of Table 2.

(1) Concrescences are concrescent subjects; they are experient, $\text{actual}_1$, self-significant, or actively self-relating. Unlike forms and concreta, concrescences have significance—meaning and importance—both in and for themselves.[17] The way in which a given concrescence becomes, i.e., decides, feels, values, integrates its data, and actualizes its $\text{potentials}_p$ (through conceptual prehension) and its $\text{potentials}_r$ (through physical prehension), makes a decisive difference to its "real internal . . . $\text{constitution}_1$"—its activity of (partial) self-creation. Conceptual prehension, the relation of concrescence to form, is *internal* (constitutive) with respect to the concrescence, though *external* with respect to the form. Similarly, physical prehension, the relation of concrescence to concretum, is *internal* with respect to the (active) concrescence, though *external* with respect to the (passive) concretum. Concrescences as $\text{actual}_1$ entities are, as Leclerc has insisted, act*ing* entities.[18]

(2) Concrescences, as *processes* of actualization, *act*, but do not *function* (passively). Unlike forms and concreta, which "are," or "have being," concrescences become, but "have no being." Put another way, whatever becomes is $\text{actual}_1$, active but-not-efficacious, $\text{actual}_p$ but not $\text{potential}_r$ (or, of course, $\text{potential}_p$): it provides *no* data of any kind. Whatever "is" or "has being" is either $\text{actual}_2$

and potential$_r$—which is the case with concreta, as entities which "have become"—or else non-actual and potential$_p$—which is the case with forms, as entities which neither become nor "have become."[19]

I interpret Whitehead's dictum that an actual entity's "'being' is constituted$_1$ by its 'becoming'" (PR 34–35 [Cat. Expl. 9]) as meaning that the *activity* of a concrescence produces, or results in, the *static being* of "its" concretum—in sense (2) of 'its' distinguished in n. 25 below. (I shall return to this point in Section X.)

In contrast to forms, which are "unconditionally dative," and to concreta, which are "conditionally dative," concrescences are *non*-dative *tout court*. Unlike forms, which provide "pure" or "general" potentiality (cf. PR 102), and concreta, which provide "real" or "empirical" potentiality, concrescences, being actual$_1$, do not function as potentials of either kind.

(3) Although every concrescence "objectifies" both forms and concreta, taking forms as objects of its conceptual prehensions and concreta as objects of its physical prehensions, it does not in any sense objectify either itself or any other concrescence. Concrescences, as active, actual$_1$ entities, as *subjects*, are non-repeatable,[20] non-objectifiable, and non-prehensible; they cannot be treated or "taken" as *objects*. The mutual non-objectifiability of concrescences is the ontological ground for the causal independence of contemporaries—a key Whiteheadian doctrine, and *one* of the conditions for the concrescent subject's freedom of decision and (partial) self-creation. All concrescences, as entities in process of (present) becoming, are contemporary. That process, once completed, issues in concreta which, as *past*, can be contemporary with no (present) concrescence whatever. For any concrescence $\alpha$ and for any concretum $b$, $b$ "is" (tenselessly) in the past of $\alpha$.

Some concreta, of course, are "contemporary" with other concreta—those, namely, the generating concrescences of which "were" (tenselessly) contemporary. Thus, if concrescences $\beta_1$ and $\beta_2$ become in the "same" present, then "their" concreta (in sense [2] of 'its concretum' distinguished in n. 25) $b_1$ and $b_2$ may be said to share the "same" past. But most concreta are non-contemporary, in "different" pasts, with most other concreta, e.g., concretum $b_1$ with $c_1, c_2, \ldots, c_n$, and $c_1$ with $d_1, d_2, \ldots, d_n$, etc.

Concrescences are temporally localized and in that sense "datable." (Cf. PR 352.) They are also "particular" in both senses of the term distinguished above (p. 114), i.e., each of them is "just what it is" and is "diverse from everything else" (PR 76). And they are atomic or "epochal": a present concrescence becomes and perishes and is superseded by another present concrescence—but, of course, this is a "new" present, a fresh "now"—which physically prehends its predecessor's concretum-product, taking it as object, as datum, for its own activity of self-realization.

(4) Concrescences are "in process" in the strong sense of being, by their very nature, "processive." A concrescence is an act or activity of concresc*ing*. In Spinozistic terms, concrescences might be characterized as *naturae naturantes*, in contrast to concreta, which would be *naturae naturatae.*

Concrescences become but do not change, unlike forms, which neither become nor change, and concreta, the *being* of which neither becomes nor changes, although their *meaning* changes with each new present. (See Section IX below.) Whitehead makes a sharp, if only implicit, distinction between what we might call the "absolute becoming" or the "becoming καθ' αὑτό" of concrescences and the change or "relative becoming"—the "becoming-$\phi$" and "becoming-$\psi$"—of an enduring entity, an Aristotelian οὐσία, which takes on now this, now that, property or attribute.[21] The absolute becoming of a concrescence is wholly unlike the becoming-yellow of a green leaf, the becoming-hot of a cool pavement, or the "becoming-present" of a timelessly "pre-existing" entity or event—such as McTaggart[22] assumed—which "becomes present" by sliding down some invisible cosmic cable into the "bright space" of the present and then, in turn, "becomes past" by slipping off along another cosmic cable into the "dark space" of the past.

Whiteheadian concrescences, since they are transient, perishing, and atomic or epochal, *become* in the absolute sense but do not *change*, do not become this-or-that. (I shall return to this question in Section X.)

(5) Concrescences are "temporally active"; they become in the present, thus producing (constituting$_1$) the temporally ordered series of past concreta—what Whitehead calls the 'extensive continuum'.[23] To avoid the vicious regress of Zeno's "dichotomy" paradox, Whitehead asserts that, although "in every act of becoming [i.e., concrescence] there is the becoming of something [i.e., a concretum] with temporal extension," still, the "act itself is not extensive, in the sense [of being] divisible into earlier and later acts of becoming which correspond to the [temporally] extensive divisibility of what has become [i.e., a concretum or group of concreta]" (PR 107). This is the essence of Whitehead's atomic or epochal theory of time, according to which the "creature is extensive, but . . . its act of becoming is not extensive" (PR 107); that is, the concretum is temporally divisible, but its generating concrescence is not, since, as Whitehead insists, the concrescent process "is not in physical time" (PR 434).

## V

The five characteristics of concreta are listed in the third column of Table 2.

(1) Concreta are post-concrescent products of concrescent processes. In contrast to a concrescence, which is an integrat*ing* of conceptual and physical prehensions—an *ens integrans*—, a concretum is an entity which has-been-integrat*ed*—an *ens integratum.* Concreta, as "post-experient" entities, lack the experiential immediacy and subjectivity, as well as the activity, of concrescences. Their integrated "feelings" are, strictly speaking, "*ex*-feelings," although Whitehead himself, and such distinguished commentators as Harts-

horne, often refer to "[present] feelings of [past] feelings."[24] Thus Whitehead speaks of a "[concrescence's] feeling which feels another [concretum's ex-]feeling" and of the "[concretum's ex-]feeling felt [by the concrescence]" (PR 362).

Concreta are characterized by ontological "publicity"—i.e., accessibility, based on repeatability and objectifiability—in contrast to the ontological "privacy"—i.e., inaccessibility, based on non-repeatability and non-objectifiability—which characterizes the concrescences (cf. PR 444–45). Concreta, as prehensible objects, are $actual_2$—efficacious but-not-active.

A concretum has significance—meaning and importance—not for itself but only for something other than itself: namely, the subsequent concrescences which causally objectify it. A given concretum "makes a difference" not to itself, or to other concreta, but only to concrescences, all of which are, of course, subsequent to it, because they are *present* whereas it is *past.* "The past has an objective existence in the *present* which lies in the [i.e., "its"] future beyond itself" (AI 246; italics added). In this and many other passages (e.g., PR 88, 126, 227, 328, 352, 379, 422, 484; AI 252, 305; MT 123, 230) '*the* future beyond itself' or 'the transcendent future' (PR 402) means ' "its" future', 'the future relative to a given past concretum'; which, in turn, means *the present.*

(2) Whitehead's system requires that concreta be $actual_2$ rather than $actual_1$, efficacious rather than active. Their "power," like that of the forms, is "static." However, there is an inconsistency in Whitehead's own statements on this issue, which will be examined separately below (Section VII). A concretum is a passive, "dative" object which is both (a) in fact objectified by a subsequent (present) concrescence and (b) in principle reobjectifiable by an indefinite series of subsequent concrescences. Forms, as passive, "dative" objects, are also objectifiable and reobjectifiable. But as we have seen (pp. 112–14 above), forms are *unconditionally* dative and *unconditionally* objectifiable, whereas concreta are *conditionally* dative and *conditionally* objectifiable. Although a form's availability for conceptual prehension does *not* presuppose any par-

ticular spatio-temporal occurrence (concrescence), that of a concretum *does*—namely, the occurrence of the concrescent process of which it is the product. In this sense, concreta provide time-bound or time-dependent data, whereas forms provide data which are not time-bound or time-dependent.

A further difference between forms and concreta is that a given form may, over an indefinite period, be unobjectified by *any* finite concrescence, being excluded, or held inoperative, through "negative conceptual prehensions" by *every* concrescence. In converting its "initial data" into "objective data," a given concrescence may exclude some forms entirely, but it cannot wholly exclude any concretum. Thus, strictly speaking, there are no "negative physical prehensions." (However, Whitehead's statements on this point are inconsistent; see pp. 127–28 and n. 29 below.) Every concrescence objectifies all of "its"[25] concreta "under limitations," i.e., "perspectivally" and "abstractively" (see p. 121 below). (With respect to the prehension of forms, one must specify "finite" or "non-divine" concrescence, since, according to Whitehead, *every* form is objectified or "envisaged" in God's infinite "primordial nature.")

As we have seen, concreta are characterized by "real" or "empirical" potentiality. Whitehead's own formulation of this point is elliptical: "[I]t belongs," he says, "to the nature of a 'being' [i.e., a non-concrescent or post-concrescent, but *not* a concrescent, entity] that it is a potential for every 'becoming' [i.e., concrescence]" (PR 33 [Cat. Expl. 4]; this formulation is repeated almost verbatim at PR 71, 101, and 252). The term 'potential', like the term 'being', is ambiguous. A fuller and less ambiguous statement of the point would be: "Every form is a potential$_p$, and every concretum a potential$_r$, for every concrescence"—with the additional qualification in the case of concreta: "*directly or indirectly*, a potential$_r$ for every *subsequent* (present) 'becoming'."

(3) Concreta, like forms, are repeatable, objectifiable or prehensible, and reobjectifiable; they do not "recur" again and again, but they can be, and are, "taken" (physically prehended) again and again. In contrast to the *unconditional* repeatability of the forms,

the repeatability of the concreta is *conditional.* In fact, a concretum may be said to be conditionally objectifiable in three respects:

(a) It cannot be objectified until the process of which it is the product—the concrescence of which it is the concretum—has occurred.

(b) It is directly objectifiable only by immediately subsequent concrescences. Its *re*objectification, through (temporally) "intermediate" concreta, is indirect. Whitehead asserts that "*A* as objectified [by and] for *B* becomes reobjectified [by and] for *C*; and so on to *D*, and throughout the line of objectifications" (PR 183).[26] However, Whitehead is inconsistent on this point as well; I shall return to it (Section VIII below).

(c) Even the "first" or initial objectification of a given concretum is partial or selective, involving abstraction and elimination (cf. PR 321). The objectification of forms, in contrast, is *not* thus selective or abstractive. However, the distinction is not sharp, since forms are inherent in all concreta and, strictly speaking, there are no "pure" physical prehensions, unmixed with conceptual prehensions (of the forms inherent in the given concreta). It follows that there are no exclusively "real" potentials, uninfected by the "pure" potentiality of the inherent forms.

Whitehead's theory of objectification is "an endeavor to express how what is settled in [past] actuality$_2$ is repeated under limitations [i.e., selectively and abstractively], so as to be 'given' for immediacy [i.e., for present concrescence]" (PR 208). Whitehead calls objectification a 'perspective' (PR 361), presumably meaning a 'placing in perspective', of the initial datum.

In the above discussion (a) stresses the extrinsic time-dependence of the objectifiability of concreta, while (b) and (c) stress the intrinsic features of the objectifying process in virtue of which concreta can be only conditionally—in the sense of "selectively and abstractively"—objectified.

(4) Concreta are "post-processive" and product-like. In Spinozistic terms, they are *naturae naturatae*, in contrast to concrescences, which are *naturae naturantes.* As "crystallizations" of being, gen-

erated by unit-processes of becoming, they themselves—in this respect like forms—neither become nor change. However, their *meaning* changes with each new (present) concrescence. (This point will be more fully explored in Section IX below.)

(5) A concretum is "temporally static" in the sense that its beginning is "fixed in the past," coinciding with the ending or "satisfaction" of the concrescence of which it is the concretum. Like concrescences, concreta begin at a definite moment of time, but, unlike concrescences, they do not cease ("perish") at any definite moment. Rather, they continue indefinitely as potentials$_r$, providing data for the self-actualizations$_1$ of an unending series of subsequent concrescences. Concreta thus differ both from forms, which are timeless (they do not become in the present and are not fixed in the past), and from concrescences, which are "temporally active" (they become in the present).

Having once occurred, a concrescence necessarily issues in a determinate concretum. And having once occurred, it cannot not have occurred, and cannot not have produced precisely the concretum that it did produce. The past—the aggregate of concreta relative to a given present—is fixed and settled, although, of course, this aggregate is not a fixed totality, since it constantly acquires new members. "The many become one [i.e., the concreta are prehensively unified] and are increased by one [i.e., by the new concrescent occasion which does the unifying]" (PR 32).

## VI

The term 'ingression', which Whitehead applies to the relation of form to concrescence, is misleading to the extent that it suggests an activity carried out by forms. Even more misleading is the use of the verb 'ingress' by some of Whitehead's major commentators[27]—even though Whitehead himself does not use it. On the other hand, some of Whitehead's language *does* incautiously imply that forms are active, e.g., his reference to their "influx" (PR 72), their "intervention" in concrescent processes (PR 337), and their "provocation of . . . activity within a [concrescent] subject" (AI 227). He misleadingly refers to forms as "agents dictating the form of composition [of a concrescence]" (MT 129) and to form as an "agent in the objectification of an $actual_2$ entity" (PR 445, 446) and an "agent whereby *A* [i.e., concretum *b*] is objectified [by and] for *B* [i.e., concrescence *α*]" (PR 447). Similarly misleading is the statement that "*A* [i.e., concretum *b*] is objectified by the eternal object *S* as a datum for *B* [i.e., concrescence *α*]" (PR 183; cf. PR 234, 352).

Forms are, to be sure, indispensable (passive) factors or ingredients in the $objectification_1$ of concreta by concrescences, since the determinateness of a concretum is due to the forms which it exhibits; but they are not active factors, not agents.

Whitehead's more cautious way of putting the point is to say that eternal objects "have" or "obtain" ingression in $actual_1$ entities (cf. SMW 230; PR 66, 245, 249, 445). His most cautious, and most accurate, way of putting it is to say that forms are "ingredient" in concrescences (cf. SMW 244; PR 482). Moreover, Whitehead's definition of 'ingression' is unexceptionable: "The term 'ingression' refers to the particular mode in which the $potentiality_p$ of an eternal object is realized in a particular $actual_1$ entity, contributing to the definiteness [i.e., determinateness] of that $actual_1$ entity" (PR 34 [Cat. Expl. 7]). To say that a given form is ingredient, or has ingression, in a particular concrescence is equivalent to saying that the concrescence actualizes, enacts, or conceptually prehends that form. It is the relation of concrescence to form which is the active relation, the relat*ing*. As Whitehead himself emphasizes, "agency belongs exclusively to $actual_1$ occasions" (PR 46). The relation of form to concrescence is a purely passive relation, a being-relat*ed*.

And the relation is internal, i.e., constitutive, with respect to the concrescence, but external, i.e., non-constitutive, with respect to the form. Whitehead states this key doctrine succinctly in the passage already quoted (n. 14 above): "[T]he relationship between [form] *A* and [concrescence] *α* is external as regards *A*, and is internal as regards $\alpha$" (SMW 231). A given concrescence is altered by the fact of its relation to (conceptual prehension of) a given form, but the form is not altered by its being related to (providing data for) that—or any other—concrescence. For example, my present (concrescent) experience of the clock on the wall includes a conceptual prehension of the geometric form of circularity which makes a difference to the quality or content of my experience. The experience would be different if the clock had been square or triangular. But the being-prehended makes no difference to the form (or even to *this* form) of circularity. The form would be just what it is whether or not my experience—or anyone else's—included it. Whitehead is committed to an epistemological, as well as an historical, realism.

Similarly, the relation of concrescence to concretum is internal with respect to the concrescence and external with respect to the concretum (cf. PR 92, 441, 470–71). A given concrescence is altered by the fact of its relation to (physical prehension of) a given concretum, but the concretum is not altered by its being related to (providing data for) that—or any other—concrescence. For example, my present memory-experience of my recently-past perceptual experience of the circularity of the clock on the wall is different because it includes just that past experience. But the past experience would have been just what it was, whether or not it had been subsequently remembered. To take a macroscopic and rather crude example[28]—that my great-great-grandfather was who he was makes a difference to *me*: I would be different if he had been different. But that I am who I am makes (and made) no difference to *him*: he would have been the same even if I had turned out to be quite different.

## VII

But does the concretum merely function to provide data in a passive way? Or are concreta—as post-concrescent entities—in *any* sense agents?

Whitehead's own answers to these questions range over a broad spectrum. There is (1) the cautious and accurate claim that the concretum is a "dead datum" from the past (PR 249), that a concrescence (actively) "originates from" a (passive) $actual_2$ world (PR 33–34 [Cat. Expl. 5]), and that concreta function (passively) as "objects for [active] prehension in the present" (AI 251; cf. PR 101).

Then there is (2) the less cautious claim that concreta perform the "function of a datum *provoking* some special activity" in subsequent concrescences (AI 226; italics added), that the data provided by the concreta are "active" (MT 123). In addition to 'provocation', Whitehead speaks of the '*intervention*' of concreta in processes of concrescence (PR 336; italics added).

Finally there is (3) the incautious claim that the "creativity of the world is the *throbbing emotion* of the past *hurling itself* into a new transcendent [i.e., subsequent, present] fact" (AI 227; italics added), and a reference to the transference from past to present of "throbs of emotional energy" (PR 178) and to the "*energizing* of the past occasion as it *claims* its self-identical existence as a living issue in the present" (AI 233–34; italics added). 'Energizing *of* past occasions' is an ambiguous expression. It might mean '*of and by* the concreta', implying that the concreta themselves actively energize, or activate, their successors; on the other hand, it might mean '*of but not by* the concreta', implying that the concreta, though themselves passive, are actively energized or activated by their successors, the present concrescences. Whitehead's *doctrine* requires the second sense; unfortunately, his *formulation* strongly suggests the first sense.

Many of Whitehead's statements on this question employ terms which seem vague, ambiguous, or both—not just verbs like 'energize', 'arise', and 'originate', but nouns like 'reception' and 'influx' —e.g., "The process of experiencing is $constituted_1$ by the reception of entities, whose being is antecedent to that process, into the complex fact which is that process itself" (AI 229). And again: "The present . . . is $constituted_1$ by the influx of *the other* into that self-identity which is the continued life of the immediate past within the immediacy of the present" (AI 233). Finally: "[T]he [categoreal] obligations [i.e., ontological conditions] imposed on the becoming of any particular $actual_1$ entity arise from the $constitutions_2$ of other [past] $actual_2$ entities" (PR 43).

There is a similar ambiguity in Whitehead's reference to the "objectification" of the concretum *for* the concrescence (e.g., PR 183). Why not *by* (or *by and for*) the concrescence? This wording would make clear that the concrescence is the (active) "subject" of objectification, while the concretum is only its (passive) "object."

However, terms like 'claim' and expressions like 'living issue' seem, if not wholly clear, at least unambiguous. They strongly, but misleadingly, suggest that the past is active, that concreta are agents. In this spirit Whitehead characterizes experience as "heavy with the contact of the things gone by, which *lay their grip* on our immediate [i.e., present, concrescent] selves" (S 44; italics added), and refers to the "real *operation* of the antecedent particulars [i.e., concreta] *imposing themselves* on the novel particular [i.e., concrescence] in process of creation" (AI 242; italics added).

On the one hand, and for good systematic reasons, Whitehead wants to characterize concreta as passive; but on the other hand, for less good, but understandable reasons, he also wants to characterize them as active. In one passage he attempts to ascribe both activity and passivity to concreta: concreta taken as a whole or conjointly are active, while concreta taken separately or in disjunction are passive: "This . . . [past] $actual_2$ world . . . , this real potentiality . . . , as a whole is active with its inherent creativity, but in its details it provides the passive objects which derive their activity from the creativity of the whole" (AI 230). And Whitehead adds: "[V]iewed in abstraction [i.e., disjunction] objects are passive, but viewed in conjunction they carry the creativity which drives the world" (AI 230–31).

In the just-quoted sentence 'objects' must be taken to refer not to forms but to concreta, not to *non*-concrescent but to *post*-concrescent entities. Forms, even in conjunction, could not possibly be said to "carry the creativity which drives the world."

I do not find the distinction between conjoint and disjoint concreta convincing. Nor do I see how an appeal to Whitehead's Principle of Creativity, the "factor of activity" (AI 230), the "ultimate metaphysical principle" governing the "advance from disjunction [of the concreta] to conjunction [of the concrescence], creating a novel [$actual_1$] entity other than the [$actual_2$] entities given in disjunction" (PR 32), would help with this problem. Whiteheadian creativity is the ground of generic Concrescence in its relation to generic Transition (cf. AI 320; PR 31, 129). Creativity so interpreted does not help us to understand Whitehead's puzzling statement that, in conjunction, concreta "carry the creativity which drives the world." They, of course, provide data for particular concrescences and thus indirectly for Concrescence as a generic process. And this process may plausibly be said to "drive the world." But concreta "carry" Concrescence (or Concrescence-plus-Transition) only in the weak sense of 'passively supporting or facilitating' it.

I have found it more helpful to distinguish between agency and efficacy. Concreta, though not active, not agents, are causally efficacious. Thus Whitehead is entirely right to say that a concrescence is, in part, the "product of [its] efficient [i.e., efficacious] past" (PR 228), and that the "earlier [i.e., the past concretum] will be immanent in the later [i.e., the present concrescence] according to the mode of efficient causality [i.e., causal efficacy]" (AI 254). As he puts it in another place: "[T]he 'power' of one $actual_2$ entity on the other [$actual_1$ entity] is simply how the former is objectified in [and by] the $constitution_1$ of the other" (PR 91).

As *potentials* concreta, though passive and "dative," are efficacious, they "make a difference" (cf. PR 101–102; AI 230). As *real* or *empirical* potentials, they provide what I call 'unrefusable data'. In Whitehead's words:

> *All* $actual_2$ entities in the [past] $actual_2$ world, relatively to a given $actual_1$ entity as "subject," are necessarily "felt" by that subject, though in general vaguely [PR 66].

Furthermore, $actuality_2$ "represents stubborn fact which *cannot be evaded*" (PR 68; italics added); and "[*a*]*ll* the $actual_2$ entities are *positively prehended*" (PR 335; italics added). Whitehead refers to the concretum as a "determinate, settled fact, stubborn and with *unavoidable consequences*" (PR 336; italics added) and states explicitly that the "actualities$_2$ *have to be felt*" (PR 366).[29]

By "requiring" the present concrescence to conform, partially, to its antecedents in the past actual$_2$ world, concreta passively exert the "causal pressure of the past." In this sense they "impose" categoreal obligations upon subsequent concrescences which the concrescences cannot fail to meet. The concreta lay down (some of) the ontological conditions necessary for the occurrence of acts of becoming.

However, the conformation of concrescence to concreta is not total; all the data provided by the concreta are prehended abstractively, hence, in a sense "negatingly"—even though, strictly speaking, they are not "negatively prehended." The expression 'in due measure' in the following quotation suggests the incompleteness of the conformation (of present to past), expressed in the "stubborn fact that whatever is settled and actual$_2$ [i.e., post-concrescent, hence past] must in due measure be conformed to by the [present] self-creative activity" (S 36–37).

In contrast to concreta, forms provide data which, though unrefusable in general, are refusable in particular. *This* form, or pattern of determinateness, may be excluded or rendered inoperative through negative conceptual prehension, but not *every* form can be so excluded. The concrescence may fail or "refuse" to exemplify *this* pattern of determinateness, but it is under a categoreal obligation to exemplify *some* determinate pattern. No concrescence can remain indeterminate.

## VIII

As we have seen, the past, as "post-concrescent," is fully determinate, whereas the future, as "pre-concrescent" (as we might call it), is indeterminate, the present being the locus of active (self-)

determination$_1$. But there is a further, and perhaps less obvious, asymmetry between past and future.

The past, as the (constantly increasing) aggregate of concreta, is ontologically homogeneous—although of course it is not equally knowable: the fine structure of the remote past may be, and may remain, beyond our cognitive grasp.

In contrast, the future is ontologically heterogeneous. The immediate future, measured in fractions of a second, is "quasi-determinate." It is "less indeterminate" or "more nearly determinate" than the more remote future. The past of half a second ago is just as completely *past*—settled, determinate, and irrevocable—as the past of half a millennium ago. But the future of half a millennium, or even half a decade, hence is much more "open" and indeterminate than the future of half a second hence.[30] There is a kind of penumbra of quasi-determinateness, a constriction in the spectrum of possibilities, in the immediate future, which shades off fairly rapidly toward the remote future, where (a non-spatial 'where') the relevant determinateness is only formal or structural, not empirical or factual.

I have suggested that only the immediate past—i.e., immediately past concreta—not the remote past, provides data for, and thus imposes categoreal obligations upon, present concrescences. This interpretation seems to be supported by the passage, already quoted, in which Whitehead refers to "*A* as objectified [by and] for *B*," and as "reobjectified [by and] for *C*; and so on to *D*, and throughout the line of objectifications" (PR 183). He adds that "for the ultimate [concrescent] subject *M* the datum includes [concretum] *A* as thus transmitted, [concretum] *B* as thus transmitted, and so on" (PR 183). Unfortunately, this passage does not unambiguously exclude the possibility of direct physical prehension by concrescence *M* (in my notation '$\alpha$') of such remote concreta as *A* ('*d*'), in addition to the indirect "reobjectifying" prehension here discussed. In other passages Whitehead seems explicitly to admit such a possibility, insisting that he is *not* committed to a denial of "direct objectification of one occasion [i.e., a concretum] in a later occasion [i.e., a concrescence] which is not [spatio-temporally] contiguous to it," adding that "the safer guess is that direct objectification is practically negligible except for contiguous occasions; but . . . this practical negligibility is a characteristic of the present cosmic epoch, without any metaphysical generality" (PR 469; cf. PR 345, 435).

The texts are clearly inconsistent. I have chosen to take the position of PR 183: that direct physical prehension is limited to immediately past concreta.

## IX

I return briefly to a topic raised earlier (p. 122): the distinction between the (unchanging) *being* and the (changing) *meaning* of the past generally, and of the concreta in particular. I wish to maintain (1) that nothing subsequent to any concretum can modify *it*, although subsequent concrescences may, and regularly do, modify *themselves*—i.e., *become* in a way different from what they might have—by objectifying past concreta in different ways; and (2) that the being, both disjoint and conjoint, of concreta is fixed and unchangeable; that only their meaning, evaluation, or interpretation changes—though such meaning in fact shifts with each new present, and some of the shifts are dramatic.

Defending a similar thesis at the International Philosophy Congress in Vienna in 1968, I was confronted by the rhetorical question: "How, in this city of Sigmund Freud, can you maintain that the past is fixed and unchanging?" The question seemed to me then, and seems to me now, to rest on a confusion between the *being* and the *meaning* (interpretation, *Deutung*) of the past—a confusion which I do not find in Freud himself. When Freudians speak of a successful psychoanalysis as involving a "reconstruction of memory" they are clearly referring to the modification of *present* memories (including fears and anxieties, as well as more "neutral" interpretations) of past "traumatic" events. It is the *present* memories, not the *past* objects of those memories, which are "reconstructed."

The case is the same with the "memory-hole" historical reductionism or nihilism so vividly pictured by George Orwell in *1984*: the "past" is continually modified for purposes of present propaganda and agitation by means of a systematic rewriting of old newspapers and other historical documents, and an equally systematic destruction of those documents which cannot be rewritten. I would argue, on Whiteheadian grounds, that even the "success" of such a staggering project would *not* involve any change in the *past*, but only in our *present* knowledge, understanding, or appreciation of an unchanged past.

However, I do not deny that there are cases—especially those which bear significantly on the history of human culture[31]—in which the relation between the being and the meaning of past events[32] is complex and even opaque. For example, a day, a year, or even half-a-dozen years after the births—on particular days in 1265, 1756, and 1879—of Dante, Mozart, and Albert Einstein, respectively, it would *not* have been possible to state that the author of the *Divine Comedy* (or even "a great poet," or even "a poet"), or the composer of *The Magic Flute*, or the formulator of the Special Theory of Relativity had been born on those particular days. The *being* of these recently past or "ex-" events did not yet have the meaning which they later came to have. One could say only that male infants of a certain description had been born in such-and-such places, of such-and-such parents, etc.

The *meaning* of all such cultural events is cumulative and slow to emerge, requiring decades in ordinary cases and centuries in extraordinary ones. In a sense, it is never completed: there is no end to the valuing "up" and the valuing "down" of the contributions to human civilization even of such geniuses as the three just named. But the *being* of ex-events such as these three births, I insist, is not affected by accretions, erosions, or other changes in their *meaning* (evaluation, interpretation).

To put the point in Whiteheadian terms: The logical subjects, which are ontological objects, viz., concreta, do not change, but the predicative patterns in which they are involved do change with each new ontological "proposition."

## X

My analysis is "Whiteheadian" with respect to four key points, on each of which I claim to take *one* of Whitehead's positions, and indeed the one that is compatible and consistent with his general speculative system. These points are: (1) elucidation and endorsement of Whitehead's profoundly original insight that all subjects (in the ontological sense) are *present*, and all objects are either *timeless* or *past*; (2) assertion of the (passive) efficacy and denial of the (active) agency of concreta; (3) denial of direct physical prehension (causal objectification) of temporally remote concreta; (4) defense of a sharp ontological—as opposed to merely functional—distinction between concrescence and concretum. This last point requires a few additional remarks.

Certain critics have maintained that the distinction between concrescence and concretum is a distinction not between different (types of) entities, as I hold, but only between different functions or manifestations of one and the same entity. William A. Christian has taken this position; and I find it consistent with his claim that Whitehead did not reject, but merely reformed, the classical category of substance (*οὐσία*). There is in Christian, as in Whitehead himself, a crypto-substantialism—expressed *inter alia* by the frequent use of 'thing' to mean 'actual entity'. Thus Whitehead refers to "*things* which are temporal" (PR 63); to "*things* that are $\text{actual}_1$" (PR 64); to "$\text{actual}_2$ *things* in process of supersession by novel $\text{actual}_1$ *things*" (PR 72); to the "real togetherness which is an $\text{actual}_1$ *thing*" (PR 147); to the "$\text{actual}_2$ *thing* for which a decision is made" and the "$\text{actual}_1$ *thing* by which that decision is made" (PR 68); and to the "becoming" and the "perishing" of "each $\text{actual}_1$ *thing*" (AI 354). He asserts that: "Each instance of concrescence is itself the novel individual '*thing*' in question" (PR

321). (Italics added or modified in *each* of these quoted phrases.)

Finally, there is Whitehead's regular use of the Cartesian expression *res vera* (pl. *rēs verae*: lit. 'true thing/s') to mean 'actual$_1$ entity/ies'. (Cf. PR viii, 32 [Cat. Exist. 1], 43, 106, 108, 116, 196, 209, 252, 254.)

I agree with such critics as Christian that Whitehead often *speaks* as though what I consider to be distinct (atomic) entities[33] are phases or functions in the career of a single enduring entity. Thus he describes the "creative advance of the world" as the "becoming, the perishing, and the objective immortalities of those things which jointly constitute stubborn fact" (PR ix; italics removed). Here the equivocal adjective 'actual', which Whitehead elsewhere uses, is replaced by the no less equivocal noun 'thing' and verb 'constitute'. (See pp. 104–105 above.) *Things*, in the sense of *concrescences*, *constitute* in the sense of *actively creating* stubborn fact, i.e., the realm of concreta; but *things*, in the sense of *concreta*, *constitute* in the sense of *passively comprising* stubborn fact.

Again, Whitehead asserts that "how an actual entity becomes [as concrescence] constitutes$_1$ what that actual entity is [as concretum]. . . . Its 'being' [as concretum] is constituted$_1$ by its 'becoming' [as concrescence]" (PR 34–35 [Cat. Expl. 9]); adding that "all actual things are alike objects [and] subjects" (PR 89), that the "atomic entity . . . is both process and outcome" (PR 129), that the "actual entity is to be conceived *both* as a subject [i.e., concrescence] presiding over its own immediacy of becoming, *and* a superject [i.e., concretum] which is the atomic creature exercising its [passive] function of objective immortality" (PR 71; italics added), and that "An actual entity is at once the subject experiencing and the superject of its experiences. It is *subject-superject*, and neither half of this description can . . . be lost sight of" (PR 43; italics added).

Finally, in at least two passages Whitehead appears to warn against the kind of ontological distinction that I am drawing between concrescence and concretum. The first is somewhat vague:

> This creature is that one emergent fact [i.e., concretum]. This fact is the self-value of the creative act [i.e., concrescence]. But there are not *two* actual entities, the creativity [concrescence] and the creature [concretum]. There is only *one* entity[,] which is the self-creating creature [RM 102; italics added].

In a second passage Whitehead asserts that his theory of prehensions entails a protest against the "bifurcation of actualities" into subject and object, private aspect and public aspect, etc., in a word, into concrescence and concretum (PR 443).

On the other hand, Whitehead's own texts supply numerous examples of a sharply drawn contrast between concrescence and concretum—e.g., between the "living present" and the "dead past." Thus he writes that the "relatedness of actualities" is

> wholly concerned with the appropriation of the dead by the living—that is to say, with "objective immortality" whereby what is divested of its own living immediacy [as concrescence] becomes [as concretum] a real component in other living immediacies of becoming [i.e., in subsequent, present concrescences] [PR ix].

In the same spirit, Whitehead contrasts the "vivifying novelty of subjective form" which characterizes the concrescence with the "dead datum" provided by the concretum (PR 249).

Such language, I would argue, strongly suggests that the distinction between concrescence and concretum is an ontological or categoreal distinction, not simply a difference of function.

However, I am doubtful that this central question can be settled exegetically, since the textual conflicts are a manifestation of an underlying tension between Whitehead's ontological atomism and his lingering crypto-substantialism. On this matter, as on others, Whitehead sometimes lapses into hyperbole. For example, rightly wishing to stress the pervasive relatedness of things, he speaks, incautiously and misleadingly, of the "mutual prehensions" of actual entities (PR 29, 35, 118, 295), and of their "real mutual prehensions of each other," referring to "feelings of *A* which feel *B*" and "feelings of *B* which feel *A*" (PR 351). This alleged mutuality of prehension or feeling is in fact precluded by the asymmetry of the prehensive relation: if concrescence *a* prehends concretum *b*, it is not possible for *b* to prehend *a*, for the interdependent reasons that (a) past entities cannot prehend present entities, (b) concreta, being passive, cannot prehend anything, and (c) concrescences, being active, cannot be prehended by anything.

In a similarly misleading way, Whitehead speaks of the "objectifications in [or 'for'] each other" of actual entities (PR 35, 91, 118), of their "mutual relatedness" (PR 394), and of actual entities as "entering into each other's constitutions" (PR 66), declaring—both hyperbolically and implausibly—that "*every* actual entity is present in *every other* actual entity" (PR 79; italics added).

In a parallel way, rightly wishing to stress the close internal or constitutive relation of subject and object, concrescence and concretum, Whitehead asserts—with hyperbole, on my view—that they are simply different functions or phases of a single actual entity. On my interpretation, I submit, there is ample theoretical space for close and constitutive relations, but such relations cannot be mutual or symmetrical. Similarly, the close and "constitutive" nature of the concrescence–concretum relation (with respect to the concrescence) seems to me a sufficient theoretical defense against the charge of a "bifurcation of actualities."[34] Moreover, the assertion of a categoreal or ontological distinction between concrescence and concretum is necessary for the defense of ontological atomism, a key Whiteheadian doctrine.

I offer four arguments in support of my interpretation: (1) an argument from the sharply contrasted characters of concrescence and concretum; (2) an argument against substantialism or "semi-substantialism" and in defense of the atomicity of becoming; (3) an argument against a given entity's playing what Whitehead calls 'disjoined roles'; and (4) an argument based on Whitehead's fundamental distinction between change and becoming.

(1) The characteristics of concrescences and concreta are not simply different; they are fundamentally opposed. Concrescences are *subjects*: experient, non-dative, non-repeatable, non-objectifiable, processive, and active in the present; whereas concreta are *objects*:

post-experient, dative, repeatable, objectifiable, product-like, passive, and fixed in the past. There is, I suppose, a theoretical possibility that even with such contrasted characteristics, concrescence and concretum *might* be functions or phases of a single enduring entity.

(2) But if concrescence and concretum, subjectivity and objectivity, activity and efficacy, are simply the contrasted functions or attributes of a single underlying entity, that entity must endure long enough to include both the epochal present and some stretch, however short, of the past. Such an enduring entity would be indistinguishable from a classical substance: an Aristotelian *οὐσία* or Cartesian *res*. But to admit enduring substances into Whitehead's speculative system is to nullify his absolutely central commitment to the *atomicity* of becoming. Whitehead calls his philosophy an "atomic theory of actuality" (PR 40), insisting that the "ultimate metaphysical truth is atomism. The creatures [i.e., concrescences] are atomic" (PR 53). He adds that "actuality$_1$ is incurably atomic" (PR 95; cf. 359–60), that "[e]ach actual$_1$ entity is a cell with atomic unity" (PR 347).[35] (See also PR 29, 96, 104, 119, 213, 383, 438, 468.)

On the substantialist interpretation, it would make no sense to say—as Whitehead repeatedly does say—that concrescences "perish" or that temporal becoming is a "perpetual perishing." Rather, one should simply say that the subject-phase of an enduring entity ("an unchanging subject of change" [PR 43], as Whitehead scornfully calls it) gives way to, or is replaced by, its object-phase; or, alternatively, that an enduring *οὐσία* simply stops functioning (actively) as a subject and starts functioning (passively) as an object. Any such formulation would involve a clear repudiation of Whitehead's ontological atomism.[36]

(3) The claim that a single self-identical entity functions in the present as subject and then in the past as object also appears to fly in the face of Whitehead's insistence that "[n]o entity—be it 'universal' or 'particular'—can play *disjoined* roles," and to contradict

his claim that "[s]elf-identity requires that every entity have *one . . . self-consistent function*" (PR 89; italics added). If the *same* actual entity in fact functioned as both active, "private," prehending subject and passive, "public," prehended object would it not be playing "disjoined"—because quite contrary—roles?

(4) The substantialist interpretation also fails to give due weight to Whitehead's insistence on the difference between change and becoming. Actual$_1$ entities, he repeatedly asserts, become and perish, but they do *not* change (PR 52, 119, 122, 508). "[T]he actual$_1$ entity 'perishes' in the passage of time, so that no actual$_1$ entity changes . . ." (PR 222).

> [T]he doctrine of internal relations makes it impossible to attribute "change" to any actual$_1$ entity. Every actual$_1$ entity is what it is, . . . determined by its internal relations to other actual$_2$ entities. 'Change' is the description of the [passive] adventures of [forms] in the evolving universe of actual$_1$ things [PR 92].

The "becoming" which Whitehead contrasts to change is the "absolute becoming" or "becoming καθ' αὑτό" of concrescences as opposed to the "relative becoming," i.e., "qualitative change," of an enduring substance, which "becomes this" and then "becomes that."[37] The green leaf "becomes" yellow and then red; the cool pavement "becomes" warm and then hot.

But this simply means, expressed colloquially, that the leaf "turns" yellow and then red; or, more solemnly, that it first exhibits (or manifests) the property (or character) of yellowness and then exhibits the property of redness. This has nothing to do with temporal or "absolute" becoming, the becoming of events or unit-processes. It would be very strange to speak of a subjective, active, "private" entity which "becomes," in the sense of "turns," objective, efficacious, passive, and "public." And it would be no less strange, though more solemn, to speak of an enduring entity which (in the present) exhibits or manifests the properties of subjectivity, activity, and "privacy" and then (in the past) exhibits the contrary properties of objectivity, passive efficacy, and "publicity."

It was precisely to avoid such unacceptable formulations, and incoherent doctrines, that Whitehead discarded the Aristotelian–Cartesian notion of *οὐσία–res*—a self-identical substance which endures through time, taking on now this, now that attribute—in favor of a theory of atomic concrescence, temporal supersession, and the reiteration of timeless forms.

My interpretation might be called 'neo-Whiteheadian' with respect to two additional—but less fundamental—points, on both of which I go beyond, or against, Whitehead's position as I understand it:

(1) questioning his sharp distinction between concrescence as "microscopic" or "microcosmic" and transition as "macroscopic" or "macrocosmic" (I claim that both kinds of process are "microscopic" or "microcosmic"—if one is to use these somewhat dubious terms at all—and that in any case they operate at the same "ontological level");

(2) suggesting that 'creativity' is only the name for the ontological ground of generic Concrescence and generic Transition in their interrelationship, and as such cannot account for that "agency" or "activity" of concreta which in some passages Whitehead appears incautiously to admit.

NOTES

1. Whitehead defines '$x$ is $\text{actual}_1$' as meaning '$x$ has significance for itself' (cf. PR 38 [Cat. Expl. 21]). To have significance for oneself, or—in slightly different terms—to be actively self-relating, is to make a decisive or "constitutive" difference to oneself. This is the case only with concrescences. Forms and concreta are "other-significant": they "make a difference" only to the concrescences which prehend them.

Passages in which '$\text{actual}_1$' and '$\text{actual}_2$' occur in close, and unsignaled, proximity also occur at PR 34 [Cat. Expl. 8]: ("the . . . mode in which the potentiality of one $\text{actual}_2$ entity is realized in another $\text{actual}_1$ entity"); PR 66 ("entity in the [past] $\text{actual}_2$ world of a concrescent $\text{actuality}_1$"); and PR 80 ("one $\text{actual}_1$ entity is constituted [i.e., 'created'—cf. p. 106] by its synthesis of other $\text{actual}_2$ entities"). Similar passages occur at PR 37, 38, 42, 43, 68, 72, 76, 88, 89, 92, 93, 95, 102, 103, 104, 119, 188, 196, 228, 252, 290, 321, 337, 339, 340, 351, 360, 364, 373, 441, 445, 486; MT 161, 165.

Nobo blurs this fundamental distinction, asserting that, for Whitehead, 'actual' means 'either *is*, or *has been*, self-realizing' (cf. Jorge Luis Nobo, "Whitehead's Principle of Process," *Process Studies*, 4 [1974], 282; italics added). What *is* self-realizing is $actual_1$ (=active but-not-efficacious); it functions actively as a subject. What *has been* self-realizing is $actual_2$ (=efficacious but-not-active); it functions passively as an object. See pp. 104–105.

In the remainder of this paper I shall continue the practice begun in this footnote, inserting subscript '1' or '2', as appropriate, following the terms 'actual' and 'actuality' in quotations from Whitehead as well as in my own discussion. Note that although in the expression '[past] actual world' '$actual_2$' is usually meant, in a few cases 'actual world' is used as a vague synonym for 'what is' or 'reality as a whole'. Cf. "the actual world is a process and . . . the process is the becoming of $actual_1$ entities" (PR 33 [Cat. Expl. 1]; cf. also PR 37 [Cat. Expl. 19]); and Whitehead's reference to "the process of the actual world" (PR 147). Sometimes Whitehead speaks—less misleadingly—of a 'world-process' (MT 128) in the sense of 'the totality of unit-processes'.

2. Although Whitehead did not use the term 'concretum', he did use a number of expressions which refer unequivocally to the "completed past $actual_2$ entity," among them: 'objectified $actual_2$ occasion' (PR 178); 'objectified $actual_2$ entity/ies' (PR 91, 407; cf. 327); '$actual_2$ entity considered . . . in respect to its existence "*objectivè*" [in the Cartesian sense of this Latin term]' (PR 335–36); 'objectified actuality/$ies_2$' (PR 78; cf. 446); 'objectified individual' (PR 229); 'objectified particular occasions' (PR 321); 'antecedent [i.e., past] . . . occasions objectified in [and by] any given [present] occasion' (PR 468); 'attained $actuality_2$' (PR 326); 'attained fact' (PR 441); 'perceived $actual_2$ entity' (PR 188; cf. 361); '$actual_2$ entities experienced' (PR 112); '$actual_2$ entity as felt' (PR 66; cf. 434); '$actual_2$ occasions felt' (PR 322); 'prehended [past] object' (AI 227; cf. AI 229); '[entities] settled in $actuality_2$' (PR 208); 'entities which are settled, $actual_2$, and already become' (PR 101); 'already-constituted [i.e., created] $actual_2$ entities' (PR 335); 'settled $actual_2$ entities' (PR 101); '$actual_2$ entities of the settled world' (PR 188); $actual_2$ entities constituting [i.e., comprising] the antecedent [i.e., past] environment' (PR 105); 'individual occasions of the past' (AI 247); 'particular occasions of the past' (AI 250); '$actual_2$ entities of the past' (PR 97; AI 251); 'past occasion' (AI 233); 'realized matter-of-fact' (MT 128). Whitehead sometimes uses the term 'creature' in this sense, e.g., at PR 30, 47, 71, 107, 108, 390. But he also uses that term as a synonym for 'concrescence', e.g., at PR 53, 523; and, more frequently, in the wider sense of 'actual entity', including both concrescence and concretum (cf. PR 33, 123, 124, 344, 347, 533).

According to the late George Burch's recently-published lecture notes, Whitehead in 1926–27 identified "three [fundamental] types of entities: eternal objects [i.e., forms], $actual_1$ entities [i.e., concrescences], and *objective occasions*," adding that "the third [type] is derivable from the other two" ("Whitehead's Harvard Lectures, 1926–27," comp. George B. Burch, ed. Dwight C. Stewart, *Process Studies*, 4 [1974], 203; italics added). Concerning the "derivative" status of concreta, see PR 46, where Whitehead refers to them as 'derivate [i.e., derivative] $actual_2$ occasions'.

3. However, Whitehead does speak of the "*efficient* conjunction" of the forms and of their "*effective* relevance to each concrescent process" (PR 64; italics added)—which comes fairly close to characterizing forms as 'efficacious'.

4. To clarify the terms of the Aristotelian polarity of ἐνέργεια / δύναμις we might write (a) '$actuality_p$' for 'actualization of a *p*otentiality' in order to distinguish 'actuality' in this sense from '$actuality_1$' and '$actuality_2$'; and (b) '$potentiality_r$' for '*r*eal potentiality (of the concreta)' as distinguished from '$potentiality_p$', the '*p*ure potentiality (of the forms)'. Although Whitehead clearly formulates this second distinction, e.g., at PR 101–102, he sometimes neglects it, as when he refers to the "timelessness of what is potential" (PR 64)—meaning, of course, '$potential_p$', but not '$potential_r$', since the latter is not timeless, but *past*.

5. Nobo, "Whitehead's Principle of Process," esp. 276–77. I shall mark the "syntactic" ambiguity by writing '$constitution_1$' for 'act of constituting' and '$constitution_2$' for 'state of having-been-constituted'; and the semantic ambiguity by writing '$constitute_1$' for 'create' and '$constitute_2$' for 'comprise'.

6. Whitehead twice quotes the passage from Locke's *Essay* (3.3.5) in which the expression 'real internal (but generally in substances unknown) constitution' occurs (PR 37 [Cat. Expl. 18], 92).

7. Cf. my "Form, Concrescence, and Concretum: A Neo-Whiteheadian Analysis," *The Southern Journal of Philosophy*, 7 (1969–70), 353 and passim.

8. However, I shall occasionally use the adjective 'abstractive' and the adverb 'abstractively'.

9. Gene Reeves clearly refers to '$concrete_1$' when he writes that "what is *concrete* in Whitehead's philosophy is not some [Aristotelian] substance . . . which may accidentally act, but the *activities themselves*" ("God and Creativity," this volume, p. 242 below; italics added). Cf. Ivor Leclerc's statement that for Whitehead "[w]hat is *concrete* is 'activity', not 'stuff' " ("Form and Actuality" in *The Relevance of Whitehead*, ed. I. Leclerc [London: Allen and Unwin; New York: Macmillan, 1961], p. 179).

10. The adjective 'concrescent' occurs more than thirty times in *Process and Reality*; the noun 'concrescence', of course, occurs much more frequently. Unfortunately, 'concrescent' is not indexed at all in the original Macmillan edition of 1929, and is indexed only for the expression 'concrescent unison' in the corrected edition (Macmillan–Free Press) of 1978 (and even here only *one* of the three pertinent page references is given). For this reason, and because of the systematic importance of the term (as a synonym for '$concrete_1$'), I list below the occurrences which I have discovered: PR 46, 64, 66, 86, 89, 91, 98, 99, 131, 133, 190, 255, 287, 343, 347, 373, 374, 420, 423, 424, 431, 435, 448, 487, 523, 532. On some of these pages the term occurs more than once.

11. Donald W. Sherburne, *A Whiteheadian Aesthetic* (New Haven: Yale University Press, 1961), pp. 22, 23. Cf. Whitehead's own characterization of a "positive [physical] prehension" as "essentially a *transition effecting a con-*

*crescence*" (PR 337; italics added). I would agree with William Garland's statement that "concrescence and transition can be seen as *complementary* aspects of creativity, which is the ultimate principle behind all process" ("The Ultimacy of Creativity," this volume, p. 226 below; italics added).

I am not convinced by Nobo's recent attempt to draw a sharp ontological distinction between concrescence and transition and to assign a peculiarly important role to the latter, but I shall not argue that point here. See his "Transition in Whitehead: A Creative Process Distinct from Concrescence," *International Philosophical Quarterly*, 19 (1979), 265–83.

12. Although Whitehead sometimes called eternal objects 'forms', he was sensitive to the Platonic coloring of the term, and insisted that his eternal objects "are not necessarily restricted to those which [Plato] would recognize as 'forms'" (PR 70).

13. Whitehead himself uses 'inherence/inherent' in three different, though loosely related, senses: (1) to refer to the traditional relation of attribute or quality to substance or substratum (cf. PR 32, 121, 219); (2) to characterize the relation of qualities ("eternal objects of the objective species") to a "presented contemporary nexus" (PR 480); (3) to name the relation of a concrescent subject to the "process of its [partial self-] production" (PR 342). Since the term does not have a single fixed usage in Whitehead's writings, I feel justified in specifying a sense for it; in fact my sense is quite close to (2) above.

14. In a few passages Whitehead says clearly and explicitly that the "relationship between [form] *A* and [concrescence] $\alpha$ is external as regards *A*, and is internal as regards $\alpha$" (SMW 231; cf. PR 92, 471). In other passages he formulates the parallel point about concreta elliptically, hence somewhat misleadingly: "Every $actual_1$ entity is what it is, . . . determined by its internal relations to other $actual_2$ entities" (PR 92). Presumably this means: 'determined by relations which are internal (constitutive) with respect to the $actual_1$ entity itself, but external with respect to "its" concreta'. Again, Whitehead refers to the "externality of [i.e., non-constitutive relation with respect to] many facts [i.e., concreta]" and to the "internality of [i.e., constitutive relation with respect to] this experiencing [subject]" (MT 159).

15. Edward Pols, *Whitehead's Metaphysics: A Critical Examination of* PROCESS AND REALITY (Carbondale: Southern Illinois University Press, 1967), passim.

16. In general Whitehead distinguishes quite clearly between *functioning* and *acting* or *being an agent.* Functioning is *passive*: a providing of data, a contributing of determination. (Cf. PR 38 [Cat. Expl. 20], 249, 445.) But he sometimes speaks of an $actual_1$ entity as functioning "in respect to its own determination" (PR 38 [Cat. Expl. 21]), which would appear to be an *active* role, as would the "self-functioning" of the concrescence, to which Whitehead refers at PR 38 (Cat. Expl. 23), and the "modes of functioning which jointly $constitute_1$ [a concrescence's] process of becoming" (AI 226).

17. On this point Whitehead is radically anti-Platonic: for him it is concrescences (the "world of becoming"), not forms (the "world of being"),

which are the locus of value. "Value is the outcome of limitation" (SMW 136). All finite concrescences—as partially self-determining processes—involve limitation and exclusion. This is consonant with Spinoza's insight that *determinatio* is at the same time *negatio* (cf. his letter No. 50 to Jarigh Jelles of June 2, 1674, in Spinoza, *Opera*, edd. J. van Vloten and J. P. N. Land, 3rd ed. [The Hague: Nijhoff, 1914], III 173).—However, in the light of Whitehead's writings after *Process and Reality*, especially his two final lectures of 1941 ("Mathematics and the Good" and "Immortality"), one would have to distinguish between concrescent (concrete$_1$) *achievings* of value and post-concrescent (concrete$_2$) value-*achievements*, on the one hand, and pre- or non-concrescent value-*ideals*, on the other.

18. Leclerc does not explicitly distinguish between Whitehead's two contrasted senses of 'actual'. See Ivor Leclerc, *Whitehead's Metaphysics* (London: Allen and Unwin; New York: Macmillan, 1958; rpt., Bloomington: Indiana University Press, 1975), passim, for the interpretation of 'actual entity' as 'acting entity'.

19. For the distinction between the potentiality$_r$ of the concreta and the potentiality$_p$ of the forms, see n. 4 above. Forms, like concreta, function datively as objects for concrescent subjects; they could, like concreta, be characterized as "efficacious but-not-active." However, unlike concreta, which, as *post*-concrescent entities, are actual$_2$ (actualized), forms, as *non*-concrescent entities, are neither actual$_1$ nor actual$_2$; in other words, they are characterized neither by actualization$_1$ (as concrescences are) nor by actualization$_2$ (as concreta are).

Since concreta are products of a process of temporal "decision"—in Whitehead's ontological sense of the term—whereas forms are products of *no* temporal process, the former might be called 'determinate' and the latter 'definite'. Although Whitehead defines 'determination$_2$' as "analyzable into 'definiteness' and 'position'" (PR 38 [Cat. Expl. 20]), he in fact makes no systematic distinction between 'determinate' and 'definite', sometimes applying 'definite' to concrescences (PR 42, 340), to "the actual" (PR 367), to concreta (PR 44); and sometimes applying both 'definite' and 'determinate' to both concrescences (PR 69) and concreta (PR 336). Certain of his uses *do* conform to the distinction here suggested, e.g., his application of 'determinate' to actual$_2$ entities (PR 393; cf. PR 322), to the "actual$_2$ world" (PR 72), and to various components of a concrescence (PR 338).

20. They are also non-recurrent: "[N]o subject experiences twice. This is what Locke ought to have meant [but did not] by his doctrine of time as a 'perpetual perishing'" (PR 43).

21. Whitehead himself offers a succinct definition of οὐσία: "an individualized particular substance (in the Aristotelian sense) which undergoes adventures of change, retaining its substantial form amid transition or accidents" (PR 87).

22. McTaggart (in 1908) introduced the now-standard distinction between "*A*-theories" of time, which regard as fundamental and irreducible the "*A*-determinations" (or 'characteristics') 'past/present/future', and "*B*-theories," which regard as fundamental and irreducible the "*B*-relations" 'before/

after' or 'earlier than/later than'. (See J. M. E. McTaggart, "Time" in *The Philosophy of Time*, ed. Richard Gale [Garden City: Doubleday Anchor Books, 1967], pp. 86–97.) Whitehead's ontology of time is perhaps best described as a 'reformed *A*-theory', since it takes the determinations 'past/present/future' as fundamental and irreducible but injects essential relationality into these determinations, insisting that the past–present relation is *internal* ("constitutive") with respect to the *present*, but *external* ("non-constitutive") with respect to the past. In contrast to traditional *A*-theorists, Whitehead treats 'past', 'present', and 'future' as *relational* predicates and past, present, and future entities as the relata of *asymmetrical* relations. Unfortunately, Whitehead sometimes lapses into the language of *B*-relations, using 'earlier/later' (S 35; PR 244, 470; AI 254; cf. PR 468, 469; AI 259) or 'antecedent/subsequent' (PR 73, 88, 105, 480; cf. PR 128; AI 229; cf. AI 242) when he clearly means 'past/present'.—Such otherwise careful commentators as Ivor Leclerc and Charles Hartshorne also say 'antecedent/subsequent' or 'prior/subsequent' when they mean 'past/present' (cf. this volume, pp. 62 and 303).

23. This point is cogently made by George Allan in his unpublished Yale dissertation, "A Whiteheadian Approach to the Philosophy of History" (1963), pp. 31–32, 47.

24. "When given, an entity [i.e., concretum] is taken into the unity of one or more experiences [i.e., concrescences], and this unity is a case of 'feeling of feeling', not a case of the [concrescent] subject's feeling the merely insentient as such" (Charles Hartshorne, "Whitehead's Novel Intuition" in *Alfred North Whitehead: Essays on His Philosophy*, ed. George L. Kline [Englewood Cliffs: Prentice-Hall, 1963], p. 20; italics added). Hartshorne is right to stress the difference between a *non*-experient and a *post*-experient object of positive physical prehensions (physical feelings); but his formulation—like some of Whitehead's—misleadingly assimilates *post*-experient entities to *experient* entities. For Whitehead the object of a subject's feelings is either a concretum's "*ex*-feelings" or a form's "*non*-feelings."

25. The expression '"its" concretum' is superficially ambiguous: (1) Where concrescence $\alpha$ prehends concretum $b$, and $b$ provides data for $\alpha$'s process of self-constitution$_1$, $b$ may, in a weak sense, be called '$\alpha$'s concretum'. (2) Where $b$ is the concretum-product of concrescence $\beta$, $b$ may, in a stronger sense, be called '$\beta$'s concretum'. In general, the '$\alpha$–$b$' (or '$\beta$–$c$') notation indicates relation (1) and the '$\beta$–$b$' (or '$\alpha$–$a$') notation indicates relation (2). (For the explanation of my notation for referring to concrescences, concreta, and forms see n. 26 below.)

26. In *Process and Reality* Whitehead adopts a notation for referring to forms, concrescences, and concreta which strikes me as misleading in two respects: (1) In some passages he represents the temporal order present-to-past by using letters in alphabetical order: the concrescence is called '*A*' and the concreta '*B*, *C*, and *D*', where *B* is the most recent of the concreta and *D* the most remote in time (PR 345–46). In other passages Whitehead reverses this order, calling the concrescence '*M*' and the concreta '*D*, *C*, *B*, and *A*', where *D* is the most recent of the concreta and *A* the most remote in time (PR 183).

In one passage, designating a concrescence as '*M*' and a concretum as '*P*', he even refers to "an $actual_1$ occasion *Q*, belonging to *M*'s *causal future*" (PR 486–87). (2) More seriously misleading is Whitehead's use of upper-case Latin letters to designate entities belonging to *four* distinct ontological categories: (a) '*A*' and '*M*' for concrescences; (b) '*A*', '*B*', '*C*', and '*D*' for concreta; (c) '*S*' for an *individual form*; (d) '*S*' (again) for a *set* of forms (PR 176–77, 183, 345–46, 351). The use of upper-case Latin letters to designate both concrescences and concreta misleadingly suggests a spatial model of temporal order, blurring the distinction between present and past—a distinction, which, in general, Whitehead was concerned to maintain.

In *Science and the Modern World* Whitehead had made a typographical distinction between the symbols for forms (upper-case Latin letters, e.g., '*A*') and those for concrescences (lower-case Greek letters, e.g., 'α') (SMW 231, 233, 245, 246). In the present essay I extend this usage: (a) upper-case Latin letters designate forms; (b) lower-case Greek letters designate concrescences; (c) lower-case Latin letters designate concreta. This convention has several advantages: (i) Different alphabets or types of letters are used to refer to entities of distinct ontological types. (ii) The common use of Latin letters for forms and concreta (distinguished by upper- and lower-case, respectively) emphasizes that both are *objects*—timeless and past objects, respectively—contrasted with concrescences, which are present *subjects* (designated by Greek letters). (iii) The community of inheritance that links concreta and concrescences is suggested through their common designation by lower-case letters, though of different alphabets. (iv) The sharpest typographical contrast, that between Greek and Latin letters, marks the crucial ontological distinction between entities which are present and active (designated by Greek letters) and those which are passive and either past or timeless (designated by Latin letters: lower-case and upper-case, respectively).

As to the *order* of letters, I have adopted that of PR 345–46, where '*A*' designates the concrescence and '*B*', '*C*', etc., the concreta—although I would rename them 'α', '*b*', and '*c*', respectively. There are two advantages to this order: (a) it suggests the ontological priority of the present—a key Whiteheadian doctrine, and (b) it avoids the suggestion conveyed by the passages at PR 176–77 and 183, where '*A*' designates the most temporally remote concretum, namely, that of a concrescence (named by the first letter of the Latin alphabet) which was "first" in the cosmic series. That there was such a cosmogonic "beginning" is an assumption which Whitehead explicitly rejects.

27. Donald Sherburne, for example, raises the question as to "which eternal objects [the $actual_1$ entity] will allow . . . to *ingress* into its concrescence" (*op. cit.*, p. 25; italics added). Cf. also Lewis S. Ford, "Whitehead's First Metaphysical Synthesis," *International Philosophical Quarterly*, 17 (1977), 261; Robert C. Neville, "Whitehead on the One and the Many," this volume, p. 259 below. William Christian rightly points out that Whitehead "*nowhere* uses the word 'ingress' either as a verb or as a noun. . . . [I]ngression means a [passive] relation, not an action, and . . . the term is generated not from a verb but from the relational adjective 'ingredient'" (*An Interpretation of Whitehead's*

*Metaphysics* [New Haven: Yale University Press, 1959], p. 185; italics added).

28. The example is crude and misleading because a living human being is not a concrescence (rather a "society of societies" of concrescences and concreta) and a no-longer-living human being is not a concretum (rather, something like a "society of societies" of concreta).

29. The five passages just quoted (from PR 66, 68, 335, 336, and 366) seem to me to amount to a clear denial of "negative physical prehensions." Unfortunately, in several other passages Whitehead appears to admit the possibility of such prehensions, referring to the "dismiss[al of] the thwarting elements [i.e., concreta] of a nexus into negative [physical] prehensions" (PR 154; cf. 161, 346, 364).

30. Cf. Lewis S. Ford, "Boethius and Whitehead on Time and Eternity," *International Philosophical Quarterly*, 8 (1968), 46–48.

31. In the case of past events involving only the natural—non-human, non-cultural—world, the relation of being and meaning is both more direct and, in general, more perspicuous than in the case of human and cultural events. The "meaning" of such events as the falling of a stone or the growth of a bud into blossom and fruit requires less time to emerge and, in typical cases, is subject to fewer and less drastic modifications than that of human and cultural events.

32. I use the expression 'past event' in the most general sense. Strictly speaking, in a Whiteheadian ontology there are no "past events," just as there are no "past concrescences." Rather, one should speak of 'ex-events', as one speaks of the 'ex-feelings' of concreta. However, because of the awkwardness of the term 'ex-event', I shall use it sparingly.

33. Concrescences are atomic *tout court*; concreta, however, though individually atomic, comprise—in their aggregate—what Whitehead calls the 'extensive continuum'. Cf. especially PR, Pt. II, Ch. 2: "The Extensive Continuum."

34. Lewis Ford has suggested, in a private communication, that the distinction between concrescence and concretum is "formal" rather than "real," a distinction apparently modeled on Whitehead's distinction between mere "intellectual disjunction" and "real separation" (PR 357). But if a merely formal distinction is like that between the convexity and the concavity of a curve, then it seems to me to apply only doubtfully to the relation between concrescence and concretum. How could two entities which are only "formally" distinguishable be related as subject and object, where the relation is internal and constitutive with respect to the subject but only external with respect to the object?

35. Defenders of the substantialist interpretation of actual entities would presumably tend to assign to 'actual$_1$' the sense of 'active but-*not-yet*-efficacious' and to 'actual$_2$' that of 'efficacious but *no-longer* active'—formulations which I have scrupulously avoided in this essay, although I incautiously used the parallel expressions 'no-longer-actual' and 'no-longer-concrescent' in its earlier version (cf. "Form, Concrescence, and Concretum," 351, 357, 359). Such formulations imply that concrescence and concretum are temporally successive phases of an enduring entity, such that one phase can be "not yet" and the other "no longer" although the entity itself is fully present.

36. Cf. Nobo: "The relation of subject to superject [i.e., of concrescence to concretum] is that of creative process to created product [but these are not] two different entities, the one creating the other [but only] one entity, *first* existing as in the process of realizing itself, and *then* existing as the static outcome of that process of self-realization. . . . [A]n actual entity *first* exists as subject, and *then* as superject [i.e., concretum-object]" ("Whitehead's Principle of Process," 279; italics added). The phrases containing the italicized terms make clear that Nobo's interpretation is a substantialist (or at least "semi-substantialist") one, incompatible with the principles of ontological atomism.

37. Cf. C. D. Broad, "Ostensible Temporality" [1938] in Gale, ed., *op. cit.*, pp. 124, 127. A full-fledged substantialist account would hold that the entity which "becomes present" (like the leaf which becomes yellow) both ("pre-dates" and "post-dates" its act of "becoming present." Christian, Nobo, Ford, et al. would presumably admit that the entity which functions as subject (in the present) and then as object (in the past) does *not* pre-date, but only post-dates, its "becoming present." Their interpretation should thus perhaps be called 'semi-substantialist' rather than 'substantialist'.

# III

# CREATIVITY, RELIGIOUS EXPERIENCE, AND GOD

8

# Religion and Solitariness

Donald A. Crosby
*Colorado State University*

"Religion is what the individual does with his own solitariness" (RM 16). Whitehead ventured this description of religion in his Lowell Lectures of 1926, and since that time it has been frequently quoted, usually disparaged, and seldom understood in anything like the way Whitehead intended. I propose in what follows to interpret the meaning of this statement in some depth, trying to give it its proper setting within Whitehead's metaphysics and his theory of religion, and to show that it is neither as one-sided, sentimental, nor vacuous as it might appear to be on casual encounter. The description is not immune from criticism, and I shall try to bring out some of its weaknesses, but my main intent will be to present its meaning as fully and sympathetically as possible.

While the social side of religion is important for Whitehead, it is not primary. The essence of religion is to be discovered, not in public dogmas, practices, or institutions, but in confrontation with "the awful ultimate fact, which is the human being, consciously alone with itself, for its own sake" (RM 16). And although religion had its historical origins in collective rituals, emotions, and beliefs, these served merely as the springboard for the emergence of religion in its finished form as what the individual does with his own solitariness. We can best get at some of Whitehead's reasons for coming to this conclusion by contrasting "communal religion,"

An earlier version of this chapter appeared in the *Journal of the American Academy of Religion* (40 [1972], 21–35).

as he conceives it, with religion which grows out of solitariness. He calls the latter "purified religion" or "rational religion," but what he actually seems to mean by these terms is religion *per se*. 'Communal religion' is thus a misleading expression since communal religion is not truly religion at all for him, but is simply a stage on the way to its development. In other words, communal religion is proto-religion, just as the speculations of Pythagoras might be termed proto-science.

## 1 · COMMUNAL RELIGION

Communal religion served several essential functions in preparing the way for religion itself. It sensitized the human consciousness to depths of emotion dissociated from the pressing demands of daily survival. It provided a vehicle for the rise of myths and beliefs which were a necessary prelude to religious concepts of a more general character. And it nurtured ethical intuition by creating a sense of social unity and mutual responsibility. But it lacks genuine religious insight because it is authoritarian, provincial, and merely pragmatic in its outlook.

Whitehead tells us that religion "runs through three stages, if it evolves to its final satisfaction. It is the transition from God the void to God the enemy, and from God the enemy to God the companion" (RM 16–17). The first stage is the stage of blind emotion, ritualistically engendered for its own sake. There is no religious object as such, but simply a "void" of feeling. The second stage is the stage of myth, uncoordinated and unrationalized. Here the predominant mood is fear; the community cowers before a deity or deities whose essence is sheer arbitrary will, and whose dread power to withhold or destroy must be continually appeased. The corollary of this conception of the divine, which is typical of communal religion in Whitehead's sense of the term, is that the religion itself tends to be *authoritarian*. It distrusts individual honesty, initiative, and self-discovery in its anxiety not to let anything disturb the tenuous and fragile relationship it has established with the gods.

Believing in gods whose capricious wills must be manipulated for the community's benefit, its leaders do not hesitate to manipulate the persons under its sway. The community, not the individual, is the unit of religion. Unless solitary men of uncommon courage and charisma arise to point the way to higher possibilities, the development of religion can easily stagnate at this point. "In fact," Whitehead observes, "this is the stage of religious evolution in which the masses of semi-civilized humanity have halted . . ." (RM 28). It is also a stage to which more highly developed religions are always reverting.

Communal religion is also *provincial*, since the horizon of its concern is the safety and cohesion of only one social group. Its concept of "rightness is mixed up with the notion of preservation" (RM 41). Thus it does not tend to occupy itself with the quest for truths and values of universal scope and application. Having learned to placate the willful gods for its own benefit, the community cherishes the notion that it is favored and blessed over all other communities, developing its religious beliefs accordingly. The limit of its sense of moral obligation is usually the boundary separating it from the remainder of human beings contemptuously dismissed as "infidels," "heathens," or some such epithet. The result is that the community may come to believe that it has a divine mandate for repressing and exploiting other peoples. Such religion, with its "morbid exaggeration of national self-consciousness," can easily become a sinister force for violence and destructiveness in the world (RM 43–44).

Not only does communal religion fail to concern itself with questions of universal truth and value, it also tends to ignore questions of intrinsic truth and value. Its orientation is *pragmatic.* The object of its highest veneration is not so much the gods as the community itself, and it is willing to pay any price to maintain the community's existence. In fact, the gods of communal religion do not morally deserve veneration, because their decisions are seen as arbitrary flashes of will, without any rationale or grounding in intrinsic good. As Paul Ricoeur phrases it, their imperatives are experienced as mere presence, not essence.[1] Hence Whitehead's dictum, "there can be very little disinterested worship among primitive folk . . ." (RM 26). Preoccupied with the community's preservation and anxiously on guard against disruptive innovation, communal religion represents "the stage of satisfactory ritual and of satisfied belief without impulse towards higher things. Such religion satisfies the pragmatic test: It works, and thereby claims that it can be awarded the prize for truth" (RM 28). But that prize is not so simply won. The spirit of genuine religious inquiry, as Whitehead conceives it, is not satisfied with techniques of current expediency. It hungers for a "permanent rightness," inherent in the nature of things (RM 61).

Taken as an objective description of a discrete stage through which all religion is supposed to have passed in its advancement toward a higher form, Whitehead's notion of communal religion is open to a number of rather obvious objections. For one thing, it assumes an evolutionary orientation, an attempt to trace the origins of religion from its earliest beginnings through clearly distinguishable stages of development. This concept has fallen into disfavor with many, if not most, modern students of cultural anthropology and the history of religions. One trouble with such an approach has been pinpointed by Ninian Smart: "Evidence of religion from prehistoric time is so slight that there cannot be as yet, and perhaps there never will be, any definitive account of the origins of the religious sentiment among mankind."[2] Also, Whitehead's description of communal religion amounts to an oversimple stereotype which does not do justice to the striking variety and complexity of particular tribal religious systems in the past and present. For instance, not all of these have personal gods, and when they do, the gods are not always of one type. Also, these systems admit of innovation by individual tribesmen in varying degrees. And their atmosphere is by no means exclusively one of terror untempered by reverence and love. Furthermore, there are pejorative overtones in Whitehead's description which ill befit an objective historical account. Finally, Whitehead cites no data for his sweeping generalizations and offers little or no argument for their historical accuracy. As John B. Cobb has noted, "For his work on religion Whitehead depended heavily on secondary sources, and his familiarity with these was limited."[3]

Although largely vitiated as an historical description, Whitehead's notion of communal religion is not without value. It is useful as an abstract type, which might apply in greater or lesser degree to particular religions. But more fundamentally, by informing us as to what religion emphatically is *not*, for Whitehead, it affords a perspective on his positive theory of what the essence of religion is. In sharp contrast with the authoritarianism, provincialism, and pragmatism which he associates with communal religion, Whitehead insists that religion in its fully developed form is founded upon commitment to the value of an individual for itself, a world-consciousness, and the concept of an essential rightness. And each of these has its point of departure in solitariness.

## II · THE VALUE OF AN INDIVIDUAL FOR ITSELF

Genuine religion, as Whitehead views it, places a premium upon individuality which is not possible in communal religion, with its overweening passion for undisturbed order. So long as individuals within a society remain other-directed, uncritically attuned to the traditions and mores of their inherited culture, they will not concern themselves with religious questions in anything like their deserved poignancy and depth. But when reflective men are enabled to break out of the confines of their tribal communities and to come into contact with the beliefs and practices of other cultures, whether through travel, conquest, or study, they will be forced to recognize the unreliability of social custom and authority for the resolution of the basic issues of life. The vise-grip of tradition upon them will be broken, and they will no longer have the sense of being at the mercy of arbitrary power (see RM 39–41). They will be thrown upon their own resources, and out of a trauma of cultural uprootedness and cosmic loneliness there will emerge, phoenix-like, the awesome realization that each man is a solitary being, unique to himself, an irreducible focus and source of freedom and value. In this mood of solitariness or existential self-discovery "the spirit asks, What, in the way of value, is the attainment of life?" (RM 60). And with this mood and question, penetrating religious inquiry begins.

This line of reasoning becomes more vivid when we consider that, in Whitehead's pluralistic vision of reality, value is not a static thing, embodied once-for-all in a deity, in society, or in nature, but something dynamic; and the source of this dynamism is the subjective experiences of individual entities. As he states it, "there is no such thing as mere value. Value is the outcome of limitation. The definite finite entity is the selected mode which is the shaping of attainment; apart from such shaping into individual matter of fact there is no attainment" (SMW 136–37).[4] The capacity for the creation of value is quite limited in the case of such societies of low-grade actual entities as crystals, rocks, and planets, where replication of past patterns, rather than novelty, is the rule. But in man's case this capacity is great, given his "soul," or regnant society of high-grade entities, set in a physiological context affording appreciable latitude for self-conscious choice.[5] For man merely to conform to past traditions or external authority would be for him to make the serious mistake of neglecting this power for the creation of value lying latent within him. Only through gaining a keen sense of his individuality and freedom can this creative power be unleashed. And until it is unleashed, a man cannot live fully as a man, but only as something lower in the scale of creatures.

But while this strong sense of individuality and personal freedom—conveyed to man in the mood of solitariness—is for Whitehead a necessary condition for a genuinely religious consciousness, it is by no means sufficient. To become acutely aware of one's freedom is also to perceive that value cannot be created *ex nihilo.* To choose meaningfully is to choose in a context transcending mere subjectivity, a context where the distinction between constructive and destructive uses of freedom can be discerned. Value, in other words, is not merely invented; it is also discovered. In Whitehead's thought it involves a triadic relationship among those possibilities objectively present in the actual world of an emergent entity, the spontaneity of the entity itself, and the initial aim of God. This last gives the original impetus for the emergence of actual entities, persuading them to that degree of intensity of subjective satisfaction which is most compatible with the full self-realization of other entities in the ongoing ferment of the world. What holds in this case for actual entities also holds, *mutatis mutandis*, for individual human beings. Because its thrust is toward the zest of individuation, and not just the maintenance of static order, God's initial aim in Whitehead's scheme stands in marked contrast with his description of the gods of communal religion, with their authoritarian distaste for individual initiative. As he sums it up, "It is the difference between the enemy you conciliate and the companion whom you imitate" (RM 41). Or even more tersely, God "is the mirror which discloses to every creature its own greatness" (RM 155). To exercise one's personal freedom with a distinct awareness of God's initial aim as the ultimate ground of value and lure for individual creativity is for Whitehead what it means to be religious.

But God's initial aim is elusive and usually felt only very dimly. What H. N. Wieman says of "creativity" applies to it as well—viz., it "is the most wonderful thing in the world and yet is so intimately and persistently with us that we scarcely ever take any note of it nor of what it is doing to us."[6] There is a close connection between this elusive character of the initial aim and Whitehead's insistence that recognition of the primary and intrinsic importance of the individual's solitary life is a precondition for its clear perception.[7] This connection is implicit in a passage of John B. Cobb's *A Christian Natural Theology*, where Cobb notes that among those conditions most likely to lead to a "heightened consciousness of God" there must be an exclusion from any important role of "the prehensions of other living persons." This is so because God is experienced only in the mode of causal efficacy (experience of the initial aim is a "hybrid physical prehension" of God), and this usually *unconscious* side of man's experience must somehow be brought into dominant awareness.[8] So long as one's life consists merely in outward responsiveness to other people, one will be distracted from meditating deeply enough upon one's experience of causal efficacy to discern the presence of divine persuasion as one of its components. This is at least one important sense in which collective emotions fail to touch the experience of the human being, consciously alone with itself. The man who knows nothing of solitude and who has not learned to value himself as an individual will have little consciousness of the role of the divine lure for his own life, even though it will continue to function below the level of consciousness as a part of his total experience of causality. And unless its role is taken consciously and seriously into account, one cannot be said to be living with religious awareness.

One final way in which commitment to the value of an individual for itself enters into Whitehead's conception of religion can be seen in his description of the experiences of the great religious prophets and teachers, and his discussion of the bearing of these experiences upon the lives of more ordinary persons. He takes it to be an important confirmation of his thesis that the "great religious conceptions which haunt the imaginations of civilized mankind are scenes of solitariness," and as examples he cites "Mahomet brooding in the desert, the meditations of the Buddha, the solitary Man on the Cross" (RM 19, 20). These conceptions are important for the religious quest of others precisely because the path to self-discovery is so arduous, and the mood of solitariness so hard to sustain. It is no great trick to be alone. But to experience solitariness, in Whitehead's sense of that term, and through that experience to come to a clear apprehension of one's freedom and of the divine conditioning of that freedom, is a formidable task.

The abilities of some men are much greater in this regard than those of others, and their accomplishments can serve as inspirations and guides for the rest:

> it is not true that all people are on a level in respect to their perceptive powers. Some people appear to realize continuously, and at a higher level, types of emotional and perceptive experience, which we recognize as corresponding to those periods of our own lives most worthy of confidence for that sort of experience. In so far as what they say interprets our own best moments, it is reasonable to trust to the evidential force of their experience [RM 125].

But the implication is not that one should trust blindly in the authority of the religious geniuses of history or rely uncritically on their announced methods or formulas, for it remains true that "religion is primarily individual, and the dogmas of religion are clarifying modes of external expression" (RM 137). The idea is, rather, that tentative use can be made of the accounts they give of their experiences, as possible aids for the enriching and deepening of one's own. In other words, religious truth cannot be appropriated in any second-hand fashion. What was conceived in the great religious teachers' times of solitude must now be brought full circle back to the test of one's own solitariness, to see whether it can help toward that consciousness which, in the final analysis, cannot be described but can only be awakened in the secret recesses of each man's private being. No sanction of tradition or external authority can make religiously meaningful dogmas or practices which fail to speak decisively to one's own condition and need. The spirit of this linkage between religion and solitary self-evaluation is captured concisely by Willard E. Arnett when he remarks that the ultimate worth of all such teachings "is derived chiefly from the vision of personal existence, freedom, responsibility, and possibility they evoke and articulate."[9]

## III · A WORLD-CONSCIOUSNESS

"The moment of religious consciousness starts from self-valuation, but it broadens into the concept of the world as a realm of adjusted values, mutually intensifying or mutually destructive" (RM 59). With these words Whitehead marks the transition from the individual to the community, from emphasis on the value of an individual for itself to a stress upon the value of the diverse individuals of the world for one another. Just as the first characteristic of religion in its true essence was said to grow out of the mood of solitariness, so does this second characteristic of world-consciousness, which contrasts with the provincial outlook of communal proto-religion. In the preceding section we saw that penetrating religious inquiry begins when man, in his solitariness, poses to himself the question, "What, in the way of value, is the attainment of life?" To that Whitehead adds, "And it can find no such value till it has merged its individual claim with that of the objective universe. Religion is world-loyalty" (RM 60). Thus would he meet the objection that his concept of religion as what man does with his solitariness is one-sided, so concerned with the solitary experience of the individual as to lose sight of the religious meaning of man's life in communion with his fellows and in relation to the cosmos as a whole. Let us see what kind of case Whitehead makes for there being an essential connection between solitariness and a world-consciousness.

To begin with, there is the contention, so fundamental to Whitehead's metaphysical outlook, that the zest of individual self-affirmation must be reconciled with the requirement of harmony and order in the world. The strength of this 'must' is partly the fact that, without harmony and order, there would be no world, since a cosmos is a pervasive order of some type. But even more germane for our purposes is the fact that individuals desperately need one another, if the highest possibilities for the zest of life for each are to be realized. The basic fallacy in the traditional doctrine of substances, from the Whiteheadian perspective, is the belief that each "requires nothing but itself in order to exist." But this is true of no entity, not even God. In fact, "every entity is in its essence social and requires the society in order to exist" (RM 108). These comments apply also to individual human beings.

Communal religion, with its externally imposed order, does violence to the integrity of individuals, thus representing one kind of glaring evil, namely, the suppression of creativity and change. But the opposite extreme is equally destructive, namely, that of anarchy, or the kind of individualism which has entities or persons working at cross-purposes, stultifying and hindering, rather than mutually enhancing, the individuality of each.[10] Over against these two forms of evil is Whitehead's aesthetic model of good as the harmonious reconcilement of these opposite tendencies of compatibility and contrast (see RM 104–105, 115). The need for compatibility shows the importance of community in religion, just as the need for contrast shows the importance of solitary self-evaluation.

Secondly, there is the role of the social medium of language and of inherited myth and symbol, whereby the individual can interpret to himself and to others the meaning of his experience of solitariness, testing the insights he has gained and the possibilities he has perceived through communication with other persons. We have already noted how much self-interpretation can be aided by the formulas in which the geniuses of religious history have expressed their own experience. There is also the fact that the individual's religious discoveries, however penetrating and novel, will be imbedded in an historical context, and will have to make use of certain historically conditioned modes of expression. And finally, the individual will find it important to safeguard himself against sentimentality and the fleeting fancies of the moment by exposing his insights to interaction with the outlooks and experiences of others, seeking to merge his personal vision into an objective, coherent view of the world. Whitehead gives these points trenchant summarization when he says,

> Expression, and in particular expression by dogma, is the return from solitariness to society. There is no such thing as absolute solitariness. Each entity requires its environment. Thus man cannot seclude himself from society. . . . But further, what is known in secret must be enjoyed in common, and must be verified in common [RM 137–38].

There will be a tension, however, between the novelty of individual religious awareness and the generality of public forms of expression. And given the solitary individual's skepticism regarding the binding authority of the conventions of his inherited social group, there will also be a tension between its ways of giving expression to the religious dimension of life and the ways to be found in other groups. The solitary individual will be characterized, therefore, by a kind of questing pluralism which transcends the interpretive categories of his own culture and seeks enrichment and illumination from those of a variety of cultures. He will be characterized, that is to say, by a world-consciousness.

Still another way in which the linkage between solitariness and world-consciousness is argued for by Whitehead lies in his observation that detachment, or disconnection from immediate surroundings, is a prerequisite for "the emergence of a religious consciousness which is universal, as distinguished from tribal, or even social" (RM 47). What he seems to be suggesting is that there must be a certain dissociation of oneself from the conventions and customs of one's own social group before one can arrive at any truly general perspective on the conventions and customs of all social groups. Without such dissociation, as Stuart Hampshire comments, man's view of himself and the world will tend to be narrowly circumscribed. He will see "his own possible forms of life as limited on two sides, by his inheritance and by his need to transmit at least some of his inheritance to his children and to their descendants. He is a station on a permanent social way." But in the mood of detachment, "it is possible to picture the span of one's own life and family and that of one's friends, not as phases in a continuing social process, but as properly to be judged in isolation and for their wholly intrinsic qualities."[11] What is true for one's family and friends in this mood is also true for mankind as a whole. From the vantage point of solitariness, with the religious sensitivity it can elicit, one is able to view other men for the first time, not as either tribesmen or aliens, or as having their relative importance conferred upon them purely by their roles within a hierarchy of social strata, but simply as human beings. To learn to value oneself as an individual is thus at one and the same time to learn to value others in the same way, to see that the situation of all men with respect to the ultimate questions is exactly like one's own. As Richard Rubenstein puts it,

> Each of us before God as the focus of ultimate concern must regard the real challenges of his personal existence as essentially the same as those of any other human being. Whether we are intellectuals, merchants, or laborers, we are born in the same way, need the same love, are capable of the same evil and will die the same death.[12]

This does not mean, however, that the diversity of backgrounds, ethnic identities, and styles of life among men is a matter of indifference. This would be valuing "mankind" in the abstract, not particular individuals. Rather, Whitehead is saying that the mood of solitariness can put one in a position to value this diversity, as part of the same concrete individuality in others that one has discovered in oneself. To learn such lessons is to find a new and more valid basis for community relationships; it is to begin to acquire the world-consciousness which Whitehead asociates with genuine religion.

But, for Whitehead, the expression 'world-consciousness' means more than a sense of human world community. It also implies a consciousness of one's interconnections with the cosmos as a whole, and a distinct feeling for it as an arena of emerging value in which no nuance of individual attainment is too petty or insignificant to be taken account of. "In fact, the society for each entity, actual or ideal, is the all inclusive universe, including its ideal forms" (RM 108). Everything exists in relatedness, and the relatedness is one of value as well as of fact. What it means to comprehend this religiously is eloquently portrayed by Whitehead when he discusses the beauty of a flower in an isolated glade in the wilderness:

> No animal has ever had the subtlety of experience to enjoy its full beauty. And yet this beauty is a grand fact in the universe. When we survey nature and think [how] flitting and superficial has been the animal enjoyment of its wonders, and when we realize how incapable the separate cells and pulsations of each flower are of enjoying the total effect—then our sense of the value of the details for the totality dawns upon our consciousness. This is the intuition of holiness, the intuition of the sacred, which is at the foundation of all religion [MT 164].

This passage suggests a vast dimension of worth beyond oneself; yet this is not a worth before which one can only stand in passive awe. It is a worth which invites one's active participation, because it is not settled or finished but depends on the contribution which each element of the universe can make to its continuing development. More will be said in the next section about this sense of worth or inherent rightness, but this much will suffice to show that for Whitehead world-consciousness extends beyond the human community to the whole structure of relationships binding the individual to the cosmos.

But if we can grant the logic of the connections which Whitehead sees between solitariness and world-consciousness, or at least their compatibility with his metaphysics, a critical problem still remains. Why does he give *primacy* in his theory of religion to the sense of solitariness? Why does he not argue instead that solitariness and the sense of community are of *equal* importance in a genuine religious consciousness? One way of answering this question would be to argue that the primacy of which Whitehead speaks is historical and psychological, rather than essential to the concept of religion itself. We have already seen that genuine religious consciousness could emerge in the course of history only when a cross-fertilization of cultures became possible, with a resulting decisive challenge to the absolute domination of communal traditions over the lives of individual men. And we have also seen that its awakening is contingent upon the psychological discovery of one's own individuality and freedom, with its accompanying recognition of the common situation of all men with respect to the basic issues of life.

But I think Whitehead wants to affirm more than these historical and psychological senses of the primacy of the solitary individual. He wants us also to understand that there is an *essential* primacy of the individual, if the nature of religion is properly understood. "The conduct of external life is conditioned by environment," he says, "but it receives its final quality, on which its worth depends, from the internal life which is the self-realization of existence. Religion is the art and the theory of the internal life of man, so far as it depends on the man himself and on what is permanent in the nature of things" (RM 16). Light is cast on this stubborn affirmation of the primacy of the individual for religion when we reflect on this passage from *Modes of Thought*:

Science is concerned with the facts of bygone transition. History relates the aim at ideals. And between Science and History, lies the

> operation of the [Divine] impulse of energy. It is the religious impulse in the world which transforms the dead facts of Science into the living drama of History. For this reason Science can never foretell the perpetual novelty of History [MT 142].

Whitehead says a great deal in this passage, but one important thing he seems to be getting at is that the province of science is peculiarly that of existing order, while the province of religion is peculiarly that of novelty and freedom. Science studies the regular, law-like, and predictable, while religion is principally concerned with the capacity of individuals to bring to bear upon the unfolding drama of history visions of possibility and value which are unique and unprecedented, because grounded in the concreteness of their own experience and freedom. This contrast between science and religion is brought out vividly by Whitehead when he bids us consider such innovators in religious history as Saint Francis of Assisi and John Wesley. "For physical science you have in these lives merely ordinary examples of the operation of the principles of physiological chemistry, and of the dynamics of nervous reactions: for religion you have lives of the most profound significance in the history of the world" (SMW 265). The same contrast is implicit in Whitehead's remark, in passing, that "most psychology is herd-psychology" (RM 16), meaning that its preoccupation as a science is with established collective norms, rather than with a thrust toward uniquely personal discoveries and ideals.

There is a primacy of individuals in Whitehead's metaphysical scheme which parallels the primacy he gives to them in his concept of religion. This primacy in the former sphere is borne out by his "ontological principle," i.e., that apart from the experiences of individual entities there can be no explanation in metaphysics (PR 28). This suggests that religion, for Whitehead, moves on a more basic level, metaphysically speaking, than does science. Science's preoccupation is with abstract description, as is shown by its primary reliance on percepta in the mode of presentational immediacy (sense data) and its interest only in those phenomena which are amenable to statistical analysis. Religion is more concrete, relying primarily on experience in the mode of causal efficacy (see the discussion of God's initial aim above) and giving its emphasis to the lives of discrete individuals. (See RM 58; PR 24.)

But when all of this has been said, it must be pointed out that Whitehead is not describing religion as it *is* when he speaks of its giving such primacy to the individual. He is characterizing it as he thinks it *ought to be.* In at least this respect his theory of religion is normative, rather than descriptive, a distinction which he seems to ignore. This fact can be made all the more apparent when we consider these words of a contemporary "radical" theologian, Sam Keen, as he contrasts an authoritarian concept of theology based on binding, external, once-for-all "revelation" with a notion of theology as finding its true value in what it can contribute to personal illumination and evolving self-discovery.

> It is *my* conviction . . . that this classical, ecclesiastical, revelational notion of theology is inadequate if not downright dangerous because *it begs the question of authority and responsibility.* To the degree that I accept the principles of my faith from the opinions, conclusions, dicta of any external authority, I am living out another person's life. To begin with a model for life which is introjected on the recommendation of an authority is to sell my soul for a role. I assume a "personality" but I lose the ability to grow as a person by continually evaluating my expanding experience.[13]

The spirit of this statement is completely compatible with Whitehead's characterization of genuine religion, and it expresses sentiments with which I am in hearty agreement. But it still remains true that the "classical, ecclesiastical, revelational" concept of which Keen speaks has long been the pervasive notion of religion in Judaeo-Christian and Islamic cultures, and that it is not without its important exemplifications in other civilized cultures as well. And it is also the case that religious institutions have tended to be conservative guardians of values inherited from the past more than they have functioned as vehicles of individual freedom and innovation. If Whitehead should want to claim that the essence of religion in such cultures and institutions is nevertheless as he describes it, then he would have to provide us with a much more convincing case, based on the relevant historical data, than he has. For the evidence against this aspect of his theory, if taken as a descriptive theory, would seem to be overwhelming.

## IV · THE CONCEPT OF AN ESSENTIAL RIGHTNESS

A persistent theme running throughout Whitehead's *Religion in the Making* is emphasis on the deeply probing character of full-fledged religious sensibility, its acute dissatisfaction with the merely pragmatic justifications of communal religion and its anxious search for "a righteousness in the nature of things, functioning as a condition, a critic, and an ideal" (RM 63). This "righteousness" or "character of permanent rightness," as he sometimes calls it (see RM 61), could be said to act in Whitehead's theory of religion as the basic predicate for which each specific religion provides a logical subject, whose nature is explicated in its doctrinal scheme.[14] His own concept of God, as developed in his metaphysics, might be construed as one such logical subject, although he clearly wishes us to regard it in a more generic way, as getting to the heart of what all religions are about. Much has been written concerning Whitehead's concept of God, and I will not go over that ground again. I shall concentrate on the three aspects of his notion of "rightness," i.e., its function as a condition, critic, and ideal.

We can best get at the idea that genuine religion is concerned with an essential rightness, taken as a "condition," by considering still another contrast between religion and science averred by Whitehead:

> science can leave its metaphysics implicit and retire behind our belief in the pragmatic value of its general descriptions. If religion does that, it admits that its dogmas are merely pleasing ideas for the purpose of stimulating its emotions. Science (at least as a temporary methodological device) can rest upon a naïve faith; religion is the longing for justification [RM 85].

What sort of "justification" does Whitehead have in mind? He answers that "religion is the longing of the spirit that the facts of existence should find their justification in the nature of existence"

(RM 85). And among those facts of existence is the eminent success of science.

Science itself can take for granted the givenness of the world. It need not inquire into the ground of the intelligible cosmic order which the success of its techniques presupposes. If those techniques work, that is justification enough. But the religious seeker, brooding in solitude upon the enigma of the world and his place within it, cannot stop with the world as given. His inquiry is by nature more penetrating. He must probe into the ultimate condition for the world-order, a condition which can among other things shed light upon the mystery of its susceptibility to theoretical analysis. The supposition that there is such a condition to be found is an important trait of the religious consciousness for Whitehead (see RM 143), and the person unable or unwilling to make it is to that extent non-religious. In Whitehead's metaphysics this supposition is highly significant, because it points to the requirement of God as that entity which brings creativity into synthesis with possibility through the harmony of his primordial vision, so as to effect the emergence of every new actuality (see RM 90, 94, 119–20).

But also among the facts of existence is the experience of value, and the justification for this sought by religion implies the search for an essential rightness functioning as both critic and ideal. The experience of value is present in our direction of practice and in our aesthetic sensibilities, and it finds its peculiarly religious focus in the individual's self-valuation and in the awareness of a vast dimension of worth beyond himself for which no words can give adequate expression. To what has already been said about the first we can add these words of Paul Ramsey, because they state succinctly an intimate connection between self-valuation and the focus of religious concern: "Loss of the sense of the Sacred or the attempt to understand one's self wholly in spatio-temporal terms leads inevitably to the debasing of man beyond measure."[15] And Whitehead's statement on the second suggests yet another contrast between religion and science: "Religion insists that the world is a mutually adjusted disposition of things, issuing in value for its own sake. This is the very point that science is always forgetting" (RM

143–44). The world, then, for the religiously sensitive person, is no mere assemblage of facts. It is an arena of value,[16] conferring rich value upon such a person and commanding his loyalty to the good and his eschewal of evil.

To speak of the concept of an essential rightness functioning as a critic is to speak of the religious awareness of evil—in oneself, in one's fellows, and in the world. "No religion which faces facts can minimize the evil in the world, not merely the moral evil, but the pain and the suffering" (RM 49). But at the same time, to be religious (and here is a difference between religion and mere morality) is to be convinced that the evil of the world is a contingent and parasitical fact, contrasting with a rightness which is essential (see RM 51, 96–97). And it is at this point that rightness as critic becomes rightness as ideal. Evil need not overwhelm man; it can be overcome. And each religion seeks to provide a way of overcoming it, centering on the promise of salvation implied by some sort of rightness or wisdom lying at the heart of the world. Whitehead's normative appraisal is that the aim of salvation from evil is not realized by all religions to the same degree; in fact, some conduce more to evil than to good (RM 17). But the intent of them all is the same: to provide a route out of hopelessness, pain, and the degradation of value into realization of the highest possibilities for good. Whitehead's concept of the consequent nature of God is a working out metaphysically of the religious assurance that good will triumph over evil. But his is a realized eschatology instead of a futuristic one, for this triumph is always taking place as God absorbs "the multiple freedom of actuality into the harmony of his own actualization" (PR 530). And here the note of individuality is struck again, for Whitehead speaks of God Himself as being "completed by the individual, fluent satisfactions of finite fact" (PR 527).

## V · CONCLUSION

Whitehead has provided us with a theory of the origin, focus, and purpose of religion. Religion's origin is in the mood of solitary self-evaluation, whence it broadens into a sense of the inherent worth of all men and a consciousness of the world as a community of value. Its focus is upon a character of rightness inherent in the nature of things, functioning as condition, critic, and ideal. And its purpose is to show the way to salvation, the way in which the power of that rightness can be appropriated for the transformation of life. It is a theory with many responsive chords in Whitehead's metaphysical system, showing the extent to which his musings on religion have influenced and been influenced by the working out of his philosophic vision. It is not a purely descriptive theory, but it does touch on a number of the characteristic traits of religious aspiration. Perhaps a lesson to be gained from this study is that no theory of a phenomenon as pervasive and multi-faceted as religion can be expected to be entirely free from debatable metaphysical assumptions. At least Whitehead has articulated his own assumptions in a system of thought which lies open for our inspection and criticism.

## NOTES

1. Paul Ricoeur, *The Symbolism of Evil* (Boston: Beacon, 1969), p. 52.

2. Ninian Smart, *The Religious Experience of Mankind*, 2nd ed. (New York: Scribners, 1976), p. 28.

3. John B. Cobb, Jr., *A Christian Natural Theology* (Philadelphia: Westminster, 1965), p. 216.

4. Cf. also RM 100: "Value is inherent in actuality itself. To be an actual entity is to have a self-interest. This self-interest is a feeling of self-valuation; it is an emotional tone."

5. For an elucidation of these ideas see Donald W. Sherburne, "Whitehead's Psychological Physiology," *Southern Journal of Philosophy*, 7 (1969–70), 401–407.

6. H. N. Wieman, "What is Most Important in Christianity?" *Religion in the Making*, 1 (1940–41), 151. Cited by Huston Smith, "The Operational View of God," *Journal of Religion*, 31 (1951), 104.

7. Cf. RM 15–16: "Life is an internal fact for its own sake, before it is an external fact relating itself to others."

8. Cobb, *A Christian Natural Theology*, pp. 235–36.

9. Willard E. Arnett, *Religion and Judgment* (New York: Appleton-Century-Crofts, 1966), p. 202. Cf. also RM 137: ". . . a dogma which fails to evoke any response in immediate apprehension stifles the religious life."

10. On the distinction between order and anarchy see FR 26–28. White-

head associates the principle of order with the physical pole of actual entities and that of anarchy with their mental pole. Reality is a harmonizing of these extremes.

11. Stuart Hampshire, "Russell, Radicalism, and Reason," *New York Review of Books*, 15, No. 6 (October 8, 1970), 6.

12. Richard Rubenstein, *After Auschwitz* (New York: Bobbs-Merrill, 1966), p. 241.

13. Sam Keen, *To a Dancing God* (New York: Harper and Row, 1970), p. 129.

14. On the difference between the basic predicate and the logical subject of basic religious proposals see William A. Christian, *Meaning and Truth in Religion* (Princeton: Princeton University Press, 1964), pp. 19–24.

15. Paul Ramsey, "No Morality without Immortality: Dostoevski and the Meaning of Atheism," *Journal of Religion*, 36 (1956), 95.

16. Another problem with Whitehead's theory of religion, if taken as an attempt at a descriptive theory, emerges at this point. He identifies value with concretion, limitation, and individuation, while a religious system like Advaita Vedanta views these things as the fruits of illusion, and the prizing of them, through ignorance, as giving rise to untold suffering. In such a view, the world is not so much an arena of value as a web of illusion, and to give the kind of metaphysical primacy to the individual that Whitehead does is simply to reinforce the illusion and its sad consequences.

# 9

# The Religious Availability of Whitehead's God: A Critical Analysis

STEPHEN LEE ELY
Late of the
*University of Wisconsin*

Today there is but one religious dogma in debate: What do you mean by 'God'?

WHITEHEAD, *Religion in the Making*, p. 67.

I

STUDENTS OF WHITEHEAD do not need to be told that his "God" is not the God of any of the supernatural or revealed religions. His "God" is primarily metaphysical. It is the purpose of this essay to describe the nature of Whitehead's "God" and to inquire whether such a "God" can serve religious ends.

---

*Editors' Note*: This essay reproduces, in its entirety, a short book of 58 pages originally published by the University of Wisconsin Press in 1942. Though the book stimulated significant discussion at the time, it has never been reprinted, partly because of the author's premature death. Although two responses to Ely's book have been republished in readily accessible anthologies, the original essay has hitherto been quite difficult to obtain.

Ely's exposition of Whitehead's concept of God is forthright, clear, and generally quite accurate. His criticisms are also well-taken. It is the consensus of several scholars, however, that the view he criticizes is not the view which Whitehead espouses. This the reader can judge for himself by comparing exposition and criticism, or he may wish to consult Charles Hartshorne, "Is Whitehead's God the God of

Whitehead's philosophy makes violent partisans. Some have confidently asserted that Whitehead has effected a new Copernican revolution in philosophy, and that *Process and Reality* is the monumental cosmology for our time and perhaps for all time. Others declare that the book is a pretentious muddle of mysticism and logic in which ancient and discredited modes of explanation, such as animism, are tricked out with meretricious mathematical finery. Such extreme opinions are no doubt uncritical; yet the fact that they are not infrequently encountered testifies to the vitality of Whitehead's thought. There is, however, another factor in the situation that deserves notice. Much of the acrimony in the discussion comes from those followers of the early Whitehead who are convinced that their loyalty has been betrayed. On the other hand, a great deal of the recent enthusiasm for Whitehead is not unconnected with gratitude for powerful support from an unexpected quarter. For Whitehead's philosophy, when in full mid-career, took a new direction. The eleventh chapter of *Science and the Modern World* marks the turning point. That chapter was entitled "God."

In his earlier books Whitehead had called for an exciting reconstruction in philosophy. The reconstruction was to be on a realistic and naturalistic basis. Errant since Descartes, philosophy was now urged to settle down in amicable understanding with modern physics and modern logic. But in that famous eleventh chapter it appeared that "God" would play an important role in the reconstruction. Philosophy must heed not only Einstein and Heisenberg and Russell but Aristotle as well.

Now, there is nothing in Whitehead's earlier books—those which established his fame as a realistic epistemologist—to suggest that "God" would appear in a modern metaphysics or cosmology.

---

Religion?" Chapter 6 of his *Whitehead's Philosophy: Selected Essays, 1935–1970* (Lincoln: University of Nebraska Press, 1972), or Bernard M. Loomer, "Ely on Whitehead's God," pp. 264–86 in *Process Philosophy and Christian Thought*, edd. Delwin Brown, Ralph E. James, Jr., and Gene Reeves (Indianapolis: Bobbs-Merrill, 1971). Additional reviews of Ely's book have been published by D. F. Bowers in the *Journal of Philosophy*, 39 (1942), 612–13, H. S. Fries in the *Journal of Liberal Religion*, 5 (1943), 96–97, and Victor Lowe in the *Review of Religion*, 7 (1943), 409–15.

The essay has been divided by the present editors into ten numbered sections.

Whitehead had repudiated idealism, and a metaphysics that includes God seems to require some brand of idealism. But Whitehead had announced that he had serious "doubts as to any form of idealism." Those doubts, he said, were based on the

> difficulty of conceiving any very close association with mind of bygone ages, when the granite was formed or when the sun first blazed. . . . We know of events whose connexion with any mental process, as we know it, appears to be doubtful, incomplete, and extremely unessential to them.
>
> That is my reason for being very shy of leaning too heavily on mind in any endeavour to express the general character of reality.[1]

Then, too, Whitehead wrote bitingly of the disastrous results "both to science and to philosophy" of the current "apathetic acquiescence" in the entirely mistaken notion that nature cannot be adequately described and explained "without dragging in its relations to mind" (CN 27). Such phrases suggested to no one that Whitehead would ever receive the acclaim of theologians.

That was in 1920, and *Science and the Modern World* with its eleventh chapter appeared in 1925. Therein God was proclaimed as a necessary metaphysical principle. On this subject Bertrand Russell wrote:

> I must confess with regret that I have failed to understand Professor Whitehead's argument on this important subject. And, speaking generally, I cannot persuade myself that his logical reconstruction of physical concepts has any such tendency as he attributes to it, to restore the consolations of religion to a world desolated by mechanism. However, before feeling any certainty on this point, we must wait until he has given us a fuller and more systematic explanation of this doctrine.[2]

The wait was four years long; *Process and Reality* was published in 1929. It is true that a little book entitled *Religion in the Making* had appeared the very year after *Science and the Modern World*, and in it the conception of God was expanded and enriched; but the treatment was from a religious rather than a philosophic standpoint, and the tone might not unfairly be termed apocalyptic.[3]

*Process and Reality* remains the principal exposition of the "philosophy of organism," as Whitehead calls his system; and in this book it becomes abundantly clear that what is called 'God' is of the most immense metaphysical and cosmological importance. In this book, moreover, new aspects of God's nature are insisted upon in an attempt to demonstrate that he is a suitable object of religious worship. Later books, it may be added, do little to explain or modify the theological conceptions of *Process and Reality.*

The indignant dismay of some of Whitehead's admirers (when it became clear that his affair with theology was no passing fancy) has enlivened many a page of the philosophical periodicals. Miss Stebbing said of *Religion in the Making* that it was "likely to be quoted in pulpits and approved by theologians, and probably only the latter will understand it."[4] But when she writes of *Process and Reality* she understands only too well, and even her sarcasm deserts her:

> Professor Whitehead's indefensible usage of language becomes nothing short of scandalous when he speaks of "God." . . . It is difficult to acquit Professor Whitehead of a deliberate desire to encourage the unclear thinking that is so common with regard to this subject.[5]

Professor A. E. Murphy resigns himself to the debacle. It would not be surprising, he thinks, if an adherent of a contemporary philosophical school such as personalism "which traditionally and professionally find[s] sermons in stones and Methodism in scientific methodology" were to talk about God as Whitehead does; but "we had hoped something else than this revival of a hoary and non-empirical eternalism from the author of *The Principles of Natural Knowledge.*"[6]

## II

Outraged feelings need no longer concern us. God is inseparable from "the philosophy of organism." Since this is so, a number of questions arise. One of the most important is this: Does Whitehead's philosophy furnish a God who is "available for religious purposes"? There is here no question, of course, of a possible identification of Whitehead's God with Yahweh, the *Ens Realissimum*, or the God of Augustine or of Calvin.[7] The question is whether Whitehead's God can serve to focus modern liberal religious feeling; whether the philosophy of organism can furnish a satisfactory basis for "The New Reformation" (the title of Chapter 10 of *Adventures of Ideas*). To answer this question we must carefully examine the role that God plays in Whitehead's system and therefore (if the philosophy of organism be true) in the cosmos. We need not take sides on the general issue concerning the tenability of Whitehead's fundamental assumptions. Our problems are such as these: Do God's religious functions follow from the necessities of the system? In any case, is he a satisfactory God, that is, can he serve as a God for contemporary religious feeling? We must inquire especially whether Whitehead's religious philosophy furnishes a real explanation of evil and a real ground for belief that his God can help man diminish that evil.

We begin with Whitehead's discussion of God in *Science and the Modern World.* It is significant, says Whitehead, that Aristotle saw the need of a Prime Mover. Aristotle was not only a most capable metaphysician, but he was (perhaps the last man so to be!) without moral and religious *arrières-pensées.*

> Accordingly on the subject of his Prime Mover, he would have no motive, except to follow his metaphysical train of thought whithersoever it led him. It did not lead him very far towards the production of a God available for religious purposes. It may be doubted whether any properly general metaphysics can ever, without the illicit introduction of other considerations, get much further than Aristotle [SMW 249–50].

This does not sound very promising. But in later books, as we shall see, Whitehead claims to know a great deal more about God than this would lead us to expect. For the present it is enough to realize that, in Whitehead's view, a sound metaphysic demands something analogous to Aristotle's Prime Mover: we reject the Prime Mover because we reject Aristotle's physics; but we still need an analogous metaphysical principle that may be called 'God'.

Stripped to its essentials, the argument for God in *Science and the Modern World*, though abstract, is fairly straightforward. We begin by assuming that the flux of events in which we find ourselves is not mere appearance, but is ultimate concrete reality. We might, of course, merely accept this reality and take it as it comes, but naïve acceptance does not suit the metaphysician. He wants reasons for reality, and such reasons ought to be, he thinks, in terms of what concrete reality means. When we say "This is a bit of concrete reality," what do we mean? We mean more than a mere assertion that "this exists now." According to Whitehead, we mean that "this" is just what it is *in contrast to* what it might possibly have been. That is what "becoming real" means—just *this* has happened, just this that *might* have been something else. At this point it might be objected that the occurrence of any event is determined by causal laws, and that therefore whatever happens could not in fact have been anything else. But this, if granted, merely pushes the inquiry a step further back. We may explain the occurrence of event $X$ by a causal law perhaps, but is not the causal law itself real? For the real particularity of the causal law itself exists only in contrast to what it might have been but in fact is not.

To explain concrete reality, then, we need several factors. We need, first, a realm of possibility, which must in some sense exist, though of course it is not concrete. Again, we need some sort of drive in the cosmos to account for the fact that anything at all happens—a sort of activity-substance that is at once the ultimate raw material, so to speak, of whatever happens, and the push that is behind all real happening. This underlying activity somehow realizes certain possibilities, and thus gets shaped into concrete reality. There are many forms that it might take, but it somehow becomes limited to just the form that it actually does take. To explain this we need a third metaphysical factor, a principle that determines which possibility the underlying activity is to realize. The activity itself, whose metaphysical essence is the possibility of becoming anything, plainly cannot limit itself, and thus by itself it could never become concrete. The bare abstract possibilities, since they are purely passive, cannot impose themselves; they must wait, so to speak, to be chosen. Hence the metaphysical situation demands some mediating agency whereby pure activity is limited to what in fact comes to pass. This agency is God, who functions as the Principle of Limitation or, as he is more frequently called, the Principle of Concretion. It is he who decides which patterns of possibility are to be realized by the underlying activity. This kind of God, thinks Whitehead, is a necessary result of sound metaphysical analysis. Further, it is the only kind of God that metaphysical reason can attain.

> What further can be known about God must be sought in the region of particular experiences, and therefore rests on an empirical basis. In respect to the interpretation of these experiences, mankind have differed profoundly. He has been named respectively, Jehovah, Allah, Brahma, Father in Heaven, Order of Heaven, First Cause, Supreme Being, Chance [SMW 257].[8]

In his later books, however, Whitehead conceives the situation differently. He claims to know a good deal more about God than this would lead us to suppose; yet he does not explicitly rely on these debatable "particular experiences." Although he may well be doing so, Whitehead does not speak as if he were drawing on his own particular store of religious or mystical experience. It is metaphysical analysis, pushed further in the later books, that is supposed to give us a Being that is much more of a God than the bare Principle of Concretion discussed in *Science and the Modern World.*

Before considering the central problem—the nature and functions of God in *Process and Reality*—one or two things about God as Principle of Concretion ought to be noticed. God is only one factor in the production of reality. He is not metaphysically ultimate. He created neither the underlying activity nor the forms of possibility, but he uses and directs them so as to bring forth the order of concrete reality that we actually find. He is, nevertheless, the final *reason*:

> God is the ultimate limitation, and His existence is the ultimate irrationality. For no reason can be given for just that limitation which it stands in His Nature to impose. God is not concrete, but He is the ground for concrete actuality. No reason can be given for the nature of God, because that nature is the ground of rationality [SMW 257].

In sum, the God of *Science and the Modern World* is the metaphysical principle that by mediating between a blind underlying will-to-exist and perfectly passive forms of possibility brings concrete reality into existence. Whitehead asserts, without any explanation, that God is good. Not a word is said of his personality, but since he is not concrete he is surely very different from the personal beings whom we usually meet. No reason is given to suppose that he would or could take any interest in either the prayers of men or the rites of churches. Emphatically he is not, according to Whitehead, "available for religious purposes."

## III

If the reader of *Science and the Modern World*, having reconciled himself to a God who is only the Principle of Concretion, should turn immediately to the closing chapter of *Process and Reality*, he would be surprised to find that God "saves" the world, that God is not only "the poet of the world, with tender patience leading it by his vision of truth, beauty, and goodness," but even that he is "the great companion—the fellow-sufferer who understands" (PR 526, 532). That a metaphysical principle can be and do all this is not immediately apparent. The answer, however, is simple enough. Only one aspect of God—a bleak metaphysical one—is discussed in *Science and the Modern World.* But God has other sides to his nature, and it is these that make him "available for religious purposes," if he can so be made. In other words, what God is in addition to the Principle of Concretion justifies us in calling him 'God' —if we are to use the word in any of its ordinary senses.

Even if we should overlook the serious shortcomings of the

Principle of Concretion as Deity—its impersonality and its imperviousness to human prayers and human ideals—there would yet be a serious difficulty. To regard God as merely the Principle of Concretion is to court the charge that God is responsible for evil. Although God is not, as we saw, metaphysically ultimate, yet he is responsible for the choice of all types of order that actually prevail, and this makes him responsible, one would suppose, for whatever happens. Whitehead appears to deny this implication, but many commentators and reviewers have told him that he has no right to do so.[9] Now, a God who creates both good and evil indiscriminately is not likely to appeal to our times. Whitehead probably recognized this, for in his later books he is much concerned with just this problem. To find his answer we must turn to the metaphysical and cosmological analysis of *Process and Reality.* In this book God's function as Principle of Concretion is barely mentioned; however, this function becomes one among several metaphysical functions that God exercises by virtue of what is now designated as his "Primordial Nature." But a God "available for religious purposes" must perform other and more specifically religious functions. Whitehead intends to supply these by what he calls the Consequent Nature of God.[10]

We shall now examine this complex conception of God in some detail, beginning with the Primordial Nature. God's various natures are not, of course, discrete; they are perfectly merged in a single Being and their distinction is one of reason only.

In *Process and Reality* the argument that leads to the Primordial Nature of God is somewhat similar to that which leads to God as Principle of Concretion. Both are based on a fundamental postulate of Whitehead's—that the possible is prior to the actual, not only logically but metaphysically. In order, however, to understand the full force of the argument in *Process and Reality* it will be necessary to sketch an outline of Whitehead's metaphysics and cosmology. This will be done as far as possible without recourse to the difficult and technical terminology which has repelled so many readers.[11]

## IV

The world is not a thing but a process. This process exemplifies certain ultimate metaphysical principles. Beyond these principles no analysis can pass, since they are the most general assertions that can be made about reality. We recognize, first of all, that the underlying drive of things expresses itself in a diversified plurality, an ever-changing, ever-renewed complex of events. Further, the underlying drive is an activity in which novelties incessantly and necessarily emerge; for whatever has already happened makes a difference to each newly born event. This does not mean that the world falls apart into a monadic pluralism. The world-process is one in which the component events so interpenetrate that each influences every other, and it is these influences thus received and felt that constitute the material out of which each nascent event is constructed. The universe, then, is solid enough (there are, strictly speaking, no external relations), but its solidarity is not that of a "block-universe." Rather, it is the ongoing solidarity of a living organism, since an organism is an arrangement of parts whereby each contributes to each, and all mutually modify one another. Moreover, the microcosm as well as the macrocosm is organic: each one of the events that together compose the universe is a tiny organism, too.

"It lies in the nature of things," says Whitehead, "that the many enter into complex unity" (PR 81). He means that the concrete events which are the integral parts of the universe forever and somehow combine to produce a new event that in a very real sense *is* the universe from a particular point of view. Like Leibniz's monad each event mirrors the universe, but unlike that monad, which has *no* windows, the Whiteheadian event is *all* window. Real influences reach it from all the items in the universe. The event, however, is not a mere passive product or reflection of the universe. Each event absorbs the many into itself, but the influences of other events are not the sole factor in deciding what the event is going to be. An event is not the mechanical resultant of many influences; it is the way these influences are *felt* that makes the event what it is. Feeling, we find, is fundamental. In fact, if it were proper to talk about the material of the world, that material would be feeling. Each event is a throb of feeling; it feels the universe, and the way it feels the universe constitutes the whole internal character of the event. The way an event feels the universe is not wholly determined by the character of the universe it feels: it is partly dependent on a free decision of the event itself, an incorrigible determination to take a hand in its own creation.

The event is not an instantaneous, static cross-section of feeling but a microcosmic process involving growth. In the first phase of the growth of an event, influences from the whole universe pour in upon it; or, to put it in another way, the event is born by feeling the many items of the universe that have already come into being. It is born into a phase of confusion and conflict, and it grows by bringing order and sanity into the welter of discordant feelings. The chaos of feelings derived from the world is, by such devices as emphasizing some feelings and subordinating others, contrasting these and combining those, worked up into an integrated and determinate single feeling of the universe. Then the event has fully become, its growth is at an end, and the microcosmic process is completed. It has grown into a stubborn fact of the universe, but by becoming a fact in the world, a something that all succeeding events must take account of, it dies to itself. Its job was to become a definite and determinate individual feeling of the world; once this has been accomplished, its work is over and its life is at an end. From then on it "lives" not for and in itself but only as an influence upon succeeding events. Thus in the internal process of the event the many become one, and then this one is added back to the many and so adds its mite to the complex of influences which are focused on the initial phases of all future events. This flux and reflux of the many and the one is a fundamental metaphysical character of the universe. Thus it has always been, and thus it will always be. God himself cannot tinker with the basic machinery of existence.[12]

To sum up and then proceed: The general metaphysical character of the blind underlying activity is not only that something shall ever go on, but that this something shall be a process whereby (1) many past events become one new event; (2) the one event in turn is added to the many that furnish the material for every other succeeding event; (3) each event is not a mere product of the many but is in a measure active and self-creative. This metaphysical groundwork, it should be noted, would be compatible with an unimaginably pure chaos. We find, however, that events are more or less ordered. Whence comes this order? It cannot be a metaphysical character of the underlying activity, for any type of order is too special, too arbitrary, so to say. Yet order must be in some sense prior to the events, for the events comply with it. We must therefore have recourse to a realm of possibility, for to characterize a thing as determinate is to imply that it has realized a possibility. If, then, there were order in the realm of possibility, if possibilities were themselves linked and graded, we should have a possible explanation of order in the actual world. We could perhaps give plausible reasons for the view that after an event had realized any given possibility, the succeeding event might be obliged to realize a possibility associated with the first possibility. This need not, of course, imply a rigid determinism, for there might be a finite number of alternative possibilities associated with the possibility that is first realized, and succeeding events could, by virtue of their own activity, choose among this set of alternatives. This would allow for freedom within the ordered processes of the universe.

## V

Let us assume that the possibilities are ordered. Then the question becomes, How did they get ordered? We might say that they can be ordered in a logical fashion by their own natures. Thus one might argue that circularity excludes squareness but not redness and one-inch-radiusness; and so on, and so on, until the whole multiplicity of possibilities is ordered into one Great Formula, bits of which are successively realized by events. But this will not do.[13] Circularity does not exclude squareness or anything else. True, an existent circle cannot be square. But a square circle is something, even if it is only a contradiction. We say that a square circle will never be realized so long as our type of geometry prevails; we cannot say that it is not a possibility at all. Indeed, possibilities are perfectly passive and completely inert to one another. They fall together as readily as they fall apart. They can be arranged into stable orders only if they can be compared and contrasted by a mind which can imagine their mutual compatibilities when realized. In a word, it takes a mind, or something very like one, to explore and exploit the real possibilities of the realm of possibility.[14]

Our metaphysical analysis thus leads to God. Before any order could enter the world there must have been some mental power to accomplish a complete ordering of the entire realm of possibility. Such an arrangement of all possibilities into groups and hierarchies must have been the logically primary task of the underlying activity. And it is this complete entertainment of all possibilities, sorted out and arranged in their relationships to whatever actuality might ever occur, that is called the 'Primordial Nature of God'. As in *Science and the Modern World*, God appears as the mediator between the blind actuality-producing world-force and the timeless realm of mere possibility. This mediating function is necessarily a mental one, though we need not attribute consciousness to it. In fact, Whitehead explicitly denies consciousness to the Primordial Nature of God.

God is the "aboriginal creature" of the underlying activity, because he must have been produced before any order could appear. This does not mean that God was created in time. God as "aboriginal" or "primordial" is logically and metaphysically posterior to the underlying activity. There never was a time when God was not. Indeed, time and space are the products of a particular type of order. Dimensionality itself may be only a characteristic of our particular "cosmic epoch"; in an unimaginably distant future, the universe may lose its dimensionality, and an entirely different fundamental type of order may supervene. But even then whatever actuality there is will be the product of the underlying activity patterning itself upon the forms of possibility ideally entertained and ordered in the primordial mind of God.

As primordial, God is timeless and eternal. He is, however, not a mere ideal or a cosmic trend; he is a real fact, just as much as any event. The ultimate reasons for anything, says Whitehead, must be ultimately traceable to something in the actual make-up of a real existent, not to a mere unrealized ideal or to an abstract possibility.[15] The very potentialities of the universe and the ordering of possibilities as relevant to realization in actual happenings must themselves reside in a real existent; they are the reasons for whatever occurs, and all reasons must be somewhere—that is, in an actually existent being. This being is the Primordial Nature of God. The special types of order which are superimposed on the fundamental metaphysical situation stem from God's intellectual grasp of the mutual relationship of possibilities.

In *Science and the Modern World* God as Principle of Concretion selects the types of order which are to be realized; God as primordial in *Process and Reality* creates all types of order whether they will ever be realized or not. But does he choose to impose all the types of order which are in fact imposed? An unconditional affirmative would imply that God is the author of evil, and this must be avoided. It can be avoided if a measure of spontaneity and self-creation is reserved to the other real existents, and this is what the philosophy of organism does. All events by metaphysical necessity are in various degrees self-creative. This postulate may not solve the problem of evil, but it will at least contribute toward a solution.

We must next consider in what way God can impose any order at all on a world made up of self-creative events. The things of the world are made up out of events or, more strictly, out of those minimal events that we might call event-atoms. But these are not "point-instants"; they are microcosmic processes which are the atoms of the macrocosmic process which is the whole sweep of cosmic history. Now, if events are organic processes, if they grow and die, it is not difficult to attribute to them a certain self-activity in the completion of their life work. And if they are self-directive, they must have a goal to aim at; in short, the microcosmic processes must be teleological. Each event aims at becoming just that determinate feeling of the universe which is the end-point of its process.

To attribute feeling, self-direction, and aim to these minute event-atoms that are the ultimate realities has been frequently characterized as the grossest sort of anthropomorphism. The usual defenses (such as the necessity of interpreting the lower in terms of the higher instead of vice versa) can be and have been made. We are not here interested in the elaborate attack and defense of this sector. This animism (if such it is) or panpsychism (which it certainly is) is inseparable from the philosophy of organism. If one cannot stomach panpsychism, one cannot assimilate the philosophy of organism. There are, however, two considerations that perhaps make Whitehead's panpsychism a trifle less unpalatable. The feeling and the teleology and so forth that characterize all events need not be conscious, for consciousness is a peculiar and highly developed mode of feeling that appears only in certain very complex organisms. Then, too, the originality and self-direction of many events are so meager that they are, *practically* speaking, absent. The events that make up a stone, for example, while theoretically self-creative, have little in their behavior that is suggestive of self-direction. For practical purposes we may neglect their spontaneity, and then explain that the stone-events "choose" to continue ever to be stony.[16]

If the most trivial event is a unity of feeling with a purpose, certainly God must be purposive too. He is; his purpose is to introduce the greatest possible amount of value into the cosmic process. Value means intensity of feeling when that intensity is attained by combining harmoniously what at first seem to be incompatible elements. The greatest value, and the highest intensity of feeling, would be present in the mind that could combine into a harmonious feeling all the most violently discordant elements in the world in such a way that they would not clash and kill one another off, but would heighten one another by effective contrast. The universe (because of God) is aimed at the production of values or (as we may as well call it) beauty, the harmonious perfection of feeling in which diversity produces intensity. The cosmic process, then, is in its deepest meaning an aesthetic process. Neither the novelty which is a metaphysical necessity, nor the order which God succeeds in imposing, nor the particular kind of creatures which emerge are ultimately valuable; at best they are a means to the production of that intensity of feeling which is beautiful.

God creates all possible types of order, and all are valuable to the degree that they promote patterned and significant beauty. If God were all-powerful, that is, if he were a metaphysical ultimate, presumably the most perfect type of order would have obtained from the beginning. Plainly this is not the case. God, therefore, is not all-powerful. He cannot repeal fundamental metaphysical laws. Each item in the universe is in its own measure self-creative according to its own internal purpose. It is free, and in exercising its freedom it may run counter to the most valuable types of order. It is the willfulness of the events of the world that frustrates God's Will to Perfect Harmony. Evil may be defined as that which obstructs God's purposes, and its source is in the freedom of the events that make up the world. Whitehead's treatment of the problem of evil requires consideration from several points of view. For the moment, only one observation need be made.

This way of dealing with the problem of evil is, of course, only a more generalized statement of the familiar theological doctrine that moral evil is the necessary result of free will in the creature. To such theological explanations it has been objected that God must have known the frightful consequences that would follow and would have benevolently withheld the curse of freedom. Such an objection would not, however, have any weight as against Whitehead's position, for the freedom of all events was not decreed by God, but is a necessary metaphysical characteristic of all realities. The blame, then, cannot be laid at God's door. We can avoid making him responsible for evil by making him a being subsidiary to the ultimate creative forces. He did not create the metaphysical basis of all being, and he cannot modify it. He, too, has to obey the fundamental rules of the metaphysical game. His aim is to produce the greatest possible harmony and beauty, given the material that he did not create and that he can but partially control. Even when he succeeds in imposing his will, the result is not always a happy one. He does the best he can under the circumstances.

> But if the best be bad, then the ruthlessness of God can be personified as *Atè*, the goddess of mischief. The chaff is burnt. What is inexorable in God is [his aim at producing] actualities with patterned intensity of feeling arising from adjusted contrasts [PR 373–74].

## VI

How can God impose order on a world of free individuals? Some theologians, both amateur and professional, are content to reply that this problem is very mysterious. Whitehead's answer, whether or not it be judged satisfactory, is at least an answer. God, through his imaginative grasp of all combinations of possibilities, must know all possible values, and must know their status in the absolute scale of value. Since his aim is the production of the greatest value, he will, in any given situation, attempt to bring to pass that possibility which he sees to have the highest value possible as the outcome of that situation. He cannot compel the situation to turn out in the way he most desires, for the situation has a will of its own. All God can do is to try to induce the event to adopt as its own the ideal goal he knows to be most valuable under the circumstances.

We must examine more precisely just how it is that God operates on the world. Reality, as we have seen, is fundamentally atomic, and each event-atom in its growth-process is governed partly by efficient and partly by final causation; that is, the event becomes what it is not only by external determinants but also by the fact that it works toward a goal it has chosen. The first phase of the atomic process is the reception into itself of influences from all the rest of the world. These influences force themselves on the nascent event; they are given for it; they are the efficient causation of the world. But the process by which the multiplicity of feelings is synthesized into the unified feeling which is the last stage of the growth is governed by final rather than by efficient causation. Throughout the process the event is guided by an ideal that it proposes to attain. In an event in which imagination is at a minimum, the ideal which it proposes to itself (unconsciously, of course) will be not much more than a reproduction of the material that the world has forced upon it. In this case the event will merely receive the influences, synthesize them in a mechanical fashion by patterning itself upon the preceding event whose influence dominates, thereby becoming a mere copy of the past and a mere vehicle for the efficient causation of the world.

The events that make up what we call non-living matter may be supposed to function in some such way. For such events, the efficient causation from without is nearly the whole story; final causation within non-living events is unoriginative and relatively unimportant. But in other events it is the efficient causation of the world which is relatively unimportant, and the final causation within the event which dominates the growth. In the events that make up a human self, for instance, this is notably the case. The difference between the events that make up a stone and the events that make up me is not that those are "material" and these "psychical," but that the former have as their ideals the mere conformation to and transmission of the past, whereas the latter are able to imagine all sorts of alternatives and choose some of these as directive ideals. In the events that compose the stone, the latter aspect is negligible. The stone stays very much as it is for countless ages, and that means that the chains of events that compose it merely enjoy and transmit a certain definite nature without alteration. If they have alternative ideals, they at least seldom choose them; for the most part they seem perfectly content in their conservatism. But the events that make up high-grade living organisms are not content merely to enjoy and transmit physical influences. The vigor of their imaginations makes them restless, and they forever seek the ideal of which they have had a vision.

Thus, all events have a dual aspect. On the one hand, they receive, enjoy, and pass on the physical causation of the world; on the other hand, under the influence of imaginative ideals, they seek to modify the given physical forces and so shape themselves into something new and different and more valuable. If we take the words in a broad sense, we may call these two aspects of every event the 'physical' and the 'mental'. We must beware, however, of misleading associations, for we do not wish to imply anything like the ordinary naïve dualism of mind and matter. There is a mental side to every stick and stone, and there is, as we shall see, a physical side to God. The distinction is a distinction of reason, for in every actuality the mental and the physical are inseparable. The physical enjoyment of being something and the mental urge to become something else are inextricably bound up together, and each unit of reality is equipped with this duality of nature.

Now, an ideal is a possibility that one proposes to realize. But where did it come from? From the mental activity of the event itself? But this would be impossible if our ideals are to be relevant ideals, that is, ideals really possible for the event to realize. For the event, though it mirrors the world, is too particularized and specialized to be able to know what all the possibilities are. To do that requires a far more powerful mental grasp. Relevant ideals, then, reside in the Primordial Nature of God. In God all possibilities are grouped and ordered, and among these will be found all the possibilities of outcome relevant to any event that will ever arise. Given the first phase of an event, all the possible outcomes are known to God. The number of possible outcomes is limited, for the physical causation that initiates the new event is a stubborn, unalterable fact. One out of all the possible outcomes will bring into being the greatest intensity of feeling and thus be the most valuable from God's point of view. Of course this outcome is the one which God wishes to bring about. He cannot, as we have seen, compel the event to turn out as he wants it to. He can only suggest that it do so. He does this by presenting to the just-born event the ideal outcome that he desires to be realized. Sometimes the nascent event finds the ideal attractive enough to be adopted and used to guide the internal process of becoming to the completion that realizes what both God and the event desire.

God's control over the atomic processes (and through them over the cosmic process) thus depends on his ability to lure the event to cooperation in the production of value. God appeals, we might say, to the event's better nature. He shows it what it might become. We know, also, that appeals to one's better nature are only too often disregarded. In such cases God is thwarted; God proposes, but the event disposes. The event always fashions itself upon an ideal which is ultimately derived from God, but it is not always the most valuable ideal, as ideals do not always seem to attract the event in proportion to their value as God estimates it. If they did, God would always have his way, and he would be responsible for whatever happens, bad as well as good. Yet, the event, even if it rejects God's first proposal, cannot cut itself off from God. If the event rejects the outcome that God proposes to it when it first enters upon its process of growth, God must offer it (reluctantly, perhaps?) other alternatives. An ideal each event must have, even if it be mere conformation to the past; and all ideals come from God.

We have been describing the primary way in which God operates on the world. We may say that in certain realms he has succeeded in overcoming the opposition furnished by the freedom of events, for instance in the realms of geometrical order and physical and chemical law. Or perhaps he is unable to stir these sluggish events to make something more of themselves. Such types of order, no doubt, have a certain value; but the highest values are not attainable merely by dependable functioning. This, I suppose, is God's tragedy. The values he most desires are contingent on the cooperation of creatures with a measure of freedom. He has been able, apparently, to impose his will on electrons and stars, but the result is not very satisfying. His will has been imposed, but only on events in which spontaneity is negligible. Their mentalities are crushed or withered or latent, and without well-developed mentality there is no well-developed value. God, then, must try to win the developed mentalities of the world to himself. This he does by presenting to the event a vision of its ideal potentiality. He spurs the event on to achievement that, by itself, it would never dream of. It is in this sense that God becomes, in a later book, the "Eros of the Universe" [cf. AI 13—eds.] and the "eternal urge of desire."

We have been speaking of God as "presenting" an ideal to a

nascent event, as if he were handing it over wrapped up and neatly addressed. In reality, however, this "presentation" is a metaphysical function, and Whitehead considers it merely an exemplification of a fundamental metaphysical principle. Each event, we have seen, becomes what it is by synthesizing the influences that come to it from all other realities. Now, God's Primordial Nature, though timeless, is aboriginally real. Therefore, each event as it arises must take account of the primordial ordering of all possibilities, which is a stubborn fact just as much as anything else. As soon as an event is born, it must take account of the relevant possibilities, for the possibilities *as relevant* are there to be taken account of. It works automatically, so to speak. We should not think of the Primordial Nature of God as being itself a conscious person. It is true that God has an aim, which is the production of value; it is true that he operates on the world by "presenting" ideals to each process as it arises; yet he is wholly unconscious. The reason for this is that the primordial ordering of all possibility is purely "conceptual" or mental, and Whitehead thinks that consciousness appears only as the result of a complex integration of the mental with the physical.

We shall discuss the physical side of God's nature in a moment; but before we do, it ought to be noted that the Primordial Nature of God, though a much richer conception than the bare Principle of Concretion, is equally unsuitable for religious purposes. God as primordial not only is unconscious and impersonal, but he has no concern for us as individuals.

> He, in his primordial nature, is unmoved by love for this particular, or that particular.... In the foundations of his being, God is indifferent alike to preservation and to novelty. He cares not whether an immediate occasion be old or new, so far as concerns derivation from its ancestry. His aim for it is depth of satisfaction as an intermediate step towards the fulfilment of his own being. His tenderness is directed towards each actual occasion, as it arises [PR 160–61].

That is, he is tender toward it only because it may give him some satisfaction. He does not care anything about individuals, except as they promote intensity of feeling—in him. But then he is unconscious, so presumably there is no moral issue involved. He works automatically in subjection to his inexorable aim at the production of intensity of feeling. Nor does this doctrine of the Primordial Nature of God seem to be a very satisfactory solution to the problem of evil. The problem demands that, if the denial of the existence of evil be ruled out, some sort of explanation be given of how God can be both all-powerful and all-good. God, we have seen, is not all-powerful. But he does not seem to be all-good, either. In fact, there has been offered, so far, no evidence that he is good at all. Goodness can hardly be identified with unconscious predilection for an aesthetic enjoyment which does not count the cost to the rest of the universe.

## VII

But God's nature is not exhausted by its primordial aspect. We have been dealing with his action on the world, and we must now determine the world's action on him. For if we adopt a metaphysical principle which demands that all actualities influence all other actualities, the actual events of the world must necessarily influence God, since he too is actual. The world is a process in time, and God's Primordial Nature (since the ordering of possibilities was done once for all) is timeless and unchanging. Although this nature influences the world, it does not appear that the world could influence it. Instead, we have recourse to another aspect of deity which is called the 'Consequent Nature of God'.

It should be remembered that the distinction of natures in God is one of reason only. God is a unity, and neither side of his nature could exist without the other. We have seen that each event has both mental and physical aspects—physical insofar as it receives and enjoys and transmits the influences of the world, mental insofar as it modifies them in order to realize an ideal possibility. God is no exception to the rule. He is mental, in that his Primordial Nature is a conceptual ordering of all possibilities; he is physical, in that the world influences him, that is, he feels it physically. It is the integration of his mental and physical aspects that produces what is called his 'Consequent Nature'. "[T]he consequent nature is the weaving of God's physical feelings upon his primordial concepts" (PR 524). According to Whitehead's metaphysics, this nature is now "fully conscious"; it undergoes becoming;[17] it changes with the world process.

A significant difference between God and the events of the world is that their processes move in opposite directions. Thus an event of the world begins with the reception of physical causation and is completed by mental functioning derived from God; whereas God is primordially a mental or conceptual ordering of possibility, and he is completed by physical influences derived from the world. God and the World are opposites, but they are contrasted opposites and mutual necessities. This is the fact that Whitehead means to emphasize by such "antitheses" as:

> It is as true to say that the World is immanent in God, as that God is immanent in the World.
>
> It is as true to say that God transcends the World, as that the World transcends God.
>
> It is as true to say that God creates the World, as that the World creates God [PR 528].[18]

Without the world, God would have no physical experience and could not consciously enjoy those triumphs of value which it is his nature to try to produce. Without God to point out the possibilities of value-achievement to each event "The course of creation would be a dead level of ineffectiveness, with all balance and intensity progressively excluded by the cross currents of incompatibility" (PR 377).

The events of the world are received into God's nature. What we have so far said about God's Consequent Nature follows pretty clearly from the metaphysical principles assumed. But such metaphysical grounding is not so evident in what we are about to say concerning the ways in which God's Consequent Nature is supposed to function. In the first place, God does not merely mirror whatever happens. He operates on events in terms of his own nature, which is preoccupied with the production of value. He "saves" the best parts of the world. He lays up in an eternally living and cumulative record all the achievements of value that the temporal world attains. No achieved values are ever lost, although individual values are no doubt constantly being merged in a larger whole that is of greater value. All past values are immediately present in God's experience. If we ask how it is possible that the past shall survive in full immediacy, Whitehead's only suggestion is that it occurs in somewhat the same way a person's past survives not in mere memory but as summed up in the present person (PR 531–32).

But what of the things of the world that are of no value or of negative value? Must these be discarded? To answer this we must determine just exactly what the opposite of value, or negative value, is. Value, we remember, is intensity of feeling arising out of a harmony in which contrasting elements set each other off. The opposite of value must then be either minimum intensity of feeling because there is no contrast (which Whitehead calls triviality of feeling) or a clash of incompatibles that kill each other off. Triviality of feeling is merely a lack of value and is too negative to be called evil; so we may appropriate the term 'evil' to the disharmony which results from "mutual obstructiveness."

For evil in this sense we cannot hold God responsible. Some of the "mutual obstructiveness" of actualities arises from their freedom, and this is metaphysically fundamental. God's Primordial Nature, in trying to lure events to the most valuable outcome possible to the given situation, is doing the best it can in its unconscious, automatic way. Either the blame for evil must lie with the autonomous individuals who refuse to cooperate with God; or, if under certain given conditions a more or less evil outcome is inevitable, there is nothing to blame but the metaphysical character of the underlying activity. And presumably this bare, blind creativity would not much care.

Thus by limiting God's power, by allowing him not an imperative but only a persuasive function, we can clear him of the responsibility for evil. Nevertheless, we have yet to show that he is all-good. A solution to the problem of evil must leave us with a

God who has religious value. Once the evil has occurred, can God do nothing about it but regret it? Certainly it is a reasonable religious demand that somehow evil shall not have the last word. It is all very well that this God saves what is valuable in the world; but what about the presumably large remainder?

Even with the real evils that exist as accomplished facts of the world there is something God can do. It is his Primordial Nature that furnishes his Consequent Nature with this ability. As soon as an evil event in the world is received into God's experience, his Primordial Nature furnishes him with a vision of how such an event may be turned to good account. Though the events of the world have turned aside from the ideal vision that God's Primordial Nature tendered them, and have stubbornly followed their own paths to destructiveness and disharmony, yet the inexhaustible richness of the primordial ordering of possibility suggests a way whereby an actual evil could be transcended—by being used, for instance, as an element in a contrast that would be valuable. Of course the evil is not really transcended in the world, for what is done is done, and God cannot unmake the past. But in the conscious mind of his Consequent Nature, God perceives all the evils in the world not as final but as having added to them their "ideal complements"; that is, he sees them in such a setting that what is itself evil performs a good function and hence helps to make up a valuable whole.[19] God sees

> every actuality for what it can be in such a perfected system—its sufferings, its sorrows, its failures, its triumphs, its immediacies of joy—woven by rightness of feeling into the harmony of the universal feeling. . . . The revolts of destructive evil, purely self-regarding, are dismissed into their triviality of merely individual facts; and yet the good they did achieve in individual joy, in individual sorrow, in the introduction of needed contrast, is yet saved by its relation to the completed whole. The image—and it is but an image—the image under which this operative growth of God's nature is best conceived, is that of a tender care that nothing be lost.
>
> The consequent nature of God is his judgment on the world. He saves the world as it passes into the immediacy of his own life. It is

> the judgment of a tenderness which loses nothing that can be saved. It is also the judgment of a wisdom which uses what in the temporal world is mere wreckage [PR 525].

God's Consequent Nature, therefore, functions in two related ways: it stores up all the achieved values so that none is ever "lost," that is, not present to God's consciousness, and it integrates the achieved evils of the world with their ideal complements into a system in which the evil character disappears as far as God is concerned.[20] Thus God turns the evils of the world to his own good account.

Here a question arises. Are both of these functions of God's Consequent Nature strictly deducible from the metaphysical assumptions? It appears that the answer differs in the two cases. That God must have a Consequent Nature is necessary, and we grant that God, by definition, aims at the production of value. But there seems to be no reason why he is metaphysically constrained to "save" values. On the other hand, it is by metaphysical necessity that God knows the "ideal complement" to all actual evils and can thus transmute them into goods for himself. We shall show that the "saving" function, which is not metaphysically deducible, has far more religious significance than the "idealizing" function, which can be so deduced.

## VIII

It must be admitted that the addition of a Consequent Nature to the Primordial Nature renders Whitehead's God far more "available for religious purposes." God as Primordial was a mere automatic urge toward the creation of value; as Consequent he is also the storehouse of achieved value. That there is in the universe a Being to whose consciousness all valuable happenings are immediately present seems to be a proposition of considerable religious and ethical import. There is, for many, comfort in the belief that whatever is valuable will inevitably be preserved. Perhaps such a belief gives additional reason for sacrificing oneself in combating evil.

Moreover, this preservative function of God is more than a mere record of successes. The successes are felt as immediately present. And the preservation of the past in full immediacy has a profound bearing on what is perhaps deeper than the specific evils that originate in "mutual obstructiveness." For "the ultimate evil in the temporal world is deeper than any specific evil. It lies in the fact that the past fades, that time is a 'perpetual perishing' " (PR 517). Although the manner in which such a thing can come to pass is not explained, it is clear that the beauty of the passing moment is captured by God and that it abides with him in all its intensity through all eternity. The deep poignancy of perishing is not a finality—not for God.

The second function of God's Consequent Nature, that of adding to each actuality an ideal counterpart whereby its value is enhanced in God's experience, does not appear to have, on the face of it, as much religious significance. It is not likely to give anyone much comfort to know that no matter what happens in this world, God can see it in an ideal setting that makes it an enjoyable sight. Anyone with ingenious imagination and little sympathy can conjure up such a setting; but when one of us mortals insists on treating evils in this way his habit is regarded as a peculiarly callous and offensive type of selfish optimism. We can hardly suppose that many will take pleasure in the reflection that God enjoys himself by making mental additions to one's pain and grief and frustration. It is no help for present ills to know that God sees them in such a way that they are valuable for him. That my ill has an ideal counterpart in God does not help me very much as long as I am on earth and God is in heaven. Paralleling my life there may be series of events in God's nature each with its ideal complement and each felt in full immediacy. This series may be very valuable to God, but it is not so to me; he experiences it, but I do not. If this transmutation of evil in God's nature has no religious value, neither does it further the solution to the problem of evil. The affirmation that what is evil for us is not evil for God does not help. For such an affirmation is merely a denial that we experience real evil, and then, of course, the real evil lies in the very fact that what is not really evil appears inexorably so to us.

Still, there is another way in which God's function of providing each event with an ideal counterpart and thus transcending its evil may be of practical and religious importance. God's Consequent Nature, which contains the perfected system in which the transmutation is effected, is after all an item in the universe, and by our metaphysical principles the world must in turn be influenced by it. There is thus a further give and take between God and the world. The actualities of the world are received into God, where they are purified and perfected (as far as possible) by God's vision of an ideal complement. But this integration, though it takes place only in God's mind, is itself a perfectly definite fact of the universe, and by metaphysical necessity the world must take account of it.

> For the perfected actuality passes back into the temporal world, and qualifies this world so that each temporal actuality includes it as an immediate fact of relevant experience. For the kingdom of heaven is with us today. The action . . . is the love of God for the world. It is the particular providence for particular occasions. What is done in the world is transformed into a reality in heaven, and the reality in heaven passes back into the world. By reason of this reciprocal relation, the love in the world passes into the love in heaven, and floods back again into the world. In this sense, God is the great companion —the fellow-sufferer who understands [PR 532].

This influence of God's Consequent Nature on the world is called, in Whitehead's peculiar terminology, the 'Superjective Nature of God'. Unfortunately, the precise mode of its functioning in the world is impossible to determine. Almost all that Whitehead says about it in *Process and Reality* is contained in the passage quoted above. Since such phrases as "particular providence" and "love in heaven" do not appear to be susceptible of technical definition in Whitehead's terms, it is likely that the passage is largely metaphor and that any analysis would be mostly guesswork.[21] The most natural interpretation of this Superjective Nature, however, does not extricate us from the difficulty already noticed: that God's ability to transmute our evils into his goods neither solves the theological problem of evil nor supports a practical faith that man can cooperate with God to eliminate what man himself finds evil.

Three considerations are relevant to the evaluation of God's Superjective functioning. First, because we do not in most or many cases see how that which seems to us incorrigibly evil can be a mere element in greater good, God's Superjective Nature operates successfully only here and there and now and then. Perhaps this unfortunate circumstance is traceable to the limited vision and imagination of most men. No matter; whatever its origin, the evil to us remains evil. At best God's Superjective Nature can at odd times ("particular providences"?) give us no more than a bare inkling of how in his mind my experience of evil becomes a factor in a greater good. Second, suppose I receive such an inkling. What then? Would even a full knowledge of how God disposes of my case and the world's case in his mind make my suffering and the world's suffering any less real? It might be argued that even a partial knowledge of the way my evil can contribute to a greater good will at least stimulate me to work toward that good. Yet the very fact that I had to suffer still remains evil to me. Third, can I be sure that what God considers a greater good would be so in my standard of values? We shall see that this tremendous doubt remains to plague you, con your Whitehead as you will. If God's values are not my values, I shall not rejoice at finding God's love "flooding back again into the world." God's Superjective Nature, then, does little to redeem the deficiencies of his Primordial and Consequent Natures.

## IX

The survey of the nature and functions of Whitehead's God is now complete. This account has already touched upon the possible religious value of such a God. A short summary will be useful before adding a few more suggestions toward a critical estimate of this conception of God.

Whitehead's God, like all other actualities, possesses both a physical and a mental aspect. On his mental side, he is the complete imaginative ordering of all possibilities, arranged in their relevance for all possible occasions. This is his Primordial Nature: finished, static, unconscious spirit. This nature operates on the world by suggesting ideal alternatives to the mental sides of the physical processes that make up the world. In doing so it is obedient to its unconscious aim, which is the promotion of the greatest intensity of harmonious feeling. The growing actualities of the world, however, have wills of their own and are free to reject the ideals offered them. Hence God's power is limited to persuasion. The developing world in turn operates on God, and its influences constitute his physical aspect. We may say that to the purely mental, primordial spirit the world contributes a body and the resultant union of spirit and body is God as a complete individual, conscious, and in direct connection with the events of the evolving world. This is God's Consequent Nature. This side of his nature stores up the values of the world as they arise; and to every negative value it adds an "ideal complement" which changes its sign to positive. This systematic saving and transmutation of the world in God's nature in turn influences the world; though exactly how is left wholly problematic.

In the same way, let us sum up Whitehead's solution to the problem of evil. In general, it is of the type that is supposed to maintain God's goodness at the expense of his power. God is only one element in every situation, and often he cannot control its outcome. The origination of evil is traceable either to metaphysical necessity in general or to the stubbornness and selfishness of temporal self-creative events.[22] But this alone does not constitute a satisfactory answer. We have shown at most that God does not will evil,[23] but we have not shown that God is good—good in any sense resembling that in which a man is good.

This is a vital issue. What evidence have we that God is truly good and that he wishes humanity well? No proof can come from a consideration of his Primordial Nature alone, since this nature is little more than an automatic device for suggesting ideal possibilities of value. This is a useful function, to be sure, if there is to be progressive realization of values, but such unconscious functioning is hardly to be identified with a benevolent God. The view that each event is ideally perfected in God's Consequent Nature, though this follows from the metaphysical assumptions, seems hardly to serve as proof of God's benevolence toward humanity. Such a function merely shows that God is very ingenious in devising ways of enjoying what seems evil to us, and this does not by any means vindicate his moral character.

It is to God's function in conserving achieved values that we must look, if anywhere, for a vindication of his goodness, even though this function is an object of faith rather than a metaphysical necessity. The evidence here is of two sorts. In the first place, if ultimate evil is defined as the "fact of perishing," and if it is declared that this is avoided in God's Consequent Nature, then God has triumphed over ultimate evil. Of course, this is proof achieved by coupling arbitrary definition with unevidenced assertion; but if we grant this we have assurance that God will not suffer ultimate defeat. In the second place, if the values which God stores up are *our* values, then he shows a concern for us that might allow us to call him good in our sense of the word.

Unfortunately, there are several aspects to be taken into account which weaken the force of these considerations to a marked degree. God may triumph over the evil of "perpetual perishing," but this does not alter the fact that, so far as we are concerned, the evil of perishing still exists. For us the ultimate evil is still ultimate. My experience of value may be laid up in heaven for God's eternal contemplation and enjoyment, but that does not help me, any more than the ideal completion whereby my suffering is transmuted into God's enjoyment helps me. In each case it seems that God's feelings alone are considered of importance, and that the actualities of the world can at best be but instruments of God's joy. Thus the individuality of finite things does not seem to count; they are only tiny fragments of a pattern that they cannot ever appreciate. And the poignancy of perishing is precisely that individuality perishes; my achieved individual values may be eternally contemplated by God, but he sees them as part of a system. Their individuality, even for God, has perished and therefore the storehouse of God's Consequent

Nature is no safeguard against the loss of my peculiar values. God can work wonders but I do not think he can merge me and my values into an indefinitely immense system and still claim that I have maintained *my* individuality and my values. Of course, if human values are not fundamentally the same as God's values, they will not be preserved in any case. Then the whole question falls, as there is in that case no possibility of showing that God is good in our sense of the term.

Again, God may, by virtue of the idealizing function of his Consequent Nature, merge me with an ideal complement so that the result is aesthetically satisfactory; but how can *I* enjoy this, and remain anything like myself? Even if I, though existent only in God's mind, retained consciousness in some incomprehensible fashion, would the knowledge that I was part of an effective contrast transmute my suffering for me? I cannot be sure that it would; and if my suffering were changed into joy, I might cease to play my part as material for effective contrast. Whitehead, however, seems to feel that recognition that one is playing a wider role will make one content with one's lot.

> The function of being a means is not disjoined from the function of being an end. The sense of worth beyond itself is immediately enjoyed as an overpowering element in the individual self-attainment. It is in this way that the immediacy of sorrow and pain is transformed into an element of triumph. This is the notion of redemption through suffering, which haunts the world. It is the generalization of its very minor exemplification as the aesthetic value of discords in art [PR 531].

This argument appears to be dubious. Granted that suffering can be redeemed by the good it accomplishes; granted that, if I know this, I may be able to suffer joyfully. But I can do this because I realize suffering to be *only* a means and *not* an end in itself. In other words, the very notion of "redemption through suffering" implies a divorce between suffering as a means and suffering as an end. Indeed, if we follow Whitehead, we can believe that, however bad the evil appears to us, God manages to use it in the construction of something valuable. We can believe that, though for us the experience of value passes, for God it is always immediately present. But this means that we can find, at best, only a vicarious joy in our sufferings and our tragedies. The actual experience of joy is God's, and we can rejoice only because God has it. The obvious but sinister implication is simply this: whatever happens is of no account in itself, since it is valuable only insofar as it contributes an element to God's experience. Such an implication sucks all the vital juices from Whitehead's basic metaphysical contention that every actuality is something for its own sake.

In fine, we may say that Whitehead does not give a satisfactory solution to the problem of evil because he has not shown that God is good in the important sense that he cherishes individuals and their values. In spite of the complicated machinery of God's nature, individual evils are not redeemed. Not even in his Consequent Nature any more than in his Primordial Nature does God care for individuals as such; he is interested only in conserving and producing values that he alone can enjoy. No matter how evil—that is, how ugly—the world is, God somehow manages to utilize it as an aspect of the beautiful picture he is eternally painting for himself. This proves him a divinely skillful painter, but it does not exhibit either human or superhuman benevolence. Whitehead's view of evil is a variant of the old conception that evil is an illusion of our short-sightedness; given the long view and the broad view—God's view—what seems to us evil is really not evil. The inadequacy of such a conception is apparent from the fact that human short-sightedness then becomes ultimate evil. We are not God, nor shall we be. To say that we suffer because we are human is to say that we suffer because we suffer, and this is not a satisfying explanation. We must conclude that Whitehead does not succeed in solving the problem of evil. God does not will the evil, perhaps; but neither is he good in any sense satisfactory to the temporal actualities of the world. But we cannot even be sure that he does not will evil—not as such, to be sure, but incidentally. What is evil to us may appear, by virtue of contrast and synthesis, beautiful to God. Perhaps World Wars are the black spots necessary for the perfection of the divine painting.

If they are, God may have lured us to courses of action that to us are unmitigatedly bad. If this has occurred, perhaps it would be just to refer it to another metaphysical aspect of God—his Diabolic Nature.

X

The reason for this dubiousness about God's moral character lies deep in the philosophy of organism. It is the metaphysical postulate that actual facts are facts of aesthetic experience. Thus feeling or experience (which corresponds to the substance of older philosophies) is not just feeling in general, but feeling for beauty. With this exaltation of aesthetic experience to cosmic significance, two of the famous trio—Truth and Goodness—lose their independent or co-ordinate status, and become valuable only insofar as they contribute to Beauty.

> . . . Beauty is a wider, and more fundamental, notion than Truth. . . . Apart from Beauty, Truth is neither good, nor bad. . . . The real world is good when it is beautiful. . . . The teleology of the Universe is directed to the production of Beauty. . . . Thus Beauty is left as the one aim which by its very nature is self-justifying [AI 341, 344, 345, 341, 342].

All values are then fundamentally aesthetic. This makes it easier to understand why God, overwhelmed with an immense vision of cosmic beauty, is not concerned with our finite sufferings, difficulties, and triumphs—except as material for aesthetic delight. God, we must say definitely, is not primarily good. He does not will the good. He wills the beautiful. Suffering humanity might well call this God's attention to the utterance, made near the close of his life, of a deeply religious man. "When a man honours beauty above goodness," said Plato, "this is nothing else than a literal and total dishonouring of the soul."[24]

A further question is whether such a Cosmic Being can reasonably be called 'God'. It might be argued that a personal, comparatively powerful, non-good being, however aesthetically inclined, does not correspond very closely to any of the usual meanings of the word 'God'. If, however, the use of the term be allowed, the problem of evil is left in an uncomfortable situation. In a sense it is disposed of, for we now have a God who is neither all-powerful nor all-good. No one who takes the problem seriously will consider this a satisfactory disposition of it.

It would be news indeed if Whitehead or anyone else were to supply a fully satisfactory answer to the ancient problem. That Whitehead does not accomplish this does not mean that his conception of God lacks all religious value. One does not have to look far afield for deities whose natures absolutely preclude any sort of reasonable answer to the problem of evil and who yet maintain considerable religious vogue. Whitehead's God promotes value—aesthetic if not moral—in his Primordial Nature and conserves it in his Consequent Nature. It has already been pointed out that the belief that there exists a powerful being who will not permit values to be wholly lost may be of considerable religious importance. All in all, if even some of our values (our aesthetic ones, for instance) are proportionately dear to God, he might be considered as a possible object of religious reverence.

Since Whitehead's God is infinite only in that his Primordial Nature grasps all possibilities, he is on the whole a finite God. That omnipotence is not a necessary attribute of divinity is no longer a novel opinion. Even in certain religious circles there seems to be a growing impression that an Absolute Existence with a set of Absolute Attributes is not a religious conception at all. We cannot say that Whitehead's use of the term 'God' is out of place merely because his God is not an omnipotent creator. As one friendly critic puts it:

> It has been suggested by more than one critic that the use of the term 'God' is not justified by the place which this entity occupies in the system. There is irony in this. For nearly two thousand years theology has invested its intellectual fortunes in the concept of the timeless absolute; and for some three hundred years, beginning especially with Spinoza, much of the best thought of modern meta-

> physicians has tended more and more irresistibly toward the conclusion that this timeless absolute is not the God of religion. . . . Now Whitehead's endeavour has been to eliminate the non-religious aspect from theology. The result, that he is accused of using the religious term with impropriety, is, I say, somewhat amusing.[25]

Whitehead has put God, via his Consequent Nature, in real relations with the world. The world is immanent in him, so that he is truly a "living God"; but at the same time his Primordial Nature, which is unchanging and complete, does justice, continues the critic, "to the motives which led medieval philosophy to exalt the non-emergent or eternal character of the Absolute." Therefore, Whitehead's God should satisfy two main types of religious demand.

That Whitehead's God can satisfy most, or all, religious demands is hardly possible. Something more, however, deserves to be said about the propriety of Whitehead's use of the term 'God'. Consider this protest of a man who is much concerned with what he conceives to be the contemporary loose usage of the word:

> It is . . . interesting to note that, while Professor Whitehead has discarded a great many traditional philosophical terms and has invented a whole new vocabulary to escape misunderstanding, he has seen fit to confuse his readers with perhaps the most equivocal term of all, namely, 'God'.[26]

This argument, though *ad hominem*, seems to have force. In the last book of the great trilogy which is composed of *Science and the Modern World*, *Process and Reality*, and *Adventures of Ideas*, Whitehead almost abandons the use of the term 'God', though he does not explain why he has done this. Nevertheless, the question persists: Is the term 'God' in *Process and Reality* really misleading? Whitehead says that he calls his cosmic being God "because the contemplation of our natures, as enjoying real feelings derived from the timeless source of all order, acquires that 'subjective form' of refreshment and companionship at which religions aim" (PR 47).[27] This leaves it for theologians to decide whether the "timeless source of all order" which is neither omnipotent nor benevolent can furnish men with "refreshment and companionship."

Whatever the verdict of religious sentiment, there remains something to be said from the standpoint of philosophy. In the first place, let us remember that, for reasons already urged, it is hardly doubtful that the Primordial Nature of God, taken by itself, ought not to be called 'God'. In the second place, on Whitehead's own admission, it is only God's Primordial Nature and perhaps the non-religious skeleton of his Consequent Nature that can be reached by philosophical analysis. When we speak of the religious functions of God's Consequent Nature, Whitehead concedes that "There is nothing . . . in the nature of proof. . . . Any cogency of argument entirely depends upon elucidation of somewhat exceptional elements in our conscious experience—those elements which may roughly be classed together as religious and moral intuitions" (PR 521). Such an admission, to be sure, need have nothing to do with the religious value of this God. Yet it leaves one, from a philosophical point of view, in a predicament. The only God that metaphysics can attain to has no religious value and presumably ought not to be called God, whereas the only Being who has a possible right to be called God can be reached only by religious and moral intuitions. Philosophers—or most philosophers—have been taught to view such intuitions with a certain distrust. In other words, when Whitehead is speaking as a philosopher he has no right to the term 'God'. When he speaks of a Being that has any resemblance to the God of the religions, he has explicitly to rely on intuitions. Nor should it be forgotten that the God given in Whitehead's intuitions is only dubiously the God of contemporary religions.

In spite of the careful distinction between God's Primordial Nature and Consequent Nature, the use of the single word 'God' is likely to result in misapprehension. Those who welcome the appearance of the word 'God' will point triumphantly to the fact that a great philosopher has felt it necessary to introduce God into modern rational cosmology. Those who resent the intrusion of the word 'God' will dwell on the equally evident fact that the God Whitehead finds necessary is a desiccated metaphysical principle. Both contentions may be justified by referring to Whitehead's books. But the real philosophical issue is this: Is there any *rational* ground for belief in a God who is "available for religious purposes"? Whitehead's use of a single term to include both what is metaphysically necessary and what is merely suggested by intuition tends to obscure this issue.

The God that Whitehead derives from metaphysical analysis is not the God of religions. Whatever religious value Whitehead's God may have depends on aspects of God that lie beyond reason—aspects that Whitehead either intuits, guesses at, or has faith in. And if this is the upshot, why should not religionists intuit, or guess at, or have faith in a God who is more of a God? For what sort of person is Whitehead's God intended? Both mystic and man in the street will refuse to undergo a long metaphysical agony which does not attain a usable God until supplemented by intuition or religious experience; they will point out that a metaphysically demonstrable God has never been a religious necessity. The philosopher, on the other hand, may not care to rely on intuition, guesswork, and faith. As for those who desire to see the problem of God's existence made clear and precise—these will be either confused or discouraged.

And so the doubt remains: Why does Whitehead, whose fertility in terminological invention is unlimited, insist on using a word that has a great variety of meanings and is, besides, so freighted with an enormous emotional load that its significance can be fathomed only in the depths that lie below language? "[T]he success of language in conveying information," Whitehead has himself remarked, "is vastly over-rated, especially in learned circles" (AI 370).

## NOTES

1. *Proceedings of the Aristotelian Society*, 22 (1921–22), 131.
2. From a review of *Science and the Modern World* in *Nation and Athenaeum*, 39 (1926), 206–207.
3. It seems likely that the puzzlingly inappropriate term 'apocalyptic' in Ely's text is an error for 'apologetic'.—Eds.
4. *Journal of Philosophical Studies*, 2 (1927), 238.
5. *Mind*, N.S. 39 (1930), 475.

6. "The Anti-Copernican Revolution," *Journal of Philosophy*, 26 (1929), 283, 295.

7. O. Martin, in the *Review of Religion*, 3 (1938), 149–60, argues that Whitehead's God cannot possibly serve for the reconstruction of Christian philosophy even though Aubrey, Morrison, and Horton may think so. Traditional Christianity demands a God with "eminent reality," and in this attribute Whitehead's God is deficient.

8. "If it must have a name," says R. B. Braithwaite in a review in *Mind*, N.S. 35 (1926), 499, ". . . the last in Dr. Whitehead's list . . . is the best."

9. For Whitehead's denial see SMW 258. The best statement of the view that he has no right to deny it is in D. J. Moxley's excellent article in the *Proceedings of the Aristotelian Society*, 34 (1933–34), 162.

10. There is also a third ("Superjective") nature of God. Reasons for regarding this element in God as secondary in importance, both for exposition and criticism, will be mentioned later.

11. Except for a few footnotes that are technical and will interest chiefly the adepts.

12. What we have been calling 'events' are the real concrete actualities of the universe. They are organic atoms of feeling; they are born, they grow, they die. After their internal processes (those which result in their becoming a definite, integrated feeling of the world) have ended, the events do not change at all, but merely become items in the world. Now what we ordinarily call events do not appear to behave this way, and perhaps it would have been better to use Whitehead's own term, 'actual occasions'. But to call them 'events' is not, I think, misleading if we remember that they are indeed minimal events. What we usually call 'an event' is a group and succession ("nexus") in space and time of these actual occasions, or event-atoms. The distinction between minimal events and their groupings, though very important in some departments of Whitehead's philosophy, is not one that is significant for our purposes.

13. In *Science and the Modern World* possibilities ("eternal objects") existed as arranged logically. "Accordingly there is a general fact of systematic mutual relatedness which is inherent in the character of possibility. The realm of eternal objects is properly described as a 'realm', because each eternal object has its status in this general systematic complex of mutual relatedness" (SMW 231). This arrangement is treated (see SMW 232) as prior to the general and particular limitations on actuality imposed by God, who chooses which set and succession of eternal objects shall be realized. But in *Process and Reality* this doctrine has been given up. Eternal objects, without God, are only a "multiplicity" which "has no unity derivative *merely* from its various components" (PR 73). The reason why the ordering of eternal objects cannot be merely a fact of the realm of possibilities is that this would violate the "ontological principle" that "everything must be somewhere; and here 'somewhere' means 'some actual entity'. Accordingly the general potentiality of the universe must be somewhere, since it retains its proximate relevance to actual entities for which it is unrealized. This 'proximate relevance' reappears in subsequent concrescence as final causation regulative of the emergence of novelty. This 'some-

where' is the non-temporal actual entity. Thus 'proximate relevance' means 'relevance as in the primordial mind of God'" (PR 73). See also PR 392: "The general relationships of eternal objects to each other . . . are their relationships in God's conceptual realization. Apart from this realization, there is mere isolation indistinguishable from nonentity."

14. If all the orderly aspects of the cosmos depend upon Mind, it is plain that those resentful disciples who have accused Whitehead of betraying their cause to Idealism have good ground for their complaints. For evidence of Whitehead's idealism, see A. E. Murphy, *New World Monthly*, 1 (1930), 81–100.

15. This important postulate is called 'the ontological principle'.

16. Whitehead prefers to speak of the self-direction, etc., that is so prominent in high-grade events as present in a latent state in humbler events. Otherwise he thinks that we run into a dualism that pushes human nature quite out of the natural world. As he says: "But any doctrine which refuses to place human experience outside nature, must find in descriptions of human experience factors which also enter into the descriptions of less specialized natural occurrences. If there be no such factors, then the doctrine of human experience as a fact within nature is mere bluff, founded upon vague phrases whose sole merit is a comforting familiarity" (AI 237).

17. It does not seem to be very clear whether God's consequent nature ought to be described as temporal. Professor H. S. Fries, to whose acute analysis of "The Functions of Whitehead's God" (*Monist*, 46 [1936], 25–58) I am greatly indebted, thinks that although this nature undergoes becoming it is not temporal, and he refers to five passages in support of his view. In the most relevant of these passages Whitehead does indeed say that in the consequent nature of God temporal actuality is "transmuted" into "living, ever-present fact," much as a person *now* sums up his own past (PR 531–32). This means, I think, that the becoming in God's nature, since it is essentially a growing and integrative organization of values, is a cumulative process. It is not temporal in the sense that it is something that becomes and then perishes. But it may well be temporal in a broad sense, just as persons are. Becoming, it seems to me, implies temporality, except in the case of the becoming of the entities that *make* time. The process whereby an actual occasion becomes is not in time, for it grows into a droplet of time. But this cannot very well apply to God, so I do not see how he can escape being temporal in some sense. The objection that time itself may be only a character of our "cosmic epoch" and that God, since he extends over all cosmic epochs, cannot be in time, would apply only to the primordial nature of God; his consequent nature is determined by the events in the world. And if this is given up, I cannot see that his consequent nature is of any use whatsoever, either metaphysically or religiously. There are one or two passages in *Adventures of Ideas* that support this view. The most explicit is: "The everlasting [i.e., consequent] nature of God, which in a sense is non-temporal and in another sense is temporal . . ." (AI 267). Presumably Professor Fries's article was written before this book appeared.

A possible solution is suggested by a phrase in Professor Charles Hartshorne's spirited defense of Whitehead (*Philosophical Review*, 44 [1935], 343): "The differentiation between the primordial nature and the endless series of consequent natures of God. . . ." Apparently his view is that God receives the influences of the world, not so as to modify his consequent nature continuously, but so as to produce an "endless series" of consequent natures. Now, Hartshorne frankly places Whitehead's God in time. This could be avoided, since each consequent nature could be complete and non-temporal, but it would be immediately succeeded by another non-temporal one. Thus God might have a cinematographic illusion of time, but the actual time of the world would not be in him, nor he in it. Against this view there is Whitehead's assertion that the consequent nature of God is ever "incomplete" (PR 524). On the whole, it seems justifiable to assert that God's consequent nature is temporal.

18. In speaking of one of these antitheses Miss [L. Susan] Stebbing remarks: "To one at least the opposition remains a flat contradiction, which reveals the hopeless confusion that lies at the base of the philosophy of organism" (*Proceedings of the Aristotelian Society*, 30 [1929–30], 299).

19. *A fortiori*, the achieved values of the world are enhanced by their "ideal complements."

20. Perhaps not everything is redeemable. Probably there are evils too malignant for God to do much with. One gathers the impression, however, that their number is negligible. Whitehead is not explicit on this point.

21. Nor is any light shed by the later book, *Adventures of Ideas.* In this book God is scarcely mentioned by name. For the phrase 'Primordial Nature of God' Whitehead usually substitutes 'the Eros of the Universe' [e.g., AI 13—eds.]. The last page or two of the book seem to speak of the Consequent Nature of God, which is now termed 'the Unity of Adventure'. I do not think that God's Superjective Nature is referred to at all; but possibly-relevant passages are written in Whitehead's most obscure and prophetic style, and I cannot be sure.

This is perhaps as good a place as any to note that it is suggested by some passages (see AI 322–23, 378–79) that God—presumably as primordial—has an epistemological function not discussed in previous books. It would not be worthwhile to explain Whitehead's complicated epistemology just in order to show how a few hints about God might fit into it, so I shall therefore merely sketch, without comment, what this new function of God seems to be.

In a developing event the first phase is the factual material given to it by the world; this may be called 'reality'. The completed event, since it is the product of the free functioning of the event itself, may be called 'appearance'. Obviously the processes in the event, especially in the higher organisms, transform the given "reality" very greatly; consequently there is a question of whether the completed "appearance" has anything significant in common with "reality." There is no metaphysical guarantee that it should have; and without this, "truth" seems to have little basis, for "truth" involves a conformation of "appearance" to "reality." Whitehead holds that the Primordial Nature of God, as the "Eros" of the universe, may well be characterized by a drive, or general tendency, to make "appearance" emphasize the significant parts of reality without too much distortion, and so make it as true as possible under the circumstances. Thus, the ultimate reason to believe, for instance, that our perceptions are "true" will be faith in the effective activity of the Primordial Nature of God—somewhat as (though Whitehead does not say so) God, in the Cartesian system, vouches for the truth of "clear and distinct" ideas. But in *Process and Reality* Whitehead does not seem to regard such a function of God with favor. See PR 289.

22. Some critics hold that the freedom of actualities is a sham, that God holds the whip hand over every event that occurs. A good case for this view can be made out when God is considered merely as Principle of Concretion as in *Science and the Modern World.* See n. 9 above. But the argument is not so convincing with regard to the elaborated divinity of *Process and Reality.* If the charge is true, then of course God is responsible for whatever happens, and no advance toward a solution of the problem of evil has been made. One thing is clear: Whitehead himself has never intended to create a God who is responsible for whatever happens. No one could speak more emphatically of the error and horror of an omnipotent creator-God. For instance, the belief in such a God is "the fallacy which has infused tragedy into the histories of Christianity and of Mahometanism" (PR 519). For equally strong statements see SMW 258, RM 55, AI 32. The discovery (which Whitehead attributes to Plato) "that the divine element in the world is to be conceived as a persuasive agency and not as a coercive agency" is "one of the greatest intellectual discoveries in the history of religion" (AI 213). All we can say is that if Whitehead's God is really an omnipotent despot, Whitehead has made him so inadvertently; for the author asserts roundly on every possible occasion that his God is not so. Accordingly I have taken seriously Whitehead's repeated assertions that the freedom from external domination that characterizes actual entities is a real freedom. See D. J. Moxley, "The Conception of God in the Philosophy of Whitehead," *Proceedings of the Aristotelian Society*, 34 (1933–34), 162, on this issue.

23. If evil is defined as a frustration of God's purpose, he cannot will evil; but that he may will what is evil to humanity is a possibility and will be mentioned later.

24. Plato, *Laws*, 727D, tr. R. G. Bury.

25. Charles Hartshorne, *Philosophical Review*, 44 (1935), 339–40.

26. Corliss Lamont, *Journal of Religion*, 14 (1934), 414.

27. It is not clear whether the reference is to both natures of God or only to the Consequent Nature.

# 10

# The Ultimacy of Creativity

WILLIAM J. GARLAND
*The University of the South*

## I

WHITEHEAD'S CONCEPT OF CREATIVITY is something of an enigma to most students of his metaphysics. It is generally acknowledged that creativity is an important notion in the development of Whitehead's thought. However, there is widespread disagreement regarding its proper role in his mature metaphysical system.[1] The problem of interpretation is intensified by the fact that Whitehead seems to waver in his own attitude toward the nature of creativity. In *Science and the Modern World* he speaks of creativity as a "substantial activity" which is individualized into a multiplicity of "modes" (SMW 254, 255), each of which corresponds to a single actual entity. This suggests that creativity is somehow more real than the actual entities into which it differentiates itself: it is a substance, whereas actual entities are merely its modes. Whitehead's explicit comparison of creativity with Spinoza's infinite substance, *Deus sive Natura*, lends additional plausibility to such an interpretation.[2] Descriptions of creativity as "substantial" have disappeared altogether by *Religion in the Making*, but creativity still assumes a central role in the metaphysics of Chapter III. It appears there as the first of three "formative elements" which

An earlier version of this chapter appeared in *The Southern Journal of Philosophy* (7 [1969–70], 361–76); as published here it is substantially revised and enlarged. I have profited greatly from critical comments by Milton Fisk, Lewis S. Ford, Charles Hartshorne, Victor Lowe, and Gene Reeves.

enter into the composition of the actual temporal world (RM 90). Thus, Whitehead's early philosophical works lead us to expect that creativity will occupy a pivotal place in a detailed statement of his metaphysical system.

Yet his treatment of creativity takes on a new perspective in *Process and Reality*, Whitehead's *magnum opus* in the field of metaphysics. Creativity retains much of its earlier importance: this is evident from the fact that it appears, along with the notions 'one' and 'many', in the Category of the Ultimate which inaugurates his categoreal scheme. Moreover, Whitehead repeatedly enunciates his earlier claim that a "creative advance into novelty" is the most fundamental feature of the universe (see, e.g., PR 340, 529). Yet he also seems eager to dispel any impression that creativity is somehow more real than the actual entities are. Although Whitehead calls creativity his 'ultimate', it does not have "final" or "eminent" reality in comparison with that of its "accidents," the individual actual entities (PR 11). Instead, these "accidents" or "modes" become the "sheer actualities" of the universe, and it is only in virtue of its embodiment in actual entities that creativity has any actuality at all (PR 10). Unlike Spinoza's God, creativity is not a substance or an "entity" of any kind.[3] Instead, it seems that 'creativity' is simply Whitehead's expression for that most general trait which all actual entities have in common. As he tells us in the categoreal scheme, it is "the universal of universals characterizing ultimate matter of fact" (PR 31). Because each actual entity is *causa sui*, each exhibits the same metaphysical character of being a particular instance of creative activity. Accordingly, the ultimacy of creativity seems to coincide with the ultimacy of the act of "self-creation" by which each actual entity comes into existence (PR 130; cf. AI 303).

These observations give rise to a significant question concerning Whitehead's metaphysics. If creativity is nothing more than a universal characteristic of actual entities, would it not be both possible and desirable to replace the term 'creativity' with the expression 'actual entities' in our most rigorous statements of Whitehead's system? *Prima facie*, such a move seems feasible, and it has been advocated by William Christian in his book and articles on Whitehead. I shall examine Christian's attempt to reduce creativity to actual entities and show why such a reduction is neither possible nor desirable. Then I shall develop an alternative interpretation of creativity which incorporates it in a positive manner into Whitehead's system.

## II

Christian's basic claim is that 'creativity' is a "pre-systematic" term which, for all purposes of "systematic explanation," is superseded by the "systematic" terms that Whitehead introduces in the Categories of Existence, Explanation, and Obligation.[4] By a "systematic" term, Christian means a term which Whitehead uses to expound the metaphysical system that he outlines in his categoreal scheme and its derivative notions (PR, Part I, Chapters 2–3). "Pre-systematic" or "non-systematic" terms are those that merely describe what Whitehead takes as the phenomenological data which his metaphysical system is designed to interpret and explain.[5] This distinction implies that Whitehead's metaphysics is contained within his "systematic" statements and their implications. Thus, we should avoid reference to "non-systematic" terms whenever we are giving a strict account of his philosophy.

Now, since 'creativity' is, according to Christian, a non-systematic term, we cannot use it to *explain* any features of the universe. It is neither a "category of explanation" nor an actual entity which can function as an ontological reason.[6] Christian sees creativity as merely an unanalyzed notion drawn from common sense which itself must be elucidated in terms of systematic concepts. Thus, he claims that "*all that can be said about creativity* can be put into systematic statements about the concrescences of actual entities."[7] If his claim is justified, then in principle we could eliminate the concept of creativity from Whitehead's metaphysics. 'Creativity' could be regarded as merely a shorthand expression for the creative activities of specific actual entities.

Christian's view implies that it is possible to translate statements about creativity into statements about individual actual entities *without loss of meaning.* We must therefore analyze a typical translation to see whether the meaning of the original statement is preserved. For instance, consider Christian's own proposal to replace the statement "Creativity is unending" by the statement "There is an infinite and unending multiplicity of actual entities."[8]

For several reasons, this translation fails to convey adequately Whitehead's doctrine of the creative advance.[9] First, Christian's translation fails to suggest that there are any connective relationships among the actual entities which are the members of this multiplicity. The requirement of an infinite and unending multiplicity of actual entities could be satisfied by a Leibnizian universe in which all actual entities exist in causal independence of one another. In the light of this problem, we must amend Christian's original translation to read, "There is an infinite and unending multiplicity of actual entities which are related through prehensions." Yet even this modified version is unsatisfactory. In particular, it does not tell us that all the actual entities which make up this multiplicity cannot exist contemporaneously with one another. As Whitehead himself points out, "A mere system of mutually prehensive occasions is compatible with the concept of a static timeless world."[10] Thus our amended translation does not express the fact that *novel* actual entities are always coming into being. Yet this is clearly a fundamental claim in Whitehead's doctrine of creativity (see, e.g., PR 31, 339–40).

Now, it could be contended that the term 'unending' already includes the requirement of novelty. On this interpretation, an "unending multiplicity of actual entities" would be one in which any given actual entity both supersedes other actual entities and is itself superseded by novel actual entities. The problem here is that such an interpretation is implicitly ruled out by Christian's principle of translation. The concept of 'supersession' is broader than the concept of 'concrescence', to which Christian insists that all translations be restricted (see n. 7). To say that one actual entity is superseded by another is to say that there is a *transition* from the completion and perishing of the old one to the becoming of the new one.[11]

Yet the concept of 'transition' cannot be expressed solely in terms of the concrescences of individual actual entities, as Christian himself points out in discussing Whitehead's categoreal scheme.[12]

In view of these considerations, we must modify Christian's original rule of translation in the following way. We must change his claim to read, "Any statement about creativity can be translated without loss of meaning into a statement about the concrescences of acual entities *and* the transitions between actual entities." For example, "Creativity is unending" could be replaced by "There is an infinite multiplicity of actual entities such that each member of this multiplicity comes into being through a process of concrescence and then perishes so as to be superseded by and prehended by novel members." Such a translation would appear to express, however awkwardly, Whitehead's doctrine of the ongoingness of time.[13]

Yet we may ask whether even this translation captures *all* that Whitehead intends to express in his doctrine of creativity. Upon analysis, we find that it does tell us that *individual actual entities* engage in creative functionings. Whitehead refers to the concrescence of an actual entity as an activity of "self-creation" (PR 130). When the actual entity completes its experience and "perishes," it passes into its function of what we may term "other-creation" (cf. AI 248) vis-à-vis the actual entities which supersede it. Thus, our translation conveys the doctrine that many different creative activities take place in the universe. Yet if we restrict ourselves, à la Christian, to statements about multiplicities of actual entities, we cannot express Whitehead's further claim that self-creation and other-creation are but two different exemplifications of a *single principle* (viz., creativity). This is the point at which Christian's project of translation must fail.

Consider one of Whitehead's most comprehensive descriptions of the creative advance: "The creativity for a creature [actual entity] becomes the creativity with the creature [actual entity], and thereby passes into another phase of itself. It is now the creativity for a new creature [actual entity]."[14] We could not translate this statement into a statement about individual actual entities without loss of meaning. Such a translation would necessarily sacrifice Whitehead's implicit claim that there is *one creative process* which connects all actual entities with one another.[15] In short, without the concept of creativity, we cannot express Whitehead's doctrine of the *unity* of all creative action in the universe. It is also awkward, though not impossible, to express his doctrine of the ongoingness of time. Thus, we must reject Christian's claim that *all that can be said about creativity* can be expressed in statements about actual entities.

## III

So far, I have argued for a relatively weak claim. Without creativity, we cannot successfully *express* certain Whiteheadian doctrines, such as those of the unity of process and the ongoingness of time. We cannot say all that we want to say (or all that Whitehead wanted to say) about these features of the universe if we restrict ourselves to the language of actual entities. Now I shall develop a stronger and more fundamental claim: creativity can be used to *explain* or to *account for* these very features of the universe which it expresses. Thus, to eliminate creativity would be to rob Whitehead's system of some of its explanatory richness.

This claim gives rise to a significant question concerning methodology. Do the rules of Whitehead's system permit us to use creativity as an explanatory concept? Let me briefly outline the case *against* using creativity in this way. It is incorrect in principle to use creativity to explain any feature of the universe, regardless of how universal and necessary a feature it might be. This is because Whitehead's ontological principle explicitly rules out this type of explanation. According to the ontological principle, only actual entities can serve as reasons for any feature of the world (see PR 36–37, quoted just below). Since explanation is commonly thought to be the giving of reasons, it would follow that only actual entities can play a legitimate role in systematic explanations. But creativity is not an actual entity, nor indeed an entity of any other kind; instead, Whitehead regularly refers to it as a "principle" (see PR 31–32). Thus, we are breaking the rules of Whitehead's system whenever we attempt to explain anything about the world by appealing to creativity. This is an argument which Christian accepts, and it undoubtedly accounts in part for his desire to eliminate creativity from Whitehead's system.[16]

In order to evaluate this objection, we must briefly examine the meaning of the ontological principle. Whitehead states it most precisely in the eighteenth Category of Explanation:

> That every condition to which the process of becoming conforms in any particular instance, has its reason *either* in the character of some actual entity in the actual world of that concrescence, *or* in the character of the subject which is in process of concrescence. This category of explanation is termed the 'ontological principle'. It could also be termed the 'principle of efficient, and final, causation'. This ontological principle means that actual entities are the only *reasons*; so that to search for a *reason* is to search for one or more actual entities [PR 36–37, Category of Explanation 18, in part].

Now, I take this to be essentially an empiricist principle. Whitehead elsewhere describes actual entities as the "final facts" in the world (PR 28), and here he says that actual entities are the only reasons. It follows that the only reasons for what happens are facts; all of our explanations must be grounded on the stubborn, irreducible facts of reality. Explanations given by citing principles are implicitly ruled out by the ontological principle.

That Whitehead is committed to the ontological principle is beyond serious question. This is clear from the emphatic way in which he repeatedly states it in *Process and Reality* (see, e.g., PR 28, 64, 73). It alone, among the Categories of Explanation, is singled out for special mention in the section immediately preceding the categoreal scheme in Part I, Chapter 2. Yet it is not quite as clear what the *scope* of the ontological principle should be. Does it rule out all possible explanations in terms of principles? I shall argue that it does not; there is one, but only one, explanatory principle that lies beyond the scope of the ontological principle. This, I contend, is the principle of creativity. Yet it cannot be said that Whitehead himself gives a clear and decisive statement in favor of my position on this topic. Indeed, the textual evidence seems to favor Christian's implicit claim that the scope of the ontological principle is unrestricted. Nonetheless, I plan to develop systematic arguments for adopting my position and not Christian's. Here I am appealing to one of Christian's own rules of interpretation: to ask what Whitehead's principles permit is not the same as to ask what Whitehead thought, or explicitly stated, that they permit.[17]

It is my contention that Whitehead operates with an implicit distinction between two fundamentally different kinds of explanation. The first kind is governed by the ontological principle, but the second kind is not. The first kind is what I shall term 'ordinary explanation'; it is explanation in which we cite specific actual entities as reasons.

There are two kinds of actual entities which we may cite in ordinary explanations—actual occasions and God. Whitehead expresses the difference between citing actual occasions as reasons and citing God as a reason this way:

> . . . the reasons for things are always to be found in the composite nature of definite actual entities—in the nature of God for reasons of the highest absoluteness, and in the nature of definite temporal actual entities for reasons which refer to a particular environment [PR 28].

Accordingly, I shall distinguish two types of ordinary explanations —"specific explanation" and "generic explanation." Actual occasions should be cited when we are giving specific explanations, while God's primordial decision should be cited when we are giving generic explanations.[18]

For example, suppose the question is raised for Whitehead, "Why does a certain actual occasion (say *A*) have the particular, contingent characteristics that it does (say *X*, *Y*, and *Z*)?" The proper reply would be to cite specific actual entities and to show precisely how they function to produce *X*, *Y*, and *Z* in *A*. These actual entities would be the actual entities in *A*'s causal past, God, and *A* itself, insofar as it serves as its "own cause" in virtue of its subjective aim. This is how we would go about explaining, for example, why *A* has a great deal of conceptual originality. We would show—to begin with the rough outlines of such an explanation—that *A* is a member of an entirely living nexus of some high-grade living society rather than being a member of some low-grade inorganic society. Note that "specific explanation" will always take the form of citing certain specific causes for the characteristics in some "particular instance" of concrescence, such as *A*, and that it will obey the ontological principle. Note also that specific explanation is a limited type of explanation. It makes no attempt to account for the generic features that *A* shares with all other actual entities; it attempts only to account for those features wherein *A* differs from at least some other actual entities.

The second type of ordinary explanation I distinguish is "generic explanation." In generic explanations, we want to explain features which all actual entities have in common. Here the proper reason to cite is God's primordial decision. Whitehead says that God's primordial nature "constitutes the metaphysical stability whereby the actual process exemplifies general principles of metaphysics, and attains the ends proper to specific types of emergent order" (PR 64). For God's "conceptual actuality at once exemplifies and establishes the categoreal conditions" (PR 522). God accounts for the generic features shared by all actual entities.

For example, suppose the question is raised for Whitehead, "Why do all actual occasions obey the nine Categoreal Obligations in their processes of concrescence?" The proper answer would be that God established these Categoreal Obligations in his primordial decision, and that every subsequent actual entity must be influenced by this decision (see PR 378). In this way, God accounts for the "metaphysical stability" of the universe.

Now I want to claim that Whitehead implicitly recognizes another legitimate type of explanation, although he never explicitly claims to be doing so. This is the type I intend to call (I hope without begging the question) 'ultimate explanation'. It appeals to the principle of creativity and not to specific actual entities; as such, it goes beyond the scope of the ontological principle. Perhaps a few examples will serve to clarify my meaning.

Suppose we are not simply asking for an account of the presence of certain specific features in some particular actual entity, and suppose we are not even asking for an account of the presence of certain generic features in all actual entities. Instead, suppose we are looking for some explanation of some all-pervasive feature of reality. For example, let us ask why it is that temporal ongoingness characterizes the universe. To translate this question into Whitehead's language, Why do new actual entities continually come into existence?

There is a generic explanation which we could put forward in response to this question, one which preserves the ontological principle by referring to God. We could appeal to God's subjective aim for satisfaction, and then we could show how temporal process is necessary to fulfill that subjective aim. Christian himself constructs the beginnings of such an explanation.[19]

Yet this generic explanation might also give rise to further, more fundamental questions. Why do God and the other actual entities aim at satisfaction? Can we give a more ultimate reason for the everlastingness of process, one that accounts for process in God as well as for process in the finite actual entities? Now I contend that we can provide such an ultimate explanation, and that we can do so by appealing to creativity. The subjective aim of any actual entity, including God, is a particular manifestation of the creative drive in the universe toward the unification of diversity. This unification, once achieved, results in the satisfaction of the entity in question. Thus, God aims at satisfaction because he, like all other actual entities, is a particular instance of the principle of creativity. A more detailed account of the ongoingness of time, but one which from the beginning avoids the appeal to God, will be provided in Section IV below.

Take another example. Suppose we ask why there is causal relatedness in the world. Why is it that the past influences the present? To translate this question into Whitehead's language, Why must each new actual entity prehend its predecessors? Here again we can give a generic explanation, one which appeals to God as the ground for the givenness of the past. A new actual entity must prehend its predecessors because God prehends all past actual entities, and the new actual entity must prehend God at the beginning of its concrescence.[20]

But suppose we then raise a more fundamental question. Why is it that any actual entity, including God, prehends other actual entities? What is it about the universe that accounts for the presence of these bonds of relatedness that connect actual entities with one another? I would claim that an ultimate explanation of relatedness can be given by appealing to creativity. Actual entities prehend their predecessors because they are all linked together as the particular "creatures" of a single creative process. A more detailed explanation of prehensive relatedness, but one which avoids the appeal to God, will also be provided in Section IV below.

I shall argue that ultimate explanations are both possible and meaningful within Whitehead's system, but first we must consider certain restrictions that apply to the construction of such explanations.

First, *all* explanation, whether ultimate explanation or ordinary explanation, is inherently limited in that it presupposes that something is *there to be explained* (see PR 67–68; cf. SMW 256–58). Thus, the question of why there is anything at all has no legitimate answer for Whitehead; it should be ruled out from the beginning as a pseudo-question.[21]

Second, no explanation can be given for the fact that creativity is Whitehead's ultimate explanatory principle. It just *is*, that is all. In fact, this is part of what we *mean* when we say that it is his *ultimate* principle. Here we see that there is also an upper limit to explanation. Whitehead uses expressions such as "*It lies in the nature of things* that the many enter into complex unity" (PR 31, italics added) to indicate that our attempts at explanation must end here. He also remarks at the end of the Category of the Ultimate, "The sole appeal is to intuition" (PR 32).[22]

Third, we should notice that ultimate explanation in terms of creativity is in certain respects a very limited type of explanation. It must never serve as a facile substitute for ordinary explanation. Instead, it should only be brought into play after we have exhausted all the specific and generic explanations at our disposal. Thus, it would be illegitimate, for example, to appeal to creativity to account for the fact that a certain actual entity has certain contingent characteristics. Here we must give a specific explanation, which is by far the most *usual* type of explanation in Whitehead's system. Thus, ultimate explanation by its very nature is appropriate only in rare cases, cases in which we are asking about the all-pervasive features of reality.

Let me now defend the legitimacy of ultimate explanations in terms of creativity. My first argument is a straightforward appeal to Whitehead's writings. From time to time, Whitehead actually does appeal to creativity as the explanation for certain very general features of the universe. For example, he refers to creativity as "the reason for the temporal character of the actual world" (RM 91). In other passages he speaks of creativity as the reason both for the becoming of each new actual entity (concrescence)[23] and for the supersession of one actual entity by others (transition).[24] Either Whitehead is simply being careless in these passages or he is implicitly granting a legitimate explanatory role to creativity. I opt for the second alternative in light of the more fundamental considerations which follow.

My second argument appeals to the place of creativity in the categoreal scheme. Creativity is the fundamental principle set forth in Whitehead's Category of the Ultimate, which precedes the other three types of categories. Whitehead says that this initial category "expresses the general principle *presupposed* in the three more special categories" of existence, explanation, and obligation (PR 31, italics added). This general principle is creativity, and it is a presupposition of all the more special principles. Thus the ontological principle, which is the methodological rule governing the categories of explanation and obligation, is logically subordinate to the principle of creativity.

Similar considerations will show us that creativity is presupposed by the concept of an actual entity. Creativity itself is not an entity, but it is one of the ultimate notions "involved in the *meaning*" of the term 'entity' (PR 31, italics added). There can be no entities, no existence, in abstraction from the creative process (see PR 321, 324); if we should deny this doctrine, Whitehead would accuse us of committing the "Fallacy of Misplaced Concreteness" (see SMW 74–77, 84–86). Likewise, creativity is the notion of "highest generality *at the base of actuality*" (PR 47, italics added), even though it is not one of the specific actual entities which make up the realm of actuality. Indeed, Whitehead sometimes refers to actual entities, God included, as the "creatures" produced by creativity in its never-ending thrust toward novelty (see, e.g., PR 47, 135). All actual entities, he tells us, are "in the grip of the ultimate metaphysical ground, the creative advance into novelty" (PR 529).

My last two arguments cite the pragmatic or "heuristic" value of allowing a legitimate explanatory role to creativity. It is my contention, to be illustrated in Section IV below, that ultimate explanations in terms of creativity can illuminate certain otherwise puzzling features of the universe. Appealing to creativity at certain crucial points helps us to make process more intelligible, and *this*, in the final analysis, is what Whitehead's metaphysics is all about.[25] For this reason, I would claim that ultimate explanations in terms of creativity are self-justifying; they do the job of explaining certain very general features of reality.

Finally, Whitehead's system achieves greater coherence if we allow an explanatory role to creativity as well as to actual entities. Here I am using the term 'coherence' in Whitehead's sense: it means that the fundamental concepts of a metaphysical system are so interrelated that they cannot be meaningfully separated from one another (see PR 5, 9). Whitehead himself explicitly applies this doctrine of coherence to creativity and the actual entities:

> But of course, there is no meaning to 'creativity' apart from its "creatures," and no meaning to 'God' apart from the creativity and the "temporal creatures," and no meaning to the temporal creatures apart from "creativity" and "God" [PR 344].

My analysis preserves this coherence in Whitehead's system, whereas Christian's analysis does not. While he wants to reduce principles to entities, my distinctions allow us to see entities and principles in their proper relationship to one another.

Here I should make one point clear. I am not claiming that creativity is somehow *more real* than actual entities are. Although it is Whitehead's ultimate principle, it must always be instantiated in specific actual entities; it has no independent reality of its own. This is what I take to be Whitehead's meaning when he says that creativity is actual only in virtue of its accidents, i.e., the actual entities (PR 10; cf. PR 339). Yet I would also assert the converse doctrine. Actual entities cannot exist except as instances of creativity; they cannot be meaningfully separated from the ultimate metaphysical principle. Indeed, Whitehead explicitly asserts that "no entity can be divorced from the notion of creativity" (PR 324; cf. PR 321–22). Neither creativity nor actual entities can be reduced to one another. Instead, taken together, they exemplify the metaphysical coherence that Whitehead values so highly.[26]

The major flaw in Christian's analysis lies in his necessarily abortive attempt to bring creativity down to the same level as Whitehead's specific entities and categories for the sake of systematic tidiness. Creativity plays a comprehensive role in Whitehead's system which cannot be expressed as a function of the roles played by any of the more limited elements. Whitehead himself admits that it is ultimately impossible to define creativity or to explain it in terms of any more specific concepts (SMW 255; PR 30, 47). We can know what creativity is only by imaginatively generalizing from our direct experience of creative energy in our own lives. Hence, Whitehead remarks at the end of his discussion of the Category of the Ultimate, "The sole appeal is to intuition" (PR 32), which for him must be the final arbiter of philosophical questions.

Yet the fact that creativity cannot be specified or defined makes it no less important as the ultimate principle which binds together all that is specific and definable.

## IV

I shall now present a positive interpretation of creativity as Whitehead's ultimate metaphysical principle, one which accounts for both the ongoingness of time and the connectedness which obtains in the universe. This interpretation is designed to overcome the inadequacies of Christian's reductive account by showing how creativity can play a legitimate explanatory role in Whitehead's metaphysics.

The notion of process or flux is the basic intuition drawn from human experience which Whitehead intends to elucidate in his metaphysical system. His constant aim in his writings is to "take time seriously."[27] In his systematic analysis of temporality, Whitehead distinguishes between two different kinds of process which take place in the universe (PR 320–23, 326–28). One kind of flux is "concrescence" or "microscopic process," which signifies the way in which a new actual entity comes into being. During concrescence, the new actual entity constructs a determinate experience for itself out of the data it receives from the past. The other type of fluency is "transition" or "macroscopic process." This term designates the movement from the completion of old actual entities to the coming-into-being of new ones. By means of transition, the determinate actual entities of the past become the data for new processes of concrescence. It is my contention that both concrescence and transition can be seen as complementary aspects of creativity, which is the ultimate principle behind all process. If my claim here is justified, then there is indeed a way in which creativity can be used to explain both novelty and unity in the universe.

It is clear that Whitehead regards creativity as the ultimate principle behind concrescence. In his account of creativity in the Category of the Ultimate he says:

> It is that ultimate principle by which the many, which are the universe disjunctively, become the one actual occasion, which is the universe conjunctively. It lies in the nature of things that the many enter into complex unity [PR 31].

Now, concrescence is the growing together of many entities into a complex unity of experience, which is a new actual entity in its role as an immediate subject. This is clear from Whitehead's remarks about concrescence in the second Category of Explanation (PR 33). But creativity, as the principle of novelty (PR 31), serves as the ontological ground of this "production of novel togetherness," which Whitehead singles out as "the ultimate notion embodied in the term 'concrescence' " (PR 32). Thus, one role of creativity is that of an "underlying activity of realisation" (SMW 102) which individualizes itself into many specific instances of creative action. Each of these instances is the concrescence of a particular actual entity. In this way, Whitehead's concept of creativity faithfully reflects the sense of the Latin verb *creare*, "to bring forth, beget, produce" (PR 324). The creative energy of the universe is constantly bringing forth new actual entities which synthesize in their own experience the many previous entities.

Yet I contend that creativity plays another role in Whitehead's system in addition to its role as the ultimate ground of concrescence. As well as being the principle behind all particular acts of self-creation, creativity also serves as a receptacle for the products of these activities. Creativity is not activity alone, but "the pure notion of the activity *conditioned by the objective immortality of the actual world*" (PR 46–47, italics added).[28] In fact, it is the very function of actual entities, in their role as objectively immortal "superjects,"[29] to "constitute the shifting character of creativity" (PR 47; cf. 129–30, 249, 344). Thus, Whitehead's doctrine that creativity characterizes actuality (PR 31) must be balanced against his doctrine that actuality characterizes creativity.[30] Since it is completely indeterminate ("protean") in itself (RM 92), creativity can act as a perfect receptacle for the determinate outcomes of all particular acts of becoming. It cannot alter these past actual entities or impose its own features upon them, for it is free from all characteristics of its own. In this sense, we may compare creativity both with Plato's Receptacle and with Aristotle's prime matter.[31] The main difference is that we cannot think of creativity as *passively* receiving the past; creativity is always a principle of *activity* (see PR 46–47, AI 230–31). Once it receives the completed superjects, it passes them on as data to be synthesized through new processes of concrescence. In receiving the past, it also provides the data for the present. Thus, creativity explains the *transition* from the completion of old actual entities to the becoming of new ones.[32]

Passages from Whitehead's writings indicate that creativity is the principle behind the transition between actual entities as well as the principle behind the concrescence of actual entities. For example, he explicitly says:

> The creativity in virtue of which any relative complete actual world is, by the nature of things, the datum for a new concrescence, is termed 'transition' [PR 322].

It should be noted that transition is just as important an aspect of the creative process as is concrescence. This point is sometimes overlooked because Whitehead discusses concrescence much more than he discusses transition. Also, he sometimes uses non-technical expressions, such as 'passing over' or 'passing on', to describe the transition phase of process:

> The process of concrescence terminates with the attainment of a fully *determinate* "satisfaction"; and the creativity thereby passes over into the "given" primary phase for the concrescence of other actual entities [PR 130; cf. PR 324].

Yet the absence of any detailed treatment of transition must not obscure its basic importance to Whitehead's doctrine of temporal ongoingness. Transition processes must occur if we are to have any new processes of concrescence, for the past must be transcended in order for novel actual entities to arise.[33] Thus, we cannot separate concrescence from transition in our full descriptions of the creative advance. During concrescence, creativity is immanent in the particular actual entity which is then coming-into-being, while in transition the individual occasion is "transcended by the creativity which it qualifies" (PR 135). Accordingly, there is a constant rhythm in the creative process as it swings back and forth between concrescence and transition.[34]

This reciprocation between the two phases of the creative process gives the ultimate explanation for the ongoingness of time promised in Section III. In concrescence, creativity moves forward from an initially indeterminate phase containing a welter of unsynthesized data to a final determinate synthesis of these data (see PR 34, 38–39). Whitehead speaks of this final synthesis as the "satisfaction" of the creative process on that occasion (PR 38, 39). In transition, creativity receives the actual entities which have already achieved satisfaction and gives them to new actual entities as initial data which again demand unification. Accordingly, a basic feature of the realm of actual entities is its radical incompletability.[35] Individual actual entities achieve completeness as "microscopic" processes, but the universe as a whole ("macroscopically") must always be regarded as "an incompletion in process of production" (PR 327). Creativity, *qua* the principle behind transition, is constantly turning the product of one concrescence into a datum for the next one. Thus, the world of settled, determinate actual entities is always being transcended by new actual entities aiming at new satisfactions. As Whitehead vividly puts it in *Adventures of Ideas*:

> The creativity of the world is the throbbing emotion of the past hurling itself into a new transcendent fact. It is the flying dart, of which Lucretius speaks, hurled beyond the bounds of the world [AI 227].

Whitehead's doctrine of creativity constitutes an emphatic rejection of any ontological version of Occam's razor. As the principle of productivity, creativity is forever multiplying entities beyond all bounds of past necessity.

As Sherburne points out, the two-fold nature of the creative advance can be succinctly expressed in terms of 'one' and 'many', the two notions that appear in the Category of the Ultimate along with creativity.[36] In the concrescent phase of the creative process, the "many" entities in the universe at that moment become "one" through their synthesis in a new actual entity. There is thereby an advance from "disjunctive diversity" to "conjunctive" unity (PR 31). Yet the final product of concrescence is a new actual entity, which adds to the "many" entities from which this process began. There is thereby a transition from conjunction to disjunction again. Consequently, Whitehead's ultimate description of the creative advance is necessarily a dual one: "The many [entities] become one [entity], and are increased by one [entity]" (PR 32). The first clause of this statement expresses the concrescence from disjunction to conjunction, while the second clause expresses the transition from conjunction back to disjunction. Since we now have another disjunction of "many" entities, the stage is set for the creative process to repeat its rhythmic cycle. It is through this basic structural pattern that creativity drives the universe forward.

Let us now indicate how creativity can give us an ultimate explanation of the unity and relatedness in the world. I claim that there are at least two senses in which creativity accounts for the unity of the universe. First, it serves as the world's "formal" principle of unity, in that each individual actual entity is ultimately describable as a concrete instance of self-creative activity (see PR 38, 321–22). All actual entities share the common property of coming into existence through a process of concrescence. They all exemplify the generic metaphysical characteristic of synthetic activity. Accordingly, Whitehead says, "The process of creation is the form of unity of the universe" (AI 231). Yet second, and most important, our preceding analysis shows that creativity is also the "material" as well as the "formal" principle of the world's unity.[37] It is not only the "universal of universals characterizing ultimate matter of fact" (PR 31), but also "the ultimate behind all forms [i.e., universals], inexplicable by forms, and conditioned by its creatures" (PR 30). In its role as the principle behind transition, creativity acts as a receptacle for all actual entities which have already attained satisfaction. It also gives these past actual entities to each new actual entity as the initial data for its act of self-formation. Creativity therefore links the past with the present as it urges the universe forward into the future.[38] In this respect, we may fruitfully compare creativity with Spinoza's one infinite substance.[39] Like the God of Spinoza, Whitehead's creativity is that ultimate principle through which the "obvious solidarity" of the world receives metaphysical elucidation (PR 10).[40] All actual entities are related to their predecessors, as asserted in Whitehead's "principle of relativity" (PR 33, 79–80), because there is but one creative process from which they all arise and to which they all make their final contributions. In this way, we can give an ultimate account (as promised in Section III above) of the presence of bonds of prehensive relatedness in the universe.

We have shown that Whitehead's principle of creativity can provide ultimate explanations for both the ongoingness of time and the prehensive relatedness of the world. It should be noted that, if we combine these two accounts, we obtain an ultimate explanation of the two features of actual entities which permit them to function as reasons in ordinary explanations (see Section III above). According to Whitehead's ontological principle, an actual entity may function in an ordinary explanation in two and only two ways: either it may act as an efficient cause of the characteristics of the actual entity in question, or it may act as the final cause of these characteristics (see PR 36–37, discussed in Section III above).

Yet the principle of creativity provides an ultimate explanation for the presence of both efficient causality and final causality in the world. There is efficient causality because creativity gives past actual entities to present ones in its role as the principle behind transition. A new actual entity must therefore begin its concrescence by prehending all the previous actual entities in its actual world. There is final causality because of the unceasing creative drive in the universe toward the unification of what is diverse. This drive manifests itself in the subjective aim at satisfaction which is inherent in the concrescence of each actual entity (see PR 41–44, 228–29). Efficient causality thus makes its appearance in processes of transition, while final causality makes its appearance in processes of concrescence (see PR 44, 320, 326–27, 423). Yet creativity is the principle behind both transition and concrescence; it is the ultimate metaphysical ground of *all* process in the world. Accordingly, creativity explains how it is that actual entities can exhibit the two types of causality which make it possible for them to be cited as reasons under the ontological principle. This is perhaps the "ultimate" in ultimate explanations.

## V

I conclude with some of my own speculations concerning the rationale behind Whitehead's choice of creativity as the ultimate principle in his metaphysics. Whitehead wants his metaphysical system to do justice to as many aspects of experience as possible. Yet experience presents us with a basic contrast at the most general level. On the one hand, it exhibits order and structure, which we can understand rationally. On the other hand, it presents process and change, which we constantly live through but which defy our attempts to divest them of their mystery and irrationality. By putting creativity into his Category of the Ultimate, Whitehead is able to acknowledge, on a very basic level, the presence of the mysterious, process-like features of existence. He is also able to provide an account of the ultimate structural patterns through which process manifests itself (see Section IV above). Having made the decision to place creativity at the center of his metaphysics, he then goes on to set down tables of entities and ontological categories to deal with the more specific structural features of the world.

Unfortunately, this way of doing metaphysics has at least an expository disadvantage. It gives *Process and Reality* the appearance of developing an abstract system of unfamiliar concepts which has little relevance to the rough-and-tumble realities of human existence. Yet such an impression is readily dispelled when we recognize the fundamental importance of creativity in Whitehead's metaphysical framework. Over and against all *entities*, which form the determinate referents of rational thought, there stands a dynamic creative *activity* which by its very nature can never be captured in the static net of conceptual definition. Although this activity works *through* entities to drive the universe forward, it can never be reduced to any set of these entities. Instead, they remain the "creatures" it produces in its never-ending thrust toward novelty-*cum*-relatedness. Of course, it would be equally wrong-headed to reduce entities to inferior "modes" of creativity, à la Spinoza. In the final analysis, we must say with Whitehead, "Process and individuality require each other" (MT 133; cf. MT 131). Creativity is needed to bring entities into concrete existence, while entities are needed to give form and definiteness to the amorphous flux of creative activity. Moreover, we need both factors in our metaphysics in order to account for both the rational structure and the non-rational process that we find in experience. A major virtue of Whitehead is his stubborn refusal to submit to the philosopher's temptation to stress one of these features of experience at the expense of the other.

Here we are brought back to Whitehead's ideal of coherence in metaphysics. I would claim that this methodological ideal has an ontological basis for Whitehead. It directs us to construct our systems of thought so that they faithfully reflect the paradoxical unity of fundamental opposites in the world (see especially Part V of *Process and Reality*). The coherence of our concepts must finally be grounded on the coherence of the ultimate features of reality, such as the features of structure (form) and process (flux) discussed above.[41] Yet both kinds of coherence are greatly endangered by all attempts to eliminate creativity from Whitehead's metaphysical system. Creativity is neither a superfluous notion nor a "pre-systematic" concept reducible to systematic ones. Rather, it embodies that "novel intuition"[42] which lies at the heart of Whitehead's process philosophy.

## NOTES

1. For example, compare the diverse interpretations proposed by Ivor Leclerc in *Whitehead's Metaphysics: An Introductory Exposition* (London: Allen and Unwin; New York: Macmillan, 1958; rpt., Bloomington: Indiana University Press, 1975), William A. Christian in *An Interpretation of Whitehead's Metaphysics* (New Haven: Yale University Press, 1959), Donald W. Sherburne in

*A Whiteheadian Aesthetic* (New Haven: Yale University Press, 1961), Victor Lowe in *Understanding Whitehead* (Baltimore: Johns Hopkins University Press, 1962), John B. Cobb, Jr., in *A Christian Natural Theology* (Philadelphia: Westminster, 1965), and Edward Pols in *Whitehead's Metaphysics: A Critical Examination of* PROCESS AND REALITY (Carbondale: Southern Illinois University Press, 1967). Even more variety appears if we take into account the articles and discussions in which references to creativity occur.

2. See SMW 102–103, 181, 255. Whitehead does not yet use the term 'creativity' in *Science and the Modern World*, but it is clear that his notion of an underlying "substantial activity" is the notion which he calls 'creativity' in *Religion in the Making*.

3. All "entities" must be specific instances of one of Whitehead's eight Categories of Existence (see PR 31), and creativity does not fit into this classification. The fact that creativity is not an entity shows that it cannot be an eternal object, despite the insistence of A. H. Johnson to the contrary. For Johnson's views on this topic, and for his evidence that Whitehead raised no objections to these views, see his *Whitehead's Theory of Reality* (Boston: Beacon, 1952; rpt., New York: Dover, 1962), pp. 69–72, 214–23, and "Whitehead as Teacher and Philosopher," *Philosophy and Phenomenological Research*, 29 (1969), 351–76. An edited version of the latter essay appears in the present volume as "Some Conversations with Whitehead Concerning God and Creativity," Chapter 1.

4. See William A. Christian, "The Concept of God as a Derivative Notion," *Process and Divinity: Philosophical Essays presented to Charles Hartshorne*, edd. William L. Reese and Eugene Freeman (LaSalle, Ill.: Open Court, 1964), pp. 182–84. Christian first enunciates this claim in the nineteenth footnote of his "Some Uses of Reason," *The Relevance of Whitehead*, ed. Ivor Leclerc (London: Allen and Unwin; New York: Macmillan, 1961), pp. 80–81.

5. "The Concept of God as a Derivative Notion," *loc. cit.* For a full account of this distinction, see Christian's "Some Uses of Reason," pp. 74–80, and "Whitehead's Explanation of the Past," *Alfred North Whitehead: Essays on His Philosophy*, ed. George L. Kline (Englewood Cliffs: Prentice-Hall, 1963), pp. 97–98. This latter article is reprinted from *The Journal of Philosophy*, 58 (1961), 534–43.

6. These points will be explained and elaborated in my discussion of Whitehead's "ontological principle" in Section III.

7. "The Concept of God as a Derivative Notion," pp. 183–84, italics added. In another place, Christian says: "(Incidentally, the [ontological] principle clearly rules out creativity as an ontological ground. It calls for actual entities, and creativity is not an actual entity, nor indeed an entity of any other systematic kind.)" ("Whitehead's Explanation of the Past," p. 98).

8. "Some Uses of Reason," p. 80*n*19. Similarly, Christian proposes that we replace Whitehead's statement in Category of Explanation 25 about the objective character of the satisfaction "for the transcendent creativity" with an equivalent statement about its character "for those other actual entities which prehend it" ("The Concept of God as a Derivative Notion," p. 183).

9. It seems safe to assume that this is the doctrine expressed by the statement "Creativity is unending." I cannot find a passage in which Whitehead explicitly says this, so presumably this statement has been invented by Christian to illustrate how any statement of this type could be translated. Since the statement does express a significant doctrine in Whitehead's thought, I shall concentrate my analysis upon it.

10. "Time," from *Proceedings of the Sixth International Congress of Philosophy* (New York: Longmans, Green, 1927); reprinted in *The Interpretation of Science*, ed. A. H. Johnson (Indianapolis and New York: Bobbs-Merrill, 1961), p. 242. Subsequent page references to this article will refer to the latter source.

11. See PR 129–30, 320–23, 326–27. Cf. "Time," *The Interpretation of Science*, pp. 240–43.

12. "The Concept of God as a Derivative Notion," p. 185, and "Whitehead's Explanation of the Past," pp. 94–95.

13. We would have to add that the concept of perishing does not apply to God. It is clear from the final chapter of *Process and Reality* that God is an actual entity which never perishes (see esp. pp. 524–32). However, God is prehended by the finite actual entities (in his "superjective" nature) and is "superseded" by them in the sense that each finite actual entity transcends God in its own immediacy of becoming (see PR 135, 339).

14. RM 92. Compare "Time," p. 243: "The creativity *for* the creature has become the creativity *with* the creature, and the creature is thereby superseded." For similar passages in *Process and Reality*, see pp. 31–32, 129–30, 249, 321–22, and 528–29.

15. See especially Whitehead's discussion of "the creative process" in RM, Ch. III, sec. vii. Also see PR 347.

16. For Christian's view of the proper relationship between creativity and the ontological principle, see *An Interpretation of Whitehead's Metaphysics*, p. 278, and "Whitehead's Explanation of the Past," p. 98.

17. See "Whitehead's Explanation of the Past," p. 97.

18. It should be noted that specific and generic explanations are ordinary explanations *within Whitehead's system*, although generic explanations are not "ordinary" ones in other contexts. Indeed, some philosophers would regard an appeal to God to explain anything as quite *extraordinary*.

19. *An Interpretation of Whitehead's Metaphysics*, pp. 277–79, 337–39.

20. In very rough outline, this is Christian's answer to the question of how the past can influence the present. See *An Interpretation of Whitehead's Metaphysics*, pp. 319–30; "Whitehead's Explanation of the Past," pp. 93–101; "On Whitehead's Explanation of Causality: A Reply," *International Philosophical Quarterly*, 2 (1962), 323–28.

21. Here I agree with the point made by Cobb, *A Christian Natural Theology*, pp. 208–209.

22. On this point I agree with Lewis Ford's remarks in "Whitehead's Differences from Hartshorne," *Two Process Philosophers: Hartshorne's Encounter*

*with Whitehead*, ed. Lewis S. Ford, AAR Studies in Religion, No. 5 (Tallahassee: American Academy of Religion, 1973), pp. 70–71.

23. See AI 230: "The initial situation includes a factor of activity which is the *reason* for the origin of that occasion of experience. This factor of activity is what I have called 'Creativity'." Cf. PR 32: "The 'creative advance' is the application of this ultimate principle of creativity to each novel situation *which it originates*." Italics added in both cases.

24. See PR 129, where Whitehead speaks of "the creativity *whereby* there is a becoming of entities superseding the one in question." Cf. "Time," p. 243, where he refers to "the creativity, *whereby* there is supersession." Italics added in both cases.

25. See PR 317: "The elucidation of [the] meaning involved in the phrase 'all things flow', is one chief task of metaphysics."

26. For two probing discussions of the intricate relationship between Whitehead's Category of the Ultimate and the ontological principle, the principle of relativity, and the principle of process, see Archie Graham, "Metaphysical Principles and the Category of the Ultimate," *Process Studies*, 7 (1977), 108–11, and David L. Schindler, "Whitehead's Challenge to Thomism on the Problems of God: The Metaphysical Issues," *International Philosophical Quarterly*, 19 (1979), 285–99. I agree with Graham and Schindler when they argue for the *coherence* of Whitehead's metaphysical categories. However, I ascribe a greater importance and explanatory power to the principle of creativity than either Graham or Schindler is willing to allow. My analysis treats creativity as Whitehead's ultimate metaphysical principle, whereas their analyses do not. Thus, I find them both guilty of the same sort of reductive account of creativity of which I have been accusing Christian.

27. "Time," p. 240.

28. "Objective immortality" is the mode in which an actual entity exists after it has completed its process of concrescence and perished (see PR 44, 335–37). The "actual world" for an actual entity includes all actual entities of the past, which function as the data for its process of concrescence (see PR 34, 101).

29. 'Superject' is another term which Whitehead uses to describe the way in which an actual entity exists after it has been "thrown up" by the creative process (see PR 43, 71, 134). An actual entity as superject exists in the mode of objective immortality.

30. See PR 44, 129–30, 249, and 344 for Whitehead's claim that actual entities supply creativity with a "character." Now, it may be urged that it is only metaphorical to speak of actual entities as "qualifications" or "characterizations" of creativity. Creativity is not an entity which can possess characteristics, nor are past actual entities universals which can be said to characterize anything. Yet Whitehead constantly questions the adequacy of the subject–predicate form of expression in dealing with ultimate metaphysical issues (see, e.g., PR 45, 76–78, 208–209). In fact, he seems to claim that, in the final analysis, *all* metaphysical language is metaphorical and must be apprehended imaginatively (see PR 6, 16, 20).

31. See PR 47, where Whitehead explicitly compares creativity with Aristotle's prime matter: "Creativity is without a character of its own in exactly the same sense in which the Aristotelian 'matter' is without a character of its own. . . . It [creativity] cannot be characterized, because all characters are more special than itself." Compare Plato's description of the complete formlessness of the Receptacle at *Timaeus* 50a–51b. As far as I know, Whitehead never explicitly compares creativity with the Receptacle. His remarks about the Receptacle in *Adventures of Ideas* (e.g., at 171–72, 192–93, 240–42) could equally suggest a comparison with the extensive continuum. But it is very appropriate to compare creativity with Plato's Receptacle. For example, while Raphael Demos does not explicitly identify creativity with the Receptacle, that would be a fair extrapolation from his careful analysis in "The Receptacle," *Philosophical Review*, 45 (1936), 535–57.

32. See PR 127, 130; AI 230–31. On my interpretation, creativity is the principle which accounts for the "givenness" of past actual entities to present ones. Thus, it is unnecessary to adopt Christian's strategy of bringing in God to bridge the "gap" between the past and the present (see note 20 above).

33. See PR 129–30, 134–35, and esp. 324, where Whitehead even asserts, "the notion of 'passing on' is more fundamental than that of a private individual fact." Compare AI 305: "Thus perishing is the initiation of becoming. How the past perishes is how the future becomes."

34. I am indebted to Donald Sherburne for his perceptive remarks about the importance of transition in *A Whiteheadian Aesthetic*, pp. 9–24. His remarks concerning the "rhythm of process" have also influenced this discussion.

35. See PR 443: ". . . nature is never complete. It is always passing beyond itself. This is the creative advance of nature." Cf. Whitehead's discussion of the concept of incompleteness in "Time," pp. 240–47.

36. *A Whiteheadian Aesthetic*, pp. 18–21; see also his *A Key to Whitehead's* PROCESS AND REALITY (New York: Macmillan, 1966; rpt., Chicago: University of Chicago Press, 1982), pp. 32–35, 218.

37. Here I am using the formal–material contrast in the traditional Aristotelian sense. I do not consider these terms inappropriate, since Whitehead himself often uses Aristotelian terms in presenting his metaphysics.

38. One of Whitehead's most forceful accounts of the continuity of the creative advance comes in an early work on philosophy of science: "The passage of nature which is only another name for the creative force of existence has no narrow ledge of definite instantaneous present within which to operate. Its operative presence which is now urging nature forward must be sought for throughout the whole, in the remotest past as well as in the narrowest breadth of any present duration. Perhaps also in the unrealised future. Perhaps also in the future which might be as well as the actual future which will be. It is impossible to meditate on time and the mystery of the creative passage of nature without an overwhelming emotion at the limitations of human intelligence" (CN 73).

39. Of course, we must keep in mind the important *differences* between Whitehead and Spinoza (see Section I above). Yet one virtue of my interpre-

tation is that it shows us the rationale behind Whitehead's remarks about his similarities with Spinoza and other monists. That the analogy with Spinoza is not confined to *Science and the Modern World* is evident from Whitehead's discussion at PR 10–11, which he prefaces with the remark, "The philosophy of organism is closely allied to Spinoza's scheme of thought."

40. Cf. PR 22, where Whitehead says that "all occasions proclaim themselves as actualities within the flux of a solid world, demanding a unity of interpretation." Cf. PR 88–89.

41. This point is implicit in Whitehead's initial discussion of coherence at PR 5.

42. This is the expression which Charles Hartshorne uses to characterize Whitehead's concept of creative synthesis in "Whitehead's Novel Intuition," *Alfred North Whitehead: Essays on His Philosophy*, ed. George L. Kline, pp. 18–26.

# 11

# God and Creativity

GENE REEVES
*Meadville – Lombard Theological School*

I

JOHN COBB'S *A Christian Natural Theology: Based on the Thought of Alfred North Whitehead*[1] is certainly an important contribution to both contemporary theology and contemporary philosophy. Cobb provides a helpful and clarifying presentation of Whitehead's views on a number of significant theological issues; he attempts to improve on Whitehead by providing a more coherent working out of some of Whitehead's principles; and he goes beyond his mentor by dealing creatively with some issues from within his own Whiteheadian perspective. At some points, especially in his development of the notion of the self and in his treatment of the relation of God to both space and time, Cobb makes major contributions to the development of philosophical theology. Certainly he has shown that Whitehead's philosophy provides an adequate and exciting philosophical basis for grappling with contemporary theological issues. With much of what Cobb has done in this book, I am in full and hearty agreement.

Nevertheless, in his treatment of the relation of God and creativity Cobb has argued for a position which is, I believe, unwarranted by his argument and inconsistent with principles of Whitehead's metaphysics which he adopts.[2] His intention is to show how

An earlier version of this chapter appeared in *The Southern Journal of Philosophy* (7 [1969–70], 377–85).

it is possible from within a Whiteheadian framework to attribute to God the "decisive" role in the creation of actual occasions. That he has not succeeded in this effort is the conclusion of the present essay.[3]

It is important to recognize at the outset that the notion of creation with which we are concerned here is the creation of actual occasions and not the initial creation of the world as such. Whitehead thought that there was no absolute beginning of the world, that there was no initial creation of the world out of nothing, and, in this sense, that the world is eternal. Though not certain that an original creation is impossible, Cobb generally agrees with Whitehead's position (CNT 205, 212). At the very least, it is clear that what Cobb is concerned with in this discussion is not an initial creation of the world but "God's power to cause actual occasions to occur" (CNT 212).

Basically, the problem of this essay has to do with the role of four formative elements—past occasions, eternal objects, creativity, and God—in the creation of actual occasions.[4] Cobb argues that while God, past occasions, and the new occasion itself are conjointly the reason for *what* an occasion becomes, God is always the decisive reason *that* each new occasion becomes (CNT 214). The argument has both a negative and a positive side: it is argued that in the coming to be of actual occasions creativity cannot be the decisive factor, and that God is the decisive factor.

In this essay it will be argued (1) that in important respects Cobb has confused Whitehead's notion of creativity; (2) that, while he is correct in arguing that exclusive decisiveness in creation cannot be attributed to creativity, on no apparent meaning of 'decisive' consistent with Whitehead's principles can such a role be attributed to God as Cobb claims; and (3) that Cobb's distinction between *what* or how an occasion becomes and *that* it becomes also fails to give God such a role.

As Garland ably demonstrates, the notion of creativity is clearly basic to Whitehead's metaphysics. Though Cobb does not give adequate attention to the importance of creativity in transition, he does recognize its importance in concrescence. As the "principle of novelty" it is coincident with the act of "self-creation" by which each actual occasion comes into existence (PR 31, 130). Actual occasions are not simply created by external agencies—within limits which are given to them, they are self-created.

With this Cobb seems to be in explicit agreement (CNT 209–11). Thus, his apparent contrast of creativity with the decisions of actual occasions is confusing and misleading. He writes, "Creativity as the material cause of actual entities, then, explains in Whitehead's philosophy neither what they are nor that they are. If the question as to why things are at all is raised in the Whiteheadian context, the answer must be in terms of the decisions of actual entities" (CNT 211). This is not wrong, but is misleading in that the decisions of actual entities are precisely what Whitehead intends by 'creativity'. "The doctrine of the philosophy of organism is that, however far the sphere of efficient causation be pushed in the determination of . . . these components there always remains the final reaction of the self-creative unity of the universe" (PR 75). That is, the decisions of actual entities are instances of creativity and should not be contrasted with it.

Whitehead also calls creativity "the ultimate" because, while each actual entity plays a role in creating itself, the act of self-creation is generic to all actual entities. Each actual occasion is an individual instance of this ultimate or absolutely general activity, and thus may even be called a "creature" of universal creativity (PR 30, 124). This does not mean, however, that creativity is some kind of a super-god, or that it is in any sense more real than the individual actual occasions. It is simply that most general feature which all actual entities have in common (PR 31). Thus it is confusing for Cobb to claim that despite the fact that "creativity as such is not concrete or actual," it is not "in the usual sense an abstraction" (CNT 210). The point is that actual decisions, *individual* instances of creativity, are not abstract; they are the ultimate concrete things of the universe; but creativity itself, considered apart from such individual instances, is abstract.

It might be instructive to point out here the sense in which Whitehead has radically revised Aristotle. For Aristotle, the basic metaphysical elements are prime matter and form. In the final analysis, it is form which is most basic; matter is pure potentiality, a basic stuff which is capable of becoming anything according to how it is formed. Action is also identified with form because mere matter cannot act. What Whitehead has done is to replace the notion of prime matter with that of actual entity. But, for him, the actual entities are actions (decisions), and the forms merely abstractions from actual entities. In this way, Whitehead completely abolishes the metaphysical notion of matter and in its place puts the notion of creativity. Like Aristotle's prime matter, Whitehead's activities take on forms and are characterized by forms. But every other characteristic of Aristotelian and traditional conceptions of matter—inertness, pure passivity, impenetrability, etc.—is gone. Thus, what is concrete in Whitehead's philosophy is not some substance or stuff which may accidentally act, but the activities themselves.[5]

II

Despite what appears to be some confusion about the nature of creativity in his own discussion, I believe that Cobb is quite correct in arguing that the priority which Whitehead himself sometimes gave to creativity will not hold up under analysis. Cobb writes:

> In Whitehead every actual occasion is a novel addition to the universe, not only a new form of the same eternal stuff. Creativity is inescapably an aspect of every such entity, but it cannot be the answer to the question as to why that entity, or any entity, occurs. The question is why new processes of creativity keep occurring, and the answer to this cannot be simply because there was creativity in the preceding occasions and that there is creativity again in the new ones [CNT 211].

Cobb goes on to show that according to Whitehead's "ontological principle" only actual entities can have efficient or final causality. He then argues that since creativity is not an actual entity, it cannot function as a cause of anything and therefore is not a creator (CNT

206). But, again, this is to confuse the meaning of creativity in Whitehead's system. Certainly creativity, as such, is abstract and neither an actuality nor a creator. But creativity basically refers to the decisions of actual occasions. Thus to call creativity a creator is simply another way of saying that actual occasions are self-creators.

Cobb also argues, somewhat more successfully, that creativity cannot answer the question of why there is and continues to be anything at all because what is is process, and creativity is another name for process (Cobb says 'change' here but obviously means 'process'). His point is that the notion of process does not include any reason for believing that process is without beginning or end (CNT 210–11).[6]

Having shown that creativity cannot be *the* decisive factor in the creation of an occasion, Cobb concludes that God is the decisive factor. But clearly this will not do.

The problem, or at least a crucially important part of it, has to do with what is meant by the term 'decisive'. On this, I do not believe that Cobb is at all clear. He wants to argue that the role of God is decisive in the formation of the initial aim of every actual entity (CNT 205), that God is the decisive factor in the creation of each new occasion (CNT 226), and thus that he "must be conceived as being the reason that entities occur at all" (CNT 211).

It can be successfully argued that any one of the four formative elements is decisive in the sense that it is necessary to the creation of any actual entity. That is, in the creation of every actual occasion, the past must be there as data, eternal objects must be involved as determinants, God must provide an initial aim, and some decision on the part of the concrescing occasion will have to be made. There is no necessity about the details, but the functioning of all four formative elements, in some way or other, is necessary. An actual occasion is initiated by a combination of its prehension of entities in its past and the ideal aim which God has for it. Its "subjective aim" is finally produced by its own decisive adaptation of the initial aim derived from God to the aims which other past entities have for it. In addition, other eternal objects which characterize past occasions will be more or less relevant to the becoming occasion. Creativity cannot be *the* answer to why an actual entity occurs because it is only a partial answer. Thus we must regard as something of an exaggeration all attempts to have creativity alone account for the ongoingness of the world. It is necessary to the becoming of any actual occasion, but it is not sufficient to create one. It is for this reason that Cobb is essentially right about the role of creativity in creation—it cannot be said to be *the* reason for actual occasions.[7] But then neither can God. He is *a* reason, a very important and essential one, but he cannot be *the* reason.

Further, in the sense of being the dominant reason for what an actual entity becomes, it is clear that it is not God but the past which is generally most influential. That is, despite the long-run importance of both God and creativity, in almost all individual instances of creation it is the past which is causally most effective. In Cobb's own view there is a gradation from nearly total conformity to the past to an upper limit of determination by the ideal given by God. Only with respect to some rare occasions of mystical experience could God be said in this sense to be *the* decisive element in the creation of actual occasions. Clearly, then, 'decisive' does not mean for Cobb 'most influential'.[8]

Cobb's claim that God is the decisive element in creation is dependent on two additional points: the role of God in determining the initial aim of occasions and a distinction between *that* and *what*. We must discuss these in turn.

According to Whitehead's philosophy, every actual occasion has a unifying factor called a "subjective aim" which governs the interplay between inherited data and conceptually felt ideals, an interplay which is the process of coming to be or creation (PR 343). But there is also a distinction between the "initial phase" (or "initial aim") of the subjective aim and later phases of the subjective aim. This initial phase, like the antecedent world, is given to the occasion. During later phases, the subjective aim is determined by the self-causation of the becoming occasion, but initially it is given (PR 373–74). Whitehead's point is that an occasion must have some basis for making its decision and therefore cannot choose just any aim for itself. There must be a principle of limitation at work whereby the occasion is pointed toward its conclusion and definitely limited as to what it can become. This principle of limitation is God, and it is by providing each occasion with a relevant initial aim that God functions in the creative process.

Cobb attempts to push beyond Whitehead's explicit writings by arguing that in the creation of an actual occasion the initial aim is not simply one among several equally important contributing factors—it is the "initiating principle" (CNT 204) or the "originating element" (CNT 205). And, since God is the source of initial aims, he has the "all-decisive role in the creation of each new occasion" (CNT 205).

Two reasons are advanced for the conclusion that the initial aim is not simply one among several equally important factors contributing to the creation of an occasion. In the first place, it is argued, the initial phase of an occasion is said by Whitehead to be constituted by the initial aim and the initial data. But it is the initial aim which determines the locus or standpoint which the occasion will occupy in the extensive continuum. Thereby it determines which occasions will be future, present, or past for the subject occasion. It follows that the initial aim determines which occasions will be in its past and thereby constitute the initial data for the occasion. In this sense, the initial aim derived from God may be said to have a kind of priority in the creation process (CNT 152–53, 204).

In the second place, it is argued, "the initial data are not a part of the becoming occasion in the same sense as the initial aim" (CNT 204). Past occasions are objects for the becoming subject. They are felt not in their role as subjects but as objectified by the new occasion. And how it objectifies them is determined by the initial aim which has been derived from God.

Both of these arguments, it seems to me, involve dubious interpretations of Whitehead. The issues involved in the first are somewhat complex and technical. Certainly, however, it is not at all apparent that Whitehead intended to assert that their initial aims determine the standpoints of actual occasions. It seems more reasonable to think of the standpoint of an occasion as being simply the occasion itself considered in relation to the extensive continuum. It is not so much that an occasion *has* a standpoint as that it *is* one (PR 434). If this is the case, the question as to what determines the standpoint of an occasion is precisely the same as the question as to what determines the occasion, and it becomes evident that Cobb's argument tends to presuppose its conclusion. At least, he will have to argue more effectively than he has, and on grounds independent of the question of the creation of an actual occasion, that the standpoint of an occasion is determined exclusively by its initial aim.

In the second argument, it seems to me, Cobb has simply misread Whitehead. In the passages to which Cobb makes reference, Whitehead says that it is the subjective aim which determines how the data are objectified. And in one passage he states that the subjective aim dominates the entire concrescent process (PR 420). But the subjective aim cannot be identified with the initial aim, as Cobb's argument seems to presuppose. An initial aim has no subjectivity but acquires it from the self-creativity of the concrescing occasion. Thus the subjective aim necessarily involves an element of self-creativity, and it is this self-creativity, guided by the aim, which determines how its data are objectified. There is no apparent reason to believe that the *initial* aim as such determines how data are objectified.

More important than these considerations is the question as to whether the two arguments, even if they did not involve questionable interpretations of Whitehead, provide an adequate basis for the conclusion that "we may properly think of the initial aim as the originating element in each new occasion" (CNT 205). Even if the initial aim does determine which occasions will be in the past of a subject occasion, it does not follow that past occasions are any less "initial" than the initial aim. Whitehead clearly believed that the analysis of an actual occasion must involve both efficient causation and final causation and that the occasion grows out of and in response to data which are initially given to it. Certainly, the initial aim derived from God is a decisive factor, but that it has a priority over the initial data such that it can be termed *the* decisive element is not clear.

Even the assumption that the initial aim does determine how the initial data are prehended will not establish the desired conclusion. It would only establish that *how* an occasion initially becomes is determined by God. The role of efficient causation by antecedent actual entities and the role of final causation by the becoming actual occasion itself are in no way diminished.

The precise meaning of 'decisive', therefore, remains unclear in Cobb's exposition. There are at least three possible meanings: In the first place, 'decisive' might refer to that which makes the decision. But in this case it is not God but the actual occasion itself which is decisive. Secondly, 'decisive' might mean 'necessary', i.e., 'required in order for there to be a concrescing occasion'. But this sense of 'decisive' does not make God's role distinct from that of the other formative elements; he is no more or less necessary than past occasions, eternal objects, and the creativity of actual entities themselves. Finally, 'decisive' might mean 'most influential' in the sense that what is more decisive has a larger role to play in determining what an actual occasion is to become. But in this case God is not more but less decisive in the creation of most actual occasions. In the overwhelming majority of cases it is the past which is most decisive in this sense. Thus, in none of these three meanings of 'decisive' can God be said to be *the* decisive element in creation.

## III

In parts of his discussion, however, Cobb seems to have something else in mind. This something else is based upon a distinction between *what* an occasion becomes and *that* it becomes at all. This distinction is related to the Aristotelian notion that if one asks why it is that there is anything at all, rather than asking why a thing is as it is, the answer must be given in terms of the eternality of prime matter. Cobb points out that Christian Aristotelians recognized that prime matter, since it is not necessary, cannot be an adequate reason for its own being and therefore that God, the necessary existent, must be conceived as the ground of all that is. Cobb then shows that "creativity" in Whitehead's system provides an even less satisfactory answer to the "radical" question of why there is anything at all (or, more accurately in this context, why there is process at all). But still the question is not a matter of God's creating a first occasion *ex nihilo*:

> . . . I am more interested in God's power to cause actual occasions to occur than in the "necessity" of his existence. It is no objection to my mind that if that which has the power to give existence requires also that it receive existence, then we are involved in an infinite regress. I assume that we are indeed involved in an endless regress. Each divine occasion . . . must receive its being from its predecessors, and I can [imagine] no beginning of such a series [CNT 212].

The question is why process keeps going, not why it began. Cobb contends that the answer to this question must be God, since it is he who always provides an initial aim for the new occasion.

A question that must be raised about this discussion is whether the distinction between the *what* and the *that* of actual occasions makes any sense in a Whiteheadian context. At first, it might seem that the answer must be no. The becoming of an actual occasion is its becoming something definite, some settled matter of fact. It does not first become and then become something definite—its being is its coming to be. There is no *that* without a *what*—no Aristotelian substance. Thus, it would seem, the reason why actual occasions are at all cannot be separated from the reasons why they are what they are.

There does seem, however, to be one sense in which the what/that distinction can be maintained. This is the distinction effectively made by Hartshorne between existence and actuality. Hartshorne's reworking of the ontological argument involves the idea that while God's existence is necessary his actuality is not. That is, God is such that he cannot fail to exist in some suitable form or other, but how he is successively actualized is a contingent matter dependent on the actual experiences he has.[9] Similarly, it can be argued that the existence of some actual occasions (some world) is necessary but that the existence of any particular actual occasion is contingent. Thus, *that* there are actual occasions is a necessary truth, but *how* occasions are actualized is dependent on a multiplicity of contingencies.[10] Whitehead hinted at this perhaps in saying that God and the world require each other as a primordial datum (PR 529).

But in this case the question of why there are actual occasions at all is a logical matter which cannot be answered by reference to any actuality, including God. 'Some actual occasions exist' is *a priori* or necessarily true simply because its negation leads to absurdities. That no actual occasions at all (no world) exist cannot be consistently conceived and obviously has no conceivable verification. In this sense, 'no actual occasions at all' is simply a meaningless notion and the alternative—'some actual occasions exist'—necessarily true. In no way does this need to involve God. What determines that actual occasions necessarily exist? Nothing. That something exists is a necessary truth due to no cause whatsoever. To make its truth dependent on something else (including God) would be to make it a contingent truth and thus destroy the original distinction.[11]

Of course in a Whiteheadian theistic system, the necessity of the world is not unrelated to God. It is the nature of God to know actual occasions and it is the nature of the actual occasions to be known by God. An actual God requires some actual world and vice versa. In this sense, God is necessarily a creator. But this does not imply, in any way that I can see, that God is *the* decisive element in the creation of actual occasions.

## IV

I have not argued that God is unimportant in the process of creation, or even that he is not more important than Whitehead sometimes seems to have allowed. Cobb's discussion of God's role in providing the initial aims of actual occasions serves both to clarify God's role as creator and to bring out its importance. In a very important sense, and one that is especially important for higher-grade occasions, God is necessary in the creation of every actual occasion. But this does not, I have attempted to argue, justify the claim that God is *the* decisive factor or *the* reason why entities occur at all.

In general a philosopher can only applaud Cobb's willingness to attempt a consistent and coherent treatment of the issues, even when this demands working out some very complicated metaphysical problems on which Whitehead was not entirely clear or always right. However, on this issue, it would seem that Cobb has not achieved the desired coherence. Undoubtedly, there are many good and sound reasons in a "Christian natural theology" for wanting to emphasize the importance of God. But the rational theologian must not allow an emphasis based on historical considerations to introduce incoherence into the rational theology, something Cobb himself has sought to avoid.

Further, I have not argued that God is not superior to everything else in the universe—to all non-divine occasions, to abstract eternal objects, and to creativity. He is vastly superior. Indeed, in a very significant sense, God's role in the creation of all other actual entities is unique. He is the only actual entity which influences in a positive way the becoming of *all* actual occasions. His creative efficacy, and only his, is strictly universal. He contributes positively to the creation of all actual entities, not just a limited few, and he contributes always, not just for a limited time. All of the other Whiteheadian formative elements, it must be remembered, are classes rather than individuals. Thus, while the class of entities covered by the term 'the past' may be more influential than God in determining a present occasion, no single occasion included in "the past" can be said to be more influential than God with respect to the class of finite actual occasions as a whole. Thus if 'creator' is taken to be an individual rather than a class designation, there is a highly legitimate sense in which God can be termed '*the* creator' within the Whiteheadian system.

A second sense in which the Whiteheadian God can be said to be uniquely creative stems from his universality. Every creature is prehended into God and made an integral part of his universal harmony. As the integrator of the multiplicity of individual finite values into a transcendent unity, God is always the final aesthetic harmony, uniquely attractive, beautiful, and worshipful. For Whitehead as for Aristotle the power of God is his beauty. But, since this responsiveness or sensitivity to all others constitutes perfect love as well as perfect beauty, God's power is also the power of love. Though any creature can to some extent reject God's aim for it, none can simply disregard God's power of beauty and love. In this sense of 'power', God is infinitely more powerful, and therefore infinitely more creative, than anything else could be.

Thus, while Cobb's analysis of God as creator must be rejected, there are good reasons from within a Whiteheadian perspective for calling God 'the creator'. At the same time, however, it should not be forgotten that in Whiteheadian philosophy the greatness of God and his superiority do not consist primarily in his efficient power as creator of actual occasions but, as Whitehead puts it, in "the worship he inspires."

## NOTES

1. (Philadelphia: Westminster, 1965). Further references, in parentheses, will be to 'CNT' with page number.

2. In this Cobb is taking on one of the major criticisms of Whitehead's philosophy made from a traditional theological position. E. L. Mascall, for example, has attacked Whitehead's conception of God for not treating God as the efficient cause of everything other than himself, and his conception of creativity for failing to provide an answer to the question as to why things are at all (*He Who Is* [London: Longmans, 1943], Chap. 11).

3. That this issue has importance beyond Cobb's own book is reflected in the fact that several Whiteheadian process theologians have adopted Cobb's position. Schubert Ogden simply asserts that God is the only necessary ground of all that exists, "the one essential cause of each moment," without attempting as Cobb has to show how this could be true within a Whiteheadian perspective (*The Reality of God* [New York: Harper & Row, 1966], pp. 63, 214). Ian Barbour simply accepts Cobb's analysis as adequate (*Issues in Science and Religion* [Englewood Cliffs: Prentice-Hall, 1966], p. 444). Richard Overman repeats Cobb's arguments as the heart of the conclusion to his own book,

*Evolution and the Christian Doctrine of Creation* (Philadelphia: Westminster, 1967), pp. 268–83.

4. In *Religion in the Making* Whitehead refers to creativity, eternal objects, and God as the "formative elements" (RM 89–90), omitting past occasions. Here past occasions are included within the notion of formative elements because it is clear that they are one of the elements which go into the formation of every actual entity. Cobb himself refers to these as the four "ultimate elements" in Whitehead's system (CNT 177).

5. See Ivor Leclerc, "Form and Actuality" in *The Relevance of Whitehead*, ed. I. Leclerc (London: Allen and Unwin; New York: Macmillan, 1961), p. 179, and *Whitehead's Metaphysics: An Introductory Exposition* (London: Allen and Unwin; New York: Macmillan, 1958; rpt., Bloomington: Indiana University Press, 1975), pp. 82–86.

6. This is disputed in Section III of the present Chapter.

7. This discussion is relevant to Donald Sherburne's claim that it is by the doctrine of creativity that Whitehead's philosophy is able to avoid "horizontal incoherence" by giving a reason for the "everlasting on-goingness" of succeeding actual occasions (*A Whiteheadian Aesthetic* [New Haven: Yale University Press, 1961], pp. 14–24).

Sherburne's and Garland's (Chapter 10 above) discussions of creativity, particularly their emphasis on the importance of creativity in relation to transition as well as to concrescence, is, I think, a very helpful interpretation of Whitehead. By seeing that creativity provides an explanation of why there is a necessary rhythm in process by which "the many become one, and are increased by one," they effectively claim a role for creativity in Whitehead's system similar to the claim that Cobb is making for God.

Unlike Cobb's, their interpretation can readily be supported by some Whitehead texts: for example, by his description of creativity as "the ultimate metaphysical ground" behind both God and actual occasions (PR 529). Creativity does indeed provide an account of the ongoingness of actual occasions. But it is important to recognize that creativity may be thought of as *the* creator of actual occasions, or as the explanation of or reason for the ongoingness of process, only if the other formative elements are presupposed. That is, within Whitehead's metaphysics it is not possible to give an adequate account of the perpetual coming to be of actual occasions without making reference to past data, eternal objects, and God, as well as to creativity.

There is, however, one respect in which creativity can be said to be uniquely the creator of actual occasions. In the concrescence of an actual occasion, as Whitehead sees it, only the actual occasion itself is active *in the present*; it decides what it will be and thus creates itself. Only in this very weak sense can creativity be said to be *the* creator of actual occasions. In contrast, eternal objects are abstract; they never act. And both God and past occasions are, relative to the becoming occasion, inactive. They *have* acted, but are now objects for the becoming occasion. This is why Whitehead so often emphasizes the idea that actual occasions are self-created, and also, I think, why he places so much emphasis on creativity. An actual occasion creates itself, but the creativity of both God and the occasions of its past which are data for the becoming occasion play a tremendously important role in its self-creation. Thus, relative to any single actual occasion, the four formative elements do have a certain order of activity: the becoming occasion which is acting, God and past occasions which have acted, and eternal objects which do not act at all.

8. Cobb's agreement with this is clear in several places in this book but especially in a discussion of mystical experience, which he regards as being the only case in which God may be more influential than the past in determining the outcome of an actual occasion (CNT 233–35).

9. See Charles Hartshorne, *Anselm's Discovery* (LaSalle, Ill.: Open Court, 1965), especially p. x.

10. That some world is necessary can also be argued on the grounds that the notion of an empty universe is itself vacuous. See L. Jonathan Cohen, *The Diversity of Meaning* (New York: Herder & Herder, 1963), pp. 260–61.

11. See Charles Hartshorne, *The Logic of Perfection* (LaSalle, Ill.: Open Court, 1962), Chap. 12, esp. pp. 282, 292–93.

# IV

# SOME CONTRASTING INTERPRETATIONS

12

# Whitehead on the One and the Many

ROBERT C. NEVILLE
*State University of New York at Stony Brook*

WHITEHEAD'S DISTINCTIVE CONTRIBUTION to the discussion of the one and the many was to assign the unifying functions traditionally ascribed to God to two different factors. On the one hand, the actual unifying of the world, the bringing of potential diversity into actual harmony, he assigned to concrete actual entities; among the actual entities is God, the rest being temporal occasions (PR 168). The actual unity of concrete facts is a function of the interaction between God and the world as described in Part V of *Process and Reality*. On the other hand, ontological creation, the unification of one and many that makes actual entities possible, was assigned to the principle of creativity in the Category of the Ultimate.

The importance of this strategy is that it underscores a distinction between two basic senses of 'cause', corresponding respectively to two basic senses of 'unity' that must be accounted for in a solution to the problem of the one and the many. One sense of 'cause' is associated with the ontological principle; the other, with the Category of the Ultimate, especially creativity. Corresponding to these, the kind of unity accounted for by the causes associated with the

---

An earlier version of Sections I–III of this chapter appeared in *The Southern Journal of Philosohy* (7 [1969–70], 387–93); Section IV is reprinted, with revisions, from Neville's *Creativity and God: A Challenge to Process Theology* (New York: Seabury Press, 1980), pp. 46–47.

ontological principle may be called 'cosmological'; the kind accounted for by the Category of the Ultimate may be called 'ontological'. The burden of this essay, however, is that the Category of the Ultimate is *not* sufficient to account for ontological unity.

## I

The explanation of the distinctions between the different senses of 'cause' and the different senses of 'unity' will lay the groundwork for this criticism of Whitehead's system.

1. The ontological principle is that any condition in any particular instance in the process of becoming is to be accounted for either in terms of the decision of some antecedent entity in its actual world, or in terms of the decision of its own concrescence (PR 36 and passim). Reference to the former kind of decision is a matter of efficient causation; to the latter, of final causation. All decisions are made in the subjective immediacy of some actual entity's experience. They involve establishing the selective emphasis of each of the data given in the initial phase of the subjective experience so that in the final objectification the experience is completely determinate (PR 38, 68). Decisions are made in accordance with the subjective aim of the experient occasions, but the subjective aim is itself subject to modification throughout the phases of the process (PR 74–75). The modification of the decisive subjective aim consists in a reaction of the experient whole on itself; in this sense each occasion gives itself its own reasons for its decisions (PR 75, 41).

The kind of *causation* associated with the ontological principle therefore is a matter of decision and of the objective results of decision. The ontological principle says that for every particular factor there is a decision somewhere that accounts for it; the corresponding kind of causal analysis involves hunting for the occasions that through their own self-creativity determine the factor to exist. Whitehead reformulated the ontological principle in many ways; all of them amount to saying that nothing enters the universe that is not the product of some actual entity's decision.

The *unity* pointed to by the ontological principle is a unity of determinate states of the cosmos, that is, of satisfactions of actual entities. The ontological principle guides our examination of any particular actual entity. And it guides our examination of the cosmos as a whole, referring to decisions in temporal actual occasions and in God's primordial and consequent natures. The primordial valuation of eternal objects is referred to God's primordial decision. The determinate satisfactions of temporal actual occasions are referred to the occasions' own decisions, to the other occasions prehended in the experience, and to the hybrid physical prehension of God's primordial valuation constituting the initial subjective aim. The satisfaction of God's experience of the world at any time is referred in its various parts to his primordial valuation, to the decisions of the actual occasions in the world, to his previous consequent decisions, and to his immediate decision. In turn, God's decisive experience of the world enters the experience of subsequent temporal occasions and must be referred to as a kind of reason in their satisfaction. The ontological principle accounts for the unity of any plurality that enters into the constitution of an actual entity; wherever there is a standpoint at which a plurality is unified, according to the ontological principle there are decisions, either in the world of the standpoint or in the standpoint itself, that account for the unity. This is the kind of unity, a unity of actual entities and ingressed eternal objects, that can be called a *cosmological* unity.

The kind of question the ontological principle interprets is how this or that ingression of eternal objects occurs, or how this or that objectification of an actual entity or nexus occurs. It does *not* answer the question why there is any decision at all, why any eternal objects ingress, why there is any objectification of actual entities, or why there are any actual entities. Yet these latter are the questions generally associated with ontology. In Whitehead's scheme, not the ontological principle, but the category of the ultimate addresses *these* questions. The ontological principle is misleadingly named. It should be called the *cosmological* principle, since it deals with the constitution of the particularities of this cosmos.

2. The ontological question as to why there exist any cosmological unities is answered, allegedly, by the Category of the Ultimate. One, many, and creativity are the notions making up the Category. They are probably what Whitehead had foremost in mind when he characterized the coherence of notions, not as the defining of each in terms of the others, but as the presupposing of each by the others "so that in isolation they are meaningless." Coherence means "that what is indefinable in one such notion cannot be abstracted from its relevance to the other notions" (PR 5). One, many, and creativity cannot be defined either by themselves or in terms of one another, but what is indefinable in each one is relevant to the others. One, according to Whitehead, "stands for the singularity of an entity" (PR 31) and, although singularity cannot be defined as such, it presupposes the notion of *many* singulars in "disjunctive diversity." Disjunctive diversity, of course, presupposes many singulars.

Most philosophers would take the system of mutual presupposition on the level of the problem of the one and the many to consist in those two notions, one and many. The heart of Whitehead's philosophy is that creativity is presupposed on the same level, as it were, and in turn presupposes both one and many.

> The ultimate metaphysical principle is the advance from disjunction to conjunction, creating a novel entity other than the entities given in disjunction. The novel entity is at once the togetherness of the "many" which it finds, and also it is one among the disjunctive "many" which it leaves. . . . The many become one, and are increased by one. In their natures, entities are disjunctively "many" in process of passage into conjunctive unity [PR 32].

It is inconceivable that there be a many or a one unless one is conceived as a unification of many and many is conceived as a disjunction of such unifications of manys. The process of unifying many into one is creativity; the process is creative since when the many is unified into one, there is one more singular than when the many is not so unified.

The kind of *causation* associated with the Category of the Ultimate is ontological. It answers the question: Why does there exist a unification of that manifold of actual entities? The answer is: Where there is a many, creativity creates a one unifying them. This differs from the cosmological causation associated with the ontological principle. There the relevant question is: Why is this satisfaction as it is? The cosmological answer is: Because of these decisions in its own coming to be and those decisions in its actual world. The cosmological inquiry is epistemologically independent of the ontological account of why there is a satisfaction given to inquire about.

The kind of unity associated with the Category of the Ultimate is correspondingly ontological. Whereas cosmological unity is a matter of objective unification of actual entities in the satisfaction of another, ontological unity is the primordial togetherness of actual entities necessary for prehension and articulated by the creativity binding many into one. The Category of the Ultimate describes the condition for the existence of any actual entity. There could be no harmonious satisfaction, expressive of the ontological principle, were there not the basic relation of ones and manys through creativity. If there were no creativity, the many would individually perish without objective trace, and no one which unifies them would be possible; of course, they in turn would have been impossible.

3. In summary, Whitehead separates the functions of creative unification usually ascribed to God, assigning the ontological ones to the Category of the Ultimate and the cosmological ones to actual entities' decisions according to the ontological principle. This reflects, in reverse order, the distinction between cosmological causation and unities, with which the ontological principle is associated, and ontological causes and unities, with which the Category of the Ultimate, especially creativity, is associated. Whitehead's characteristic emphasis on the freedom of every actual entity to be self-creative in relative independence from every other actual entity, including God, rests on this separation. In the more usual view of creative unification, God in some sense is the source of both onto-

logical and cosmological unity, while created entities are the cause of the latter in some different but complementary sense. But along with the more usual view goes a commitment to the thesis that God is intimately present as creator to every creature even in the subjectivity of the creature's free self-constitution. On the usual view men are not free from God's creativity, whereas on Whitehead's view God's creative influence is limited to the provision of data for the finite actual occasions to objectify.

II

The separation of the functions of creative unity depends on the Category of the Ultimate to give an adequate account of ontological unity. There is good reason to think that this account is inadequate; this section will examine the reason.

Creativity is the principle that every plurality of actual entities is creatively unified into a new actual entity. But there is a dilemma: in what sense is creativity a "principle"? It might be an empirical generalization, stating that in fact all pluralities get creatively unified; but this would fail to account for the ontological problem of *why* they get unified. Or creativity might be interpreted as a principle in a more normative sense, to the effect that pluralities *must* get unified; but Whitehead's theory precludes this interpretation. These points will be elaborated in turn.

1. Consider the alternative that the notion of creativity merely generalizes the descriptive fact that every occasion is a creative unification of initial data. This is an inadequate ontological account because it does not give a reason for the existence of processes of creative unification. In effect it fails to advance ontologically beyond the ontological principle, which, taking for granted the creative unification, accounts for the specific form of the unification in terms of decisions. The ontological principle by itself simply assumes that the events of creative unification take place, and if the Category of the Ultimate is merely an empirical generalization,

then it is not necessary at all. With it or without it, the ontological question is begged.

2. Consider then that the Category of the Ultimate is a normative principle determining that there must be creative unifications of manys. Whitehead was clear, however, that creativity is indeterminate in abstraction from concrete events that exhibit it (PR 47 and passim). As the universal of universals, creativity is grasped by intuition in specific occasions and has no describable character apart from them. The actual creativity of any occasion is a matter of the decisions making it up. But then if creativity apart from specific occasions is completely indeterminate, it cannot be normative in any sense that would necessitate creativity in specific occasions.

Two rebuttals of this objection are to be expected.

First, it might be said that the sense in which Whitehead held creativity to be indeterminate is solely a function of the difficulties of conceptualization and not a matter of complete lack of character in creativity itself. After all, the reason why creativity cannot be described is that any description must be more special than it, and hence distorting. Whitehead intended that there be content to the intuition of creativity over and above the cosmological character of the specific entities in which it is embodied.

The difficulty with this rebuttal, however, is that the determinate character needed for creativity is one constitutive of a necessity for creative unification in entities; this necessity must be contrastable with the contingency that there be no creative unification (even if the latter is self-contradictory) and such a contrast would indeed be describable, at least as a contrast. But then it could not be a matter of intuition, and creativity could not be the universal of universals; rather, the ground of the contrast would be the universal of universals. To respond to the basic ontological problem, the category of the ultimate would have to show why there is creativity instead of nothing.

The second rebuttal is that creativity *by itself* need not be normative for specific occasions. Rather, it is normative only *relative* to specific occasions, and the relevance is contributed by God in his primordial nature (PR 46). God can be said to determine not only the relevance of eternal objects as possibilities for the unification but also the necessity that there be a creative event of unification. The difficulty here, however, is the self-referential one. Creativity is required to explain why there is any creative actuality, even the creation of the primordial created fact of relevance. It cannot be that God creates the normative relevance of the Category of the Ultimate according to the Category of the Ultimate. There would be no normative relevance of the Category for that primordial creative act; that act would be an exception to the Category. It would illustrate it, and this would allow it *not* to be an exception *if* the Category were only an empirical generalization; but if the Category is normative, the primordial divine creative act is an exception to its obligatoriness. Put another way, the unification of actual entities with the Category of the Ultimate that might be normative for them must be the product of some decision, as required by the ontological principle; but the reason for there being any decision at all is what the Category of the Ultimate is supposed to explain.

3. The conclusion to be drawn is that the Category of the Ultimate does not genuinely address the ontological question but only records the ontological situation, namely, that there are actual entities whose being consists in constituting themselves as unifications of manys. In effect, the Category of the Ultimate is only an empirical generalization. This accords with Whitehead's description of cosmology as imaginative generalization in the first chapter of *Process and Reality* and with his specific application of this interpretation of speculative philosophy to creativity (PR 30).

## III

What conclusions are we to draw about Whitehead's contribution to the discussion of the one and the many? We might simply note that he would reject the ontological question. He would claim that it is impossible to say why there are real things, why there are creative actual entities.[1] But our conclusion must indicate whether he is entitled to stop there.

1. The basic ontological problem is to account for the unity of many and one through creativity. The Category of the Ultimate is a statement of the ontological problem, not the answer to it. The ontological unity is *de facto*, not *de jure.* Every actual entity is an instance of ontological unity as well as an enjoyment of its specific cosmological unity; it is a unification through creativity of its initial data as such into an objective satisfaction as such, as well as a unification of the specific characters of its initial data into the specific character of its satisfaction. According to the ontological principle, there ought to be somewhere a creative decision responsible for any unification. But the decisions of all actual entities, precisely because they are creative, cannot constitute the ontological unity as the condition for creativity. There could be no creative actual entities if there were no unity of one and many through creativity. Not even God's primordial decision could constitute this ontological unity in his own creativity or in others' creativity, since that decision, being creative, depends on a prior ontological unity of many and one in creativity. Therefore, *given the ontological principle*, with no possibility of an ontological decision, the ontological unity of many and one in creativity is impossible. Any attempt to exempt the Category of the Ultimate from criticism at this point is only special pleading. Whitehead is not entitled to reject the ontological question.

Whitehead's response would have to be that the ontological principle does not apply to ontological unity in the sense described. There is no decision responsible for the basic togetherness of one and many in creativity. Precisely because the Category of the Ultimate is the universal of universals there can be nothing "responsible" for it. Creativity must simply be accepted as something given.

2. The issue here is whether the irrationality of the Category of the Ultimate must be accepted.[2] Whitehead was right to see that any complex unity is contingent and needs to be accounted for. The cosmological unities of actual satisfactions are contingent upon

and accounted for by actual decisions; but that kind of account cannot suffice for ontological unity. Ontological unity is a contingent complexity in its own way, a complex of one and many in creative process. Of course, neither ones nor manys nor creativity could exist except as together; but the question is why they exist at all. If Whitehead accepts the irrationality of the Category of the Ultimate, he accepts an irrationality in one place yet does not accept it in an analogous place; he might as well say that events happen with pure spontaneity and no causation.

We rightly boggle at this. It is a betrayal of rational faith (PR 67).

3. The criticism of Whitehead made here would be only a complaint about inelegance in his theory if it went no further than it has. It might simply be the case that no account of ontological unity as exhibited in the Category of the Ultimate can be given. This seems not to be the case, however. Another account is possible, and it rests on a different construction of the primitive notion of creativity.

Whitehead took creativity to be the bringing about of a one that unifies a many through its own creative self-constitution. This may in fact be descriptive of the cosmological process; but it cannot be descriptive of the grounding of the ontological unity.

The alternative conception is that creativity is the bringing about of a many in an act that constitutes the creative source to be a unified agent, a one for the created product. The creative source is admittedly indeterminate apart from any connection with creation. But in the act of creating, the source constitutes itself as creator and as unified. This kind of creativity does not presuppose an ontological unity because it is not a reduction of a multiplicity to unity through a novel entity, or a production of a multiplicity out of a unity. It is the creation of both unity and multiplicity *ex nihilo*, the creation of determinateness as such.

4. The latter conception of creativity can legitimately be called ontological creativity, because it can account for ontological unity.[3]

Whitehead's conception of creativity cannot account for ontological unity, because it is defined on a par with one and many. The alternative conception is that one and many are both the products of the creative act, along with the cosmological creativity that relates them, if Whitehead's description of process is correct. The very interrelation of one, many, and cosmological creativity that makes Whitehead's Category of the Ultimate irrational indicates that the notions and what they signify are contingent upon ontological creativity.

Since ontological creativity is productive of all determinate plurality, including its own character, it cannot proceed according to any pre-established principles. In this sense, then, there is no explanation of why this world that has process in it, rather than one without process, has been created. Whitehead was correct that philosophy must accept concrete fact and explain the abstractions from it. At root philosophy is empirical, and its object is the world that happens to be one of process. But the advance made by appealing to ontological creativity is that in this way it can be explained how such a world is possible; such a world is ontologically created, not by decisions within its own process—that would be self-referentially absurd—but by a transcendent creator who makes himself creator in the act of creating. Although this advance does not give a reason why there is this world rather than that, it gives a reason how there could be any world.

5. Whitehead's system must be reassessed if the idea of ontological creativity is valid over and above the cosmological creativity in the Category of the Ultimate. Two points of reassessment may be mentioned in conclusion.

First, the distinction between ontological and cosmological creativity should be clearly maintained. They are non-competing notions, and every actual entity would have to exhibit both kinds. Each entity would be both (a) cosmologically creative in its own right and (b) the product, together with the entities which it prehends and those which prehend it, of ontological creation. In some respects the recognition of ontological creativity is merely complementary to Whitehead's system as it stands. In other respects at least rhetorical qualifications may have to be introduced; for instance, regarding freedom, actual entities would be self-creative only in the cosmological sense—in the ontological sense they would be wholly dependent.

Second, Whitehead's conception of God as an actual entity functioning relative to the world in the cosmological ways described in Part V of *Process and Reality* must be set alongside the conception of the ontological creator who constitutes himself the creator of the world by creating it. Certainly the latter is closer than Whitehead's conception to what the Western tradition has regarded as the God of religion. If Whitehead's theory in fact requires the recognition of an ontological creator as well as an infinite actual entity, then the question as to which should be called God must be reopened.[4] Of course, in this essay we have not raised the question whether Whitehead's description of the cosmological process is in fact correct or whether his notion of God as an infinite actual entity makes sense.

6. The argument of this essay has been that Whitehead's separation of the unifying creative functions usually ascribed to a transcendent creator into the Category of the Ultimate and the decisions of actual entities entails that he is able to account only for cosmological unity. But his own account entails that there is an ontological unity described by the Category of the Ultimate. This latter is the locus of the problem of the one and the many on the ontological level and Whitehead's system cannot account for it. That this irrationality ought not to be accepted was argued by suggesting a conception of God that does account for it.

## IV

A profound metaphysical issue underlies the discussion of this essay. It concerns the nature of an ultimately satisfying explanation.

There are two broad types of sensibility regarding this which are so diverse as to be virtually impossible to mediate.

On the one hand, there is the rationalist's view that an ultimately satisfying explanation is a reduction of things to first principles. Things are explained by being shown to exhibit characters necessitated by certain determinate first principles. The first principles explain by virtue of their own determinate character. If it is asked how the first principles themselves are to be accounted for, the answer is that they do not need to be accounted for if indeed they are "first"—the ultimate and primordial explanatory principles. The Hartshornean line of philosophical theology is clearly within this rationalist sensibility. Whitehead's Category of the Ultimate, if it is accurately analyzed as an empirical generalization, is also of this sort.

On the other hand, there is the empiricist's view that an ultimately satisfying explanation consists in locating the decisive actions from which things take their form. To be satisfied is to see the loci of decisive determination. A theory of an ontological creator surely falls within the scope of this sensibility regarding explanation, for it claims that even the first principles, being determinate, need an account, and the only thing that could account for them is an ontologically creative act.[5] Whitehead's ontological principle, emphasizing that actual entities are to be accounted for by reference to decisions in various actual entities, accords with this sensibility on the cosmological level. But Whitehead fails to extend the reference to decision to the ontological level, and thereby slips into rationalism. Or at least Whitehead opened the door to addressing the ontological question in a rationalist way, even though he did not do so himself.

The difficulty alleged against the empiricist sensibility is that there is nothing in the character of the ontologically creative act that accounts for the product of the act (as indeed there cannot be if all determination must be within the product); therefore, explanation by reference to a decisive action is not an explanation at all, but merely a pointing at what needs explanation. But then, this objection begs the question in favor of the rationalist sensibility, since only a rationalist would want something determinate in the character of the explanatory principle that would explain the determinateness of things. Being of the empiricist persuasion, I can only point out that the rationalist approach cannot account for existence, for the ontological issues, because it must presuppose the normative existence of the explanatory first principles. Only the empiricist approach can address the problem of accounting for the reality of things. If philosophical theology is to account for the reality of things, then it should have a bias toward the empiricist sensibility. Surely the existential quality of religious experience is empiricistic in this sense!

## NOTES

1. Whitehead writes: "In other words, philosophy is explanatory of abstraction, and not of concreteness. . . . Each fact is more than its forms, and each form 'participates' throughout the world of facts. The definiteness of fact is due to its forms; but the individual fact is a creature, and creativity is the ultimate behind all forms, inexplicable by forms, and conditioned by its creatures" (PR 30).

2. The Category of the Ultimate is an abstraction, and therefore to be accounted for, even though its reference is to the most concrete of facts.

3. This conception is given abstract formulation and detailed defense in my *God the Creator* (Chicago: University of Chicago Press, 1968), Pts. I and II. The argument there is that anything determinate is created, in the ontological sense. Applied to Whitehead's system creativity is determinate vis-à-vis one and many in the Category of the Ultimate; and therefore the ultimate category descriptive of the world, and the ontological character of the world it describes, are created in the ontological sense.

4. I have drawn some negative conclusions regarding the "religious availability" of a similar conception of God, defended by Schubert Ogden, in "Neoclassical Metaphysics and Christianity: A Critical Study of Ogden's *Reality of God*," *International Philosophical Quarterly*, 9 (1969), 605–24. These conclusions are, I think, relevant to Whitehead's own technical formulations.

Regarding the possible relation between the ontological creator and the infinite actual entity in whom the world is saved and unified cosmologically, see my article "Creation and the Trinity," *Theological Studies*, 30 (1969), 3–26. The argument there is that as a contingent fact, witnessed by religious testimony, the creator has created an actual element in the world, the logos, in which the world receives its dynamic unification and by which its creation is raised to a contingent but glorious peak of fulfillment. The problem of that paper is to identify this created logos with the person of Jesus and with God as well, not to elaborate the philosophical categories of the relation between this created divinity and the rest of the world. It might be interesting to examine Whitehead's concept of God relative to an ontological creator in Trinitarian, or at least Binitarian, terms. The emphasis on grace in the theological tradition accords well with Whitehead's emphasis on the createdness of God in his primordial and consequent natures; the point of the present essay is that the decision constituting God's primordial nature is itself created in a sense different from Whitehead's sense of creativity.

5. My early attempt to formulate this view may be found in *God the Creator*, Chaps. 5 and 7.

# 13

# Neville's Interpretation of Creativity

LEWIS S. FORD
*Old Dominion University*

IN THE PREVIOUS ESSAY Robert C. Neville proposes that we distinguish between two types of creativity, cosmological and ontological. Cosmological creativity explains why any particular actual unity is what it is in terms of the ontological principle, which locates the reasons for that unity either in prior decisions by the actual entities prehended by the concrescent occasion, or in the decision of that occasion itself. But the question why there are occasions at all, Neville contends, is not thereby answered, and requires appeal to another kind of creativity, which he designates as 'ontological'.

This proposal makes good sense in terms of Neville's larger project, which adopts Whitehead's philosophical orientation only in the restricted sense as applying to the character of the world. How that world came to be, by contrast, is explained in terms of a transcendent creator, in himself indeterminate, who becomes determinate only insofar as he is the creator of this particular world. Thus Whitehead's principle of creativity, and his ontological principle, are interpreted as applying to actualities, presumed to have been already created, while ontological creativity mediates between the transcendent creator and his creation.

This project, it should be recognized at the outset, is quite foreign to Whitehead's own intentions. This creator God must be transcendent to all experience and its categories, and thus be quite unknowable. Such a God is akin to the "causal nature" behind the scenes that Whitehead had rejected in his earlier books on the philosophy of nature. Whitehead's whole effort to achieve maximum coherence takes the form of trying to conceive of all actualities, including God, within one set of common categories. Creativity itself is not an exception to this effort.

Partly in order to avoid the dualism inherent in traditional theories of divine creation, Whitehead's first metaphysical proposal was quite naturalistic.[1] He rejected the notion of an ultimate creator to explain the order of nature:

> [A]ny summary conclusion jumping from our conviction of the existence of such an order of nature to the easy assumption that there is an ultimate reality which, in some unexplained way, is to be appealed to for the removal of perplexity, constitutes the great refusal of rationality to assert its rights. We have to search whether nature does not in its very being show itself as self-explanatory. By this I mean, that the sheer statement, of what things are, may contain elements explanatory of why things are [SMW 134–35].

We cannot look behind the scenes, as if this would do us any good. In the final metaphysical proposal of *Science and the Modern World*, God was conceived as having an essential role as the principle of limitation, but this is not a creative role.

In Whitehead's later writings creativity is carefully distinguished from God, and assigned primarily to the activity of the actual occasions. Each concrescent occasion is conceived to be an act of becoming, whereby a new actuality is brought into being, or created. It is created, however, by its own act of synthesizing its inherited past. The many occasions of its causal past are thus unified by its own concrescent activity. The reasons why the present occasion is as it is and not otherwise are to be found either in these many past occasions or in its own creative decision to be the particular synthesis which it is. Thus each occasion simultaneously exemplifies the ontological principle and the principle of creativity, for each is an instance of the many becoming one. Here the transcendent creator of traditional theism has been replaced by an immanent process of creation in which all creatures share. The world is essentially self-created. God is creative only in the sense that he also is an actual entity, and shares in the creativity which all actual entities possess. He is thus a creature of self-creativity, although its chief exemplification.

Neville's cosmological interpretation tends to veil this intimate relationship between the ontological principle and creation. It is precisely *because* every actuality is self-creative that it can function as a reason, in partial explanation either of itself or of those of its successors which it causally influences. For every determinate aspect of any actuality must first come into being (i.e., be created), either in itself or in its causal predecessors.

While foreign to the Whiteheadian enterprise as such, Neville's moves do make sense as an attempt to incorporate Whitehead's metaphysics within the scope of classical notions of divine creation. Neville is proposing a way of reinterpreting that metaphysics, including its principle of creativity, as a "cosmology," i.e., as an account of the world created by God. Insofar as creativity resists limitation to the created order, it is understood as "ontological creativity," exercised by the creator. This is one way of securing the advantages of Whitehead's contemporary philosophy for a more classical understanding of creation, and it offers Neville a peculiarly advantageous standpoint from which to criticize Whitehead's own theory of creation. Hence it is important for us to evaluate these two different theories of creation in terms of their coherence and intelligibility.

Neville questions the ultimacy of Whitehead's Category of the Ultimate. This category has three principles, one, many, and creativity, all on a par with one another. Does not this triplicity, he asks, require further explanation in terms of that which created it? Yet Neville himself must make use of a triplicity of concepts: the creator, the creative act, and the creature. If the creature were identified with either the creative act or the creator, (then, on Neville's own principles) we would have being but no creation. For the creature is only a creature if it is the outcome of creation distinct from itself; otherwise we would have self-creativity. If we identify the creator with the creative act, then God's being is exhausted in the process of bringing that particular creation into being.

This triplicity is harmless, Neville would argue, for it results from the creative act, which determines the creator (otherwise indeterminate) as the creator of that particular creature, and the creature as the outcome of that act. Yet we should likewise recognize that the one, in Whitehead's Category of the Ultimate, is also the outcome of the creative act. Instead of assuming a creator distinct from both the creative act and the resultant creature, Whitehead ascribes the activity of creation to the very synthesizing process whereby the occasion emerges from its causal past. Thus the creator of that creative act is not different from the creature resulting from that act.

The two theories thus differ primarily with respect to the third term, the many out of which, according to Whitehead, the one is created. This is the difference between theories of total creation and theories of partial creation. It is also the difference between theories of external creation and theories of self-creation, for the notion of a total self-creation *ex nihilo* makes no sense. The creative act needs two termini: the situation prior to (and independent of) the act of creation, and the situation which results from that act. Creation *ex nihilo* presupposes the prior existence of at least the creator. This would be impossible if the creator were himself to be created by that act.

The theory of partial creation, whereby only a part of the creaturely occasion is newly created, the other parts deriving from past being, also militates against a theory of external creation. Neville's own view seems to be that the events of the world are continuously being created in their entirety as they emerge in the present. If so, past efficient causation, if it could really introduce elements of past being into those occasions now being created, would be quite redundant.

Suppose, however, that only the novel synthesis were now being created. This possibility is emphasized by Neville's careful analysis of spontaneity insofar as it is experienced as now being created.[2] If this creative act were external to the elements of past being, it is difficult to see how it could be so finely tuned to the contours of that past being as to serve as its apparent synthesis. The new being emerges precisely *as* the synthesis of the old. Moreover, if the creator is now creating the new synthesis out of the old, how does this creating differ from the occasion's own (partial) self-creativity? Insofar as we have any conscious awareness of this process, we experience it as our own exercise of freedom. Since all the objective factors of our experience belong to its past (or timeless) components, the present components by contrast must constitute our own subjectivity.

Whitehead's metaphysical innovation lies in vesting present synthesizing with the activity traditionally vested in past efficient causation. This synthesizing activity, moreover, is conceived as productive of novelty. If the new is more than simply a recombination of the old, something new has come into being. That novel element has been created by the process of synthesis itself. A theory of self-creation befits this metaphysical innovation, just as a theory of external creation befits traditional notions of efficient causation.

Which of these two theories is the more intelligible? If by this we mean: which can be explained in terms of exemplifying first principles, partial creation is the more intelligible. For if every concrescent occasion, in the way it prehensively unifies its past, is partially self-creative, self-creation exemplifies the necessary principles exemplified by such concrescence. External creation, by transcending those principles, is radically unintelligible in their terms. But Neville sees this as begging the question, since the creator creates those principles as well, and serves as the reason why those principles are what they are.

Here we seem to have a theoretical stand-off. In the final section of his essay Neville reflects on two different metaphysical sensibilities concerning the nature of an ultimately satisfying explanation. For the rationalist, it is a matter of reducing things to first principles. These first principles cannot be explained in terms of anything more ultimate; otherwise they would not be "first." "On the other hand, there is the empiricist's view that an ultimately satisfying explanation consists in locating the decisive actions from which things take their form. To be satisfied is to see the loci of decisive determination."[3] From this point of view, first principles need to be explained, and only creation will suffice as an explanation.

This account, we submit, stretches the notion of "empiricism" beyond the breaking point. Granted, things can be explained in terms of those things which produced them. Hence, in terms of traditional theories, there is an incessant search for efficient causes. But if this search is to result in an intelligible theory, we search for causes of a single type, following the maxim that "like produces like." Otherwise our empiricism results in mere historical chronicle, not in theoretical explanation. The loci of decisive determination must exhibit common features, and be subsumable under first principles. If we then seek to explain these first principles in terms of some more ultimate creative act, we leave the bounds of all possible experience far behind.

On Neville's analysis, we experience only what is created; we do not experience the creative act itself. If this is the case, could we ever determine that this world is created, and hence requires a creator? Now, this is not a problem peculiar to Neville's position, but applies to every theory of creation *ex nihilo*. We have no experience of such creation, nor any analogue to it. Partial creation, however, can be experienced. We experience such creation insofar as we experience our own self-creation, our own subjectivity. The distinction between what creates and what is created is precisely the distinction between the subjective and the objective.

Although we question Neville's use of 'empiricism' to describe his alternative, there is truth in his claim that first principles, being determinate, are in need of further explanation, just as there is truth in the claim that creation, to be intelligible, should exemplify first principles. Whenever we attack this problem one-sidedly, some element of the truth will be neglected. Whitehead's solution tries to do justice to both sides.

For one thing, the ontological principle is hardly rationalistic, in Neville's sense of 'rationalism'. It demands that all reasons be vested in decisions. The principle would have been less exceptionable if Whitehead had substituted the word 'cause' for 'reason'. Then the principle would simply mean that every actuality must be totally caused. Yet Whitehead chose the term 'reason', adopting the rationalist's proclivity for classifying activity according to principles. His "reasons" are not adventitious, because the causes for a particular outcome are all of a particular sort, subsumable under a particular principle. Insofar as any occasion exemplifies the metaphysical order, it conforms to the common order inherited from all of its antecedent actualities. Yet the reason why that timeless order is the order it is must be vested in some decision, which can only be God's primordial, non-temporal envisagement. In one explanation of the ontological principle Whitehead writes that "the reasons for things are always to be found in the composite nature of definite actual entities—in the nature of God for reasons of the highest absoluteness, and in the nature of definite temporal actual entities for reasons which refer to a particular environment" (PR 28).

On the other hand, the strict coherence of Whitehead's philosophy demands that even the creative act must be intelligible in terms of first principles. This is possible because God's non-temporal envisagement "at once exemplifies and establishes the categoreal conditions" (PR 522). Just as on Neville's own alternative, first principles are ultimately explained as created. But that creative act need not be unintelligible. This is possible only if we abandon the notion of a unique act of total creation in favor of a plurality of partial creative acts, of which God's is chief.

Creation *ex nihilo* is unintelligible in yet another sense, if we grant any rationality or truth to the ancient maxim, "*ex nihilo nihil fit.*" The two principles are diametrically opposed. We seem forced here to choose between creation and rationality. On its most extreme interpretation, "*ex nihilo nihil fit*" means that the new is only apparently new, for it can only be a recombination of the old. The ontological principle, however, restates that maxim, and so qualifies it as to permit partial creation. The reasons for every feature of an actuality are to be found *either* in past actualities (as the principle of *ex nihilo nihil fit* claims) *or* in the present self-creative decision of the concrescing occasion. Whitehead's genius lay in recognizing that the synthesis itself is creative, productive of new being.

NOTES

1. On this point see my essay "Whitehead's First Metaphysical Synthesis," *International Philosophical Quarterly*, 17 (1977), 251–64.

2. Robert C. Neville, *Soldier, Sage, Saint* (New York: Fordham University Press, 1978), Chap. 5.

3. Robert C. Neville, "Whitehead on the One and the Many," this volume, p. 269 above. Cf. also his *Creativity and God: A Challenge to Process Theology* (New York: Seabury Press, 1980), pp. 46–47.

# 14

# On a Strain of Arbitrariness in Whitehead's System

JUSTUS BUCHLER
*State University of New York
at Stony Brook,*
Emeritus

## I

A SYSTEM LIKE WHITEHEAD'S, and perhaps any major philosophic system, arises primarily, not from the cultivation of diverse interests or from reasoned pronouncement on a large number and variety of problems, but from a new mode of discriminating complexes of nature, one which intrinsically aims to translate itself into a discipline of generalization. (It just is not satisfactory to speak in terms of a "new way of seeing." Besides perpetuating the age-old bias toward sight as paradigm, this expression is not more applicable to systematic than to non-systematic invention in philosophy.) The specific discriminations that exemplify the mode take the shape of a body of ideas dealing with complexes as such, though sometimes, as in Whitehead, also with the way the complexes have come to be discerned or framed. A system is kindled, in other words, not by a desire to give answers to standing problems, but by a demanding form of awareness that requires conceptual ramification. Inevitably, specific problems are coped with—both those which

An earlier version of this chapter appeared in *The Journal of Philosophy* (66 [1969], 589–601).

the new mode of discrimination itself breeds and those which it construes as traditional. The very source of a system's problems lies in its gestation and application: there are discrepancies among its assertions, there is darkness in the evolving portrayal; the scope of its categories recurrently becomes uncertain; the categories need clarification. I do not know of any systematic philosopher who has been more concerned to provide alternative formulation, contextual restatement, than Whitehead; nor of any who has striven more assiduously to make his results available in the language of other systems.

In Whitehead's theoretic exposure of the traits he deems fundamental, I find two distinct trends. These are interlaced in the texture of his thinking, but it is imperative to enunciate them, because they represent profoundly different ways in which a mode of discrimination can work itself out. They represent philosophic impulses which cohabit uneasily, and not only in Whitehead's system but in systems quite different from his. I shall speak of Trend I and Trend II, and I shall contrast them not all at once but progressively, in connection with specific Whiteheadian theses.

In Trend I Whitehead seeks to define and justify a set of major concepts, together with their derivatives; to show their amplitude, their appositeness to both common and special forms of experience, and their ordered collective value for philosophic understanding. These concepts are designed to distinguish "types of entities" (types of "existence") and to explain their interrelation. In Trend II, on the other hand, Whitehead is concerned, not to delineate with increasing refinement the traits of the various types of entities, whether in specific detail or in large patterns, but to determine how "real" the various entities are. He sees each type as possessing an absolute role or function in the universe, in accordance with its mode and degree of reality.

In Trend I the analysis of traits is accomplished by the articulation of various "principles." In Trend II the assignment of absolute roles is accomplished by accentuating a small number of these principles, but especially a principle in a class by itself, "the ultimate metaphysical principle."

In Trend I the types of "existence" are shown to differ in scope or range. For example, actual entities or occasions are necessarily more comprehensive than subjective forms. Actual entities and eternal objects, on the other hand, are comparable in scope: each is of greater comprehensiveness than any of the other types of being. But *as* a type of being, neither is more fundamental than the other. And all the types, whatever their scope, equally "are." In Trend II, however, the ultimate cosmic role belonging to each of the types of being, in virtue of their respective degrees of reality, implies much more. It implies the primacy or centrality of one type, in contrast with all the others. This primacy belongs to actual entities. Their privileged role defines a basic direction in the universe, and it is to them that all other kinds of being, including eternal objects, minister.

In Trend I interrelations and interdependencies are affirmed with an eye to evidential support from major forms of constructive imagination—science, art, religious probing—as well as from tenacious convictions of common experience. In Trend II, although these sources of evidence are scarcely left unexploited, there is an overriding appeal to "the nature of things." The nature of things presumably is epitomized in the "ultimate metaphysical principle." This is a principle of "creativity," in accordance with which novel beings are created. Since there cannot be novel eternal objects, the ultimate principle is inherently addressed to actual entities. It is to the continuous creation of individual actualities that everything else is subsidiary or accessory. Everything else is defined and explained with reference to them, and everything else *is* for their becoming ("all entities" are "potentials for the process of becoming" [PR 44]). And even God, the ground of all possibility, is "in the grip of the ultimate metaphysical ground, the creative advance into novelty" (PR 529).

Whitehead declares "the primary method of philosophy" to be "descriptive generalization" (PR 15–16). If this method, in whatever respect, is embodied in his work, it can only be embodied in Trend I. Trend II is characteristically revealed by his abundant use of phrases intended to express degrees of reality. Although he dislikes the term 'unreal', he resorts over and over again to "more real," "really real," "final realities," "deficient reality," "completely real things," "final real things," "an absolute reality," "absolute individuality," "sheer individuality," "complete actuality," "deficiently actual," "complete matter of fact." These phrases add nothing to any accounts that could conceivably be called descriptive, accounts that constitute theory in Trend I. What they are intended to subserve is an affirmation of ultimate roles and positions, of priority and posteriority in the universe.

No doubt, Whitehead's metaphysics, like that of anyone else, is shaped in part by aesthetic and moral factors; and I shall not overlook this point. But it is beside my purpose to explain why the two trends coexist or why they are not perceived as two by Whitehead himself. The main question is whether Trend II weakens the structure to which it contributes; whether it casts a shadow of crude myth upon a remarkably intricate tissue of distinctions and generalizations; whether it spawns a formidable strain of arbitrariness in a system above all designed to avoid arbitrariness.

## II

If there is any notion to which Whitehead is addicted, it is the notion of "concreteness." In Trend I the broadest and most pervasive theme of his system is the interplay of possibility and actuality. In the "ultimate" reckoning of Trend II, possibility is secondary to actuality, and actuality as such is secondary to "concrete" actuality. A society, or other nexus, is "less" concrete than the actual occasions that compose it. The latter are the true individuals, each of which, as a process of becoming, as a synthesis or concrescence of everything in the universe into one actuality, is a true unity.

The two trends emerge sharply in two versions of a comparison between the reality of a nexus and the reality of its component actual entities. Trend I is exemplified when Whitehead says that a nexus of actual entities should be regarded as "real, individual, and particular" in the same sense as an actual entity (PR 29–30), or when he says that a society "is its own reason" (AI 261). But Trend II is exemplified when Whitehead conceives of a nexus as a "grouping" of actual entities, and contrasts the nexus with the "absolute reality" (AI 227), indeed the "sole reality" (AI 228) of the actual entities in their individual immediacy; only the latter are the "completely real things" (AI 262). In this trend, an actual entity is regarded as more real than a society of which it is a component, but also more real than any of its own components (e.g., a prehension). The actual entity is more concrete than its concrete components, while the society is less concrete than its concrete components. And *among* the components of the actual entity, some can be regarded as "most concrete."[1]

If we ask why pure possibilities (eternal objects) should be secondary and actual entities primary, when it is repeatedly stated that neither of these two kinds of being is conceivable apart from the other; what it means for one actuality to be "more" concrete or "less" concrete than another actuality; why any kind of unity or oneness is "more" of a unity, a truer oneness than any other; why individuals are "more real" than societies, why they "make up the sole reality of the universe," when non-individual actualities have been discriminated just as decisively; what it means to be a "completely real thing"—we find no answers. We find reiterations galore, and plenty of equivalent statements ingeniously formulated. But we find no answers in the way that we do when we ask, for instance, why perception in the mode of presentational immediacy should not be the only mode of perception, or why becoming is necessarily distinguished from change. It would not be an answer—e.g., to the question why concrete elements of certain composites are held to be more concrete than the concrete elements of other composites—to say that some composites (societies) are extensive, or extensively divisible, while others (actual occasions in their becoming) are not, and that therefore only the latter are truly concrete. This kind of answer is a disguised iteration, begging the question. It may hammer home a supposed difference between *kinds* of concreteness. But it does not explain the notion of *degrees* of concreteness. Nor can we provide an answer to the question why a society is less concrete than its component occasions by saying that a social composite "illustrates its qualities passively" while "[t]he activity belongs to the individual actualities" (AI 274). What makes activity more concrete than passivity?

The "concrete" has long been a shibboleth in philosophy. Most recently, both pragmatism and existentialism have been described in terms of it; the former as an "appeal" to the concrete, the latter as a "search" for the concrete. In Whitehead the problem, it would seem, is to provide adequate theoretical recognition of the concrete. And such recognition is expected, not only to achieve continuity with everyday feeling about what is "really real," but to guide and refine it. Like Whitehead, most philosophers of this century claim support from the grass roots, from "human orthodoxy" (Santayana); they see themselves as patient purifiers of a coarse primeval wisdom. Notwithstanding the claim, Whitehead's opinions about the concrete lean in an opposite direction from the "common" opinion. The latter attributes concreteness mainly to the occurrences and the gross enduring objects of everyday life, whereas Whitehead attributes it not to such occurrences and objects, which for him are societies, but to atomic actualities that become and perish. And whereas traditionally concreteness may be blind, nonrational, or directionless, Whitehead finds it to be that which *par excellence* manifests value, aim, self-creativity, self-realization.

"An actual entity," says Whitehead, "is concrete because it is . . . a particular concrescence of the universe" (PR 80). The impression is conveyed that in this system the meaning of 'concreteness' is derived from the meaning of 'concrescence'. But it is *not* thus derived, as we can see at once from the consideration that concreteness admits of more and less, while concrescence does not. To say, for example, that an actual entity is more concrete than a society and incomparably more concrete than a proposition, is to make Whiteheadian sense. But we cannot say that an actual entity is "more concrescent" than other kinds of entities. It alone, among the kinds of entities, is concrescent; it *is* a concrescence.[2] Then should we, perhaps, say that the parallel to degrees of concreteness is not degrees of concrescence but degrees of proximity to or involvement in concrescence—in the process of becoming? This, however, is made meaningless by more than one of Whitehead's principles. Actual *and* non-actual entities, non-individual actualities *and* possibilities, alike are involved in the becoming of any actual entity. We can speak of the nature, but not the degree, of such an involvement.

Both in Whitehead and in historical usage, concreteness is naturally contrasted with abstractness. In Whitehead there are different levels of meaning for the term 'abstract'. But there is a sense produced by a class of pronouncements that is plainly relevant to the issue of ontological degree. It is taken for granted in this sense that abstractness (like concreteness) belongs to entities and not merely to expressions about entities.[3] What, we may ask, constitutes an entity's being abstract? Certainly not that it is a possibility rather than an actuality. An actual entity which has perished in its immediacy, which is existing "objectively," is said by Whitehead to be "existing abstractly" (S 27). Moreover, there are degrees of abstractness, and for Whitehead the difference between a possibility as such and an actuality as such is not one of degree. It is accurate to say that a possibility is more abstract than an actuality, that one kind of possibility is more abstract than another, and that one kind of actuality is more abstract than another. If there is a scale of being in terms of greater and lesser abstractness, with eternal objects at one end and individual actualities at the other, the intermediate range of possibilities and actualities must be represented. Now, to speak, says Whitehead, of the abstractness of an eternal object means that "what an eternal object is in itself—that is to say, its essence—is comprehensible without reference to some one particular occasion of experience" (SMW 228). Does this state a criterion of relative abstractness in terms of comprehensibility? How such a criterion would be applied to descending degrees of abstract being is far from clear. If we try to apply it at the opposite end of the scale, to non-abstractness, to the actual entity or "one particular occasion of experience," what can we say? That the one occasion is comprehensible in terms of itself? That the one occasion is not comprehensible in terms of itself? Any occasion is related to the rest of the universe, but its individual comprehensibility in that capacity is another matter. Does it make sense at all to say that a given occasion is "comprehensible"? The notion of an occasion is comprehensible, but is a particular occasion? And although an occasion prehends (positively or negatively) all that there is, what can we mean here if we speak of the occasion "itself"? The occasion considered in its moment of satisfaction? The occasion insofar as eternal objects are ingredient in it? The statement that seems the safest to make in this context seems also to be the most paradoxical: what is "really real" (the occasion) is less comprehensible "in itself" than what is "merely real" (the eternal object). The notion of relative comprehensibility is not very helpful as the basis of a criterion for ascertaining the relative abstractness of entities.

According to Whitehead, a man in one occasion (act, moment) of his experience is that man in his most truly individual, "most concrete" being. What we call the man's life is a historic route of moments or occasions, in each of which he "concentrates in himself the colour of his own past." And therefore, "The 'man in his whole life-history' is an abstraction compared to the 'man in one such moment'" (S 27). 'Abstraction' here carries the sense of remoteness from the concrete atoms, the living elements, of a life. The whole known as a life-history, with all its changes, is depicted as a relatively abstract actuality; the component whole discerned as a becoming is depicted as free of all abstractness. The former (the history) is an imperfect unity; the latter (the occasion), a perfect unity. Despite Whitehead's commitment to the position that neither kind of unity is simple or unanalyzable, he regards the kind of whole that endures as being less concrete than the kind of whole that becomes. It does not strike him as relevant that, in another and well-established sense, only the whole of a man's history (the society of all his acts) may provide the adequate framework for the *understanding* of the man-at-one-moment. We arrive once again at the result that what is called "most concrete" and therefore really real may also be least intelligible (or comprehensible) in its concreteness. And it may be least intelligible to the very man-at-one-moment, to the same man as a continuing society of moments, or to another man with resources for interpretation. If Whitehead does not believe that a complete history is required in order to reveal adequately the being of a human occasion in that history, what accounts for his belief that "A reference to the complete actuality is required to give the reason why . . . a prehension is what it is in respect to its subjective form" (PR 29)? The answer is simply that in this system a history, unlike any of its atomic components, is not regarded as a "complete actuality." Whitehead plainly takes his conception of the man-in-one-moment to be what each of his positive conceptions aspires to be, namely, an instance of "the welding of imagination and common sense" (PR 26). But the appeal in issues of this kind surely cannot be to common experience construed as a fund of belief requiring only articulate recognition. At best it is to the spontaneous testimony of everyman's intuitings. By deferring to the same fickle guide, a philosopher could easily be persuaded that Whitehead's actual occasions—unencounterable, not identifiable in the way that "common objects" are—have the status of dubious inferred entities, or that the concept of a monadic occasion is akin to the most extravagant of speculative fictions.

## III

The conception of the centrality or primacy of actual occasions is set forth in several vigorous statements exemplifying one or another of Whitehead's principles, especially the "ontological principle." Usually there is more than a trace of conscious contention; witness the statement that "in separation from actual entities there is nothing, merely nonentity" (PR 68). One could ruminate over the precise force of the phrase 'in separation from', and then render it as 'except in relation to'. But the important observation to make is that, in spite of the emphasis intended, the Whiteheadian scheme permits us to say with equal validity: in separation from eternal objects there is nothing, merely nonentity. Another of Whitehead's statements in this vein employs the phrase 'apart from' instead of 'in separation from'. Thus, "apart from the experiences of subjects there is nothing, nothing, nothing, bare nothingness" (PR 254). The repetitive pounding does not help to supply a reason for the ontological primacy of "subjects." The assertion would remain valid and would retain the same kind of significance if we substituted 'the ingressions of eternal objects' for 'the experiences of subjects'. Whitehead fails to perceive that contentions of the preceding type, characteristic of Trend II, are in effect perspectival versions of what his system legitimates as truths. The statability of other and equally fundamental perspectives, compatible with those selected for emphasis, vitiates the claim of ontological priority. Is it an argument for the priority of actual entities to point out that each actual entity positively or negatively prehends everything that constitutes the universe, including the infinite realm of eternal objects? No more than it is an argument for the priority of eternal objects to point out that each eternal object is internally related to every other and necessarily has ingression, positive or negative, in every actual entity.

Consider four other variations on the theme of ontological primacy:

1. "[N]o things *are*, in any sense of 'are', except as components in experience or as immediacies of process . . ." (AI 304). But a parallel statement with a reverse orientation can be validated in the system. For example: No things *are*, in any sense of 'are', except as possibilities or as factors and conditions in their actualization. Since the frameworks which the system provides for this kind of formulation allow the expression of complementary perspectives, Whitehead's choice of one perspective as privileged is gratuitous.

2. "[T]he general metaphysical character of being an entity is 'to be a determinant in the becoming of actualities' " (PR 392). This appears to be an uncompromising pronouncement. But we can validate statements that are ostensibly excluded. For example: The general metaphysical character of being an entity is to be a con-

stituent in (a condition relevant to) the actualizing of possibilities. These statements embody the intent of the system's categories, but they emanate as it were from opposite directions. We can speak either of the conditions that make for the becoming of actualities or of the conditions that make for the actualizing of possibilities. (Strictly speaking, neither Whitehead's own statement nor the one with which I have matched it seems adequate to embrace every conceivable manifestation of "being an entity" in his system. But either is as adequate as the other.) The bidirectional emphasis (exemplifying Trend I) is expressed by Whitehead himself in various ways. From one direction, "each eternal object has a definite, effective relevance to each concrescent process" (PR 64). From the other direction, "The things which are temporal arise by their participation in the things which are eternal" (PR 63).

3. "[T]he endeavour to understand eternal objects in complete abstraction from the actual world results in reducing them to mere undifferentiated nonentities" (PR 392). But not less basic to Whitehead is an appropriately stated reversal: The endeavor to understand actual occasions in complete isolation from the world of possibility results in reducing them to mere unrelated nonentities.

4. "All relatedness has its foundation in the relatedness of actualities . . ." (PR ix). By the most indispensable standards of the system, this statement is not only arbitrary but rash. The term 'foundation' as here used is unclear; yet whatever its limits of meaning may be, the chances of emerging with a statement that is valid in the system are at least as good if we substitute 'eternal objects' for 'actualities' as they are if we leave the statement intact. And if *Science and the Modern World* is the book we select for evidence, the substitution even seems to be desirable.

Trend II subordinates whatever fails to conform to selected ontological conditions. Trend I delineates whatever conforms to these conditions. The temper of Trend I is not to find that "nothing is *except* in such-and-such a way" but to find that "something *is* in such-and-such a way"—in whatever other way it is. Or, more specifically, not that no things are except as components of "experience," but that all things are, in one respect, components of experience; not that apart from actual occasions there is nothing, but that whatever there is can be described in terms of the becoming of actual occasions—in whatever other way it can be described.

Whitehead favors his actual occasions as the really real beings on another account. It is of them that he thinks irresistibly when he deals with certain attributes which have acquired honorific status in the history of philosophy—to wit, individuality, efficacy, and determinateness. And yet the range of his own thought makes the issue of when and how these attributes prevail a knotty one, one which in fact yields small comfort to the thesis of ontological primacy.

So far as *individuality* is concerned, it is attributed by Whitehead to eternal objects as well as to actual occasions. Each eternal object is an individual; it has its own "individual essence" (SMW 229). And if there are thus abstract individuals and concrete individuals, which shall we crown as the "true" individuals? Trend I represents Whitehead undertaking to discriminate two manifestations of individuality, analyzing each, conveying the integrity of each, and comparing traits. Trend II represents Whitehead's inclination to discriminate not just two forms but primary and secondary forms of individuality, with a view to cosmic ranking.

*Efficacy* is associated by Whitehead with "reasons" and "causes." One of the ways in which he states his so-called ontological principle is "that actual entities are the only *reasons*" (PR 37). This is the "principle of efficient, and final, causation" (PR 36–37). The indicated conclusion is that efficacy is an attribute of concrete actuality. But there is the other side of the matter. Whitehead says that to "function" means "to contribute determination to the actual entities in the nexus of some actual world" (PR 38). And it is essential, in his language, to attribute "functioning" to actualities and eternal objects alike. Both alike are "determinants." The "effective relevance" of eternal objects to concrescences has already been cited. Whitehead does not even hesitate to call eternal objects "agents": the mode of ingression of certain eternal objects is "to be an agent in objectification" (PR 445). We are warned by some experts on Whitehead not to take him seriously when he uses terms like 'agent' in connection with eternal objects. I am not unreceptive to such warnings. Whitehead does say, in the same work, that "agency belongs exclusively to actual occasions" (PR 46). I am less concerned, however, with the concept of "agency" than with the broader concept of efficacy, having myself suggested elsewhere that efficacy belongs to all natural complexes whatever. And I am of course mainly concerned with the (two) trends that may help to show how or why Whitehead vacillates in the way he does.[4] In any event, it seems to me that, if we make our context Whitehead's system as a whole (precarious and difficult as it may be to do this), then so far as the concept of efficacy *as such* is concerned, there is no way, and no need, to distinguish between the effective relevance of an actual entity and the effective relevance of an eternal object. To assign efficacy in this system solely to actual entities would reflect not an analysis but a decree. And if the decree is ascribable to Whitehead, it is no less ungrounded in the system.

The notion of *determinateness* is elusive in Whitehead. From one angle we can find a contrast between the possible as the indeterminate and the actual as the determinate, and a corollary contrast between the determinate and the fully determinate. The latter is one more guise of the really real; it is identified with "the culmination of the concrescence into a completely determinate matter of fact" (PR 322). This culmination is the satisfaction of the actual entity, its "final unity" or "concrete unity of feeling." But from another angle the basic contrast is not between the possible as the indeterminate and the actual as the determinate; it is between determinate and indeterminate aspects of the possible, on the one hand, and determinate and indeterminate aspects of the actual, on the other. Thus (omitting for brevity's sake "real" possibilities and "impure" possibilities, or propositions) eternal objects are determinate with respect to their individuality, their mode of ingression into actual entities, and their internal relatedness to one another; they are indeterminate so far as "their own natures do not in themselves disclose in what actual entities [the] potentiality of ingression is realized" (PR 44). Actual entities are determinate in their "formal constitutions"; they are indeterminate (for example) with respect to the interrelation of their components in the stages antecedent to their satisfaction (PR 322).

IV

To a certain extent we can think of Trend II as a tendency in Whitehead to dramatize metaphysical inquiry. His entity-types come to be interrelated in the way the characters of a narrative or a drama are. Sometimes he even speaks the language of one engaged in a quasi-narrative undertaking. "Cosmological story, in every part and in every chapter, relates the interplay of the static vision and the dynamic history. But the whole story is comprised within the account of the subjective concrescence of *rēs verae*" (PR 254). From the epic or dramatic standpoint it is clear why the "whole story" must be an account of concrescence; why actual entity must play the central role and occupy the central location. A story has a plot. There must be action. And action or activity most directly suggests actual entity. The other entity-types play their roles, but their roles are defined by the destiny of the central being, the individual that unifies the multifariousness of the world. The note of tragedy is sounded. Actual entity perishes in the fulfillment of its subjective being. But, immortal in its objectivity, it contributes itself to endless generations. Without it there is no life and nothing to record or recount. It is the bearer of novelty, which is the measure of direction. As metaphysical hero, it receives the accolades of being: true unity, complete individuality, final reality, pure actuality, concreteness in the highest. These emerge as heavily charged conceptions, mirroring the philosopher's moral reaction to what is. Eternal object, stiff and immobile, gets second billing. But it makes a vivid impact. Whereas actual entity harbors an "internal principle of unrest" (PR 44), eternal object undergoes "adventures" (e.g., PR 92), and "suffer[s] changing relations" (PR

44). The ways that obtain between the eternal and the actual form the core of the complicated story. These ways are constituted by the dramatic mediation of God.

Remembering, always, Whitehead's underlying assumption that such concepts as feeling, aim, experience, freedom, subjectivity, and value do not have pre-eminently human relevance, there is no reason to think of the cosmic drama as a figurative aspect of the system. But there is good reason to think that, by insisting on the rise, fall, and immortality of actual entities as the all-encompassing theme, Whitehead has involuntarily curtailed the imaginative power of this system. My feeling is that if Trend I had gained the ascendancy, with its mere relentless scrutiny of discriminanda, its independence of ultimate rankings and destinies, there would have emerged a structure equally majestic, freer from disparity and gratuitousness, and more subtle in its exhibitive dimension.

NOTES

1. "The analysis of an actual entity into 'prehensions' is that mode of analysis which exhibits the most concrete elements in the nature of actual entities" (PR 28). Whether elliptically or not, Whitehead speaks also of the "most concrete mode of analysis" (PR 29).

2. Consider also: "Whenever the 'all or none' principle holds, we are in some way dealing with one actual entity, and not with a society of such entities, nor with the analysis of components contributory to one such entity" (S 28).

3. The entities are also described, in a confusing way, as "abstract from" concrete particulars (PR 30).

4. Where it is justifiable (as I have been arguing it is here) to think of a body of thought in terms of different and deep-seated inclinations, we are spared the awkward, ad hoc procedure of dismissing as "unfortunate" or "unhappy" those passages which are hard to account for in a particular interpretation of Whitehead—and which are left unaccounted for.

15

# Ontological Primacy: A Reply to Buchler

CHARLES HARTSHORNE
*University of Texas at Austin,*
Emeritus

JUSTUS BUCHLER HAS GIVEN US a brilliant critique of Whitehead's metaphysics. I wish to say at the beginning that I go some part of the way with his criticisms. I think that "eternal objects," as Whitehead characterizes them, are not wholly congruous with the most distinctive features of the Whiteheadian account of creative becoming and of actuality. I also think that Whitehead has not sufficiently clarified the apparent paradox in saying that "societies," genetically connected groups of actualities, are less concrete than the single actualities composing them.

I hold, however, that the right way to overcome these deficiencies is not to give up what Professor Buchler calls 'Trend II', and what Whitehead calls 'the ontological principle' (that "actual entities" are primary), but rather to restrict the meaning of 'eternal object', and to make more clear than Whitehead has done that a society, as referred to in any given instance, is nothing over and above its objectification in some actual entity doing the referring (including the de facto actual state of Deity in which alone the full truth about the society is adequately embraced).

Buchler is wonderfully ingenious in finding ways of reversing

An earlier version of this chapter appeared in *The Journal of Philosophy* (67 [1970], 979–86).

claims made for the basic role of actual entities, in favor, now of eternal objects, now of possibilities, now of societies. Thus: apart from actual entities there is nothing; but also, apart from eternal objects [or possibilities, or societies] there is nothing. Of course. But the sense in which the eternal requires the actual or temporal is different from the sense in which the temporal requires the eternal. To see this we must take distinctions of logical level into account. The eternal is the (completely) universal, universals exist only through instances (as a minimum, someone thinking the universal). However, while the universal requires only that there *be* instances, the instances require not just that there be universals, but the very universals which they instantiate. In general, polar contrasts, such as abstract/concrete, universal/particular, object/subject, are symmetrical correlatives only so long as we think simply of the categories themselves, as concepts, and not of what they may be used to refer to or describe.[1] The moment we think of the latter, the symmetrical interdependence is replaced by a radical asymmetry. Thus the universal, abstract, or (at the extreme) eternal is the common factor of diverse particulars, and since the latter *also* possess their differences, they are richer in qualities than the universal. Nor can the differences in question be reduced to additional eternal universals. For eternal objects do not exhaustively characterize even the humblest actual entity, whose unique unity is something additional. This statement cannot be reversed: all eternal objects (and all so far actualized entities) are fully included in the character of the latest actuality, including that stage of the divine actuality which prehends both the eternal and the temporal universe as so far actualized. Eternal objects are not additional to actualities, if divine actuality is taken into account; but every actuality is something more than eternal objects. I admit that to carry this asymmetry through it is probably necessary to reduce "eternal objects" so that the idea denotes much less than Whitehead seems to have in mind; for instance, so as not to include "red" or "sweet." But I do not wish here to discuss my difference from Whitehead on this point. I think that a fairly strong rebuttal of some of Buchler's most serious charges (I shall not try to deal with all of them) is possible in abstraction from this issue.

The essential meaning of 'concrete' is 'definite' or 'determinate' (a term Buchler finds "elusive"). "Definiteness is the soul of actuality" expresses a basic Whiteheadian conviction. One aspect of this doctrine is found in Leibniz, in his "in esse" principle. The definiteness of truth presupposes the definiteness of reality, and a pluralistic ontology holds that there must be at least several definite entities. Universals are all indefinite, compared to their instances. *This man* is more definite than the property *human.* Whitehead differs from Leibniz, however, above all in holding that *this man now* is more definite than *this man*, since until a man is dead his career is partly indeterminate, and even after he is dead we can say that the same man could have acted and experienced differently than he did. His actual history is definite, but "he" is not. A second disagreement with the earlier philosopher is that Whitehead takes a possibility to be less definite than its actualization. Here Whitehead agrees with Bergson and other philosophers of process: before an experience occurs, the unique quality of that experience was neither possible nor impossible; there was no such quality, with any status whatever. Possibilities are always more or less universal, non-particular. Thus there is a basic asymmetry between the definiteness of the particular, actual, or concrete, and the partial indefiniteness, by comparison, of the universal, possible, or abstract.

The idea of degrees of concreteness which bothers Buchler is the ontological correlate of the familiar notion (somewhat generalized, as we shall see) of degrees of universality or abstractness. It is also very different from doctrines (Bradley, Sankara, Plotinus) of the unreality of concrete particulars—indeed, it is nearly the opposite of this. The fullness of reality, including all its value, is in actual experiences, not in any mere thought, timeless form, or being. This view is common to almost the entire group of process philosophers, e.g., Nietzsche,[2] Bergson, James, Dewey, Mead, Peirce, and Whitehead. (The last, however, seems to me to exaggerate the definiteness of the abstract, and *in this respect* to be inferior to the others.)

Buchler sees that Whitehead wants to assert the asymmetry between definite actualities and indefinite possibilities, but he tries to show that the system also implies symmetry. Thus:

> [E]ternal objects are determinate with respect to their individuality, their mode of ingression into actual entities, and their internal relatedness to each other; they are indeterminate so far as "their own natures do not in themselves disclose in what actual entities . . . ingression is realized." [Similarly,] actual entities are determinate in their "formal constitutions"; they are indeterminate (for example) with respect to the interrelation of their components in the stages antecedent to their satisfaction [pp. 292–93].

What is overlooked here is that the determinateness of a satisfaction includes (by positive and negative prehensions) that of all eternal objects (and their indeterminateness as well) plus the indeterminateness of the "incomplete" stages of realization (Principle of Process: an actuality sums up its own becoming).

Over and over we find Buchler obscuring this, the essential point. Thus, referring to the definition of being as "potential for becoming," he says: "We can speak either of the conditions that make for the becoming of actualities or of the conditions that make for the actualizing of possibilities" (p. 290). Ah, but an actuality prehends its conditions, and so possesses their definiteness, while a possibility neither prehends *nor in any sense whatever possesses* "its" actualizations. A possibility does not change when it is actualized; simply there is a new determinate instance of a certain partly indeterminate universal.

I fully grant that Whitehead's exposition is somewhat inadequate in the extent to which it opens the way to Buchler's attack. The role of asymmetry is not nearly enough stressed, and indeed in some passages seems contradicted. There is much talk about internal relations, only a little about external relations. But both are essential and entirely relevant to Buchler's problem. Whitehead does say that eternal objects have internally no relations to any particular actual entity. (They are internally related to God, but only in his primordial aspect, which is "abstract," "deficient in actuality," that is, in richness of determinations.) Moreover, and above all, it is made entirely clear that prehension is a radically one-way dependence of an actuality upon "antecedent" conditions, that is, temporally prior actualities. It is also stated many times that prehending is a form of including, whereby reality is enriched, "increased" in multiplicity of factors. "The many become one and are *increased* by one." Reality is protean and cumulative, as Bergson said. If any Whiteheadian statement conflicts with this, then I think it is to be discarded. For the formula just quoted is said to characterize the "ultimate" principle. And if this principle goes, then I see not much need for Whitehead.

Given that *A* succeeds and prehends *B*, the relation between the two terms is internal to *A* but not to *B*. It follows that *A* is *more* than *B*, for it includes relation-to-*B*, this relatedness having a *how* of subjective form into which the nature of *B* enters, but only as prehended datum, not as the entirety of the new actuality. "Subjective forms" always include their data, but never vice versa. Universals, as such, are essentially data (primordially for God) and nothing more.

It might be replied that actualities also are destined to become data, and all but the latest are already such. Yes, but they are data for later actualities, not for eternal objects. The latter are either common constituents of their instances, or else thoughts, or concepts, primordially "divine concepts." And thoughts are real only in experiences of some kind, that is, actualities. Not only Aristotle but the entire nominalistic tradition is behind Whitehead in this. The ontological principle is thus a long way from a mere Whiteheadian eccentricity. Renouncing it, as Paul Weiss has done, leads to proliferation of basic "modes of being," none really telling us what makes truth true.

Buchler does not see how relations of actualities can be the foundation of all relatedness, including relations between universals, and thinks that the latter could as well be the foundation. And he complains, with some justification, that 'foundation' is a vague or ambiguous term. However, as Whitehead repeatedly tells us, universals are merely ways in which actualities can relate themselves to other actualities. All relations have to be internal to something, and relations of particular, temporal actualities could not be internal to universal and eternal possibilities. Nor could the relations of possibilities to the actualities be internal to the former. To know what relations obtain one must find the relations contributing to the definiteness of some entity for which they are constitutive, and this will not be an entity prior to the obtaining of the relations, and therefore it will not be eternal, for the eternal is prior to any temporal entity you please (though not to all such entities, for these are not finite in number).

We are told that if eternal objects are not comprehensible apart from actualities, neither are actualities apart from eternal objects. But this is only to say that the contrast abstract/concrete is ultimate; nevertheless the concrete entities include the abstract ones, not vice versa. Thus it is the concrete that enjoys the contrast. The concrete is the whole story; the abstract is a partial version of that story. An actuality is comprehended by comparing and otherwise relating it in thought to other actualities; and the comparing is done by actualities. Universals are only aspects of this process. A full analysis of a given actuality would disclose all antecedent reality, in its concreteness as well as in its abstract aspects. But even an ideally complete analysis of eternal objects would not arrive at Justus Buchler or me or at our experiences from moment to moment. The ideal divine "envisagement" of eternal objects was "complete" before there were the entities mentioned, even as distinct possibilities. And this can be so only because God was already and always actual—though also open to increase in definite content. (I incline to take this as meaning that God is a society, not a single actuality. Here too I seem to differ from Whitehead and some of his admirers.)

To Whitehead's "apart from the experiences of subjects there is nothing" Buchler retorts: "The assertion would remain valid and would retain the same kind of significance if we substituted 'the ingressions of eternal objects' for 'the experiences of subjects' " (p. 289). But for an eternal object *O* to be ingredient in an actual entity *AE* is nothing for *O*, for which it is an external, and one might even say a merely nominal, relation. It is not *what O is* that makes it *true* to say that *AE* contains or embodies *O*, but only what *AE* is. This was Leibniz's "in esse," a poorly understood but in itself sound doctrine.

If there are any ideas without which Whitehead is negligible they are prehension and creativity. Both are nothing without a radical distinction between internal and external relationships, a radical asymmetry between the independent and the dependent, or the less and the more, the non-inclusive and the inclusive. Whitehead himself points out that the relation of earlier actualities to subsequent ones is analogous to that between universals and instances. Thus the distinction between universal and particular is "blurred" or, better, given many degrees. An actuality is a potential datum for subsequent becoming in general, and so any *AE* establishes the universal "prehends *AE*," of which there will be innumerable instances.

Possibility is a way of looking at the foregoing. Real possibility is simply the destiny of actualities to be objectified by subsequent actualities. Every actualization of the possibility "prehending *AE*" includes it and more besides. The actualization has additional definiteness. This is just an application and generalization of the familiar logical doctrine that assertions of particular instances of universals are "logically stronger" than the mere assertion that the universals exist, or have some instances or other. "There is a man" is weaker than "There is a man named Chang who has qualities *F*, *G*, *H*. . . ." But specifying the present state of Chang, that he is now sick with a high fever, say, gives more definite information than merely specifying his fixed characters. And Chang's self-awareness prehends more than any set of universals. Similarly, that someone is aware of Plato is less definite than that I now think of Plato in a certain way peculiar to me as I now am.

That societies are less concrete than actual entities is a more difficult matter. It does not mean, taking basic principles of the system into account, that a given sequence of actual entities is abstract. This would, I think, be absurd. However, (1) the identity of a society depends not upon its entire actual history (for to claim this is to accept the Leibnizian exclusion of real contingency from the temporal process) but upon its "defining characteristic," this being abstract enough to allow for the appropriate degree of indeterminacy in becoming. Moreover, (2) a sequence of events is always summed up in its latest member (apart from God, always with partly negative or abstractive prehensions). Past actualities have being only as prehended items in later actualities. Being past is not an absolute but a relative status. Nothing is past just in itself, or "perished" just in itself. (Here I seem to differ somewhat from certain interpreters.) To become past and to become objectified by later actualities is but one transaction. Also, (3) in a process philosophy one cannot refer to a sequence of actualities from a timeless perspective. "The universe," says Whitehead, is a "demonstrative pronoun," meaning *the universe as past for a certain actuality*, plus what is implied about contemporaries and successors by that past universe. Each time we say "the universe" we refer to a partly different set of entities. This holds for a local society also.

There is partial agreement on this point between Whitehead and Mead. Everything must somehow be in the present. But since Whitehead does not limit his account to human or manlike presents, but believes in a sort of divine present, man's invincible limitations of remembering and reconstructing the past are not for Whitehead "the measure of things." Only in the divine actuality is the full definiteness, concreteness or actuality, of the past, and of all reality, contained. There are difficulties in this, as the mention of relativity physics should make manifest. Whether and how the difficulties can be satisfactorily dealt with is indeed a grave question, one which always reminds me of my limited grasp of certain mathematical and physical conceptions.

My conclusion is not that Buchler is simply wrong, but that he is seriously wrong at some points, and that what he has so cleverly shown is not quite what he thinks he has, namely, that to reach a sound view one can and should purify the Whiteheadian vision of what he calls Trend II, summed up in the ontological principle that the concrete and inclusive realities are actual entities, everything else being these entities in some partial aspect or constituent. (Once more the ingredience of a universal in an instance is neither a constituent of the universal nor an aspect of it in the sense here intended. It is not a relation which the universal has, but a relation which has it.) What Buchler has shown, to my satisfaction at any rate, is only that Whitehead's exposition and, to some extent, his actual meanings are not wholly satisfactory, but chiefly for the basic reason that the asymmetry between abstract and concrete, indefinite and definite, prehended and prehending, universal and particular, prior and subsequent, possible and actual, included and including, is not sufficiently emphasized, and not altogether consistently developed, in Whitehead's system.

The trouble is partly rhetorical. Whitehead does not believe that one can incorporate all needed qualifications into assertions; and I suspect that at times he makes this skepticism a justification for excessively one-sided or oversimple affirmations, including apparent admissions of symmetry where radical asymmetries are required. But I would not, for all that, assume that Whitehead was free from real inconsistency or confusion. Indeed, he says himself that this is scarcely possible for our human "ape-like consciousness," with its language which is always but a stage in our individual and collective mental development. I think his system is, not so much very good as, in the famous phrase of R. M. Hutchins about the University of Chicago, "simply the best" that down to its time had existed. If we are to go back into the past at all, it seems absurd to ignore Whitehead. Professor Buchler has not done this.

NOTES

1. See my *Creative Synthesis and Philosophic Method* (London: Student Christian Movement Press; LaSalle, Ill.: Open Court, 1970; rpt., Washington: University Press of America, 1983), Chap. VI, "A Logic of Ultimate Contrasts."

2. In a fascinating passage (called to my attention by Grayson Douglas Browning) in *The Twilight of the Idols* Nietzsche scolds philosophers for their "hatred of the very idea of becoming" and refers to the idea of being as "an empty fiction." See *The Portable Nietzsche*, ed. Walter Kaufmann (New York: Viking, 1954), pp. 479–83.

# AFTERWORD

# A Sampling of Other Interpretations

Lewis S. Ford
*Old Dominion University*

The essays collected in this volume are representative of the best work that has been done on Whitehead's philosophy in recent years, but they by no means show the full scope and variety of concerns that his thought has evoked. Hence it has seemed advisable to round out the volume with an informal critical survey of some of the studies which we were unable to include here.[1] This survey is not intended to be exhaustive; it is only a sampling of the Whitehead literature, and mainly of the literature which antedates the establishment of the journal *Process Studies* in 1971. That journal, which is devoted to the study of Whitehead and other important process philosophers, in effect carries on—in its articles, abstracts, and reviews—the task of surveying the current Whitehead literature.

This sampling is organized around three topics: (I) Metaphysics (or Speculative Philosophy), (II) Panpsychism (or "Pansubjectivism"), and (III) Theism. It is Whitehead's joint commitment to all three of these positions, against the grain of much contemporary philosophy, which largely explains why he is so widely disregarded in philosophical circles. The situation in theological circles is now quite different; an indication of the change is that we are now exhorted to read Reinhold Niebuhr because of his affinities with Whitehead, rather than vice versa.[2] The collapse of the fideistic and anti-metaphysical assumptions of neo-orthodoxy, widely advertised by the "death of God" theologians, has prompted many theologians to re-examine the possibility of a revised natural theology. For this task Whitehead offers rich resources. Among philosophers, however, interest in Whitehead's thought needs to be reawakened. Many philosophers are concerned with the revitalization of metaphysics, and a substantial number are willing to consider theism a live option. A few take panpsychism (or pansubjectivism) seriously. But very few combine all three commitments. Whitehead's positive espousal of all three positions may cause him to be viewed as a thinker whose thought is "out of season." But this of course says nothing about the truth of his philosophy. To determine that we need to examine each of these topics closely.

## I · METAPHYSICS (OR, SPECULATIVE PHILOSOPHY)

The contemporary revolt against metaphysics takes many forms. The positivist–linguistic veto is well known, whether in its early form, as the claim that, to be cognitively meaningful, an utterance must be either tautologous or empirically verifiable in principle; or in its later efforts to reconceive philosophy's task as the disentanglement of linguistic confusions. Earlier, pragmatists had objected to theoretical, *a priori*, deductive undertakings based upon absolutely certain starting points. Phenomenologists have sought to evade metaphysical concerns by "bracketing" the question of existence. Heidegger and others have argued that the enterprise of metaphysics reached its conclusion in the thought of Hegel and Nietzsche, and that now "fundamental ontology" must search out the deeper meaning of Being.[3]

We cannot begin to discuss adequately even this partial list of criticisms, but must focus upon more particular objections to Whitehead's form of metaphysics. Here the most pressing objection is the claim that it is too Leibnizian—that it is a dogmatic, pre-critical enterprise which refuses to take Kant's transcendental turn seriously.

On one level this is true. Whitehead recognizes that his philosophy involves "a recurrence to pre-Kantian modes of thought" (PR vi). He refuses to accept Kant's conclusions insofar as they depend upon Hume's analysis of sensation and experience. He adopts the radical empiricism of William James,[4] which is being re-examined in phenomenological circles,[5] and argues that sense-experience includes patterns and relations, in particular causal relations, as well as isolated sensory impressions. Experience brings with itself the means of its own organization, and does not require the alien imposition of any transcendental machinery to render it intelligible. This does not mean that Hume's analysis is mistaken in detail, for Whitehead agrees that the mode of perception which Hume examines does consist in essentially unrelated sense-images. In concentrating upon this clear and distinct foreground of "presentational immediacy," illustrating external space contemporary with ourselves, Hume ignores the vague and massive "causal efficacy" derived from the immediate past. Since, according to relativity physics, contemporary entities cannot be causally related,[6] we should expect Hume's denial of any intrinsic causal connections as long as perception is identified with the clear and distinct deliverances of "presentational immediacy." As phenomenology shows, however, there is little reason to assume that experience can be restricted to those aspects important to scientific empiricism, ignoring all others.

Whitehead's basic objection runs deeper, and applies generally to the whole epistemological preoccupation inaugurated by Descartes. Whitehead endorses the Cartesian subjectivist turn, but sees it as incompletely assimilated by its discoverer. Descartes

> laid down the principle, that those substances which are the subjects enjoying conscious experiences, provide the primary data for philosophy, namely, themselves as in the enjoyment of such experience. This is the famous subjectivist bias which entered into modern philosophy through Descartes. In this doctrine Descartes undoubtedly

> made the greatest philosophical discovery since the age of Plato and Aristotle. For his doctrine directly traversed the notion that the proposition, "This stone is grey," expresses a primary form of known fact from which metaphysics can start its generalizations. If we are to go back to the subjective enjoyment of experience, the type of primary starting point is "my perception of this stone as grey" [PR 241].

The proposition "This stone is grey" has basically a subject/predicate form of expression, reflecting a substance/quality metaphysics. The subject/predicate form distorts the underlying structure of "my perception of this stone as grey," which is a two-term asymmetrical relation connecting perceiver and perceived. Descartes and his successors tried to articulate the subjectivist turn within the inherited subject/predicate form of expression by replacing "substance" with "subject" and "quality" with "perception." The older doctrine of independent substances with their dependent attributes now gave rise to individual subjects enjoying their own private perceptions. The intrinsically relational character of perceptions as inseparably connecting the perceived to the perceiver is undercut when these relations are reduced to one-term properties of substance-subjects. As long as perceptions are conceived to be nothing but the properties of independently existing subjects, they can only be private sensations, however much they are said to "mirror" or "represent" external reality. The solipsism of immediate experience, foreshadowed in the unknowability of the thing-in-itself, is the necessary consequence of trying to take the subjectivist turn while retaining substance/quality assumptions. Hume and Kant are no less enmeshed in these problems than Descartes. Only a relational metaphysics, Whitehead argues, in which actualities are conceived as nothing but unities (or better, unifications) of relations, can adequately account for the subjectivist turn.

These criticisms of Kant, however, ought not to obscure the senses in which Whitehead does accept the transcendental turn. As a valid extension of the subjectivist turn, it may be phrased in the form of a normative judgment: instead of investigating the generic structure of reality, philosophy should seek to determine the generic structure of experience. Faced with these exclusive alternatives, Whitehead opts for experience rather than reality: "Speculative Philosophy is the *endeavour* to frame a coherent, logical, necessary system of general ideas in terms of which every *element of our experience* can be interpreted" (PR 4, italics added). He repudiates the efforts of classical metaphysics on two fronts: its insistence upon absolutely secure foundations in self-evident propositions, and its rational construction of theoretical entities transcending experience. Whatever general structures metaphysics uncovers must be discernible wholly within experience. So stated, however, these propositions may be misleading insofar as Whitehead does not grant that any reality lies wholly outside experience. In experience we truly grasp reality, being truly related to it; and yet that reality is not exhausted in our experience of it. This is taken to be, not a speculative inference, but a feature of the experience itself: in perceiving the surface of the table, I experience the table as being something more than its surface, even though the qualitative character of the excluded aspects is hidden from me. Whitehead's claim that we actually grasp reality in experience follows partly from his relational metaphysics, and partly from his insistence that reality and experience are not incommensurables, but opposite sides of the same coin. Experience is the present subjective immediacy of reality, and reality is experience objectified as past fact. The defense of this claim must be postponed until we discuss panpsychism, but these comments should suffice to indicate that it is these considerations, and not resistance to the transcendental turn itself, which give Whitehead the appearance of being precritical. From Whitehead's point of view, many thinkers who have taken the transcendental turn have not gone far enough, for they do not see that the experience/reality distinction must be made within experience, understood as a distinction between two of its temporal modalities. They remain haunted by the idea, whether expressed or not, of a reality lurking beyond the bounds of experience.

Kant's transcendental philosophy is coupled with a critique of traditional metaphysics as caught in irresolvable antinomies, because it sought to extend the categories beyond the bounds of possible experience. Hegel argues that the contradictions lie in the categoreal concepts themselves, and not in the mode of their employment. Concepts are necessarily one-sided and exclusive, and cannot individually express the concrete totality of reality. Only by developing the contradictions which are dialectically inherent in our metaphysical concepts can we arrive at the concrete universal, which adequately mediates the many-sided nature of the whole. Hegelians cannot chide Whitehead for indulging in metaphysics, but they can look askance at his non-dialectical approach.

The question is whether Whitehead's method is pre-dialectical or post-dialectical. If a metaphysics is based on clear and distinct ideas, each independently meaningful by itself, then the one-sided, exclusive character of these concepts calls for a dialectical development. Whitehead, however, is committed to the idea of coherence. This

> means that the fundamental ideas, in terms of which the scheme is developed, presuppose each other so that in isolation they are meaningless. This requirement . . . means that what is indefinable in one such notion cannot be abstracted from its relevance to the other notions. It is the ideal of speculative philosophy that its fundamental notions shall not seem capable of abstraction from each other [PR 5].

This demand for coherence explains Whitehead's opposition to all dualisms in terms of which one kind of entity is fully explicable without reference to the other kind (cf. PR 9–10); it also explains why *Process and Reality* is such a hard book to read and to teach. Since no basic concept is fully intelligible without all the other basic concepts, one must grasp them all together in their interplay with one another before one has understood any one of them individually. But to grasp all the basic concepts together in their mutual interplay is, in Hegel's terms, to understand the *Begriff*. Whitehead's counterpart of the "concrete universal" is the organic unity of the entire scheme of his categoreal concepts, none of which is individually exclusive since none is independently intelligible.

Whitehead differs from Hegel in his understanding of the whole, the totality. It always has an indexical quality relative to the ever-changing present. Each actual entity, in its turn, is the summation of the entire universe, and there is no way in which we can designate the togetherness of all things except from the standpoint of some actuality. Thus the task of metaphysics is not to comprehend the whole *simpliciter*, but "to conceive a complete . . . fact" (AI 203). It is to discern all the generic features which in the organic interplay of their particular contingent exemplifications constitute a single particular concrete actuality. In his understanding of the "concrete universal," Whitehead puts the emphasis upon the universal, limiting himself in metaphysics to those generic features exemplified by all actualities whatsoever, from God to "the most trivial puff of existence in far-off empty space" (PR 28). Only these generic features are considered, but they are discussed in their organic unity. Hegel's emphasis is upon the "concrete," leading him to a more relaxed understanding of the "universe," as that which is intelligible or rationally justifiable. In the extreme this leads him to try to explain the inexplicable contingencies of brute facticity, and to explain away the grounds for existential decision. But if the universal is understood most rigorously, then our basic metaphysical concepts must be non-dialectical or univocal in order to ensure that they are exemplified by every actuality whatsoever.

There are, however, some important affinities. Creativity has been likened to Thomas Aquinas' *esse-ipsum* and Paul Tillich's being-itself in terms of its intrinsic dynamism, its all-pervasiveness, its analogical embodiments, and its power to create and sustain actualities in being. Yet it shares an additional dimension with the emergence of Hegel's spirit. Creativity is inherently subjective in its activity. Both Whitehead and Hegel conceive "substance" as process which is at root subject. Whitehead's philosophy may thus be regarded as a non-dialectical, pluralistic account of Hegelian spirit. His categoreal scheme is formally analogous to Hegel's *Logic*, for both are the unified non-temporal expressions of spirit: in Whitehead's case, of creativity as instantiated in God's primordial envisagement. If the *Phenomenology* is the reflection of the categories of the *Logic* in human experience, then there may be important parallels with Whitehead's analysis of human experience as the clue to the basic metaphysical categories. Hegel and Whitehead differ, of course, with respect to their philosophies of nature and of spirit. Where Hegel sees the necessary unfolding of absolute spirit in time and in history, Whitehead sees a vast multiplicity of contingent instantiations of creativity, partly conflicting with one another, and partly coordinated by the directing activity of divine persuasion. Such persuasion, when successful, explains the plausibility of much of Hegel's account, but its fragmentariness limits the Hegelian thrust toward total explanation.

Heidegger's criticism of metaphysics had not been specifically applied to Whitehead, although one could readily imagine how it might be. Philosophy, since the time of Plato, according to this critique, has subtly but basically distorted the underlying question of being into what it means to be *a* being. This shift has narrowed the most general philosophical question to the metaphysical search for the proper categories to describe all beings generically. Rather, it is urged, we must break out of the narrow restrictions which metaphysics has imposed upon us and ask the question of being anew, in terms of a fundamental ontology. We must go back beyond Plato to the pre-Socratics.[7]

Whether or not this critique is justified, Whitehead's philosophy is often conceived as an example of metaphysics as categoreal analysis, just the sort of thing that Heidegger is challenging. Ivor Leclerc's vigorous defense of the ontological principle[8] as the core of Whitehead's thought may be construed as a brilliant response to this sort of question. Following Aristotle, Leclerc argues that the question of being can only be formulated in terms of what it means to be a particular actuality or *οὐσία*, or what it means to be an entity which is fully actual, in Whitehead's terminology. Then the ontological principle is reinterpreted in terms of the general Aristotelian principle that only actual entities are fully existent, while other entities, such as forms or eternal objects, are only derivatively existent, dependent upon actual entities for their instantiation. On this point Whitehead is definitely an Aristotelian and not a Platonist, as Leclerc convincingly shows.

Yet this is only a secondary function of the ontological principle, which basically shows that efficient and final causation must be grounded in actualities. Leclerc mentions this role, but inverts the order of these two features. The fundamental and pervasive role of creativity, moreover, suggests that Whitehead's philosophy cannot be construed as restricted to a metaphysics in the Heideggerian sense. The discussion of creativity moves on a level more fundamental than that of the other categories. Instead of conceiving the categoreal scheme as the principles of the metaphysical system, we may distinguish between an ontological level, expressed by the Category of the Ultimate, and a metaphysical level, expressed by the Categories of Explanation and the Categoreal Obligations. The reason why the metaphysical principles are as they are and not otherwise may be found in the primordial decision of God, yet that decision itself exemplifies the creative unification of the many eternal objects into a single order of possibility (PR 28, 64, 522). If this is so, we may argue that Whitehead has a minimal, yet sufficient, ontology to ground his metaphysical analysis of actuality.

Thus Whitehead's quarrel with Heidegger is not whether metaphysics needs an ontology but whether ontology can replace metaphysics. Neither enterprise can be abandoned, in Whitehead's view, for they require each other. Ontology, as adumbrated in the Category of the Ultimate, can be rendered precise and definite only in terms of a metaphysical scheme, which then can be tested in terms of its adequacy and applicability to our experience. Metaphysics, on the other hand, needs to be grounded in an ontology as its ultimate source, from which it can be generated.

Leclerc's book, however, serves as a most useful introduction to Whitehead's metaphysics. His exposition is an excellent illustration of pedagogic skill. It deftly cuts the tight circular structure of Whitehead's system, and presents its elements in the order of ascending complexity, allowing the novice to master each in turn. It makes a good companion to the *Key to Whitehead's* PROCESS AND REALITY compiled by Donald W. Sherburne.[9] Sherburne took approximately two-fifths of Whitehead's text, re-arranging it in an order designed to introduce the reader step by step to the fundamental concepts of the system in Whitehead's own words. It all flows very well, except for the first chapter, in which we are immediately plunged into Whitehead's subjectivistic talk of actual occasions. Why should Whitehead be concerned with such microscopic events, and why should he describe these events as having "feelings," of all things? The *Key* offers no answer, but Leclerc does. First, he shows us how Whitehead is concerned about metaphysics in the tradition of Aristotle, endeavoring to conceive of the generic properties of a primary existent. But this actual entity, this primary existent, is an atomic spatio-temporal event rather than an Aristotelian enduring substance. By the time we are introduced to the atomicity of becoming which governs the coming into being of these actual occasions, the reasons for Whitehead's subjectivistic approach to such microscopic events (reasons which we shall explore in the next section) have been made clear. Thus the two books can be used side by side to illuminate each other.[10]

Turning now from continental to Anglo-American resistance to process metaphysics, we shall concentrate on the criticisms advanced by two former Whiteheadians who have made the linguistic turn. The first we may note briefly, for it has been sufficiently refuted by David A. Sipfle.[11] V. C. Chappell correctly notes serious confusions and difficulties in the notion of "instantaneous becoming," which, however, he mistakenly ascribes to Whitehead.[12] The crucial inference occurs in these two sentences: "To say that a certain act or process of becoming is not extensive . . . would seem to imply that the becoming does not take any time to occur, that it is an act or process that extends through no time. The becoming may still occur at a time, i.e., at a certain instant, but only at that instant; hence it will be an instantaneous becoming."[13] Now, an act of becoming is not extensive "in the sense that it is divisible into earlier and later acts of becoming" (PR 107). The actual occasion is the unit of "epochal" passage from past to future; time requires the succession of occasions. No time can elapse until at least one occasion has been succeeded by another. This, however, need not mean that the occasion is instantaneous. Whitehead rejects the common assumption that if *a* is earlier than *b*, *a* must lie in the past of *b*. Each occasion is "temporally thick" in the sense that its spatio-temporal region can be formally analyzed into a series of instants, each earlier than its successor, yet all co-present. The act of becoming occupies the entire region, not just one of its instants, because it occupies the entire present. The temporal continuum is infinitely divisible in terms of the abstract relation of "earlier than" (or "later than"), but time is atomic in terms of the "epochal" passage from past to future. Thus, though each occasion comes into being "all at once," there is no instantaneous becoming, and the problems which Chappell has with this difficult and perhaps self-contradictory concept simply do not apply to Whitehead's theory.

A second critic, Richard Rorty, cannot be charged with misunderstanding Whitehead. His essay "Matter and Event" gives the best account available of the systematic importance of decisiveness for Whitehead's analysis of actuality and potentiality.[14] Rorty contrasts realism and reductionism as a way of stating the basic controversy between Aristotelians and post-Cartesians over the past three hundred years. Reductionism is the attempt to dissolve things (unrepeatables) into properties (repeatables). Realists resist this attempt by means of the form/matter distinction, arguing that the unrepeatable is an indissoluble unity of form and matter. But the fatal flaw in Aristotle's analysis is his identification of actuality with definiteness, for whatever is definite can be analyzed into a congeries of properties. Thus Locke can analyze a substance as a set of properties inhering in an unknown substratum, and Berkeley can dispense with the substratum. By taking time seriously, Whitehead can make decisiveness rather than definiteness the criterion for actuality. The presentness of this actual decision is unrepeatable, but its objective outcome can be repeated as the past becomes ingredient in subsequent present actualities.

'Actuality' and 'potentiality' thereby become relative terms, for whatever is actual in itself (in its own present becoming) is also potential for all subsequent actualities. Moreover, whatever is potential was in itself actual, and this holds true even for pure potentials or possibilities (i.e., the eternal objects). On Whitehead's view, the realm of possibilities is the outcome of God's non-temporal decision (the primordial envisagement), which is *his* actuality.

In "The Subjectivist Principle and the Linguistic Turn,"[15] published the same year (1963) but representing a tremendous transformation of perspective, Rorty undertakes to criticize Whitehead in order to justify making the linguistic turn. The focus is again on the problem of realism within a post-Cartesian framework, i.e., within a framework which accepts the methodological form of the subjectivist principle, "that nothing may be used as a philosophical explanation which is not, in some sense, an object of possible experience."[16] This poses a serious problem for doctrines of substance. "For if the experience of substances discloses only repeatables, then substances, since they are unrepeatables, are not disclosed in experience."[17] Whitehead sought a different paradigm in an entity which, though unrepeatable, could be experienced: the present, experient subject. Once past, however, it is the object of many subsequent possible experiences, and as such quite repeatable.

By this move every unrepeatable falls within experience, for each actuality is for itself an experienced togetherness (PR 288–89). But this experience is its own, not one which in principle could possibly be mine, or that of another human being, unless of course, it were our own experienced subjectivity. It satisfies the Cartesian subjectivist turn, broadly conceived. But Rorty sees the linguistic turn as insisting upon a stricter interpretation of what it means to be "an object of possible experience," one which entails the possibility of description. Unrepeatable present actualities must then be thought of as capable of describing themselves, since they are the subjects of their own experiences. The only unrepeatables we could ever describe would be ourselves, for whatever else we describe would already be repeatable: either as objectified actualities or as eternal objects. At this point Whitehead distrusts the subject–predicate structure of ordinary language. If that structure creates our problems, it would be self-defeating to forbid us to transcend the categories built into that structure to solve our problems.

The key question for Rorty then becomes: "Is Whitehead right in saying that an account of knowledge which preserves the realism of common sense must postulate the existence of entities which are describable neither in ordinary language nor in an extension of ordinary language?"[18] Should philosophy make any appeal to experience which is "too concrete to be expressed in language"? Rorty thinks not, because realism can be reconciled with the subjectivist principle without going beyond the bounds of ordinary language. He devotes the rest of his essay to sketching out an argument proposed by Wilfrid Sellars purporting to do just that. While divergent in methodology, particularly with respect to ordinary language, the two strategies share a common thesis, "that our knowledge may be about an independent reality without its being the case that it is even logically possible that this reality should be described independently of the observer's perspective." Rorty takes the defense of this thesis to be the central task of contemporary philosophy. "Whitehead's attempt to break free from the substance–property framework and thereby show that temporal perspectives are internal to the nature of concrete actualities was the last, and the most important, attempt to perform this task prior to the 'linguistic turn'. But once this turn is taken, new methods of carrying out this task become available."[19]

An analogue of Ockham's razor is operative in this argument: language should not be stretched beyond necessity. The rule is justified as a clarification of the subjectivist principle, for language serves as our ordinary guide to what is an object of possible experience, and we ought to have compelling reasons for modifying its structure. Philosophical controversy will rage around whether, and to what extent, language must be stretched to resolve persistent conceptual difficulties, but if Rorty is correct, no stretching is required in this particular case. Whether this is sufficient grounds for abandoning Whitehead's metaphysics will depend, I suspect, largely on whether the reconciliation of realism with the subjectivist principle is *the* central issue. It is unquestionably an important issue, and looms large in the history of philosophy. From the perspective of process metaphysics, however, it may well be a derivative issue, at least in the sense that its resolution may be the happy by-product of a much deeper concern, the reconceptualization of causation and subjectivity.

We shall turn directly to these topics in our discussion of panpsychism, but first we should note that for Whitehead it is not actuality, strictly speaking, which is unrepeatable, but subjectivity. If the core meaning of actuality is decisiveness (cf. PR 68), then past decisions are just as actual as are present decisions. To be sure, they are no longer deciding, and hence lack subjectivity, but this does not mean that they cease to be, as Rorty suggests.[20] Whitehead speaks of a perishing of subjective immediacy, but this only means that the subjective process of deciding is terminated in the being of the decision.

Whitehead's world gives the impression of being populated exclusively by momentary beings which vanish almost as soon as they appear, utterly lacking persistence. This impression arises from his preoccupation with the problem of becoming, the novel and more fundamental element in his philosophy, and his relative neglect of the complementary role played by being. Becoming is necessarily transitory, for every process exclusively geared to the production of one entity must cease in the achievement of that entity. The becoming is a process of unification which terminates in the unity achieved. The being necessarily survives the perishing of becoming, because otherwise the becoming cannot become something, some being. Since becoming and being are identified with subjectivity and objectivity, respectively, this is the reason why occasions subjectively perish, and yet are objectively immortal. Now the being so achieved need not be momentary, and its persistence in successive momentary occasions is itself continuous.

Unfortunately, Whitehead himself seems not to have achieved sufficient clarity concerning this distinction between the perishing of becoming and the persistence of being. He was fascinated with Locke's observation that time is a "perpetual perishing." Obviously this applies to becoming, as the present perishes in becoming past; but it also applies to the continuity of the past, as it gradually fades into a common background which is no longer distinctly taken up into the present (cf. PR 517).

William A. Christian, in his monumental study of Whitehead's metaphysics,[21] carefully distinguishes between becoming and being, but implicitly applies the doctrine of perishing to both. This book has so revolutionized our understanding of Whitehead that all "recent" studies must be dated from it. Christian has his own set of questions, centering on transcendence and immanence, with which to interrogate the text, but his interpretations are balanced, fair, accurate, authoritative, and solidly documented. They have worn so well during the intervening years that one hesitates to criticize any minor idiosyncrasies. In a detailed scrutiny of his study I was able to isolate only four, three of which are intrinsically related to the alleged perishing of being:

(1) Christian dismisses Whitehead's talk about creativity as presystematic discourse translatable without remainder into the systematic language of actual entities, prehensions, etc.[22]

(2) He claims that the satisfaction of an occasion represents a pause in the midst of flux, which contains the whole temporal thickness of the occasion.[23]

(3) According to Christian, God functions as the ground of the givenness of the past, providing the continuity whereby present occasions can prehend past ones. This idiosyncrasy has been widely noticed and criticized, among others by Sherburne, whose criticism I shall consider in the section on theism.[24] Christian has modified his original stance considerably, and has carefully reformulated his position.[25]

(4) Christian argues that Whitehead abandoned the doctrine of a realm of eternal objects once espoused in *Science and the Modern World* (Chapter 10). Instead, in *Process and Reality* Whitehead speaks of a "multiplicity" (PR 46, 69, 73), whereby he seeks to deny any fixed order or unity inhering in the eternal objects.[26]

These features have been noticed individually several times, but the intrinsic connection of the first three has not. They are closely connected to the implicit assumption of the perishing of being, as the second requires it, and the third provides for the causal continuity which it undercuts.

The primary reason for claiming that God is the ground of the givenness of the past is that such grounding is metaphysically necessary. God must sustain the past in being, Christian argues, because otherwise it could not be prehended. Since on his view actual occasions cease to be before new occasions arise, they cannot be prehended by the new generation of occasions (apart from the activity of God) simply because there is nothing there to prehend.

Yet why should we assume that the being of occasions simply ceases? Christian does not identify becoming with being, such that the perishing of becoming in being also means the perishing of being. In fact, he sharply distinguishes between the concrescence, which is the coming into being of an occasion, and the occasion's subjective enjoyment of that completed being in its satisfaction. This satisfaction is not the instantaneous completion of one act of becoming before creativity moves beyond that occasion in the initiation of the next,[27] but has a definite temporal thickness or duration. "Indeed the satisfaction contains, one might say, the whole of the *temporal* duration of the occasion. For the genetic process that produces the satisfaction is not itself in physical time."[28]

If we can accept Johnson's report on this issue, Christian's statement does not represent Whitehead's own view as of 1936. Johnson had been describing the ceaseless coming into being and perishing of occasions, and then asked:

QUESTION: "Is this a fair statement [of your position] or do you hold that for a 'split second' the *complete* actual entity pauses to enjoy itself as fully complete—before passing on?"

WHITEHEAD: "Yes[,] it is a fair statement. I do not accept the alternative."[29]

Since in satisfaction the occasion has achieved determinate unity, presumably God could prehend it during this duration. This would mean, however, that in its satisfaction the occasion would be both subjective and objective at the same time, undercutting Whitehead's double identification of this contrast with present and past, and with becoming and being.

Only the instant of transition between the present and the immediate past can be both subjective and objective, just as there is only an instant wherein becoming or unification completes itself in being or unity. When he assumes that the occasion subjectively enjoys its satisfaction for a duration *after* it has fully come into being, Christian makes it impossible to identify becoming with subjectivity or to interpret the perishing of subjective immediacy as the termination of becoming in being. Rather the perishing of immediacy must mean the termination of this being as subjectively felt in the satisfaction. Yet if this satisfaction can endure for a while, what prevents it from enduring indefinitely? Christian offers no reason why this enduring satisfaction must necessarily perish, but if it does, it must be the perishing of the occasion's being, and not just of its becoming.

Were that true, of course, we would have to invoke some sort of *deus ex machina* to explain how the past can be prehended by the present, but we need not suppose that this is entailed by Whitehead's own theory. If the perishing of subjective immediacy is simply the completion of subjective becoming in objective being, it is just this being, persisting into its future, which is prehended as causally efficacious by succeeding occasions. According to the rhythm of creativity, the many become one, and are increased by one (PR 32). The many "perish" by becoming the one, but that one is now an item in the new many in process of becoming one. If the one also ceased to be in the perishing of the many, there could be no new many emerging from these new ones, and creativity would cease. The ongoingness of time and creativity, and the real causal efficacy of the past, are strong reasons for supposing that the past continues to persist into the present, and only an unnecessarily severe interpretation of the perishing of subjective immediacy prevents Christian from asserting this. The continuity provided by the rhythm of creativity is overlooked by Christian, for he claims that creativity can be exhaustively understood in terms of the systematic properties of individual actual occasions. Since these cease to be before any new ones can arise, an atomism of occasions replaces the continuity of creativity. Yet it is this continuity which is the real ground of the givenness of the past.

As we noted in discussing the fourth distinctive feature listed above, Christian denies that Whitehead's mature philosophy has any strong doctrine of a realm of eternal objects. It replaces any fixed order of the eternal objects with a bare "multiplicity." Yet this interpretation ignores the role of relational essences, which reappear in *Process and Reality* in the guise of "patterns" (PR 174–76) and "eternal objects of the objective species" (PR 445–47). There is a contrast with his earlier approach, but its significance lies elsewhere. In *Science and the Modern World* the eternal objects are ordered independently of God. For Whitehead, God first functioned as "the principle of limitation," deciding which of this vast multitude of eternal objects are fit possibilities for temporal actualization. In *Process and Reality*, the eternal objects are organized together and given their respective "relational essences" by the primordial or non-temporal activity of God. *Apart from God*, these eternal objects form a mere "multiplicity," which is not a proper entity, lacking even a derivative existence of its own (PR 44–45). All togetherness or unity is togetherness in experience (PR 288–89), and the togetherness of the pure eternal objects is "in" God's primordial envisagement. In order to call attention to this divine organizing activity, Whitehead says that, apart from God, they form a bare "multiplicity." As experienced by occasions, however, these eternal objects are ordered in a realm just as much as in the account given in *Science and the Modern World.* But this ordered realm of eternal objects offers an infinity of possible alternatives, and is not marked by the kind of constricting closure which Christian fears.

## II · PANPSYCHISM OR PANSUBJECTIVISM

In one of its forms panpsychism is essentially a pluralistic variant of idealism. Given the problem of the relation between mind and matter, we seem to have three doctrinal possibilities: idealism, materialism, and dualism. We may derive matter from mind, derive mind from matter, or treat both as independent. The dualistic hypothesis seems most plausible when applied to common experience, but it suffers from the incoherence of the arbitrary disjunction of first principles. If both are equally primitive, then there is no reason why the world should contain both: the world could have been solely mental or solely physical. On the other hand, it is difficult to see how life and consciousness can be explained purely in terms of matter, while matter can be understood as a useful abstraction from the fullness of experience. This does not mean that everything must be regarded as conscious in the ordinary sense. There may be sentience or feeling or vague awareness, with only very few beings having full consciousness. Moreover, only individual actualities need be regarded as sentient. Most things in everyday experience may be quite lifeless, consisting of vast aggregates of actualities. It is only the ultimate constituents of such aggregates that need be considered as possessing any degree of awareness.

This is the sort of panpsychism espoused by Charles Hartshorne,[30] and it has an important place within process philosophy. Yet it is distinct from Whitehead's theory, which has a different genesis, rational support, and outcome.[31]

The root of Whitehead's panpsychism must be seen in his shift from the philosophy of nature to metaphysics. In his earlier writings, such as *The Concept of Nature* (1920), Whitehead deliberately restricts his concern to nature understood as that which is perceived through the senses. He contrasts this concern with that of metaphysics, which seeks to take into account the perceiver and his relationship to the perceived. Whitehead's programmatic aim was to find acceptable substitutes for the pre-relativistic elements of nature: space, time, and matter. Yet, could this program be successfully carried out within the bounds of the perceived?

A problem arises concerning present immediacy: can it be perceived? If seems that it cannot, for the events we perceive must already have occurred in order to be perceived. Perceiving shares in the subjective immediacy of the perceiver, in contrast to the perceived objects deriving from the past, even though that past may be only a split second prior to the immediate present. If this is so, then the immediate present cannot be part of nature objectively defined in terms of the perceived, and it is impossible to do justice to all the modalities of time within the confines of the philosophy of nature. Present immediacy introduces the element of subjectivity. In fact, it suggests a way of reinterpreting the subjective/objective contrast which then becomes decisive for Whitehead's metaphysics: subjectivity may be identified with presentness, and objectivity (at least with respect to actualities) with pastness. Presentness must be subjective because it can be "experienced" only as the subjective immediacy of perceiving, while subjectivity is presentness because it is always "experienced" as present immediacy.

This reconceptualization of subjectivity and objectivity is reinforced by their future identification with becoming and being. Present and past, if considered homogeneously, solely in terms of being, are too similar to bear the weight of the subjective/objective distinction. Two events, simply considered in terms of their being, differ only in their time coordinates. Yet whatever exists must have come into being, and that becoming is prior to its being. If the present is subjective and the past objective, this shift from subjectivity to objectivity may be understood as the shift from becoming to being, for this is a definite shift in ontological modality. What now exists, i.e., that which has being in the present, is not the present but the objective past ingredient within the subjective becoming of the present. Moreover, once becoming is introduced, the "epochal" theory of time, designed to avoid Zeno's paradoxes, applies only to becoming, not to being, which is continuously persistent and hence infinitely divisible. It is the act of becoming which cannot be infinitely subdivided into "earlier and later acts of becoming" (PR 107), as if each such act presupposed some portion of itself as that which brings it into being. Such a regress would be infinite, and nothing would ever come into being, since whatever sub-event we specify depends upon some earlier event for its being.[32] By the same token, the act of becoming cannot be indefinitely prolonged; it must terminate in some being, since it must become something. Thus becoming generates its own rhythm with being, ensuring a constant temporal passage from present subjectivity to past objectivity.

This analysis is based upon what Whitehead calls the 'principle of process': "*how* an actual entity *becomes* constitutes *what* that actual entity *is*; so that the two descriptions of an actual entity are not independent. Its 'being' is constituted by its 'becoming' " (PR 34–35). We take this to mean that what an actuality is, which is what can be prehended as causally efficacious in subsequent actualities, is necessarily dependent upon the private act of becoming which brought it into being. That act is absolutely individual and unique. It comes, and is gone forever. It is unrepeatable, for while there may be similar acts, none of them can ever be *that* act of becoming.[33] But the act of becoming leaves its mark in the being it produces, for that being could not be the sort of being that it is except as the outcome of that particular act of becoming.

This principle of process is sometimes interpreted differently, as meaning that the mode of existing for actual occasions is becoming. When becoming "constitutes" being, does this mean that becoming *produces* being, or that becoming *is* (identical with) being? Leclerc claims that the latter interpretation is supported by another text from Whitehead: " 'existence' (in any of its senses) cannot be abstracted from 'process'. The notions of 'process' and 'existence' presuppose each other" (MT 131).[34] But Whitehead cannot mean that process is equivalent to existence in all of its senses, for the eternal objects or forms have a derivative existence, even though they cannot undergo process. I take him to mean that there is no being except as ingredient in becoming, nor any becoming which does not result in being. Being and becoming presuppose each other, but they are ontologically distinct.[35]

Hartshorne interprets the principle of process to mean that "the entity *is* its activity" and then is troubled by Whitehead's talk of "perishing," which he takes to be an unfortunate metaphor.[36] This "suggests becoming lifeless, whereas the final word of *Process and Reality* is that occasions 'perish and yet live forevermore', to which Hartshorne says he will hold, whether Whitehead always did or not."[37] In identifying becoming and being, Hartshorne interprets becoming as the being of events: their dynamic happening, occurring. Events are constantly changing, and it is this dynamic instability that is meant by becoming. Since these events are causally efficacious, they persist, "perishing" only insofar as they are no longer causally efficacious. This is the fading of being we described earlier, the only sort of "perishing" Hartshorne can permit. Whitehead, however, also holds that "[c]ompletion is the perishing of immediacy: 'It never really is' " (PR 130) because immediacy is unrepeatable and hence never prehensible. Actual entities become and "perish, but do not change; they are what they are" (PR 52; cf. PR 122). They do not change, because change is the difference between successive occasions (PR 113–14).

Donald W. Sherburne also interprets the principle of process as asserting an identity, but draws the opposite conclusion about perishing, since he interprets the perishing of becoming as entailing the annihilation of being. If, upon completion of becoming, the actuality perishes and is no longer actual, it can no longer be causally efficacious. Hence he proposes to modify Whitehead's doctrine by allowing only immediately past, contiguous occasions to be causally efficacious, since on the interface between two occasions, at that instant in which the first completes, and the second initiates, its becoming, the first occasion can be both becoming and causing at the same time.[38] This implies that two occasions overlap insofar as they must share a common interface, while Whitehead's theory of external connection (PR 453) suggests that two contiguous acts of becoming are so close as to allow no points in between, but share no common region whatever. Moreover, it is difficult to see how the first occasion as objectified can continue to persist in the second as a causal factor in its final satisfaction, if it instantly ceases to be at the outset of concrescence. All these difficulties can be avoided, however, if being and becoming are not identified; then we can simply hold that the being persists as objectively prehended after its becoming has been completed in bringing forth that being.

If this rhythm of becoming and being is ontologically fundamental, and can be identified with subjectivity and objectivity, then subjectivity must be drastically reconceived. Its scope of application must be considerably widened, while at the same time its meaning must be purified of the parochial connotations associated with specifically human experience. Ordinarily subjectivity is restricted largely to human persons, with some allowances for those animals whose behavior we can perceive to be analogous to our own. If, however, every spatio-temporal event must have come into being as exercising its own present immediacy, and this present immediacy of becoming is what we mean by subjectivity, then every being must have enjoyed its own subjectivity in becoming. This pansubjectivity is absolute, admitting of no exceptions and of no degrees. By the same token, however, subjectivity must be clearly understood to mean nothing more than this present immediacy of becoming. In particular it must be distinguished from mentality and from consciousness.

Conscious human experience holds the key to our understanding of subjectivity, not because it is mental or conscious, but solely because it is *immediate.* We can have no other experiential access to the present. Even so, it is not human experience as such that is immediate, but only *my* experience. We habitually generalize from the character of our own experience to that of human conscious experience, while Whitehead presses us to generalize further, to include experience as such. We know many kinds of being, but only one kind of becoming, our own. Hence, in order to understand the general properties of becoming, we must so generalize our own experience of subjectivity as to make it appropriate to every kind of being. The resistance felt against panpsychist (here, more properly, pansubjectivist) theories of being often stems from the sense of inappropriateness in ascribing certain features of human experience to other beings. This inappropriateness may simply mean, however, that we have not been rigorous enough in our generalization. Because our experience happens to be highly mental and conscious, we assume that mentality and consciousness must be features of all subjective becoming.

If, however, mentality is distinguished from subjectivity, it refers to the degree of novelty and spontaneity inherent in an occasion as opposed to the degree of determination exercised by its past. Inorganic physical things are quite habitual in their behavior; each successive occasion blindly repeats the character received from its predecessors. Novelty matching the novelty in the environment first makes its significance apparent in the emergence of life. Nonetheless, we must conceive of mentality as belonging to all occasions, even if the degree is negligible, since all have some degrees of spontaneity insofar as they do not conform totally to their past, just as all have some degree of habit insofar as they generally do conform to it. Consciousness, however, is a highly contingent factor. On Whitehead's analysis, it arises only in the felt contrast between what is and what might be, and there is no reason to suppose that many occasions are sufficiently complex to entertain such feelings. While there are certainly degrees of consciousness, and there may be considerably more low-level consciousness in the world than we are wont to suppose, there is no metaphysical reason to assume it to be all-pervasive. The estimation of the extent of consciousness in the world is primarily an empirical undertaking beyond the scope of metaphysical reflection.

Basically, Whitehead's commitment to an event-ontology which identifies subjectivity with present immediacy makes his language sound strange. The point can be made, and defended, easily enough within the framework of ordinary language, but the precise analysis of becoming requires new words such as 'prehension' (i.e., 'unconscious apprehension') or new uses for old words such as 'experience' and 'feeling'. This does not mean that ordinary language cannot handle the insights which Whitehead seeks to convey, but only that it is unaccustomed to doing so, since the language of subjectivity is habitually restricted to human contexts. Language can be systematically misused, as when contrastive terms are used in contexts which preclude the application of the contrast, for example, when we speak of the world as being *completely* mental, or material. Here, however, while the lines between the subjective and the objective may be redrawn, the basic contrast is retained. Every act of becoming, subjective in its present immediacy, produces an objective being for *all* subsequent subjects.

The coming into being of any present actuality *is* its (partial) self-causation. Since on Whitehead's principles becoming is to be identified with subjectivity, subjectivity must be intrinsic to self-causation. Here we may adopt the model of perception, suitably generalized in terms of prehension. Prehension means any (conscious or unconscious) "taking account" of another, such that the prehender is affected by what is prehended. The way *B* prehends *A* is the way *A* is causally efficacious for *B*. An individual concrescing occasion is the unification of its prehended data, just as an effect is analyzed as the outcome of its causes. The difference, however, is that the unity of these causes is not simply an unexplained accident, for if the model of perception is adopted, experience may be understood in a quasi-Kantian way as the manner in which the subject "spontaneously" organizes and unifies its data into a single coherent whole. If Kant's insight is thus generalized, the Cartesian dualism between physical causation and mental perception can be overcome.

This same reinterpretation of causation can be achieved, however, without any appeal to subjectivity. Causes are traditionally held to produce their effects: the cause is the active agency; the effect, its passive outcome. On this model, the rational ideal of complete causal explanation entails determinism, for the effect can be nothing more than the outcome of the joint activity of all of its causes. However, if the causal relationship is analyzed in terms of successive actual occasions, one of which is the partial or total efficient cause of its successor, we encounter a problem. When the successor occasion is coming into being, its causal predecessor must be past, since the efficient cause must precede its effect in time. On the other hand, its predecessor cannot be past if it is to be the active agency producing the effect, since all activity must occur in the present. Whitehead resolves the problem by assigning the active agency inherent in the present to the effect, that is, to the successor occasion now coming into being, thereby treating the cause as passive. The causes constitute the way in which the past is ingredient in the present, but the activity ordinarily vested in the efficient causes is transferred to the effect. Instead of the causes producing the effect, the effect produces itself out of its causes. In one sense, then, the effect is *causa sui* in that its immediate present activity is its productive cause, but this activity *per se* is radically indeterminate, a mere drive toward unity, which requires past occasions, functioning as determinate data for prehensive unification. The causal past is thus an essential factor in the process of causation, but it is neither the total factor nor the active factor.

If this is so, then the standard objection to a causal future falls. The future cannot cause, it is objected, because it does not yet exist. To be sure, the future is not yet actual, and hence possesses no active agency, but it does exist as possible in the form of inert, passive, objective real possibilities. If past actualities are causally efficacious even though they are merely passive objective factors, there seems no reason in principle why possibilities concerning the future cannot also be causally efficacious. Moreover, unless past causes determine the way in which their incompatibilities are eliminated and the way in which they are unified in the present event, the ideal of total causal explanation requires the introduction of future causes. But past causes cannot now determine how they are to be unified in the present event, since they are no longer active. It is the present event which determines how it will appropriate the past, but it can do so only insofar as it is guided by some future ideal of itself as to what it should become.

Causal determinism assumes an ontological parity between past and present. It assumes that the past is wholly adequate to explain the present. Theories of radical novelty and of creative freedom are sensitive to dimensions of experience over which the deterministic account rides roughshod; they seek to do justice to these by assuming that the present embodies an ontological advance over the past: genuine novelty emerges *ex nihilo* and is inexplicable in terms of the past. Such fidelity to our sense of emergent novelty, however, must be purchased at the price of curtailing the rational principle *ex nihilo nihil fit*. In contrast to both, Whitehead holds that the past and future provide more than can be contained in the present.

The past occasions prehended by a present occasion contain conflicting tendencies and tensions which must be resolved by a selective, perspectival appropriation of that past in a way which enables them to fit together as constituting the present actuality. Moreover, only one of the many real possibilities for that occasion can be actualized by it: the others must be discarded. The freedom of the occasion lies in this interplay between the past and the future as ingredient in the present, for it is by means of some possible ideal of itself that the occasion producing itself selectively appropriates from the past, as it is by means of the past which it is appropriating that it selects which real possibility it shall actualize. If there were only one real possibility which it could actualize, that one possibility would determine what the occasion appropriates from its past. On the other hand, if there were no way to appropriate selectively from the past in accordance with some real possibility, then the past would determine the occasion's actuality. The occasion's freedom lies in its decision, that is, in the way it cuts off unwanted aspects of the past in terms of a future ideal, and in the way it cuts off unwanted real possibilities for the future in terms of its appropriated past.

If occasions thus produce themselves by selectively unifying their causes, these acts of unification must be unrepeatable, even while the entities so unified may be repeatable as that which can be taken up into subsequent acts of causal unification. The unification is unrepeatable because never again will just those causes present themselves for unification. Subsequent acts must include that unification as part of their causal past. Moreover, the present immediacy of that act of unification passes and is gone forever. Thus from his analysis of both causation and subjectivity Whitehead can derive the repeatability/unrepeatability distinction that concerned Rorty. Whatever stretching of language Whitehead undertakes is to be seen in the way he redesigns the subject/object contrast, and this is one way of approaching his solution to the repeatability question. Since, however, it is possible to derive his resolution of that question from his analysis of causation, and because it is possible to formulate his analysis of causation without an appeal to subjectivity, we may argue that no stretching of language is needed to provide a Whiteheadian solution to Rorty's problem, though it is needed for other important purposes.

## III · THEISM

In analyzing the concept of an event producing itself out of its causal data, we noted the need for an ideal possibility serving as the criterion for the appropriation of the past. If efficient causal determinism is to be overcome without violating the principle of complete rational explanation, final causation must be introduced. Ideals in the form of real possibilities for the future can be such final causal factors, since the agency investing such objective components with causal power is the present occasion in its act of becoming. It actualizes the potentiality derived from its past by means of the real possibility entertained for its future. We have not said, however, where these future ideals come from. In some cases, particularly in human experience, they may come from antecedent occasions in the same personal society or sequence of occasions. Ultimately, however, Whitehead argues, they must derive from an actuality which is not any one of the occasions of the past. Since it is the ultimate source of all values, and hence properly worthy of worship, Whitehead calls this non-temporal actuality 'God'.

Whitehead's analysis of present immediacy in terms of a succession of acts of becoming focuses attention on the problem of subjectivity, particularly upon the way it must originate anew in every moment. In part this is understood in terms of creativity, the ceaseless activity of the many past causal factors converging into one effect, itself thereby becoming an additional causal factor among many for the superseding moment. But creativity by itself is simply blind activity, supplying the drive but not the focus for such convergence. Without an ideal for the process to aim at, there is no reason why creativity would not be just as divergent as it is convergent, achieving unity only accidentally if at all. Subjectivity is not merely sheer activity; it must be unitive in order to have a subject, and to be unitive it must be purposive to some degree. Whitehead therefore suggests that subjectivity is a purposive process of unification originating from the ideal at which it aims. This subjective aim must be derived from somewhere, and as identical with the future possibility just considered, it derives from God.

Thus Whitehead's distinctive analysis of causation in terms of an event producing itself out of its past, coupled with his identification of subjectivity with present immediacy, generates a new argument for the existence of God. This was a surprising result, for Whitehead began his reflections on the philosophy of nature as an agnostic. In the process of introducing God into his thought he alienated several enthusiastic early supporters, such as Susan Stebbing, who expressed shocked dismay in her review of *Process and Reality*.[39] In many ways this has been most unfortunate, for the easiest way to evade the conclusion of an argument is to reject its premisses. In the present non-theistic climate of opinion, it has prevented many philosophers from examining Whitehead's premisses independently on their own merits.

This melancholy result has led some critics to propose a non-theistic or "naturalistic" version of Whitehead's philosophy.[40] Donald W. Sherburne calls for the elimination of the concept of God as both inconsistent and unnecessary. According to Whitehead's principles, an actual occasion cannot be prehended during its act of becoming, for then it is not yet determinate. For differing reasons, both Sherburne and Christian hold that the total occasion ceases to be upon the completion of its act of becoming. When can the past occasion be prehended, if neither during its becoming nor at any instant thereafter? Christian suggests that God preserves the past occasions, and thus is the ground of the givenness of the past.[41] But if past occasions cannot be prehended, how can God prehend them without being an exception to the categoreal principles? This is the basic inconsistency which Sherburne finds in the introduction of God into Whitehead's system;[42] but it remains to be shown that the difficulty is really in Whitehead's position rather than in Christian's interpretation of that position. An adequate understanding of "perishing," whereby only the process of unification ceases to be in its attainment of a prehensible unity, removes the problem.

Actually, it would be enough to show that the concept of God is unnecessary in the system. This would give us an appropriate

Whiteheadian non-theism as a possible option. It would also convict Whitehead's system of incoherence, the arbitrary disjunction of first principles (cf. PR 9–10). If we could only show that the subjective aim of each occasion might be derived from some source other than God, God would be dispensable within this philosophy. Sherburne makes some suggestions in this direction, which I have reformulated as five distinct alternatives. The subjective aim for a given individual actual occasion might be derived from: (1) a dominant past occasion occupying the same spatial coordinates, or (2) a dominant occasion belonging to the same personally ordered society, or (3) all the past occasions of its actual world. Alternatively, we may conceive of (4) subjective aim belonging only to the more complex occasions, being absent from the simpler ones. Finally (5), we may suppose that each occasion spontaneously generates its own aim. These would seem to exhaust the alternatives; but all have been tried and found wanting, suggesting that the derivation of subjective aim from a non-temporal actual entity is the most acceptable alternative after all.[43]

Although it is not central to his intent, Robert C. Neville comes closer than other recent commentators to offering an acceptable Whiteheadian non-theism in *The Cosmology of Freedom*.[44] He is decidedly a theist himself, but he must get rid of Whitehead's conception of God in order to make room for a particular understanding of God as that which is radically indeterminate. On his view God becomes determinate only insofar as he becomes our creator.[45] If God is radically indeterminate, then it would seem that he cannot exemplify the metaphysical principles as a being, or as an actual entity, among others. But Whitehead's God "at once exemplifies and establishes the categoreal conditions" (PR 522).[46] However this may be, Neville obviates the need for Whitehead's concept of God by describing freedom and temporal passage in ways that come very close to Whitehead's characteristic claims, yet which eliminate the necessity for the subjective aim and its transcendent source.

Thus it would appear that Whitehead's pansubjectivism and theism stand or fall together, and many philosophers who are sympathetic to Neville's presentation of creativity as temporal self-constitution will be relieved that he has managed to avoid these two controversial assumptions. At this juncture everything depends on whether our defense of pansubjectivism is cogent, and whether Whitehead's temporalistic reconception of subjectivity in terms of present immediacy breaks the stranglehold that the subject–object dichotomy has exercised these past few centuries. If subjectivity is to be identified with present immediacy, such that each moment is a fresh expression of an intrinsic activity requiring an inner aim, then a transcendent, non-temporal source of this aim seems inescapable.

Others have objected to designating this dynamic source of values as God. Proponents of classical theism often refuse to recognize anything other than the traditional conception of God as "God." Thus Cornelio Fabro and Arthur Gibson regard Whitehead as an atheist, because what Whitehead terms 'God' is dependent for his concrete experience upon the ongoing activity of the world.[47] Fabro ignores the traditional element in Whitehead's conception—the claim that God in his primordial or non-temporal nature is infinite, unchanging, and totally independent of the world (much like Aristotle's unmoved mover "thinking on thinking")—and concentrates solely on its novel aspects. Following Kuspit,[48] he sees strong affinities between Whitehead and Samuel Alexander, and tends to criticize Whitehead in terms more appropriate to Alexander.[49] Not every Thomistic response to Whitehead, however, remains at this level. Norris Clarke has cogently defended the doctrine of the immutability of God against the full force of the process challenge.[50] Heretofore the standard critique of the Thomistic tradition of God's immutability has been Charles Hartshorne's *The Divine Relativity*.[51] This critique has been extended in further detail by Burton Z. Cooper,[52] but an adequate response to Father Clarke's argument requires an entirely new level of sophistication.[53]

Another source of opposition, this time from the side of convinced atheists, has been based on the problem of evil. The God of classical omnipotence fails to explain the presence of so much unnecessary evil in the world, and Whitehead's revision is pre-eminently designed to correct this difficulty. Now, however, Madden and Hare charge that Whitehead's God is "too weak" to ensure the ultimate triumph of good, a central expectation of traditional theism.[54] Hartshorne has responded to this charge,[55] and I have suggested that genuine religious commitment requires that the future be an open risk, not something absolutely guaranteed in advance.[56] In their revision, Madden and Hare have softened the original phrase, 'triumph of good', to 'growth of value'.[57] Yet, as the ultimate source of value, God is responsible for whatever growth of value takes place, since he must first provide any particular emergent value as a real possibility before it can be actualized. He does not control the process, to be sure, and cannot therefore force a growth of value, but the multiplicity of free decisions which he coordinates will inevitably yield an increase in the complexity of its actualizations in the long run. Some creatures will be persuaded to follow the divine prompting, and this is sufficient.[58]

Within process theism itself, the major area of controversy has centered on whether God should be conceived as a single actuality or actual entity, as Whitehead intended, or reconceived as a personally ordered society of occasions, that is, a temporally ordered linear series of momentary events, as Hartshorne has proposed. This apparently quite abstruse question has very complex roots. It began innocently enough as a suggestion of Hartshorne's intended to make Whitehead's system more consistent.[59] Yet the interpretation is also more consonant with Hartshorne's own philosophy, which has a separate origin and differs subtly from Whitehead's on this point.[60] Hartshorne's theistic philosophy is resolutely temporalistic, far more temporalistic than Whitehead's, who characteristically referred to God as the non-temporal actual entity.[61] In his non-temporal nature Whitehead's God is the complete, infinite ordering of all pure possibilities, which he integrates with his temporal experience of the past to create and evaluate the range of real possibilities confronting each emergent occasion. In this way God indirectly influences each occasion by providing it with its own subjective aim, which is that valued real possibility toward which it strives. Thus God is the ultimate power of the future, teleologically influencing the occasion's self-creativity as to how it will appropriate the past actualities which it has prehended to create its own actuality.

The present occasion is the integration of the future (i.e., the one real possibility selected as its "form") and the past (i.e., the many past actual occasions which make up its "content" or "matter"). Hartshorne's nominalism reduces the infinite multiplicity of pure possibilities which undergirds God's role as the power of the future to one single abstract necessary aspect, and God's concreteness is conceived in terms of individual concrete changing states continually succeeding one another. Instead of influencing a present occasion as the source of its future possibilities, the immediately previous state of God's concrete experience causally influences that occasion as one member among others in its past.

One curious difficulty which Hartshorne's conception raises concerns relativity physics. Each of the divine occasions constitutes a simultaneous cross-section of the universe in a single brief moment, and this forms a privileged designation of simultaneity contrary to the special theory of relativity. Whitehead's God is exempt from this incompatibility, since he is the one non-temporal actuality, and is prehended not as an item in the nascent occasion's past world, but as the ultimate source of possibility constituting the inner standpoint from which it prehends that past world.[62]

Many students of Whitehead, conscious of Whitehead's own emphatic insistence that God is not an exception to the central metaphysical principles (PR 521), have been embarrassed by the apparent anomaly that God is so different from all other actual occasions. Previously Cobb proposed a systematic revision of Whitehead's philosophical theology to make God conform as much as possible to the principles governing actual occasions, and reaffirmed Hartshorne's proposal of reconceiving God as a series of momentary divine occasions.[63] Yet the effort could never be totally successful: either God would be partly different from the actual occasions, and to that extent an exception to the necessary principles governing them, or he would completely exemplify those principles, differing from other occasions only in contingent respects. Yet if God is only contingently different from finite occasions, it is possible that any of these differences could be eliminated, thereby undercutting God's necessary existence, infinity, everlastingness, etc. We seem caught in a dilemma: God must be necessarily different from the finite, contingent actual occasions; but if so, is he not an exception to the general metaphysical principles?

As is well recognized, Whitehead does make a terminological distinction: God is the only actual entity that is not also an actual occasion (PR 135). It seems to be mere evasion when Whitehead claims that the categoreal principles apply to all actual entities, not just to the actual occasions. Yet close examination of the various Categories of Explanation (PR 33–39) indicates that these apply equally to God and to the other actual entities.[64] The crucial difference between God and the actual occasions does not appear on this categoreal level. Technically speaking, this difference concerns the priority of the mental or the physical pole. Actual occasions originate by means of their physical poles, that is, by their derivation from other past actualities. God alone originates by means of his mental pole. In this context this means that conceptual activity—the contemplating of pure possibilities—is primary, and God's experience of other actualities is derivative. From this basic difference all the others flow. Here it is important to recognize that God is not an anomalous member of the class of actual occasions, but that there are really two distinct classes of actual entities, each required by, and each requiring, the other. In the one class, however, there is necessarily only one member, God, who is infinite and non-temporal. The other class, which comprises the World, has a vast multiplicity of finite, temporal members. Only by this elaborate strategy could Whitehead both maintain metaphysical intelligibility by having God exemplify the most general metaphysical principles and yet show that God systematically and necessarily differs from the World.[65]

Few philosophers have appreciated how deep this contrast between God and the World runs for Whitehead. It can account for the subtitle of *Process and Reality*: "An Essay in Cosmology." The customary understanding of Whitehead's distinction between metaphysics and cosmology has been well expressed by Dorothy Emmet: "Metaphysics deals with the general nature of Being as such; cosmology with the particular type of being of our world, and so brings in empirical elements. A cosmic epoch is a particular dominant type of world order. . . . But this may not be metaphysically necessary."[66] Surely the distinction between metaphysical principles and the contingent features of particular cosmic epochs is central to Whitehead's thought, but it may be questioned whether he understands by 'cosmology' the study of this present cosmic epoch. In considering the human epistemological preconditions for his philosophy, he does consider the various modes of conscious perception, which may apply only to a few cosmic epochs. On the whole, however, he seems to be concerned with purely metaphysical issues and not with broad empirical generalizations which are only contingently applicable to the world.

In one place Whitehead notes that his discussion (in PR 147–67) will be restricted to "the hierarchy of societies composing our present epoch" (PR 147). Here would be an excellent opportunity to make the distinction between metaphysical generality and cosmological particularity, if this were his distinction. On the contrary, he identifies cosmology with the same type of generic necessity that metaphysics enjoys:

> It is to be carefully noted that we are now deserting metaphysical generality. We shall be considering the more special possibilities of explanation consistent with our general cosmological doctrine, but not necessitated by it [PR 147].

In Whitehead's philosophical vision cosmology is a branch of metaphysics, required by the internal dialectic between God and the World. This means that *Process and Reality* is primarily a work in metaphysics devoted to the topic of the World, the realm of actual occasions, mentioning God only so far as necessary to explain the

World. If the system is coherent, each side requires the other, and neither can be explained apart from the other, although Whitehead's own professed concern is with the actual occasions.

There is a radical incompleteness in *Process and Reality.* While the basic principles are presented, only one half of Whitehead's vision is worked out in detail. Rather than seeking to adapt this discussion of finite actual occasions to God, process thinkers should be trying to construct an analogue to Whitehead's cosmology, a philosophical theology appropriate to the general categoreal scheme. That task has hardly been begun.

## NOTES

1. For the sake of completeness in the discussion of certain topics, reference will also be made to one or two essays that *are* included in the present volume, e.g., Rorty's "Matter and Event" and Garland's "The Ultimacy of Creativity" (see Chapters 6 and 10 above).

2. David Griffin, "Whitehead and Niebuhr on God, Man, and the World," *Journal of Religion*, 53 (1973), 149–75, esp. 175.

3. Here it is claimed that the meaning of being cannot be exhaustively determined by discovering what it means to be a typical being, yet the latter has been the traditional quest of metaphysics. See, e.g., Gottfried Martin, "Metaphysics as *Scientia Universalis* and as *Ontologia Generalis,*" pp. 218–31 in *The Relevance of Whitehead*, ed. Ivor Leclerc (London: Allen and Unwin; New York: Macmillan, 1961). The focus of Whitehead's concerns in framing a categoreal scheme is clearly metaphysical in the sense of *scientia universalis*, seeking to determine precisely what a typical being, an actual entity, is. But this need not mean that questions of general ontology are excluded or neglected, unless creativity is understood to be merely a pre-systematic description of the activity of actual entities.

4. See Craig R. Eisendrath, *The Unifying Moment: The Psychological Philosophy of William James and Alfred North Whitehead* (Cambridge: Harvard University Press, 1971), and also Calvin O. Schrag, "Struktur der Erfahrung in der Philosophie von James und Whitehead," *Zeitschrift für philosophische Forschung*, 23 (1969), 479–94.

5. See James M. Edie, "William James and Phenomenology," *Review of Metaphysics*, 23 (1970), 481–526, and the literature he discusses there.

6. Since the causal past of a given event includes all those events affecting it, and its causal future includes all those events it will affect, its contemporaries are defined by this property of causal independence.

7. See Raymond J. Devetterre, "Whitehead's Metaphysics and Heidegger's Critique," *Cross Currents*, 30 (1980), 309–22.

8. *Whitehead's Metaphysics: An Introductory Exposition* (London: Allen and Unwin; New York: Macmillan, 1958; rpt., Bloomington: Indiana University Press, 1975), Chap. 2.

9. (New York: Macmillan, 1966; rpt., Bloomington: Indiana University Press, 1972; rpt., Chicago: University of Chicago Press, 1982).

10. Victor Lowe, *Understanding Whitehead* (Baltimore: Johns Hopkins University Press, 1962) also offers a good, somewhat more informal, introduction. Part II offers what is probably the best general survey of the development of Whitehead's thought from its earliest beginnings in mathematics to his final address on "Immortality."

11. "On the Intelligibility of the Epochal Theory of Time," *The Monist*, 53 (1969), 505–18.

12. "Whitehead's Theory of Becoming," *Journal of Philosophy*, 58 (1961), 516–28; reprinted in *Alfred North Whitehead: Essays on His Philosophy*, ed. George L. Kline (Englewood Cliffs: Prentice-Hall, 1963), pp. 70–80.

13. Ibid., pp. 73–74.

14. I include this brief characterization of Chapter 6 above to show its relationship to Rorty's next essay on Whitehead, which is not reprinted in the present volume.

15. In Kline, ed. (n. 12), pp. 134–57.

16. Ibid., p. 135.

17. *Loc. cit.*

18. Ibid., p. 146.

19. Ibid., p. 153.

20. Ibid., p. 139.

21. *An Interpretation of Whitehead's Metaphysics* (New Haven: Yale University Press, 1959).

22. See William Garland's essay in the present volume, "The Ultimacy of Creativity," concerning this point.

23. Interpretation, pp. 29–30. I have argued against this reading in "Genetic and Coordinate Division Correlated," *Process Studies*, 1 (1971), 199–209, as has Robison B. James, "Is Whitehead's 'Actual Entity' a Contradiction in Terms?" *Process Studies*, 2 (1972), 112–25.

24. See, e.g., D. F. Gustafson, "Christian on Causal Objectification in Whitehead," *International Philosophical Quarterly*, 1 (1961), 683–96.

25. "Whitehead's Explanation of the Past," pp. 93–101 in Kline, ed. (n. 12).

26. *Interpretation*, pp. 258–77.

27. As Robison B. James and I claim: see n. 23 above.

28. Christian, *Interpretation*, p. 30.

29. A. H. Johnson, "Whitehead as Teacher and Philosopher," *Philosophy and Phenomenological Research*, 29 (1968–69), 363. (This exchange is omitted from the excerpted version of Johnson's article published as Chapter 1 above.)

30. See, e.g., Eugene M. Peters, *Hartshorne and Neoclassical Metaphysics* (Lincoln: University of Nebraska Press, 1970), Chap. 3.

31. Johnson reports from his 1936 conversations: "Whitehead replied that he is a panpsychist in the sense [of holding] that every actual entity has a vague feeling of other [actual entities] (as when you are waking up in the morning and become aware of other things). This is the only sense in which he is a panpsychist. He refuses to accept the theory that all things are of the nature of a 'high class' soul, or self. He doesn't like to use [the] word 'awareness' instead of 'prehension'. It suggests 'consciousness'. This is what most panpsychists hold[,] in his opinion" ("Whitehead as Teacher and Philosopher," p. 354; italics removed. This passage is also omitted from our excerpted version of Johnson's article.)

32. For a further elaboration of this point, see my essay on "The Duration of the Present," *Philosophy and Phenomenological Research*, 35 (1974–75), 100–106, esp. 103–106.

33. See Ivor Leclerc, "Whitehead and the Theory of Form" in *Process and Divinity*, edd. William L. Reese and Eugene Freeman (LaSalle, Ill.: Open Court, 1964), p. 128.

34. *Whitehead's Metaphysics*, p. 69.

35. My position is strongly supported by the careful and exhaustive analysis of the texts which Jorge L. Nobo has carried out in "Whitehead's Principle of Process," *Process Studies*, 4 (1974), 275–84.

36. "Whitehead's Novel Intuition" in Kline, ed. (n. 12), p. 22; reprinted in Hartshorne's *Whitehead's Philosophy: Selected Essays, 1935–1970* (Lincoln: University of Nebraska Press, 1972), p. 165.

37. David R. Griffin, "Hartshorne's Difference from Whitehead" in *Two Process Philosophers: Hartshorne's Encounter with Whitehead*, ed. Lewis S. Ford (Tallahassee: American Academy of Religion, 1973), p. 54.

38. "Whitehead Without God" in *Process Philosophy and Christian Thought*, edd. Delwin Brown, Ralph E. James, Jr., and Gene Reeves (Indianapolis: Bobbs-Merrill, 1971), esp. pp. 320–23; reprinted, with revisions, from *The Christian Scholar*, 50 (1967), 251–72.

39. L. S. Stebbing, Review of *Process and Reality* in *Mind*, 39 (1930), 466–75.

40. See the early suggestions by H. K. Wells, *Process and Unreality* (New York: King's Crown Press, 1950; rpt., New York: Gordian Press, 1975), and E. Shahan, *Whitehead's Theory of Experience* (New York: King's Crown Press, 1950), pp. 128–30.

41. *Interpretation*, pp. 319–30.

42. See "Whitehead Without God," pp. 307–309.

43. On this point see my essay on "An Appraisal of Whiteheadian Nontheism," *The Southern Journal of Philosophy*, 15 (1977), 27–35.

44. (New Haven: Yale University Press, 1974).

45. See *God the Creator: On the Transcendence and Presence of God* (Chicago: University of Chicago Press, 1968).

46. For the application of Neville's dialectic to Whitehead's concept of

God see my essay "Whitehead's Categoreal Derivation of Divine Existence," *The Monist*, 54 (1970), 374–400; our exchange in the *Proceedings of the American Catholic Philosophical Association*, 44 (1970) [Ford: "The Viability of Whitehead's God for Christian Theology," 141–53; Neville: "The Impossibility of Whitehead's God for Christian Theology," 130–40]; my essay "Neville on the One and the Many," *The Southern Journal of Philosophy*, 10 (1972–73), 79–84; and our exchange appearing in the present volume as Chapters 12 and 13.

47. Fabro, "Concrescence or Dispersion of God into the World (Whitehead)" in *God in Exile*, trans. Arthur Gibson (Westminster, Md.: Newman, 1968), Pt. 6, Chap. 4 (pp. 804–35); Arthur Gibson, *The Faith of the Atheist* (New York: Harper and Row, 1968), Chap. 7.

48. Donald B. Kuspit, "Whitehead on Divinity," *Archiv für Philosophie*, 11 (1961), 64–171. Kuspit carefully develops Whitehead's claim that God is the chief exemplification of the categories (cf. PR 521). God is the ontological correlative of the world, needed for a full explication of the categories. Yet Kuspit fails to endow God, so conceived, with the independence and particularity which the Western religious tradition has generally ascribed to him, because Kuspit does not see that God—like *any* other actual entity—is *both* the exemplification of more general principles *and* something more, something peculiarly dependent on that entity's own subjective decision. For Kuspit, God is nothing but the way in which God exemplifies the categories, and hence the conception of God is simply an abstract description of reality. The most interesting part of Kuspit's study is the initial section, which develops some illuminating comparisons with Samuel Alexander (64–84).

49. See my article "In What Sense Is God Infinite? A Process Perspective," *The Thomist*, 42 (1978), 1–13.

50. W. Norris Clarke, S.J., "A New Look at the Immutability of God" in *God Knowable and Unknowable*, ed. Robert J. Roth, S.J. (New York: Fordham University Press, 1973), pp. 43–72.

51. (New Haven: Yale University Press, 1948).

52. *The Idea of God: A Whiteheadian Critique of St. Thomas Aquinas' Concept of God* (The Hague: Nijhoff, 1974).

53. On this point, see my "The Immutable God and Father Clarke," *The New Scholasticism*, 49 (1975), 189–99, and the masterly summary in Clarke's *The Philosophical Approach to God: A Neo-Thomist Perspective* (Winston-Salem: Wake Forest University Department of Philosophy, 1979), Chap. 3 (pp. 66–109).

54. Edward H. Madden and Peter H. Hare, "Evil and Unlimited Power," *The Review of Metaphysics*, 20 (1966), 278–89.

55. "The Dipolar Conception of Deity," *The Review of Metaphysics*, 21 (1967), esp. 282–89.

56. "Divine Persuasion and the Triumph of Good," *Process Philosophy and Christian Thought*, pp. 287–304, at p. 297.

57. Contained in Hare and Madden, *Evil and the Concept of God* (Springfield, Ill.: Thomas, 1968).

58. The debate continues: Hare and Madden, "Evil and Persuasive Power," *Process Studies*, 2 (1972), 44–48, responded to by J. E. Barnhart, "Persuasive and Coercive Power in Process Metaphysics," *Process Studies*, 3 (1973), 153–57, and Dalton D. Baldwin, "Evil and Persuasive Power: A Response to Hare and Madden," *Process Studies*, 3 (1973), 259–72. For a discussion of the problem of evil within a process context, see also John B. Cobb, Jr., *God and the World* (Philadelphia: Westminster, 1969), Chap. 4 (pp. 87–102), and David R. Griffin, *God, Power, and Evil: A Process Theodicy* (Philadelphia: Westminster, 1976).

59. "Whitehead's Idea of God [1941]" in *The Philosophy of Alfred North Whitehead*, ed. Paul A. Schilpp, Library of Living Philosophers, 2nd ed. (New York: Tudor, 1951), pp. 513–60, esp. pp. 546–50; rpt. in Hartshorne's *Whitehead's Philosophy* (Lincoln: University of Nebraska Press, 1972), pp. 63–97.

60. For its separate origin, see William Lad Sessions, "Hartshorne's Early Philosophy" in *Two Process Philosophers*, pp. 10–34, and for the differences, my essay on "Whitehead's Differences from Hartshorne," pp. 58–83 in the same volume.

61. On the importance of this term for the primacy of the primordial nature, see my "The Non-Temporality of Whitehead's God," *International Philosophical Quarterly*, 13 (1973), 347–76.

62. John T. Wilcox, "A Question from Physics for Certain Theists," *The Journal of Religion*, 4 (1961), 293–300; Lewis S. Ford, "Is Process Theism Compatible with Relativity Theory?" *The Journal of Religion*, 48 (1968), 124–35; Paul Fitzgerald, "Relativity Physics and the God of Process Philosophy," *Process Studies*, 2 (1972), 251–76; Frederic F. Fost, "Relativity Theory and Hartshorne's Dipolar Theism" in *Two Process Philosophers*, pp. 89–99. These discussions all involve the special theory of relativity, about which Whitehead and Hartshorne had agreed with Einstein, but recently there has been interest in the general theory, about which Whitehead and Einstein disagree. See Robert A. Ariel, "Recent Empirical Disconfirmation of Whitehead's Relativity Theory," with a critical reply by Dean R. Fowler: *Process Studies*, 4 (1974), 285–90; Francis Seaman, "Note on Whitehead and the Order of Nature," *Process Studies*, 5 (1975), 129–33; and Dean R. Fowler, "Whitehead's Theory of Relativity," *Process Studies*, 5 (1975), 159–74. Hartshorne has stated his more recent views in "Bell's Theorem and Stapp's Revised View of Space–Time," *Process Studies*, 7 (1977), 183–91.

63. John B. Cobb, Jr., *A Christian Natural Theology, Based on the Thought of Alfred North Whitehead* (Philadelphia: Westminster, 1965), esp. Chap. 5.

64. This appears not to be true of the nine Categoreal Obligations (PR 39–41), which seem to be framed as the necessary conditions for finite concrescence, described in *Process and Reality*, Pt. III. We are simply not told what the conditions for divine concrescence are.

65. This derivation and mutual implication of God and the World is discussed in my essay "Whitehead's Categoreal Derivation of Divine Existence" (n. 46 above). See also Marjorie Suchocki, "The Metaphysical Ground of the

Whiteheadian God," *Process Studies*, 5 (1975), 237–46. Kenneth F. Thompson, Jr., *Whitehead's Philosophy of Religion* (The Hague: Mouton, 1971), defends Whitehead's original proposal against Cobb's objections. See also William A. Christian, "The Concept of God as a Derivative Notion," *Process and Divinity*, pp. 181–204.

66. *Whitehead's Philosophy of Organism* (London: Macmillan, 1932, 1966), p. 172*n*1.

# INDEX